British Institute of International and Comparative Law and
SMU Dedman School of Law (SMU—London Forum Initiative)

REPRESENTATIONAL FAIRNESS IN WTO RULE-MAKING

British Institute of International and Comparative Law
and
SMU Dedman School of Law
(SMU—London Forum Initiative)

Representational Fairness in WTO Rule-Making

Negotiating, Implementing, and Disputing the TRIPS Pharmaceutical-Related Provisions

MOHAMED OMAR GAD

British Institute of International and Comparative Law

THE SMU DEDMAN SCHOOL OF LAW
www.law.smu.edu

Published and Distributed by
British Institute of International and Comparative Law
Charles Clore House, 17 Russell Square, London WC1B 5JP
and
The SMU Dedman School of Law

British Library Cataloguing in Publication Data
A Catalogue record of this book is available from the British Library

ISBN 1–905221–04–5

Typeset by Cambrian Typesetters
Frimley, Surrey
Printed in Great Britain by Biddles Ltd
King's Lynn

Contents

List of Tables and Diagrams

PART ONE

MULTINATIONAL ENTERPRISES, DEVELOPING COUNTRIES, INTERNATIONAL RULE-MAKING, AND THE TRIPS AGREEMENT

Chapter 1

Introduction

Multinational enterprises (MNEs),[1] which are most often based in industrialized countries (ICs), are a dominant force in the global economy,[2] responsible for a considerable proportion of global innovation and possessing intellectual property rights in state of the art technology and processes.[3] This economic muscle, knowledge base, and considerable organizational sophistication, endows multinational enterprises with highly valuable resources that entail elements of political power.[4] While MNEs understandably use this power to affect conditions that bolster their economic interests in their markets, there are also instances where they have deployed their power indirectly (ie through lobbying on the domestic, cross-border and international levels) to condition the regulatory environment in pursuit of their economic interests.

Given the spread of their economic activities and the trend towards regulatory globalization,[5] there are increasing instances of interference by MNEs in the international economic regulatory environment.[6] Indeed, the profusion of international economic regulatory systems, as a reflection of

1 For a proper definition of the term 'multinational enterprises', please refer to Ch 3.

2 For a brief historical overview of the contributions of MNEs to the global economy, see Mira Wilkins *Multinational Enterprises and Economic Change* 38 AUSTL ECON HIST R 103 (1998). On MNEs and innovation, see GILLES BERTIN AND SALLY WYATT, MULTINATIONALS AND INDUSTRIAL PROPERTY: THE CONTROL OF THE WORLD'S TECHNOLOGY (1988).

3 There are seven types of intellectual property rights recognized under the Agreement on Trade Related Aspects of Intellectual Property Rights (TRIPS): patents, copyrights, trademarks, geographical indications, industrial designs, layout designs (topographies) of integrated circuits, and undisclosed information.

4 Ch 3 examines the influence of MNEs on international economic regulation, and specifically considers their role as political actors.

5 On the globalization of regulation, and the role of MNEs therein, see JOHN BRAITHWAITE AND PETER DRAHOS, GLOBAL BUSINESS REGULATION (2000); and REGULATING INTERNATIONAL BUSINESS (Sol Picciotto and Ruth Mayne eds 1999).

6 MNEs affect external legal environments through lobbying their home state policy before international organizations and other multilateral fora. See Peter T Muchlinski *'Global Bukowina' Examined: Viewing the Multinational Enterprise as a Transnational Law-Making Community* in GLOBAL LAW WITHOUT A STATE 79–108 (Gunther Teubner ed 1997). *See also* Peter Malanczuk *Multinational Enterprises and Treaty-Making—A Contribution to the Discussion on Non-State Actors and the 'Subjects' of International Law* in MULTILATERAL TREATY-MAKING: THE CURRENT STATUS OF CHALLENGES TO AND REFORMS NEEDED IN THE INTERNATIONAL LEGISLATIVE PROCESS 45–72 (Vera Gowlland-Debbas ed 2000).

the globalization of law, has been described as 'an integral part of enabling and facilitating global corporate initiatives and strategies'.[7]

However, this active engagement by MNEs in the rule-making processes at the international and other levels, and consequently in the implementation of agreed international standards or best practices into domestic legislation, may be at odds with the no less legitimate policy interests of developing countries (DCs). Some viable level of representational fairness for DCs in the rule-making process at these levels—particularly at the international level—would appear to be both desirable and necessary, less the legitimacy, integrity, transparency and (above all) fairness of the international regulatory process be skewed, producing bottom-up retorting action by developing countries and thus giving rise to a proliferation of disputes and of disturbances within the international rule-making framework. Such would not be in the best interest of this framework nor of the MNEs and DCs.

Multinational Enterprises champion regulatory standards and prerogatives that reflect their interests which are in numerous cases substantially different from those advocated by DCs.[8] As a result, in instances when MNEs succeed in influencing the regulatory environment, DCs face regulatory norms that may hamper their ability to pursue their own public policy aims in the given field of regulation. This might result not only in adverse effects on legitimate DC interests, but might often be disruptive to the international economic regulatory system itself. In this regard, the case of the negotiation and implementation of the Agreement on Trade-Related Aspects of Intellectual Property Rights (TRIPS) is a good example of this adversity and disruption.[9] The TRIPS Agreement and specifically its pharmaceutical-related patent provisions, has been perceived by DC governments and their local stakeholders, among others, as creating major difficulties in their pursuit of domestic public policies. In addition, the Agreement has generated substantial difficulties for the World Trade Organization (WTO) system at large.

The TRIPS Agreement was negotiated during the Uruguay Round (1986–94) of the General Agreement on Tariffs and Trade (GATT), and was signed as part and parcel of the Final Act of the Uruguay Round, coming

[7] A Claire Cutler *Globalization, Law and Transnational Corporations: a Deepening of Market Discipline* in POWER IN THE GLOBAL ERA: GROUNDING GLOBALIZATION 55 (Theodore H Cohn, Stephen McBride, and John Wiseman eds 2000). On the globalization of law in the area of intellectual property, and the influence of MNEs therein, see Raymond T Nimmer and Patricia Ann Krauthaus *Globalisation of Law in Intellectual Property and Related Commercial Contexts* 10 LAW IN CONTEXT 80 (1992).

[8] On MNEs regulatory preferences, see HELEN V MILNER, RESISTING PROTECTIONISM: GLOBAL INDUSTRIES AND THE POLITICS OF INTERNATIONAL TRADE (1988).

[9] Agreement on Trade-Related Aspects of Intellectual Property Rights (15 Apr 1994) 33 ILM 1197 (1994) [hereinafter TRIPS Agreement].

into effect on 1 January 1995.[10] While an ambitious and a potentially positive contribution to the world trading system, the TRIPS Agreement has proven to be a controversial development in the international regulation of intellectual property rights, specifically with regard to patent rights generally, and to pharmaceutical-related patent rights specifically. By setting minimum standards for the protection of intellectual property rights (IPRs), it created an upward harmonization in Member States' regulations towards the standards prevalent in ICs. Accordingly, it can be reasonably argued that the TRIPS patent and related provisions codify regulatory standards that tilt the balance of rights and obligations towards the interests of IC-based pharmaceutical MNEs, at the expense of DC interests. At the centre of this 'imbalance controversy', are the effects resulting from the implementation of the TRIPS Agreement's provisions pertaining to the patenting of pharmaceutical products.[11] The role of pharmaceutical MNEs in lobbying the negotiation and implementation of these patent and related provisions and the ensuing legal and political disputes generated between DC and IC WTO members over their implementation, or lack thereof, forms the subject of this book.

(I) STAKEHOLDERS AND THE DIFFERING PERSPECTIVES

(A) Multinational Enterprises' Perspective

Viewed as private rights,[12] the vast majority of pharmaceutical product patents are owned by MNEs, and it is precisely in such ownership that reside the main assets of pharmaceutical MNEs. Understandably, pharmaceutical MNEs have been among the most vociferous promoters of high protectionist standards in the provisions of the TRIPS Agreement.[13] The codification of these patent provisions and other standards proved a considerable victory for the pharmaceutical MNEs.[14] Furthermore, through promoting the establishment of TRIPS as part and parcel of the universe of agreements and instruments constituting the multilateral trading system,

[10] Final Act Embodying the Results of the Uruguay Round of Multilateral Trade Negotiations (15 Apr 1994) 33 ILM 1125 (1994) [hereinafter Final Act].

[11] *See* Julio Nogues *Patents and Pharmaceutical Drugs: Understanding the Pressures on Developing Countries* 24 J WORLD TRADE 81 (1990); Julio Nogues *Social Costs and Benefits of Introducing Patent Protection for Pharmaceutical Drugs in Developing Countries* 31 DEV ECON 24 (1993); and Richard P Rozek *The Consequences of Pharmaceutical Product Patenting: A Critique* 16 WORLD COMPETITION L AND ECON REV 91 (1993).

[12] 'Recognizing that intellectual property rights are private rights'; preamble to the TRIPS Agreement.

[13] *See* INTERNATIONAL FEDERATION OF PHARMACEUTICAL MANUFACTURERS ASSOCIATIONS, GATT TRIPS AND THE PHARMACEUTICAL INDUSTRY: A REVIEW (1995).

[14] *See* Philippe Bennett *TRIPs—a Victory for US Industry* 66 PAT WORLD 31 (1994).

MNEs have succeeded not only in guaranteeing adherence to the agreement, but have also guaranteed the observance of its provisions as they are incorporated as one of the covered agreements of the WTO's effective dispute settlement (DSU) mechanism.[15]

(B) Developing Countries' Perspective

On the other hand, the success of the pharmaceutical MNEs to influence the negotiation of the TRIPS Agreement, as well as to lobby for its rapid implementation by DCs can be viewed as having adversely affected the interests of the latter.[16] The standards codified in TRIPS entail restriction on DCs' ability to manage their domestic intellectual property policy, and more specifically patent policy, as a component of their broader public policies designed to advance sustainable developmental and social objectives. This might involve, for example, specific damage to their public health policy, which depends on the availability of affordable medicines, as well as to the growth of their local pharmaceutical industry when faced with competition from pharmaceutical MNEs. The resulting 'rub' from the perspective of DCs is an imbalance in the rights and obligations of patent owners on the one hand, and patent users on the other, and consequently in their own ability to pursue certain public policy options. Diagram 1.1 below graphically depicts the relationship of the TRIPS Agreement to DCs.

(C) Industrialized Countries' Perspective

The ability of the pharmaceutical MNEs to integrate their interests into the TRIPS Agreement was ultimately the result of supportive ICs' positions. In this regard, the United States was the single most effective IC in supporting the inclusion, negotiation and implementation of the IP standards favoured by the pharmaceutical MNEs.[17] The EC, and to a lesser extent Japan and Switzerland also performed important roles during the latter phases of the

[15] Understanding on Rules and Procedures Governing the Settlement of Disputes, Annex 2, Marrakesh Agreement Establishing the World Trade Organization, art 1(1) (15 Apr 1994) 33 ILM 1226 (1994).

[16] *See* D BHORALI, GATT AGREEMENT OR DUNKEL DRAFT TREATY: ITS IMPACT ON AGRICULTURE INDUSTRY TRIPS AND TRIMS AND DRUG INDUSTRY (1994); GATT: CRITICAL ANALYSIS OF GENERAL AGREEMENT ON TARIFFS AND TRADE (A Kulshreshtha, K Trivedi and R Kumar eds 1994). *See also* A Samuel Oddi *TRIPS—Natural Rights and a 'Polite Form of Economic Imperialis'* 29 VAND J TRANSNAT'L L 415 (1996).

[17] Harrelson notes that US-based pharmaceutical MNEs are the leaders by far in drug innovation, where 45 per cent of new pharmaceuticals were developed by them, followed by 14 per cent for UK-based pharmaceutical MNEs, and 9 per cent for their Swiss-based counterparts. *See* John A Harrelson *TRIPS, Pharmaceutical Patents, and the HIV/AIDS Crisis: Finding the Proper Balance Between Intellectual Property Rights and Compassion* 7 WIDENER L SYMP J 175, fn 82 (2001).

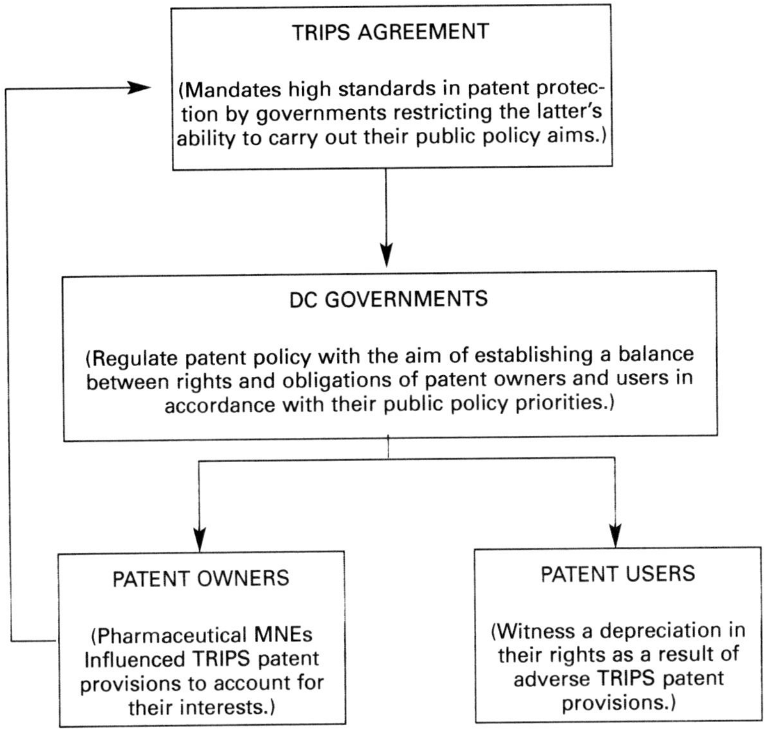

Diagram 1.1: Conceptual View of the TRIPS Agreement's Effects on DC Public Policy

UR negotiations on TRIPS, and in ensuing developments concerning implementation and disputes.[18] Nonetheless, the US remains the key IC player on this issue, and will consequently be the focus of study with regard to the role of ICs. A main avenue whereby the United States was successful in negotiating and implementing TRIPS has been its ability to engage in bilateral pressure on DCs, including in latter stages, its resort to the WTO DSU mechanism. Table 1.1 below lists selected disputes and instances of IC pressure applied on DCs to bring their domestic legislation and policies into conformity with the TRIPS patent standards, as will be covered in this book.

[18] On the role of the EC during the Uruguay Round negotiations, see European Communities Council of Ministers (1986) 'Overall Approach: New Round of Trade Negotiations in Defence of Open Multilateral Trade' EEC Doc No 7748/86, PV/CONS.33 Ext 1 GATT 107 (June 1986); and HUGO PAEMEN AND ALEXANDRA BENSCH, FROM GATT TO THE WTO: THE EUROPEAN COMMUNITY IN THE URUGUAY ROUND (1995). An excellent work on the negotiation of the TRIPS Agreement that analyses the role of the EC therein is Duncan Matthews GLOBALISING INTELLECTUAL PROPERTY RIGHTS: THE TRIPS AGREEMENT 29–43 (2002).

Table 1.1: Selected Disputes and Pressures that have Arisen Concerning Product Patent Protection for Pharmaceuticals in Five Developing Countries Since the Mid-1980s

	Selected Disputes and Pressures on Five DCs
Argentina	Initiation of a US Section 301 investigation (1988). USTR placement of Argentina on the Special 301 Priority Watch List (1996–2002). Two Requests for Consultation by the US under the WTO DSU rules (1999 and 2000).
Brazil	Request for Consultation by the US under the WTO DSU rules (2000). Initiation of US Section 301 investigations (1987 and 1993). Imposition of sanctions following the 1987 Section 301 investigation (1988). USTR placement of Brazil on the Special 301 Priority Watch List (1995 and 2002). USTR placement of Brazil on the Special 301 Watch List (1996, 1997, 1999–2001).
Egypt	USTR placement of Egypt on the Special 301 Priority Watch List (1997–2002). USTR placement of Egypt on the Special 301 Watch List (1995–6).
India	Initiation of a US Section 301 investigation (1991). USTR placement of India on the Special 301 Priority Watch List (1995–2002). Dispute with the US under the WTO DSU system (1996). Dispute with the EC under the WTO DSU system (1997).
South Africa	Case submitted by the South African Pharmaceutical Manufacturers' Association against the government of South Africa (1998). USTR placement of South Africa on the Special 301 Watch List (1995, 1998–9).

(D) World Trade Organization Perspective

Furthermore, this problem of the constraint on DCs' public policies may have repercussions that go beyond the DC arena and affect the WTO system itself. Dissatisfied with the TRIPS Agreement provisions afflicting their ability to forge independent health policies, DCs have become increasingly disconcerted with the WTO. In this vein, at the request of the African Group,[19] the WTO's TRIPS Council held a special discussion in 2001 on 'Intellectual Property and Access to Medicines' to discuss the implications of TRIPS on access to medicines.[20] Pronouncements on the 'imbalance' and/or indeterminacy of those provisions were debated and resulted in the Declaration on the TRIPS Agreement and Public Health being adopted at the WTO's Doha Ministerial Conference.[21] Equally, the legitimacy of the WTO's TRIPS Agreement has come under severe attacks from global civil society represented by Non-Governmental Organizations (NGOs).[22] Yet, more remarkably, certain TRIPS provisions have been cited within the ambit of the United Nations system as possibly infringing human rights. Specifically, in August 2000, the Sub-Commission on the Promotion and Protection of Human Rights of the UN Commission on Human Rights adopted a resolution on 'Intellectual Property Rights and Human Rights', which declared that 'there are apparent conflicts between the intellectual property rights regime embodied in the TRIPS Agreement, on the one hand, and international human rights law, on the other'.[23] Such instances of DC action, civil society attacks, and UN criticism put considerable strain on the foundations of legitimacy that the WTO strives to maintain.

[19] An informal grouping of African WTO Member States.

[20] The special discussion was held on 18–21 June, 25 July, and 19–21 Sept 2001. See Press Release, World Trade Organization TRIPS Council Meeting on Access to Medicines: WTO Members to Press On, Following 'Rich Debate' on Medicines (22 June 2001) Press/233. *See* WTO *TRIPS Council, Submission by the African Group, Barbados, Bolivia, Brazil, Cuba, Dominican Republic, Ecuador, Honduras, India, Indonesia, Jamaica, Pakistan, Paraguay, Philippines, Peru, Sri Lanka, Thailand and Venezuela* IP/C/W/296 (29 June 2001).

[21] WTO *Ministerial Conference Fourth Session, Doha 9–14 November 2001, Declaration on the TRIPS Agreement and Public Health* WT/MIN(01)/DEC/2 (20 Nov 2001) [hereinafter Doha Declaration].

[22] *See* Oxfam *WTO Patent Rules and Access to Medicines: The Pressure Mounts* OXFAM POLICY PAPER (June 2001) <http://www.oxfam.org.uk/policy/papers/wtorules/wtorules.htm> (last visited 7 Feb 2002). See also Oxfam *'Cut the Cost' Campaign* <http://www.oxfam.org.uk/cutthecost/index.html> (last visited 7 Feb 2002); and Medecins Sans Frontieres *Campaign for Access to Essential Medicines* <http://www.accessmed-msf.org/index.asp> (last visited 7 Feb 2002).

[23] United Nations Commission on Human Rights, Sub-commission on the Promotion and Protection of Human Rights 'Intellectual Property Rights and Human Rights' Res No 2000/7 E/CN.4/SUB.2/RES/2000/7 (17 Aug 2000).

(E) Other Perspectives

The problems generated by the TRIPS patent provisions as they impact on DCs have been explained and debated both in the formal setting of the WTO, as well as in the academic literature. Furthermore, a number of international organizations, most notably the United Nations Conference on Trade and Development (UNCTAD), the World Intellectual Property Organization (WIPO) and the South Centre,[24] have addressed the constraints facing DC public policy, and have produced studies on how solutions might be forged at the domestic level of DC legislation implementing the agreement, so as to minimize their adverse impact.[25] Such solutions, while undoubtedly a worthwhile effort, tackle the TRIPS dilemma subsequent to the fact, that is, they transfer the problem to DCs to attempt to extricate themselves from this 'imbalance' against their interests. Consequently, there is a need to address in a structured analysis, the specific problem of the fundamental role of pharmaceutical MNEs' lobbying in creating the constraints effect on DC public policy of the TRIPS patent and related provisions. Therefore, it is the lynchpin of the argument of this book, (that is, the role of MNEs), which drives its approach on this issue.

(II) SIGNIFICANCE OF THE PROBLEM

The problem addressed in this book therefore manifests a number of interrelated issues that imbue it with significance in the field of international economic law. Primarily, this problem concerns the ability of DCs to address their public policy independently, and most importantly, in a manner consistent with the right of their population to proper access to health care, among others. Second, the problem relates to the impact that MNEs have on international economic regulation, and most notably on the GATT/WTO system, where their impact vis-à-vis DC interests and the broader interests of the WTO system has thus far been controversial. Finally, as it is the direct impact of the TRIPS provisions that is affecting

[24] The South Centre was established in 1995 as an inter-governmental body of developing countries to meet the need for analysis of development problems and experience, as well as to provide intellectual and policy support required by developing countries for collective and individual action in the international arena. It is headquartered in Geneva.

[25] *See* UNCTAD THE TRIPS AGREEMENT AND DEVELOPING COUNTRIES (1996); W Lesser *The Effects of TRIPS-Mandated Intellectual Property Rights on Economic Activities in Developing Countries* WIPO STUDIES ON INTELLECTUAL PROPERTY (2001) <http://www.wipo.int/about-ip/en/studies/pdf/ssa_lesser_trips.pdf> (last visited 24 Jan 2002); SOUTH CENTRE, INTEGRATING PUBLIC HEALTH CONCERNS INTO PATENT LEGISLATION IN DEVELOPING COUNTRIES (2000); and Frederick M Abbott *The TRIPS Agreement, Access to Medicines and the WTO Doha Ministerial Conference* QUAKER UNITED NATIONS OFFICE—GENEVA, OCCASIONAL PAPER NO 7 (2001).

DC interests, the problem points directly to the Agreement, as well as its institutional context within the WTO, and addresses the issue of 'fairness' in that system.

During the negotiation of the TRIPS provisions, and particularly the extension of patent protection to pharmaceutical products, DCs and other independent experts have signalled a concern as to the adverse effects such provisions would have on DCs' ability to pursue independent public policies.[26] However, it is the public health crisis, particularly with regard to the HIV/AIDS pandemic in certain DCs, most notably South Africa and Brazil, which has highlighted the clash between the TRIPS provisions and DC policies and legislation necessary for addressing their obligations towards their populations. Furthermore, in the case of South Africa, representatives of the multinational pharmaceutical industry endeavoured to actively outlaw specific legislation by the South African Government addressing the HIV/AIDS pandemic, as inconsistent with its TRIPS obligations.[27] Similar policies by the Brazilian Government have been reported by the multinational pharmaceutical industry to the US Government seeking the application of US pressure on Brazil to reverse what the industry considered as a violation of its rights under TRIPS.[28] Such interference exhibits MNEs' ability not only to manipulate the codification of multilateral regulatory standards, but also to pursue their implementation to the detriment of DC public policy duties towards their citizens.

In the same vein, although on a less urgent scale, the TRIPS patent provisions threaten adverse effects on the local pharmaceutical industries of

26 The *travaux préparatoires* of the TRIPS Agreement negotiations contain a wealth of developing countries' concerns in this regard. In the very first meeting of the Negotiating Group on TRIPS, the need was expressed 'for the Group in its work to balance the interests of technology importers and exporters and of more advanced and less-developed countries, particularly as regards the transfer of technology, and to recognize the legitimate different national interests and policy objectives in the area of intellectual property rights'. *See* GATT *Meeting of the Negotiating Group on Trade-Related Aspects of Intellectual Property Rights, including Trade in Counterfeit Goods* (25 March 1987) para 12 MTN.GNG/NG11/1 (10 Apr 1987).

27 Medicines and Related Substances Control Amendment Act No 90 (1997) <http://www.gov.za/acts/1997/a90-97.pdf> (last visited 7 Feb 2001). On 18 Feb 1998, action was brought by the Pharmaceutical Manufacturers' Association of South Africa and others (including the world's major pharmaceutical MNEs) against the President of South Africa and others, on the premise that the abovementioned Act is unconstitutional and violated South Africa's obligations under the TRIPS Agreement. See *Pharmaceutical Manufacturers' Association of South Africa et al v Nelson Mandela, President of the Republic of South Africa et al* Case No 4183/98 (Transvaal Provincial Division filed 18 Feb 1998). Under intense pressure, the applicants withdrew their case on 19 Apr 2001.

28 In June 2000, the US initiated the first step of the WTO dispute settlement system (consultation) with Brazil on its measures affecting patent protection. See WTO *Brazil—Measures Affecting Patent Protection, Request for Consultations by the United States* WT/DS199/1 (8 June 2000). A mutually agreed solution was reached nonetheless in July 2001. See WTO *Brazil—Measures Affecting Patent Protection, Notification of Mutually Agreed Solution* WT/DS199/4 (19 July 2001).

developing countries. In Argentina,[29] Egypt,[30] Brazil,[31] and India,[32] among others, the local generic pharmaceutical industry is a highly successful industry that contributes significantly to the domestic economy in terms of employment opportunities and export earnings. It has been a conscious policy of such DC governments to provide these industries with a legislative framework to allow them to grow and protect them from unfair competition from the pharmaceutical MNEs. However, pharmaceutical MNEs are engaging in intense lobbying to apply TRIPS provisions, and indeed 'TRIPS-plus'[33] provisions to protect their interests at the expense of the local generic industry.

With regard to the impact of pharmaceutical MNEs, they have played a principal role in the problem relating to the TRIPS provisions on pharmaceutical product patent protection. As described, they have had an impact on influencing the negotiations codifying those standards, and have actively pursued their observance and implementation by developing countries. This is an interesting example of the role of MNEs as political actors and their influence on international economic regulation. The influence they exerted and continue to exert over the TRIPS provisions and their implementation is an area of research that has caught the attention of scholars in different disciplines.[34]

[29] See PM CHALLU, ADAPTATION OF NATIONAL LEGISLATION TO THE TRIPS AGREEMENT OF GATT'S URUGUAY ROUND, AIMED AT ASSURING INHABITANTS BEST ACCESSIBILITY TO PHARMACEUTICALS (1995); and Wendy S Vicente *Questionable Victory for Coerced Argentine Pharmaceutical Patent Legislation* 19 U PA J INT'L ECON L 1101 (1998).

[30] See A ABOUELENEIN, TRADE-RELATED ASPECTS OF INTELLECTUAL PROPERTY RIGHTS (TRIPS) AND THE PHARMACEUTICAL INDUSTRY IN EGYPT (1996).

[31] See Christopher S Mayer *The Brazilian Pharmaceutical Industry Goes Walking From Ipanema to Prosperity: Will the New Intellectual Property Law Spur Domestic Investment?* 12 TEMP INT'L AND COMP L J 377 (1998).

[32] See Sudhir Ahuja *GATT and TRIPS—the Impact on the Indian Pharmaceutical Industry* 65 PAT. WORLD 28 (1994); and S Karandikar INDIAN DRUG INDUSTRY AFTER GATT (1994).

[33] 'TRIPS-plus' refers to standards that go beyond the minimum required by TRIPS. Recently, under pressure from the US and EU, some developing countries have been encouraged to go beyond theses minimum standards required by TRIPS. See James L Bikoff and David I Wilson *Intellectual Property Protection Under NAFTA and TRIPS and the Future of Bilateral Intellectual Property Initiatives—Part I* 66 PAT WORLD 21 (1994); and James L Bikoff and David I Wilson *Intellectual Property Protection Under NAFTA and TRIPS and the Future of Bilateral Intellectual Property Initiatives—Part II* 66 PAT WORLD 31 (1994).

[34] See Susan K Sell *Multinational Corporations as Agents of Change: The Globalization of Intellectual Property Rights* in PRIVATE AUTHORITY AND INTERNATIONAL AFFAIRS 169–197 (A Claire Cutler, Virginia Haufler and Tony Porter eds 1999); Susan K Sell *Structures, Agents and Institutions: Private Corporate Power and the Globalisation of Intellectual Property Rights* in NON-STATE ACTORS AND AUTHORITY IN THE GLOBAL SYSTEM 91–106 (Richard Higgott, Geoffrey RD Underhill and Andreas Bieler eds 1999); Susan K Sell *The Origins of a Trade-Based Approach to Intellectual Property Protection: the Role of Industry Associations* 17 SCI COMM 163 (1995); Frank Emmert *Intellectual Property in the Uruguay Round—Negotiating Strategies of the Western Industrialized Countries* 11 MICH J INT'L L 1317 (1990).

Finally, the significance of the research problem derives from the impact of the TRIPS Agreement provisions and the wider institutional context of the WTO system on DC interests. The balance of rights and obligations of members of the TRIPS Agreement, and indeed the 'fairness' of TRIPS is a matter of great importance. And given the link between TRIPS and wider WTO instruments, the legitimacy of the WTO system is also an issue for consideration, given the need not only for the ability of members to freely conduct their public policy priorities, but also bearing in mind the principle of differential treatment provided for DCs in the GATT/WTO system.[35] Notwithstanding, there is also the issue of the relationship of the TRIPS provisions to the wider system of public international law and the rights of states, people and individuals therein.[36]

(III) APPROACH TO THE PROBLEM

This book examines the problem generated by pharmaceutical MNEs in lobbying the negotiation and implementation of TRIPS, characterizing it as 'top-down' rule-making, and argues that as this leads to the creation of public policy impediments to DCs, results in 'bottom-up' retorting action on their part. The book ultimately presents that this problem, representing an instance of the broader dilemma concerning representational fairness in GATT/WTO rule-making and the impact of MNEs therein, can and should be addressed for the interests not only of DCs, but also for those of the TRIPS Agreement, the WTO system, and indeed for the long-term benefit of MNEs themselves.[37] The book ultimately argues that addressing this problem necessitates a solution based on a preventative strategy relating to the WTO rule-making process, and the impact of MNE interests vis-à-vis those of DCs.

35 The principle of 'differential and more favourable treatment' to developing countries was a long running practice in GATT, with its roots in Art XVIII, and part IV of GATT 1947. Most recently, it has been codified in the Tokyo Round. *See* GATT *Differential and More Favourable Treatment, Reciprocity and Fuller Participation of Developing Countries* (28 Nov 1979) BISD 26S/203 (1980).

36 See Richard Elliott *TRIPS and Rights: International Human Rights Law, Access to Medicines, and the Interpretation of the WTO Agreement on Trade-Related Aspects of Intellectual Property Rights* CANADIAN HIV/AIDS LEGAL NETWORK (Nov 2001) <http://www.aidslaw.ca/Maincontent/issues/cts/briefs/TRIPS-human-rights-briefPDF.pdf> (last visited 7 Feb 2002).

37 Pharmaceutical MNEs have been subjected to adverse publicity on account of the TRIPS Agreement. See Oxfam *Dare to Lead: Public Health and Company Wealth—Oxfam Briefing Paper on Glaxo Smith Kline* <http://www.oxfam.org.uk> (last visited 18 Feb 2002); and Oxfam *Preventing the Cure: Corporate Lobbying and Fair Access to Medicines—Oxfam Briefing Paper on Pfizer* <http://www.oxfam.org.uk> (last visited 18 Feb 2002).

The disproportionate influence of pharmaceutical MNEs on the TRIPS negotiation process is in part the result of the GATT/WTO negotiation process. In this regard, reforming the WTO rule-making process necessitates a more transparent procedure, and it is proposed that a powerful tool in achieving balanced results in the outcome of multilateral instruments and their implementation in domestic jurisdictions is to open up the process to meaningful public debate that can guard against the predominance of influence from one particular lobby, in our case the pharmaceutical industry lobby. Furthermore, addressing the causes also entails encouraging dialogue between MNEs and DCs. In this sense, a dialogue between pharmaceutical MNEs and developing countries' authorities and other actors in the field must be engaged in an effort to fashion provisions and implementation procedures that take into account the interests of all parties involved.[38]

The starting point in this inquiry will focus on the rule-making process, or the negotiating history of the TRIPS Agreement. In this endeavour, our focus will be on the role of the pharmaceutical MNEs in formulating their patent standards and regime preferences, and consequently, in their intense lobbying of the major negotiating parties, chiefly the United States and to a lesser extent the EC. In carrying out this task, this book will aim to understand and demonstrate the level of influence enjoyed by the pharmaceutical MNEs over the TRIPS negotiations and the standards adopted in the eventual Agreement. This task will be carried out in Part Two.

The second task is to examine the TRIPS implementation process in DCs. The focus will be on the response to the effects of the implementation of the TRIPS patent and related provisions perceived by DCs and their stakeholders as they impact upon their ability to pursue their public policy priorities. The pressures exerted during this implementation process by pharmaceutical MNEs and ICs will also be examined. A main part of the treatment will then focus on the implementation process as it transpired in the case of Egypt, examining in greater detail its legislative enactment of a new IP law. General comparisons of pre- and post-TRIPS patent legislation in selected DCs will comprise part of this assessment. This task will be undertaken in Part Three.

The third task of this book relates to the impasse between DCs on the one hand, and the pharmaceutical MNEs and ICs on the other, and the resulting disputes generated over the implementation and interpretation of the TRIPS patent provisions. In treating this task, we will take stock of the increasing number of legal and political disputes at the level of the WTO dispute settlement system, at the domestic and bilateral levels, as well as at

[38] The Duke Law School has initiated such a dialogue by bringing together developing country officials and MNE representatives to bargain around the provisions of the TRIPS Agreement. See David Lange *Public-Private Initiatives After TRIPS: Designing a Global Agenda* 9 DUKE J COMP AND INT'L L 1 (1998).

the level of the WTO's political organs. Moreover, we will also account for the arguments being made from both sides, as well as the political pressures being applied, including the significant voice of the international NGO community on the issue. Similarly, in carrying out this task, the book will highlight the adverse effects that the proliferation of disputes and the continuing constraints on DCs' public policies have on the legitimacy of TRIPS and the WTO system. This task will be covered in Part Four.

Finally, Part Five concludes our discussion of the argument presented that a disadvantageous 'top-down' rule-making process of TRIPS ultimately leads to untoward 'bottom-up' retorting action by aggrieved DC interests. In so doing, a set of selective suggestions on addressing the problem of the lack of representational fairness between the interests of MNEs and DCs will be presented. This final task will therefore aim to re-anchor the practical focus of the book to the broader dilemma it entails.

In structuring the analysis of the book, it is acknowledged that the impact of the TRIPS patent and other related provisions differ widely from one country to the other. The emphasis will be on the impact as it affects DCs, yet admittedly, even among these, the impact still varies substantially. In this regard, the data analysis will be directed variably to five key developing countries: Argentina, Brazil, Egypt, India, and South Africa. Arguably, these countries give a wide sample of the effects faced by DCs during the negotiation, implementation and disputes on the TRIPS patent provisions. South Africa and Brazil are at the vanguard of countries with a major health pandemic (HIV/AIDS) that necessitates a patent regime that appears to conflict with TRIPS standards. Furthermore, Argentina, Brazil, Egypt, and India are examples of DCs with vibrant local pharmaceutical industries that are now threatened by the TRIPS patent standards. Moreover, at least three of these countries (Brazil, India, and Egypt) were at the vanguard of opposition to the standards sought during the negotiation of TRIPS. Finally, at least two of these countries (India and Brazil) offer some of the most lucrative markets for pharmaceutical MNEs expansion.

Bearing in mind that the broader dilemma this book examines concerns the issue of international rule-making and the influence of MNEs therein, Part One, in its Chapters 2 and 3, discusses a multi-disciplinary evaluation of the process of international rule-making; and a conceptual understanding of the role of MNEs in international economic regulation. In Chapter 4, the issue of patent protection is discussed, with an overview of the development of the concept and the earlier attempts at international regulation. The discussion will then focus on the TRIPS Agreement with an emphasis on its general provisions, its patent provisions, and other provisions of relevance.

Chapter 2

International Rule-Making: A Multi-disciplinary Evaluation

This chapter will aim to develop a conceptual understanding of the role of non-state actors in international rule-making, necessitating an appreciation of wider theoretical analysis of international regulation. This is an issue addressed by international legal theory, international relations theory, and regulation theory.[1] Apart from theoretical studies, the wealth of empirical research conducted on the role of non-state actors in international regulation is to be found across the three disciplines, and in fact, it is quite rare to find empirical work that does not include cross citation from at least one other discipline. Initially however, and given the focus of this book on multilateral treaty-making as the instance of international rule-making examined, we cannot ignore the definition of treaty-making as currently practiced under international law doctrine.[2] Nonetheless, it will be argued that such a definition, based on a legal positivist approach, does not capture the essence of the context within which we seek to examine the role of MNEs, and neither is it a sufficiently broad approach to capture and explain the process through which international rules emerge.

[1] Apart from regulation theory, which explicitly acknowledges its interdisciplinary nature, there has been a nascent interdisciplinary approach between the fields of international law and international relations that seeks to combine elements of both traditions into theoretical appreciation of empirical phenomena. See Kenneth W Abbott *Modern International Relations Theory: A Prospectus for International Lawyers* 14 YALE J INT'L L 335 (1989); Anne-Marie Slaughter, Andrew S Tulumello, and Stepan Wood *International Law and International Relations Theory: A New Generation of Interdisciplinary Scholarship* 92 AM J INT'L L 367 (1998); and Harold Koh *Transnational Legal Process* 75 NEB L REV 181 (1996). Nonetheless, this approach, predominantly American, has been vehemently criticized elsewhere, see most notably Martti Koskenniemi *Carl Schmitt, Hans Morgenthau, and the Image of Law in International Relations* in THE ROLE OF LAW IN INTERNATIONAL POLITICS: ESSAYS IN INTERNATIONAL RELATIONS AND INTERNATIONAL LAW (Michael Byers ed 2000).

[2] For discussions of international treaty-making under the current international law doctrine, see Paul Reuter INTRODUCTION TO THE LAW OF TREATIES (1989); ANTHONY I AUST, MODERN TREATY LAW AND PRACTICE (2000); United Nations REVIEW OF THE MULTILATERAL TREATY-MAKING PROCESS (1985). For accounts that examine the role of non-state actors in international treaty-making, see Malgosia Fitzmaurice *Actors and Factors in the Evolution of Treaty Norms: An Empirical Study* 4 AUST REV INT'L AND EUR L 481 (1999); and MULTILATERAL TREATY-MAKING: THE CURRENT STATUS OF CHALLENGES TO AND REFORMS NEEDED IN THE INTERNATIONAL LEGISLATIVE PROCESS (Vera Gowlland-Debbas ed 2000).

(I) DEFINING 'TREATY-MAKING'

Both Fitzmaurice and Gowlland-Debbas argue that the question of who are the actors involved in the process of multilateral treaty-making depends on the definition of this treaty-making process.[3] Therefore, in our definition exercise, we will first explain the positivist, more restrictive, definition of the process. This will then be followed by reference to another less restrictive account that envisions a role for non-state actors in the process.

Current international legal doctrine prescribes that the process of multilateral treaty-making is governed by the provisions of the 1969 Vienna Convention.[4] Article 2(1)(a) of the Convention defines a 'treaty' as 'an international agreement concluded between States in written form and governed by international law, whether embodied in a single instrument or in two or more related instruments and whatever its particular designation.'[5] As far as the issue of treaty-making is concerned, the Convention addresses only one aspect of this process in its second part, the 'conclusion of treaties'. It identifies the actors involved in the process as states and how they are to be represented in the process (Articles 6 and 7 respectively),[6] it then proceeds to a discussion of the adoption of the text (Article 9), its authentication (Article 10), the consent of the parties to be bound by a treaty (Articles 11–15), and finally the exchange of the instruments of ratification, acceptance, etc (Article 16). Clearly, this is a definition of the treaty-making process that does not account for any role for non-state actors. Another instance of the positivist approach, offering a more inclusive vision of the multilateral treaty-making process is contained in the report of the Secretary General of the United Nations to the General Assembly on the techniques and procedures used in the elaboration of multilateral treaties.[7]

In his report, the Secretary General outlines five stages in the multilateral treaty-making process: the initiation of treaty-making, the formulation of multilateral treaties, the adoption of multilateral treaties, the post-adoption concerns, and supplementing and updating treaties. Throughout these stages, the report details processes that are conducted solely by States and

[3] Fitzmaurice (1999) 2; and Gowlland-Debbas (ed) (2000) 5.

[4] Vienna Convention on the Law of Treaties (23 May 1969) 8 ILM 679 (1969).

[5] The 1986 Vienna Convention offers the same definition with the added provision of the inclusion of international organizations as possible parties. See Vienna Convention on the Law of Treaties Between States and International Organizations or Between International Organizations 25 ILM 543 (1986) Art 2(1) (a) [hereinafter 1986 Vienna Convention].

[6] Article 6 of the 1986 Vienna Convention confers capacity of international organisations to conclude treaties.

[7] United Nations (1985) (n 2) 15–38. For another discussion of the formal process of the conclusion of multilateral treaties, see Reuter (1989) (n 2) 48–51.

intergovernmental organizations (IGOs), except for an interesting and significant deviation. In the first stage of the process, the 'initiation of treaty-making', the report presents the first step as the 'proposal', and adds

> proposals for new treaty instruments originate with many different types of sources; for example, Governments (individually or jointly), subsidiary organs, expert groups, the Secretariat, conferences convened to deal with other related subjects, treaty organs and other inter-governmental or *non-governmental organizations*.[8]

However, the report briskly backtracks to positivist orthodoxy as it comments that it

> does not appear possible to attribute to the origin of the proposal any particular significance in respect to the devolution of the subsequent treaty-making process, or to suggest any practical changes in procedures relating to the making or reception of such proposals.[9]

Hence, notwithstanding its admission that NGOs may be the initiators of a multilateral treaty,[10] and indeed, including within it's definitional ambit of the treaty-making process more than is accounted for under the Vienna Convention, yet it still denies non-state actors any consequent part in the process, nor does it attribute any privilege to that initiation.

On the other hand, the less restrictive definition of the process of treaty-making is presented by more recent academic international law scholarship. In a study on the evolution of treaty norms, Fitzmaurice poses the question of the definition of that process, particularly as to what stages should be included within its ambit.[11] She notes that:

> the treaty-making process is a predominantly political one which is focused on the pursuit by the parties of their own conflicting and competing interests with a view toward achieving maximum benefit.[12]

[8] United Nations (1985) (n 2) 24. Emphasis added.

[9] ibid.

[10] This would include business NGOs but not individual MNEs, as the UN's definition of an NGO, for purposes of consultations under Art 71 of the UN Charter, includes associations of business.

[11] Malgosia Fitzmaurice (1999) (n 2) 2.

[12] ibid 4.

In this same spirit, and in contradistinction to the positivist definition of the treaty-making process, Doswald-Beck provides a definitional vision that accounts for the participation of NGOs.[13] She defines their role as occurring before the initiation of the diplomatic conference, as well as during the diplomatic conference itself. In the earlier phase, the mechanisms of influence of NGOs are: fact finding; and creating State interest through individual effort, coalition formation, and/or mobilizing public opinion. The significance of this phase is that NGOs, and MNEs for our purposes, can prepare the ground for the formal negotiations by shaping States' perceptions of the issue involved through the provision of facts, and lobbying key decision-making organs of States. In the second phase, occurring during the official negotiation of the treaty, the influence of NGOs derives from: their participation in deliberations; their provision of information; contacting state representatives; and their reporting in press briefings and conferences. This is also a very important phase in the treaty-making process as it allows non-state actors both feedback to developments that is essential if they are to influence the process, and more significantly, opportunities for direct lobbying of the formal participants. Both phases of the treaty-making process are clearly important to MNEs, the former in providing them the opportunity of setting the agenda, and the latter in allowing them to remain abreast of developments and to respond accordingly.

Having stated both definitional accounts, it is argued here that there is no inherent conflict between them. While the latter account offers a more encompassing approach that acknowledges the pursuit by non-state actors of their aims through publicity and lobbying, it also acknowledges the limitations imposed by the diplomatic practice of States (and IGOs) being the only parties to formal negotiations. Likewise, this book adopts a similar outlook as it presents that the influence of non-state actors on State policy is an essential component of their strategy in influencing the process.

Finally and before engaging in a theoretical discussion of the process of international regulation, a few words on the issue of the focus of the book being on economic rather than other forms of international regulation are due. Hancher and Moran argue that understanding economic regulation entails understanding 'a process of intermediation and bargaining between large and powerful organizations spanning what are conventionally termed the public and private domains of decision-making'.[14] Arguably, it is the emphasis on the public–private nexus that is essential for understanding the difference between international economic regulation and the more traditional regulation of the political and security aspects of inter-state relations.

[13] Louise Doswald-Beck *Participation of Non-Governmental Entities in Treaty-Making: The Case of Conventional Weapons* in Gowlland-Debbas (ed) (2000) (n 2) 41–4.

[14] Leigh Hancher and Michael Moran *Organizing Regulatory Space* in CAPITALISM, CULTURE, AND ECONOMIC REGULATION 272 (Leigh Hancher and Michael Moran eds 1989).

In other words, the role of private actors in international economic regulation is more pronounced than in 'high-politics' international regulation due to the fact that more of their direct interests are at stake. There are of course instances where non-state actors engage in attempts to influence international security regulation, particularly arms control regimes,[15] yet these instances are not comparable to their engagement over international economic regulation, neither in terms of the preponderance of these instances, nor in the diversity of specific interests represented in the attempts.

(II) THE VIEW OF INTERNATIONAL LEGAL THEORY

The dominant paradigm of international law is the rule-oriented approach of legal positivism, as expounded by scholars such as Kelsen and Hart.[16] The positivist approach stresses a rule-orientation to the vision of international law, arguing that only through an objective examination of the sources of law (with emphasis on treaties and custom), will we reach a proper assessment of the standards that are to be considered 'law'.[17] As such, this paradigm of international legal theory, presents that international law has a strong normative content in the sense of the enforceability of clear and specified rules, but limited scope in the sense of the limitations of 'law' to those rules only. This conceptual framework, naturally, does not treat non-state actors as subjects of international law, a category reserved only to sovereign States, and more recently, IGOs. Hence, the treatment of non-state actors emanates from their view as subjects of their home-states.[18] Treatment is thus carried out under the doctrines of 'diplomatic protection' and 'State responsibility'.[19] More recently, and in view of the difficulty of

[15] For a brief discussion of the influence of Chemical Industry MNEs on Chemical Weapons Treaties, see Fleur Johns *The Invisibility of the Transnational Corporation: An Analysis of International Law and Legal Theory* 19 MELB U L REV 893, 902–3 (1994).

[16] *See* HANS KELSEN, INTRODUCTION TO THE PROBLEMS OF LEGAL THEORY (1992); HLA HART, THE CONCEPT OF LAW (1994). For a more recent treatment of the rule-oriented approach, see Prosper Weil *Towards Relative Normativitiy in International Law?* 77 AM J INT'L L 413 (1983). For a review of other theoretical traditions in international law, see THE STRUCTURE AND PROCESS OF INTERNATIONAL LAW: ESSAYS IN LEGAL PHILOSOPHY DOCTRINE AND THEORY Part I, 15–176 (Ronald St J Macdonald, and Douglas M Johnston eds 1983). For a more recent bibliographical account of modern approaches to international law, see David Kennedy and Chris Tennant *New Approaches to International Law: A Bibliography* 35 HARV INT'L L J 417 (1994).

[17] MARTTI KOSKENNIEMI, FROM APOLOGY TO UTOPIA: THE STRUCTURE OF INTERNATIONAL LEGAL ARGUMENT 160 (1989). For a critique of legal positivism, see David Dyzenhaus *Positivism's Stagnant Research Programme* 20 OXFORD J LEGAL STUD 703 (2000).

[18] Barcelona Traction Light and Power Co (*Belg v Spain*) ICJ 3 (5 February 1970).

[19] See Fleur Johns (1994) (n 15) 894–6; and PETER MUCHLINSKI, MULTINATIONAL ENTERPRISES AND THE LAW 503–14 (1999).

treating non-state actors, and particularly MNEs, as subjects of their home-states, there emerged a form of direct regulation of MNEs, internationally as well as regionally.[20] However, MNEs as such, not even defined as business associations, let alone other less powerful non-state actors, are not seen as possessing the necessary standing to influence international regulation.[21]

This vision of the international legal order, dominated by sovereign states, is currently facing challenges that deem its interpretative power incapable of satisfactorily accounting for recent trends. New categories of issues to contend with, interdependence, the increasing power of non-state actors, both in new and older issue areas, and the increasing artificiality of segregating the domestic order from the international, are the factors underlying the challenges facing positivist IL theory.[22] It is in the area of international economic law that this complexity is most evident. Indeed, it has been argued that

> as international economic law issues increasingly arise to challenge the Westphalian system, it is being transformed. Its basic concepts of sovereignty, of *domaine reservé*, of sovereign equality, and of territorial jurisdiction must be revised.[23]

In opposition to positivist theory, lies the process-oriented approach, which is useful as a framework for accounting for the current complexity of the international regulatory system.[24] This approach argues that the view

[20] See Peter Muchlinski (1999) (n 19) ch 16. For a review of the problems encountered by international law in dealing with the MNE phenomenon, see Detlev F Vagts *The Multinational Enterprise: A New Challenge for Transnational Law* 83 HARVARD L REV 739 (1970). Nonetheless, many instances of international regulation of MNEs involve 'soft law'; this category is not recognized as 'law' by the rule oriented approach when it entails a 'sub-legal' obligation as in codes of conduct, on that, see Prosper Weil (1983) (n 16) 414–15.

[21] Nonetheless, recent developments in the practice of international law, seems to confer a limited degree of recognition to MNEs. See Fleur Johns (1994) (n 15) 899–903.

[22] For an account that describes and argues for the importance of non-state actors in the international legal system, see GLOBAL LAW WITHOUT A STATE (Gunther Teubner ed 1997).

[23] Joel P Trachtman *The International Economic Law Revolution* 17 U PA J INT'L ECON L 33, 48 (1996). From a purely positivist social science approach, this depiction is largely correct. The danger lies when such an argument is presented normatively to advocate a duality in the international legal system between 'liberal' and 'non-liberal' States. See A-M Slaughter *International Law in a World of Liberal States* 6 EUR J INT'L L 503. This agenda is reminiscent of the historical depiction of international law as that between 'civilised states'. For a perceptive discussion of this threat, see David Kennedy *The International Style in Postwar Law and Policy* 1994 UTAH L REV 7 (1994).

[24] The process-oriented approach to law found its most forceful proponents in the New Haven School, founded by Professors Myres S McDougal and Harold Lasswell at the Yale Law School. It must be noted however that a process-oriented approach to law is by no means the invention of the New Haven School, rather it is rooted in the Sociological Movement, which found earlier expressions, most notably in Legal Realism. See ALAN HUNT, THE SOCIOLOGICAL MOVEMENT IN LAW (1978). On a recent review of the approach, see ROSALYN HIGGINS, PROBLEMS AND PROCESS: INTERNATIONAL LAW AND HOW WE USE IT (1994). See also HAROLD D LASSWELL AND MYRES S MCDOUGAL, JURISPRUDENCE FOR A FREE SOCIETY Vol I (1992).

of international law should include not only 'rules' but also the process of 'effective control', hence it seeks to encompass within its purview the decisions that formulate and apply rules that affect community values and emanate from a variety of decision-makers—'formal authority conjoined with effective control'.[25] Hence, it conceives of 'law' as normatively weak, but entailing a wide scope. The significance of this approach for our purposes lies in two of its distinguishing features: primarily, its inclusion in the process of international regulation the domestic level; and secondly, its willingness to account for non-state actors in that process.

As Judge Higgins posits, 'international law is a continuing process of authoritative decisions. This view rejects the notion of law merely as the impartial application of rules. International law is the entire decision-making process, and not just the reference to the trend of past decisions which are termed 'rules'.'[26] It therefore conceptualizes a 'world social process' within which legal normativity resides as the 'trend of past decisions'. While the positivist legal tradition focuses on the rules of law, it considers their origin, the political and societal forces that bear upon their formulation, as well as the degree of their legitimate authority as derived from society, as matters considered 'political' rather than 'legal'.[27] The New Haven School on the other hand admits them as within the purview of the legal process and incorporates them within the community context of decision-making. Given that the essence of the process of international law is that it decides on how values are to be distributed in a given community, the participants in this value allocation process exist at all levels of the process, including at the domestic level.

With regard to participants in the international legal process, the New Haven School recognizes participants in the international legal process not by their possession of the attribute of 'sovereignty', but rather by whether they possess 'formal authority' and/or 'effective control'. This, according to the New Haven School, is determined by three criteria: influence, stability of influence, and ability to apply sanctions.[28] The New Haven School of course recognizes that a considerable proportion of international regulation is indeed influenced by formal authority. While under normal circumstances States possess 'formal authority', they are not the only actors to possess it,

[25] Myres S McDougal *International Law, Power and Policy: A Contemporary Conception* 82 RECUEIL DES COURS 137, 181 (1953).

[26] Rosalyn Higgins *Policy Considerations and the International Judicial Process* 17 INT'L AND COMP L Q 58, 58–9 (1968).

[27] Richard A Falk, Rosalyn C Higgins, W Michael Reisman and Burns H Weston *Myres Smith McDougal (1906–1998)* 92 AM J INT'L L 729, 730 (1998).

[28] Myres S McDougal and Harold D Lasswell *The Identification and Appraisal of Diverse Systems of Public Order* in INTERNATIONAL RULES: APPROACHES FROM INTERNATIONAL LAW AND INTERNATIONAL RELATIONS 119 (Robert J Beck, Anthony Clark Arend, and Robert D Vander Lugt eds 1996).

and indeed more importantly, even if they enjoy the advantage of 'formal authority', this does not necessarily imply their possession of 'effective control'. Decision-making for this School is a dynamic venture where decision-makers of every type and location are engaged in regulation.

The point we wish to underline is that any description of the world power process which would concern itself with effects in the real world, rather than with illusion, must inquire not merely into the structure of formal authority but also into that of effective control and, thus, consider not only 'governmental' participants but other participants who in fact perform the functions of government.[29]

While it does not account for the role of MNEs as individual enterprises, yet it accounts for them in the sense of business associations. The New Haven School defines them as 'transnational pressure groups,' which are

> unofficial bodies or groups that are organised by private associations or private individuals for controlling or influencing decision-makers with respect to particular value demands.[30]

This class of participants, as any other participant, seek to deploy base-values through practices in order to achieve scope values (their posited goals).[31]

The New Haven School is a complicated, yet extremely rich tradition of international legal theory. As all rich traditions, it has its strong adherents, but it has also been met with vehement criticism. We begin by alluding to these criticisms where it affects our purposes the most. The more problematic element in the New Haven School involves its methodology. Not only is its methodology linked to the normative aim—akin to a crusading mission—for the attainment of human dignity as the ultimate aim of any law-making effort, which leads us into the throes of cultural relativism,[32] but it also places us into the straight jacket of a highly complicated methodology, which we are 'forced' to follow.[33] As Mullerson notes in his critique

[29] McDougal (1953) (n 25) 173.

[30] ibid 244.

[31] The terminology of the New Haven School is complicated, but an integral part of it. In short, 'base values' are the resources available to participants; 'practices' are the means through which they deploy those resources; and 'scope values' are the desired outcome of the participants' actions.

[32] For criticisms of this value-orientation, see Gerald Fitzmaurice *Vae Victis or Woe to the Negotiators! Your Treaty or Our 'Interpretation of It?'* 65 AM J INT'L L 358, 370–3 (1971); and Koskenniemi (1989) (n 17) 175–6.

[33] On the New Haven School's methodology see McDougal (1953) (n 25) 140–1, and 186–8. For a recent application of that methodology on a study of human rights, see Curtis Francis Doebbler 'The Individual in the Process of International Human Rights Law: A Value-Oriented Policy Approach' (1997) (unpublished PhD dissertation, University of London). For criticism of the methodology, see Koskenniemi (1989) (n 17) 170–8.

of the New Haven School, its strength lies in its inclusiveness, yet that is also where its weakness lies.[34] The methodology of the School, its 'map of inquiry', seeks to integrate not only the contextual examination of past decisions, but also the utilization of all the techniques of social sciences. This he deems, rightly so, an almost impossible task. He adds:

> [t]he map of inquiry, proposed by Professor McDougal and his associates, 'both comprehensive and selective,' seems to be, on the one hand, too wide including practically everything that may be relevant for the study and application of international law and, on the other hand, too rigid if meant to be always applied. Therefore, it looks more like a menu (very useful, I believe) from which, depending on circumstances, a researcher can choose, or guidelines not to be forgotten rather than a rigorous theory.[35]

Another major sustained attack on the New Haven School has been waged from none other than the legal positivists. This criticism is levelled against its fundamental conception of law as a process. To make law equivalent to a process, the critics argue, ignores the fact that at a given point in time, 'certain concrete *rules* can be identified.'[36] This is a criticism that we do not accept. The New Haven School, we present, does indeed take account of rules as the 'trend of past decisions', however, it goes beyond them in its conception of the international legal system. Indeed, the critics' argument could be turned around, when we can appreciate that what they are offering entails a definition of law as a series of stills in time. A process-oriented approach would transform those infinite number of stills into a continuous dynamic venture. In that sense, our treatment of the TRIPS Agreement involves an appreciation of its 'course' or 'life' from how it was being negotiated, its implementation, the conflicts it generates and the proposals for its review.

(III) THE VIEW FROM INTERNATIONAL RELATIONS THEORY

The study of international relations has passed through a series of discourses pitting rival camps over the interpretation of certain phenomena in the international system.[37] One such discourse, of relevance in our

[34] REIN MULLERSON, ORDERING ANARCHY: INTERNATIONAL LAW IN INTERNATIONAL SOCIETY 33–37 (2000).

[35] ibid 36.

[36] Arend Beck and Vander Lugt (eds) (1996) (n 28) 290.

[37] Steve Smith identifies ten such discourses. Although his classification is not mutually exclusive, it is more a classification of how different IR theorists have pitted their respective

context, focused on identifying the actors in the international system, with the rise of accounts attacking the predominance of the State in state-centric accounts, while placing more importance on the role of non-state actors.[38] We can synthesize two particular positions that are fundamental to the above and other similar discourses, the realist and the pluralist tradition in international relations theory. Realist theory is premised on four basic assumptions.[39] First, that States are the principal actors, and that they represent the main unit of analysis. Second, the State is viewed as a unitary actor, facing the outside world as an integrated unit. Third, the State is seen essentially as a rational actor. Finally, there is an assumption of a hierarchy of international issues, with national security atop other priorities.[40] At the other end of the theoretical spectrum from realism, in terms of the units of analysis of the international system, lies the pluralist paradigm.[41] Pluralists make four key assumptions about international relations.[42] Primarily, non-state actors are important entities in world politics. Secondly, the State is not looked upon as a unified actor, rather, competition, coalition building, and compromise between various interest groups including multinational enterprises will eventually culminate into a 'decision' announced in the name of the State. Thirdly, pluralists challenge the realist assumption of the State as a rational actor, and this derives from the second assumption where the clash of competing interests may not always provide for a rational decision-making process. Finally, the nature of the international agenda is

positions against rival accounts. See Steve Smith *The Self-Images of a Discipline: A Genealogy of International Relations Theory* in INTERNATIONAL RELATIONS THEORY TODAY 7–30 (Ken Booth and Steve Smith eds 1995).

[38] See TRANSNATIONAL RELATIONS AND WORLD POLITICS (Robert O Keohane and Joseph S Nye Jr eds 1971). See also RICHARD W MANSBACH, YALE H FERGUSON, AND DONALD E LAMPERT, THE WEB OF WORLD POLITICS: NONSTATE ACTORS IN THE GLOBAL SYSTEM (1976). For a more recent account and slightly altered work in this tradition, see BRINGING TRANSNATIONAL RELATIONS BACK IN: NON-STATE ACTORS, DOMESTIC STRUCTURES AND INTERNATIONAL INSTITUTIONS (Thomas Risse-Kappen ed 1995).

[39] The founding works of realist thinking in international relations theory are: E H CARR, THE TWENTY YEARS CRISIS, 1919–1939: AN INTRODUCTION TO THE STUDY OF INTERNATIONAL RELATIONS (1939); and HANS J MORGENTHAU, POLITICS AMONG NATIONS: THE STRUGGLE FOR POWER AND PEACE (1948). The neo-realist tradition was presented in KENNETH N WALTZ, THEORY OF INTERNATIONAL POLITICS (1979).

[40] PAUL R VIOTTI AND MARK V KAUPPI, INTERNATIONAL RELATIONS THEORY: REALISM, PLURALISM, GLOBALISM 5–7 (1993).

[41] Pluralism covers a myriad of theoretical approaches including 'transnationalism', 'domestic politics' and 'interdependence'. On the pluralist paradigm, see Keohane and Nye (1971) (n 38); GRAHAM ALLISON, ESSENCE OF DECISION: EXPLAINING THE CUBAN MISSILE CRISIS (1971), in which Allison traces the bureaucratic politics involved in the critical decision-making process of the US response during the Cuban Missile Crisis; JAMES N ROSENAU, THE STUDY OF GLOBAL INTERDEPENDENCE: ESSAYS ON THE TRANSNATIONALISATION OF WORLD AFFAIRS (1980); and ROBERT O KEOHANE AND JOSEPH S NYE, POWER AND INTERDEPENDENCE (2nd edn 1989).

[42] Viotti and Kauppi (1993) (n 40) 228–9.

extensive and includes issues of national security as well as economic, social and environmental issues.

Two important elements in this debate within international relations are of direct interest for our purposes, both supported by the pluralist vision. The first element is the importance of accounting for non-state actors in the study of the international system. The second element involves what is referred to as the level of analysis problem, enquiring at what level we seek to base our understanding of international phenomena. 'The 'level of analysis problem' is about how to identify and treat different types of location in which sources of explanation for observed phenomena can be found.'[43] While realist international relations theory advocates a systemic explanation of international phenomena, deriving from its assumption of the State as a unitary actor, we are more inclined towards pluralist analysis that integrates domestic influences as factors to be accounted for in explaining these international phenomena—international rule-making in our case.[44]

Domestic politics accounts vary, with observers identifying three such subcategories:[45] 'society-centred' accounts that appreciate the influence of domestic interest groups;[46] 'state-centred' accounts that focus on the decision-making process within the executive branch;[47] and 'state-society relations' which focuses on the institutions linking state and society.[48] While working in the 'state-centred' account, yet to date, the most sophisticated model developed to integrate domestic and systemic explanations is Putnam's two-level game analysis.[49] Putnam argued that 'we need to move beyond the mere observation that domestic factors influence international affairs and vice versa, and beyond simple catalogues of instances of such influence, to seek theories that integrate both spheres, accounting for the areas of entanglement between them.'[50] In pursuing this aim, he developed his model from insights on the Bonn Summit of 1978. In this model, the politics of international negotiations occurs as a two level-game, the first is a game of domestic interest group politics, and the second is the international

[43] Barry Buzan *The Level of Analysis Problem in International Relations Reconsidered* in Booth and Smith eds (1995) (n 37) 199.

[44] For an excellent literature review of attempts to integrate international and domestic politics, see Andrew Moravcsik *Introduction: Integrating International and Domestic Theories of International Bargaining* in DOUBLE-EDGED DIPLOMACY: INTERNATIONAL BARGAINING AND DOMESTIC POLITICS (Peter Evans, Harold Jacobson, and Robert Putnam eds 1993).

[45] ibid 6.

[46] *See* RAYMOND A BAUER, ITHIEL DE SOLA POOL AND LEWIS A DEXTER, AMERICAN BUSINESS AND PUBLIC POLICY (1963).

[47] See Allison (1971) (n 41).

[48] On this account, see PETER KATZENSTEIN, BETWEEN POWER AND PLENTY: THE FOREIGN ECONOMIC POLICIES OF ADVANCED INDUSTRIAL STATES (1978).

[49] Robert D Putnam *Diplomacy and Domestic Politics: The Logic of Two-Level Games* 42 INT'L ORGb 427 (1988).

[50] ibid 433.

deal-making process more familiar to realist analysis with its eye on the 'national interest'. Putnam presents a perceptive visualization of this two-level game:

> Each national political leader appears at both game boards. Across the international table sit his foreign counterparts, and at his elbows sit diplomats and other international advisers. Around the domestic table behind him sit party and parliamentary figures, spokespersons for domestic agencies, representatives of key interest groups, and the leader's own political advisers.[51]

In modern day political systems, particularly so in Western-style democracies, his model presents that the main goal for negotiators is to achieve a negotiated outcome that would be capable of ratification in the national legislature. This process therefore entails two stages, inter-state bargaining, which it is hoped, will develop into a tentative agreement, described as Level I, and secondly, achieving the support of domestic groups for that tentative agreement with the aim of ratification, what he describes as Level II.[52] Clearly, this is an oversimplification of the empirical reality of negotiations as domestic discussions often precede international negotiations as is posited in this current study. The achievement of the necessary domestic support for a given tentative agreement depends on the size of the 'win-set', which is defined as all possible level I agreements that would 'win', meaning capable of achieving ratification.[53] Putnam goes on to consider three factors that determine the size of these 'win-sets', namely: level II preferences and coalitions; nature of level II institutions; and the strategies adopted by the negotiator at level I.

Putnam's analysis presents an insightful model for explaining the interaction of domestic and international politics. It is particularly useful for the purposes of our study in that it attaches the domestic context to international negotiations, which encompasses international economic negotiations over a treaty instrument. Nonetheless, there are two additional criticisms that we level against his model. Primarily, his focus on 'ratification' as the arbiter of the domestic influence on international negotiations, characterizes it with a negative force, which precludes a more positive conceptualization of the power of the domestic factors in directly shaping those negotiations. In other words, it gives priority to level I in shaping the outcome, subject to modification to satisfy level II requirements. What we are after in this book is the reverse, with level II largely shaping the outcome, subject to modification to satisfy level I agreement.

[51] ibid 434. [52] ibid 436. [53] ibid 437.

Secondly, and more significantly, we raise an objection to Putnam's zealous focus on the statesman as the negotiator sitting on both tables. This emphasis emanates from the assumption of rational-choice theory.[54] What we may find is that this assumption is contrary to the evidence, and perhaps what we are dealing with what can best be explained by a public-choice account, where MNEs and/or other interest groups produce more influence than accounted for under rational-choice. Evans presents this point eloquently in his commentary on case-studies following the model:

> The obvious challenge is created by the vision of the constrained but still relatively autonomous chief executive as the fulcrum for an integrative analysis. This 'state-centric' vision emerged out of the cases almost in spite of the project's preconceptions. Even among those who accept the importance of developing an integrative approach, many will want to challenge this COG-centred view, suggesting instead ways of linking domestic and international factors more directly, with less intermediation through the pinnacles of the state apparatus.[55]

(IV) THE VIEW FROM A REGULATION THEORY PERSPECTIVE[56]

There is no single definition of the concept of 'regulation'. Baldwin et al account for three meanings offered in the literature: regulation as 'targeted rules', as 'direct state intervention in the economy', and as 'encompassing all mechanisms of social control by whomsoever exercised'.[57] Although discussing regulation in the national context, Baldwin et al's first meaning of the term as 'targeted rules', satisfies our purpose in dealing with international

[54] See Moravcsik (1993) (n 44) 16.

[55] Peter Evans *Building an Integrative Approach to International and Domestic Politics: Reflections and Projections* in DOUBLE-EDGED DIPLOMACY: INTERNATIONAL BARGAINING AND DOMESTIC POLITICS 401 (Peter Evans, Harold Jacobson, and Robert Putnam eds 1993).

[56] As a subject, regulation dates from the18th-century 'police science', and is peculiarly characterized by the fact that it does not belong, in the sense of being 'owned', to any particular academic discipline. Nonetheless, it has been described as a political process exhibiting a main feature of political studies, that is the contest of power, but it simultaneously delves into legal issues; hence it is also a legal process. See CHRISTOPHER HOOD, EXPLAINING ECONOMIC POLICY REVERSALS 20 (1994); and Hancher and Moran eds (1989) (n 14) 4.

[57] A READER ON REGULATION 2–4 (Robert Baldwin, Colin Scott and Christopher Hood eds 1998). See also ROBERT BALDWIN AND MARTIN CAVE, UNDERSTANDING REGULATION: THEORY, STRATEGY, AND PRACTICE 1–2 (1999). Apart from the three definitions of the term 'regulation', there is also a definitional rift between American and European usages of the term. American usage implies a specific kind of policy-making designed for interference with markets, whereas the European usage is taken as a synonym for governance. See DE-REGULATION OR RE-REGULATION? REGULATORY REFORM IN EUROPE AND THE UNITED STATES 1–2 (Giandomenico Majone ed 1989); Giandomenico Majone *The Rise of the Regulatory State in Europe* (1994) W EUR POL 77, 78 (1994); and Hood (1994) (n 56) 19.

regulation. They state that 'at its simplest, regulation refers to the promulgation of an authoritative set of rules, accompanied by some mechanism, typically a public agency, for monitoring and promoting compliance with these rules.'[58] In this sense then and for our purposes, international economic regulation refers to the overwhelming variety of transnational, international, and indeed national[59] rules and processes designed to regulate the global economy, including domestic economies. Indeed, international economic regulation has been hailed as a new species of regulation involving rule-making at the supranational level and rule-implementation at the national level.[60]

There are various theoretical explanations of regulation, a considerable number of which are explanations that examine the external influences on regulatory regimes and are based on the notion of 'interest'.[61] For our purposes, a special category of regulatory theory explains regulation in terms that account for the role of MNEs. This group of theories referred to by Baldwin and Cave as 'private interest theories' views regulation as driven by the pursuit of private interests, rather than public or group interest.[62] Among the most important concepts of this group is regulatory 'capture'. This concept, deriving from a realist view of regulation with 'power' as a focal issue, describes how the regulatory agencies set up to regulate particular activities, have been effectively controlled by those whom they were meant to regulate.[63] As Hood would put it, 'the mice ended up in charge of the cheese.'[64] A category of this group, the 'public choice' theory,[65] based on an economic model of regulation, presents the vision that regulation is initiated originally not in the pursuit of public interest, but rather originates in the self-interested pursuits of business for government intervention in the economy on behalf of their interests. In return, politicians would sell regulatory policy to those interests capable of providing votes directly or through campaign contributions.

[58] Baldwin et al (1998) (n 57) 3.

[59] Most notably those with an extraterritorial effect.

[60] Baldwin et al (1998) (n 57) 29.

[61] Baldwin and Cave (1999) (n 57) 18–19, and ch 3 for a review of Regulation theories. See also BARRY M MITNICK, THE POLITICAL ECONOMY OF REGULATION: CREATING, DESIGNING, AND REMOVING REGULATORY FORMS ch 3 (1980); and STEPHEN BREYER, REGULATION AND ITS REFORM ch 1 (1982).

[62] Baldwin and Cave (1999) (n 57) 21–22.

[63] See Toni Makkai and John Braithwaite *In and Out of the Revolving Door: Making Sense of Regulatory Capture* in Baldwin, Scott and Hood eds (1998) (n 57).

[64] Hood (1994) (n 56) 21.

[65] This approach is developed in MANCUR OLSON, THE LOGIC OF COLLECTIVE ACTION: PUBLIC GOODS AND THEORY OF GROUPS (1965); George J Stigler *The Theory of Economic Regulation* 2 BELL J ECON 3 (1971); and Richard A Posner *Theories of Economic Regulation* 5 BELL J ECON 335 (1974).

One particular work of direct relevance to this study, seeks to integrate the insights of public choice theory to the explanation of international economic law.[66] Applying it to four problem areas: executive power; currency controls; trade and the environment; and protection of culture, the author concludes that its application (public choice theory),

> tends to undermine the logical appeal to implicit norms that often makes up the heart of legal analysis, and it poses questions that require empirical responses. It suggests that appetites more than ideals might dominate the lawmaking process. . . .'[67]

Yet, he commends its application, where it augurs a much clearer comprehension of the problems of international economic law.

However, just as there is no precise definition of the concept of regulation; theories of regulation do not offer sharp distinctive visions of the regulatory enterprise. Rather, they can accommodate different aspects between them, and hence, works on regulation need not necessarily be attributed solely to a particular theory. Braithwaite and Drahos's research on the globalization of business regulation, is an example of such a work cutting across different accounts of regulation.[68] In their approach, they present us with a particular vision of the impact of globalization on international economic regulation. An explanatory and descriptive approach of how international economic rules have been made, primarily, in the post-Second World War era, although they trace the roots of some regulatory areas to much earlier epochs. For them, globalization is the driving force of the homogenization of regulation where its content is converging onto a single global standard, although not in a necessarily linear fashion as they caution (pp 23–4). In this sense, they view the globalization of regulation as essentially the harmonization of regulation. Apart from the explanation of regulation, their work contains (indeed is based upon) a strong, normative element, where they espouse 'citizen sovereignty' as an ideal that can and should be advanced in the globalization of regulation. Within their descriptive and explanatory scholarship, they present us with a method whereby 'weaker' actors can attempt to influence the regulatory course—chiefly through the mechanism of modelling.

On the other hand, they identify three modes of business (MNE) influence in the regulatory process (pp 488–94). Primarily, through shaping the behaviour of States and international organizations where they account for

[66] Paul B Stephan III *Barbarians Inside the Gate: Public Choice Theory and International Economic Law* 10 Am U J Int'l L and Pol'y 745 (1995).

[67] ibid 767.

[68] John Braithwaite and Peter Drahos, Global Business Regulation (2000). Further references to this work will be indicated within brackets in the text below.

the concept of regulatory capture. A particularly clear case of regulatory capture that they discuss is Motorola Corporation's chairing of the committee setting telecom standards in the International Telecommunication Union (p 4). They note in particular that amongst MNEs,

> US corporations exert more power in the world system than corporations of other states because they can enrol the support of the most powerful state in the world, which is prepared to deal directly with the corporations (partly due to the fund-raising methods of US political campaigns). . . . The other advantage of US companies is that the Washington political environment (as opposed to the Brussels or Tokyo environment) is hospitable to ad hoc groupings of like-minded companies setting up a Washington lobbying office and gaining political access at the highest levels (p 490).

The second mode of MNE influence in the regulatory process is by shaping regulation directly. They note that one of the major findings in their research is that global regulatory norms follow globalizing self-regulatory practice (p 491). It is in this regard that modelling, a mechanism emphasized as effective by the authors, has been well utilized by international business, as they model their own practices across national borders. And they warn against the perception of 'standard-setting at an international organization as the decisive moment in the history of the globalization of a form of regulation,' rather, it merely formalizes a consistently practised informal regulatory reality (p 492). Finally, Braithwaite and Drahos present as the third mode of MNE influence, their ability to shape regulation by regulating other businesses or states, referring to private organizations such as the New York Stock Exchange (NYSE), or the ICC Court of Arbitration, which establish regulatory frameworks for other actors to follow.

With this brief analysis of regulation theory, and the introduction of the argument of an important work of relevance to this book, in addition to the earlier sections on international legal theory and international relations theory, we hope we have adequately introduced the most important conceptual evaluations of the structure and process of international rule-making.

Chapter 3

Influence of MNEs on International Economic Regulation

The TRIPS Agreement was negotiated within the intergovernmental forum of the GATT. However, as this book argues, the pervasive influence of MNEs, and particularly the pharmaceutical MNE lobby in alliance with other business interests was fundamental in launching the negotiations, and in carrying them toward their eventual culmination into the TRIPS Agreement. This chapter will therefore address the issue of the influence of MNEs on international economic regulation.

(I) DEFINING MULTINATIONAL ENTERPRISES

Primarily, we have to properly define what exactly we mean when we apply the term 'multinational enterprises'. Fieldhouse argues that the earliest appellation of the term 'multinational corporation' is traceable to David E Lilienthal, onetime head of the Tennessee Valley Authority, who defined them as 'corporations—which have their home in one country but which operate and live under the laws and customs of other countries as well.'[1] On the other hand, Strange attributes the term 'multinational' as allegedly first used by the Public Relations division of IBM in the early 1960s to conceal or divert attention from the fact that it was an American enterprise, even though it was seeking market access throughout the world.[2] Apart from these earlier roots of the use of the term 'multinational,' there are three broad definition attempts: the economists' definition; the definition of the UN; and the definition of the OECD.[3]

The economists tend to offer an inclusive definition of the term where 'a multinational enterprise is a corporation which owns (in whole or in part), controls and manages income-generating assets in more than one country. In so doing it engages in international production, namely production

[1] Quoted in D K Fieldhouse *The Multinational: A Critique of a Concept* in MULTINATIONAL ENTERPRISE IN HISTORICAL PERSPECTIVE 10 (Alice Teichova, Maurice Levy-Leboyer and Helga Nussbaum eds 1986).

[2] SUSAN STRANGE, THE RETREAT OF THE STATE: THE DIFFUSION OF POWER IN THE WORLD ECONOMY xiii (1996).

[3] P T MUCHLINSKI, MULTINATIONAL ENTERPRISES AND THE LAW 12–15 (1999).

across national boundaries financed by foreign direct investment.'[4] In UN parlance, the term 'transnational' is favoured, and is used to refer to the extent of operations or activities, rather than ownership, which the term 'multinational' refers to.[5] The OECD definition focuses on the nature of influence or control, where it stresses the ability of one company to control the activities of another located in another country.[6] Apart from definitions with regard to ownership or control, distinctions also take into account the nature of the enterprise's operations. In a recent edition on non-state actors in the global system, the editors distinguish between transnational corporations (TNCs) and multinational corporations (MNCs), where the former is seen to be engaged in a 'world-wide intra-firm division of labour,' and the latter 'replicates production within a number of regions.'[7] On the other hand, the use of 'enterprise' rather than 'company' or 'corporation' is intended to imply a legally neutral description since the multinational as an entity is not a company or corporation in the legal sense, but 'an aggregate group or network of corporate and non-corporate entities, established under the domestic laws of different nations.'[8] Finally, the International Law Institute states that 'Enterprises which consist of a decision-making centre located in one country and of operating centres, with or without legal personality, situated in one or more countries should, in law, be considered as multinational enterprises.'[9]

Multinational enterprises also represent a particular strand of the universe of actors that are defined by what they are not, rather than by what they are, as 'non-state actors.' Higgott et al classify TNCs and MNCs as 'private sector corporate actors' representing one strand of non-state actors to be differentiated from non-governmental organizations (NGOs).[10] But while NGOs clearly do not include MNEs as such, they include groupings or associations of MNEs, and of business generally, organized to advance the interests of their MNE members on certain issues.[11] The latter

[4] NEIL HOOD AND STEPHEN YOUNG, THE ECONOMICS OF MULTINATIONAL ENTERPRISE 3 (1979).

[5] CYNTHIA DAY WALLACE, LEGAL CONTROL OF THE MULTINATIONAL ENTERPRISE: NATIONAL REGULATORY TECHNIQUES AND THE PROSPECTS FOR INTERNATIONAL CONTROLS 11–12 (1983).

[6] Muchlinski (1999) (n 3) 13.

[7] Richard A Higgott, Geoffrey R D Underhill and Andreas Bieler *Introduction: Globalisation and Non-State Actors* in NON-STATE ACTORS AND AUTHORITY IN THE GLOBAL SYSTEM 1 (Richard A Higgott, Geoffrey RD Underhill and Andreas Bieler eds 1999). They base this differentiation on Ruigrok and van Tulder's distinction between firms adopting a 'globalization' strategy and those following a 'glocalization' strategy. See WINFRIED RUIGROK AND ROB VAN TULDER, THE LOGIC OF INTERNATIONAL RESTRUCTURING 9 (1995).

[8] Wallace (1983) (n 5) 10.

[9] Quoted in Wallace (1983) 13. Writing in 1983, Wallace cautioned that this definition had not enjoyed wide acceptance as an official definition.

[10] Higgott et al (1999) (n 7) 1–2.

[11] Steve Charnovitz *Two Centuries of Participation: NGOs and International Governance* 18 MICH J INT'L L 183, 187 (1997).

form of business association has been referred to by Archer as BINGOs, short for Business International Non-Governmental Organizations.[12]

Having defined multinational enterprises, we devote the remainder of this chapter to theories developed to explain MNEs as political actors. An important point to bear in mind while approaching theoretical work on the multinational enterprise is the linchpin of analysis. Two approaches are conceivable: primarily, to understand the MNE as an 'agent' from within—a sort of endogenous theorizing of the firm and hence in this instance, the focus is on the MNE as a structure in which interactions within it—mainly organizational—are the focus of interest.[13] Alternatively, there is the view of the MNE as an 'agent' in an exogenous structure.

(II) MULTINATIONAL ENTERPRISES AS POLITICAL ACTORS

As the treaty-making process is essentially a political process,[14] a political examination of MNEs is essential for understanding their influence on multilateral rule-making. We must be cautious however, in noting that a political theory of MNEs does not refer merely to the tools deployed by MNEs in their action, rather, it refers to the aims for which MNEs are pursuing a given course of action, for which they can deploy economic (material resources and money) as well as political power such as bargaining and lobbying.[15] Theories of the political activities of the MNE as they relate to their interactions with governments can be roughly divided into macro- and micro-approaches.[16] It must be noted that both approaches are not mutually exclusive, for example, the adoption of a bargaining model (a micro-approach) could be informed by a liberal, dependency or neo-mercantilist worldview (the three macro-approaches). The approaches (macro and micro) are merely methods of categorizing aggregated data phenomenon rather than a theoretical standpoint.

The macro-approach is informed by the three grand traditions of international political economy: the liberal (or orthodox) perspective, also known as the sovereignty-at-bay model; the Marxist (or dependency school) perspective; and the nationalist (or neo-mercantilist)

[12] CLIVE ARCHER, INTERNATIONAL ORGANIZATIONS 43 (2nd edn 1992).

[13] This is the approach of the microeconomic theory of the firm.

[14] Malgosia Fitzmaurice *Actors and Factors in the Evolution of Treaty Norms: An Empirical Study* 4 AUS REV INT'L AND EUR L 1, 3 (1999).

[15] Jean J Boddewyn *Political Aspects of MNE Theory* 19 J INT'L BUS STUD 341, 342–3 (1988).

[16] Thomas L Brewer *An Issue-Area Approach to the Analysis of MNE-Government Relations* 23 J INT'L BUS STUD 295, 296–300 (1992).

perspective.[17] The liberal approach to MNE-government relations traces its roots to the seminal work of Raymond Vernon, *Sovereignty at Bay*.[18]This approach argues that the nature of MNEs as powerful economic entities that operate across borders with a high degree of flexibility and sophisticated managerial systems has severely curtailed the sovereignty of States due to the inflexibility of the nation-state system. With regard to home states, due to the activities of their MNEs, national economic policy has largely lost its relevance and effect.[19] Furthermore, MNEs also pose a threat to the sovereignty of host countries in their control over their national economies, whether in the developed countries, as documented in Servan-Schreiber's account on the impact of US MNEs in Europe,[20] or in the less developed countries where MNEs can create relations of dependence and distort their development paths.[21] Hence, the nature of MNE-government relations are antagonistic and conflictual, with the MNE posited as the stronger party. However, in his most recent work, Professor Vernon has backtracked from this rather fatalist approach, presenting that through cooperation, this conflict of interest can be accommodated by both parties.[22]

The second macro-approach, the dependency school of MNE-government relations, assumes MNEs to be in alliance with home governments and in a conflictual relationship with host governments in DCs.[23] Furthermore, DCs are assumed to be in a weaker, more dependent position vis-à-vis the multinationals. This analysis is informed by dependency theory's vision of the world as composed of a 'core' that includes the industrialized countries of the north, dominating a 'periphery' composed of developing countries. MNEs are seen in such a model as agents of this 'exploitative' condition, seeking to extend their interests at the expense of the DC hosts, and largely independent of their IC home state governments which they can bring into action on their behalf.[24] The weakness of the

[17] ROBERT GILPIN, THE POLITICAL ECONOMY OF INTERNATIONAL RELATIONS 241 (1987). For a good summary of the three approaches, see Shah M Tarzi *Multinational Corporations and American Foreign Policy: Radical, Sovereignty-at-Bay, and State-Centric Approaches* 28 INT'L STUD 359 (1991). See also Brewer (1992) (n 16) 298–9.

[18] RAYMOND VERNON, SOVEREIGNTY AT BAY: THE MULTINATIONAL SPREAD OF US BUSINESS (1971).

[19] ibid 16–18.

[20] J-J SERVAN-SCHREIBER, THE AMERICAN CHALLENGE (1979). See also RAYMOND VERNON, STORM OVER THE MULTINATIONALS: THE REAL ISSUES ch 6 (1977).

[21] Vernon (1971) (n 18) 181–6; and Vernon (1977) (n 18) ch 7.

[22] RAYMOND VERNON, IN THE HURRICANE'S EYE: THE TROUBLED PROSPECTS OF MULTINATIONAL ENTERPRISES ch 6 (1998).

[23] See RICHARD J BARNET AND RONALD E MULLER, GLOBAL REACH: THE POWER OF THE MULTINATIONAL CORPORATION (1974); and ROBERT W COX, PRODUCTION, POWER AND WORLD ORDER: SOCIAL FORCES IN THE MAKING OF HISTORY (1987).

[24] See Barnet and Muller (1974) (n 23) 72–104.

dependency approach however, is that its treatment of MNEs is assumed within the larger treatment of development, or rather, underdevelopment. Similarly, it focuses its treatment on DCs to the exclusion of ICs, currently, the primary location of MNE activity.[25]

Finally, the third macro-approach, the nationalist approach to MNE-government relations, was most clearly developed by Robert Gilpin.[26] In his work, Gilpin argues that the liberal and Marxist views of MNEs operating either independently of governmental policies or controlling them are inadequate, rather he favours a neo-mercantilist interpretation where the governments of both home and host countries try to bend the behaviour of inward and outward investors to their domestic and international purposes. MNEs have been able to penetrate foreign markets, because it is in the interest of the dominant State for them to do so. His work has a parallel normative aim in advocating that the US government should weigh the benefits as well as losses from its own MNEs, and not assume that MNE and US interests automatically coincide. This perspective, in tandem with Gilpin's thought, is influenced by realist international relations theory, where power is thought to ultimately reside with the state.

On the other hand, the micro-approach to MNE-government relations is dominated by bargaining theory, as applied to MNE-government negotiations in international business (IB), and international political economy (IPE) scholarships.[27] Another more nascent micro-approach seeks to integrate the political behaviour of MNEs into economic models of the MNE, namely the 'eclectic paradigm.'[28]

Bargaining theory has been the most popular perspective on MNE-government relations, to the extent that it has been described as '*the* currently accepted paradigm of HC [Host Country]—MNC relations in international political economy'.[29] The bargaining relationship has been defined as that where 'two (or more) parties seek through cooperation to achieve goals that each cannot gain by themselves'.[30] Hence, in game theory terminology, the outcome of the bargain is dependent on the benefits sought

25 See GRAZIA IETTO-GILLIES, INTERNATIONAL PRODUCTION: TRENDS, THEORIES, EFFECTS 74–75 (1992).

26 ROBERT GILPIN, US POWER AND THE MULTINATIONAL CORPORATION (1975).

27 For a good recent review, see Robert Grosse and Jack N Behrman *Theory in International Business* 1 TRANSNAT'L CORP 93 (1992). See also THEODORE MORAN, MULTINATIONAL CORPORATIONS AND THE POLITICS OF DEPENDENCE: COPPER IN CHILE (1974).

28 See Jean J Boddewyn (1988) (n 15).

29 Stephen J Kobrin *Testing the Bargaining Hypothesis in the Manufacturing Sector in Developing Countries* 41 INT'L ORG 609, 610 (1987). For a further discussion of this approach, see Moran (1974) (n 27); Nathan Fagre and Louis T Wells *Bargaining Power of Multinationals and Host Governments*, 13 J INT'L BUS STUD 9 (1982); and JN BEHRMAN AND ROBERT E GROSSE, INTERNATIONAL BUSINESS AND GOVERNMENTS: ISSUES AND INSTITUTIONS (1990).

30 Behrman and Grosse (1990) (n 27) 7.

by each player, compared to the contributions the other is prepared to offer, subject to the stakes involved for either player, as well as the goal congruence of both players.[31] Theodore Moran argued that contrary to the dependency perspective, DC hosts can have a stronger bargaining position vis-à-vis MNEs.[32] He argued that while MNEs' bargaining power is strongest in entry negotiations, their power declines considerably while that of the host country rises once the MNE has established its plant.[33] While Moran discussed his finding with regard to FDI in the extractive industries, yet in the manufacturing sector, these were not found to be totally conclusive, where MNEs possess more bargaining advantages than host States.[34]

Moran's thesis that governments have a stronger bargaining position, remains a strong view of the bargaining relationship between MNEs and governments. Walter, in a study on FDI, concludes along Moran's line that the 'structural power'[35] of MNEs (represented in what he describes as the 'convergence hypothesis'), has been exaggerated, and that in fact, based on his empirical work, developing host State governments do maintain an advantaged bargaining position.[36] Furthermore, the structural weakness of MNEs limits the ability of their home governments to negotiate stronger international investment agreements with developing country hosts.[37] Finally, Walter adds that to engage in political lobbying activities, MNEs are thereby confirming their structural weakness.[38]

Contrary to the views presented by Moran and Walter, there was, and continues to be, a divergence in the literature as to which actor possesses a stronger bargaining position. Presenting the opposite argument, Stopford and Strange state:

> [o]ur conclusion is that governments as a group have indeed lost bargaining power to the multinationals as the possibilities for collective action have diminished. Intensifying competition among states seems to have been a more important force for weakening their bargaining power than have the changes in global competition among firms.[39]

[31] ibid 8–14.

[32] Moran (1974) (n 27).

[33] This phenomenon described as the 'obsolescing bargain' was further developed in Vernon (1977) (n 20).

[34] Kobrin (1987) (n 29).

[35] For a description of the term, see Susan Strange (1996) (n 2) 25–7.

[36] Andrew Walter *Globalization and Policy Convergence: The Case of Direct Investment Rules* in NON-STATE ACTORS AND AUTHORITY IN THE GLOBAL SYSTEM 51–73 (Richard Higgott, Geoffrey R D Underhill and Andreas Bieler eds 1999).

[37] ibid 70.

[38] A similar account presents the inability of MNEs to effectively influence the course of the negotiations of the draft Multilateral Agreement on Investment within the OECD (MAI). See Elizabeth Smythe *State Authority and Investment Security: Non-State Actors and the Negotiation of the Multilateral Agreement on Investment at the OECD* in NON-STATE ACTORS AND AUTHORITY IN THE GLOBAL SYSTEM (Richard Higgott, Geoffrey RD Underhill and Andreas Bieler eds 1999).

[39] JOHN STOPFORD, SUSAN STRANGE AND JOHN S HENLEY, RIVAL STATE, RIVAL FIRMS: COMPETITION FOR WORLD MARKET SHARES 215 (1991).

This analysis by Stopford and Strange, representing the 'convergence hypothesis' referred to by Walter, must be qualified by the latter's conclusion, that MNEs have also suffered from collective action problems, and as a whole, it is MNEs rather than States that have lost out in the power relation. Nonetheless, Walter's treatment is to be further qualified by his limiting his study to the issue of FDI, to the exclusion of other issues of interest to MNEs, as well as by his study's exclusion from empirical investigation of MNE lobbying.[40]

Despite its popularity as an approach explaining the political behaviour of MNEs, yet we must ask the question as to what extent is bargaining theory—in the vast majority of works where it has been applied—of relevance for our purposes.[41] Bargaining theory has mostly been applied to relations between MNEs and developing host countries on the issue of foreign direct investment. Its fundamental premise, as outlined by Moran, is a quid pro quo relationship between MNEs and States (mostly developing). In this vein, these studies develop limited analysis for the specific purposes of our research problem. A more valuable use of the bargaining approach could be found in those studies focusing on particular legislation which involved lobbying on the part of MNEs. One such example was presented by DeVos in his study on the role of MNEs attempts to derail social legislation (the Vredeling Proposal) at the level of the then EEC.[42]

Finally, the second micro-approach to the political behaviour of MNEs, developed in large part by Boddewyn, seeks to 'enrich Dunning's eclectic paradigm by explicitly incorporating political elements in the consideration of ownership (O), internalization (I) and location (L) advantages.'[43] The model argues that contrary to the assumption of economists, that the regulatory environment in a particular market is a 'given,' it is often the case that it is in fact a 'taken', 'with significant implications for the nature of ownership advantages and the internalisation of external agents'.[44]

Primarily, Boddewyn in dealing with the 'O' advantages, presents that they can include advantages pertaining to tackling the non-market environment, mainly: better intelligence about political actors and opportunities; readier access to political opinion and decision makers; and 'superior influence skills'.[45] Secondly, with regard to 'I' advantages, it seeks to explain

[40] Walter (1999) (n 36) 52.

[41] For a criticism of bargaining theory with regard to relations between MNEs and states, see Stopford, Strange and Henley (1991) (n 39) 134–6.

[42] See TON DEVOS, MULTINATIONAL CORPORATIONS IN DEMOCRATIC HOST COUNTRIES: US MULTINATIONALS AND THE VREDELING PROPOSAL (1989); and M Nelson, *The Vredeling Directive—the EEC's Failed Attempt to Regulate Multinational Enterprises and Organize Collective Bargaining*, 20 NYU J INT'L L AND POL 967 (1988).

[43] Jean J Boddewyn (1988) (n 15) 341–2.

[44] ibid 344.

[45] ibid 348.

why the 'O' advantages outlined above are built into the MNE hierarchy rather than bought and sold through arms length transactions in the market. Essentially, there are two types of political intermediate products, knowledge/expertise about political and social conditions, and that of 'beneficial government decisions'. On the longer run, it is in the interest of MNEs to seek to internalize them due to the nature of the external market not guaranteeing long-term 'supply'.[46] Finally, with regard to the 'L' advantages, the model presents that home and host location advantages can also include political factors. While he presents the inclusion of an environment conducive to political activity by MNEs as a factor influencing the willingness of MNEs to engage in FDI. Similarly, we can present that the 'L' advantages can also exist with regard to MNEs engaging in efforts to influence international economic regulation, namely those with their headquarters in the 'paradigm-setting states (most notably American MNEs) have the advantage of better access to shaping the policy position of their home States.

As elegant as the above classification into macro- and micro-approaches to MNE political activity might be, there are certain scholarly traditions that cannot be easily compartmentalized within its bounds. Most notably in this regard, is the work of Stopford and Strange which advocates that the nature of the relation between states and firms has changed due to the exigencies of the changing international system, what they describe as structural changes. Both actors are involved in a competition that revolves around the creation of wealth, and that is affected equally by the interaction between States, between firms, and between States and firms. Hence, a triangular diplomacy is what best describes interaction in the international political economy.[47] Their analyses prods governments to perceive the game of competition over wealth as entailing the necessity of forging alliances with some MNEs, and they caution that similar to international security arrangements, the choice of which MNEs to pick as allies is fundamental.

Another work of significance is Sally's study of French and German MNEs, which argues that in the distribution of wealth and power, MNEs are at the interface of domestic structures, and the process of internationalization within global political economic structures.[48] Sally argues that the MNE is at the vortex of a myriad of relationships with other actors including different levels of government. The linkages it creates in the regional and domestic setting, in turn, can assist it in 'influencing variables of power

[46] ibid 349–354.

[47] Stopford, Strange and Henley (1991) (n 39) 19–29.

[48] RAZEEN SALLY, STATES AND FIRMS: MULTINATIONAL ENTERPRISES IN INSTITUTIONAL COMPETITION (1995). See also Razeen Sally *Multinational Enterprises, Political Economy and Institutional Theory: Domestic Embeddedness in the Context of Internationalization* 1 REV INT'L POL ECON 161 (1994).

and public policy process and outcome in the international political economy.'[49]

The above two models in particular draw a more encompassing approach to viewing MNE-government relations, than the majority of work conducted within bargaining theory. Hence, they can be classified, if we so choose, under the macro-approaches to the political behaviour of firms. Indeed, Sally's work is adaptable to being placed under the liberal macro-approach. Nonetheless, their insights are particularly powerful due to their treatment of the conditioning international environment within which the political activities of MNEs occur. This then draws our attention to the importance of this factor of examining MNE activity within the outer structure of regulation in our context of the TRIPS negotiations.

[49] Sally (1994) 162.

Chapter 4

Patent Protection and the TRIPS Agreement

(I) AN INTRODUCTION TO PATENT PROTECTION

The term 'patent' derives from Latin meaning 'open' as used in 'Letters Patent' in England since the 14th century granting the inventor or importer of a new device or method the right of sole use for a certain period of time.[1] Cornish defines 'patents' as intellectual property rights granted by a State or regional patent office for a particular invention, ie technological improvement, which contains a degree of inventiveness over what was previously known.[2] Patents last for a set period of time and require the invention to be publicly described in the patent specification. On the other hand, a patent has also been defined as a 'limited monopoly' granted in return for the disclosure of technical information sufficient so that it can be used or 'worked' by someone 'skilled in the art'.[3] This limited monopoly confers on the owner of the patent the exclusive right to control the way their patented invention is exploited for a period of time, to be guaranteed by the State.[4] On the other hand, the World Intellectual Property Organization (WIPO) defines a patent as 'an exclusive right granted for an invention, which is a product or a process that provides, in general, a new way of doing something, or offers a new technical solution to a problem.'[5] Finally, Article 27.1 of the TRIPS Agreement stipulates that patents shall be available 'for any inventions, whether products or processes, in all fields of technology, provided that they are new, involve an inventive step and are capable of industrial application.' While the above definitions concentrate on defining the right in patent protection, a different definition of IPRs has been advanced by Maskus, arguing that in defining patents, we should not only pay attention to the rights conferred to the owners of patents, but also to the users of the patents, hence, he characterizes intellectual property

[1] Daniel Gervais, The TRIPS Agreement: Drafting History and Analysis 65 (1998).

[2] WR Cornish, Intellectual Property: Patents, Copyright, Trade Marks and Allied Rights 7 (4th edn 1999).

[3] Lionel Bently and Brad Sherman, Intellectual Property Law 309 (2001).

[4] ibid

[5] See WIPO <http://www.wipo.int/patentscape/en/patents_faq.html#patent> (last visited 3 Mar 2006).

rights as 'society's attempt to achieve a balance in this fundamental tension among information providers and users.'[6]

The roots of the modern, essentially 'Western' system of intellectual property protection are to be found in the early 15th century in the Italian republics of Florence and Venice.[7] The first patent for invention was granted in 1421 for an architect who invented a barge-like device with hoisting gear used for the transport of marble for construction purposes.[8] However, the first patent law is traceable to Venice in 1469.[9] The patent system was slow to develop in Europe, mainly due to the opposition of the powerful force of the guilds in the economic life of late medieval Europe. Indeed, it was mainly through royal patronage that the system of patent grants was sustained, gradually spreading from the Italian city-states into France, Germany, Holland and Belgium, and into England.[10] In England, the practice of granting a patent derived from the sovereign's power of grant, which entailed an often-abusive monopoly in exchange for revenue for the sovereign until, however, this came to an end in the *Case of Monopolies* in 1602.[11] The result of that case was to effectively place limitations on the sovereign prerogative of granting patent monopoly privileges.[12] These limitations were soon to be codified into the Statute of Monopolies of 1623, and are considered the foundation of English patent law.[13]

The history of international patent regulation, on the other hand, has its roots in the mid-19th century. By that time, most of the leading European economies as well as the United States had adopted quite similar patent systems. However, the problem arose in respect of the protection of the patent of a national in another State.[14] The background to this problem revolved around a raging controversy between three groups over the patent system:[15] the anti-patent movement striving to abolish the patent system and led by Germany; the recognition of patents as private property, led by the United States and Britain; and the recognition of patents as an instru-

[6] Keith E Maskus *Normative Concerns in the International Protection of Intellectual Property Rights* in THE WORLD TRADING SYSTEM: CRITICAL PERSPECTIVES ON THE WORLD ECONOMY, VOL IV, THE URUGUAY ROUND AND BEYOND 15 (Robert Howse ed 1998).

[7] Maximilian Frumkin *The Early History of Patents for Inventions* 26 TRANSACTIONS OF THE NEWCOMEN SOC'Y 47, 48 (1947). See also ASSAFA ENDESHAW, INTELLECTUAL PROPERTY POLICY FOR NON-INDUSTRIAL COUNTRIES ch 3 (1996).

[8] Frumkin (1947) (n 7) 48.

[9] Endeshaw (1996) (n 7) 55.

[10] ibid 56–7.

[11] PETER DRAHOS, A PHILOSOPHY OF INTELLECTUAL PROPERTY RIGHTS 29–30 (1996).

[12] *Darcy v Allen* 72 Eng Rep 830 (KB 1602).

[13] WILLIAM HOLDSWORTH, A HISTORY OF ENGLISH LAW, VOL IV 349–53 (1937).

[14] See Endeshaw (1996) (n 7) 68–9.

[15] See F Machlup and E Penrose *The Patent Controversy in the Nineteenth Century*, 10 J ECON HIST 1 (1950); *and* Heinrich Kronstein and Irene Till *A Re-evaluation of the International Patent Convention*, 12 LAW AND CONTEMP PROBS 765 (1947).

ment of public policy, led by France.[16] While initially the anti-patent movement seemed to gain more ground, and included influential voices, most remarkably *The Economist* magazine,[17] basing their arguments on the importance of free-trade, it was eventually the patent rights movement that prevailed. It is remarkable how similar the lobbying methods of the patent rights movement during the 1860s and 1870s, before the negotiation of the Paris Convention, were to those of the business lobbies that helped fashion and vigorously supported the TRIPS negotiations in the 1980s and 1990s:

> The advocates of the patent system organized a mighty counteroffensive. The techniques of propaganda employed in the years between 1867 and 1877 were quite remarkable for the time. New societies for patent protection were formed, resolutions were drafted and distributed to the daily press, speakers were delegated to professional and trade association meetings, floods of pamphlets and leaflets were released, articles were planted in trade journals and reproduced in daily papers, public competitions were announced with prizes for the best papers in defense of the patent system, petitions were submitted to governments and legislatures, international meetings were arranged, and compromises were made with groups inclined to endorse liberal patent reforms.[18]

As a result of the victory of the patent rights advocates, the Paris Convention for the Protection of Industrial Property was signed in 1883.[19] The Paris Convention, apart from regulating specific issues in industrial property law, established two primary rights: guarantees to the 'right of national treatment'; and guarantees to the 'right of priority'.[20] The Convention was revised four times, the last revision being at Stockholm in 1967 when the World Intellectual Property Organization was established,[21] and amended in 1979. Since 1967, the Convention has been managed by WIPO.

Given the advantage enjoyed by DCs in WIPO as a forum, and bearing in mind its lack of an effective enforcement mechanism, MNEs sought a different forum for negotiating a new international intellectual property

[16] Kronstein and Till 766; and Endeshaw (1996) (n 7) 74.

[17] Machlup and Penrose (1950) (n 15) 3.

[18] ibid 5–6.

[19] Paris Convention for the Protection of Industrial Property 21 UNTS 305 (20 Mar 1883) [hereinafter Paris Convention].

[20] For a leading commentary on the Paris Convention, see GHC Bodenhausen, Guide to the Application of the Paris Convention for the Protection of Industrial Property, as Revised at Stockholm in 1967 (1968).

[21] Convention Establishing the World Intellectual Property Organization (14 July 1967) 828 UNTS 3 (as amended on 28 Sept 1979).

regime.[22] In this regard, GATT provided a convenient venue, and it was through ingenious legal engineering that the linkage between trade and IP was established. The negotiation of the TRIPS Agreement, and particularly its patent provisions, during the Uruguay Round was accompanied by what may be described as a forceful ideological campaign praising the virtues of a strong system of international intellectual property protection.[23] This campaign, in part, was a component of the strategy of MNEs to influence the negotiations on intellectual property in the Uruguay Round. Below, the main provisions of the Agreement will be introduced.

(II) THE TRIPS AGREEMENT

> 'Of all the measures contained in the TRIPS Agreement, the patent provisions may be the most significant in terms of economic implications for developing countries.' UNCTAD[24]

The TRIPS Agreement is composed of Parts I–VII, covering 73 articles. The preamble to the TRIPS Agreement states that the aim of the agreement is to '*reduce distortions and impediments to international trade*'. Being an agreement within the framework of the institutional context of the GATT/WTO, it emphasizes its links to trade. On the other hand, it is only in '*taking into account the need to promote effective and adequate protection of intellectual property rights*', that the protection of IPRs is first introduced into the preambular language of the Agreement. This section will analyse selected provisions of the TRIPS Agreement that are of most relevance to this book in terms of their constraining effects on DC public policy options. Relevant provisions will also be contrasted to existing international standards prior to TRIPS, mainly the Paris Convention.

(A) General Provisions

The general provisions of the TRIPS Agreement are contained in Part I entitled 'General Provisions and Basic Principles', which defines the general scope of intellectual property protection, and identifies the Agreement's objectives and principles. **Article 1.1** spells the 'minimum standards' philosophy of TRIPS, where '*Members may, but shall not be obliged to, imple-*

22 See SUSAN SELL, POWER AND IDEAS: NORTH-SOUTH POLITICS OF INTELLECTUAL PROPERTY AND ANTITRUST (1998).

23 See INTELLECTUAL PROPERTY RIGHTS: GLOBAL CONSENSUS, GLOBAL CONFLICT? (R Michael Gadbaw and Timothy J Richards eds 1988).

24 UNCTAD, THE TRIPS AGREEMENT AND DEVELOPING COUNTRIES 30 (1996).

ment in their law more extensive protection than is required by this Agreement.' Commentators have argued that the use of the positive form '*Members may*' is indicative of the fact that some negotiating countries wished to include higher standards of IP protection but were unable to do so.[25] Nonetheless, should members pursue the implementation of higher standards into their national legislation; such standards may not contravene the provisions of TRIPS. Hence, the TRIPS Agreement can be seen as an instrument establishing a 'standstill' in IP legislation, with an acquiescence in measures designed to go beyond its standards—what are know as 'TRIPS-plus' provisions.[26]

The TRIPS Agreement, under **Article 2**, incorporates reference to Articles 1 through 12 and 19 of the Paris Convention, as Members are required to comply with their provisions in respect to Parts II, III, and IV of TRIPS. Those mentioned provisions of the Paris Convention relate most importantly to National Treatment (Article 2), basic norms in the protection of patents, utility models, industrial designs, marks, and inventors' certificates (Articles 4–11), and to the obligation to establish a special industrial property service and a central office for relevant communication to the public (Article 12). In that sense, TRIPS has interestingly been described as a 'Paris-plus' arrangement.[27]

Articles 3 and 4 of TRIPS incorporate the fundamental GATT principles of National Treatment (NT) and Most Favoured Nation (MFN) Treatment. Article 3 on NT however, is incorporated more as an established principle in intellectual property conventions, since it departs from GATT practice in bestowing this treatment to persons rather than to goods.[28] Under this article, Members are required to '*accord to the nationals of other Members treatment no less favourable than that it accords to its own nationals with regard to the protection of intellectual property. . . .*' Protection as defined by the footnote to Article 3 covers matters affecting the '*availability, acquisition, scope, maintenance and enforcement of intellectual property rights as well as those matters affecting the use of intellectual property rights specifically addressed in this Agreement.*' On the other hand, one of the main innovations in international IP law brought about by TRIPS is the

25 Gervais (1998) (n 1) 42.

26 On TRIPS-plus, see JH Reichman and David Lange *Bargaining Around the TRIPS Agreement: the Case for Ongoing Public-Private Initiatives to Facilitate Worldwide Intellectual Property Transactions* 9 DUKE J COMP AND INT'L L 11, fns 17–19 (1998) and accompanying text.

27 Gervais (1998) (n 1) 45.

28 The incorporation in Art 3 of NT as an established principle of IP conventions is perhaps superfluous since this principle established in Art 2 of the Paris Convention (1967) is already incorporated in TRIPS art 2(1). However, Blakeney argues that TRIPS Art 3 performs the 'important symbolic role of emphasising the continuation of a long established principle of intellectual property protection.' See MICHAEL BLAKENEY, TRADE RELATED ASPECTS OF INTELLECTUAL PROPERTY RIGHTS: A CONCISE GUIDE TO THE TRIPS AGREEMENT 40 (1996).

incorporation of the MFN principle in Article 4. This innovation is undoubtedly the result of the influence of GATT practice and principles. Under its provisions, and subject to listed exemptions, in the area of intellectual property protection '*any advantage, favour, privilege or immunity granted by a Member to the nationals of any other country shall be accorded immediately and unconditionally to the nationals of all other Members*'.

Article 6 of TRIPS addresses the controversial issue of the exhaustion of intellectual property rights. More accurately perhaps, it precludes addressing it by stating that, '*for the purposes of dispute settlement under this Agreement, subject to the provisions of Articles 3 and 4 nothing in this Agreement shall be used to address the issue of the exhaustion of intellectual property rights*'. The background to this article was the debate that raged during the TRIPS negotiation on whether to adopt the principle of international exhaustion. International exhaustion refers to the ability to import into a country a product that is protected by intellectual property rights after it has been legally placed in a foreign market.[29] The advantages accruing to DCs from such a practice, as opposed to that of 'local exhaustion', is clearly that they may search the global marketplace for the lowest prices of protected products and import the cheapest available if it is at a price lower than that charged for the protected product in the home market. This is often possible due to MNEs engaging in the practice of differential pricing across different markets—this is particularly true in pharmaceuticals.[30] The principle of international exhaustion had developed as a necessity for European integration, but had been bitterly opposed by certain business interests during the TRIPS negotiations—most particularly by the trademark and copyright lobbies that wished to continue the practice of price discrimination.[31]

As will be discussed further below in discussions of Article 28, MNE interests have argued that Article 28.1 (a) of TRIPS prohibits the importation of patented products, as 'importing' was one of the enumerated rights conferred by that article to the patentee. It must be noted however that Article 28.1 (a) does not address the issue of the exhaustion of rights, and moreover, it is subject to the provisions of Article 6 as indicated by an

[29] These imports are referred to as 'parallel imports'. For further discussion, see Marco Bronckers *The Exhaustion of Patent Rights Under World Trade Organization Law* 32 J World Trade L 32 (1998); and Stefan Szymanski *International Exhaustion: A Review of the Economic Issues* Paper Prepared for the Intellectual Property Institute (Feb 1999) (on file with author).

[30] See Keith E Maskus *Parallel Imports in Pharmaceuticals: Implications for Competition and Prices in Developing Countries* WIPO Studies on Intellectual Property (2001) <http://www.wipo.int/about-ip/en/studies/pdf/ssa_maskus_pi.pdf> (last visited 3 Mar 2006).

[31] Blakeney (1996) (n 28) 42.

attached footnote.[32] The compromise solution thus reached in the TRIPS text of Article 6 is that as long as there was no violation of the principles of NT and MFN treatment, countries' practice on the issue of exhaustion would not be subject to the dispute settlement process. Nonetheless, it has been presented that this waiver does not entail sanctioning a 'free hand' for countries to adopt whichever regime they preferred, and that the restraint on the use of unilateral measures required by the WTO regime does not apply to this issue, and hence the argument carries, the US may be justified in using bilateral pressure under Section 301 to address exhaustion issues.[33]

Articles 7 and 8 on the Objectives and Principles of the Agreement respectively, are the two most relevant articles in upholding considerations of public policy for DCs in the conduct of their intellectual property policy. Indeed, their inclusion in the text of the Agreement during the negotiation was fervently advocated by DCs seeking to stress the underlying developmental and social factors in the formulation of intellectual property policy.[34] Article 7 states that the '*protection and enforcement of intellectual property rights should contribute to the promotion of technological innovation and to the transfer and dissemination of technology, to the mutual advantage of producers and users of technological knowledge and in a manner conducive to social and economic welfare, and to a balance of rights and obligations*'. This is a codification into the text of the Agreement of what was recognized in its preamble as the '*underlying public policy objectives of national systems for the protection of intellectual property, including developmental and technological objectives*'. Hence, this article indicates that the protection of intellectual property rights is not an absolute exercise unto itself, rather, its objective is: (i) to promote technological innovation and, (ii) the transfer and dissemination of technology. Moreover, this is subject to the qualifications that it is: (a) to the mutual advantage of producers and users of technological knowledge, (b) conducive to social and economic welfare, and (c) conducive to a balance of rights and obligations. It has therefore been argued that this

> clearly indicates the subordination of the protection of intellectual property rights to public policy objectives in other areas of the state's activity, especially social and economic welfare, which depends in part on national health and social policies.[35]

[32] See also Frederick M Abbott *The TRIPS Agreement, Access to Medicines and the WTO Doha Ministerial Conference* QUAKER UNITED NATIONS OFFICE—GENEVA, OCCASIONAL PAPER NO 7, 17–22 (2001).

[33] JACQUES J GORLIN, AN ANALYSIS OF THE PHARMACEUTICAL-RELATED PROVISIONS OF THE WTO TRIPS (INTELLECTUAL PROPERTY) AGREEMENT 17–18 (1999).

[34] See ibid 16; and Gervais (1998) (n 1) 64.

[35] G Velasquez and P Boulet *Globalization and Access to Drugs: Perspectives on the*

Even the International Intellectual Property Institute, with its pro-IPR protection policies, interprets this provision as stating that intellectual property protection is not an end by itself, 'but should be balanced to benefit society as a whole'.[36]

Article 8 on the other hand, lays down the principles of the Agreement. Under the provisions of paragraph 1, Members, in formulating or amending their legislation, are allowed to '*adopt measures necessary to protect public health and nutrition, and to promote the public interest in sectors of vital importance to their socio-economic and technological development*', this is however, subject to the qualification that those measures do not conflict with the provisions of the Agreement. Furthermore, under paragraph 2, Members are given the freedom to adopt appropriate measures '*to prevent the abuse of intellectual property rights by right holders or the resort to practices which unreasonably restrain trade or adversely affect the international transfer of technology*'. Again this is subject to those measures being consistent with the provisions of the Agreement. This article can be seen to reflect the Preamble's pronouncement particularly '*the special needs of the least-developed country Members in respect of maximum flexibility in the domestic implementation of laws and regulations in order to enable them to create a sound and viable technological base*'.

Articles 7 and 8 of TRIPS have recently been the subject of speculation as to their operational value in the Agreement. Writing in 1996, Blakeney noted that the generality of Article 7 contrasts uneasily with the specificity of the standards of protection detailed in Part II of the agreement, and cautioned that it is yet to be seen 'what reliance will be placed upon this Article by countries seeking, for example, to implement policies for the compulsory licensing of intellectual property rights'.[37] On one extreme, lies the position, which argues that Articles 7 and 8 have no operational value in the agreement, and are merely hortatory.[38]

The issue of whether Article 7 has any operational significance was not raised in the course of the negotiations out of fear that the LDCs would insist on changing the language to explicitly make it operational. As a result, and EC efforts, during the course of the negotiations on the Article, which were described by one negotiator as more UNCTAD that GATT-like,

WTO/TRIPS Agreement Report to the World Health Organization, 18 (1999) <http://www.who.int/medicinedocs/collect/edmweb/pdf/whozip35e/whozip35e.pdf> (last visited 3 Mar 2006).

36 International Intellectual Property Institute (IIPI) *Patent Protection and Access to HIV/AIDS Pharmaceuticals in Sub-Saharan Africa* Report Prepared for the World Intellectual Property Organization, 27 (2000) <http://www.wipo.int/about-ip/en/studies/pdf/iipi_hiv.pdf> (last visited 3 Mar 2006).

37 Blakeney (1996) (n 28) 43.

38 Gorlin attributes this observation to US and EC negotiators, and indeed to an official from the WTO Secretariat. See Gorlin (1999) (n 33) 16.

were aimed at making the language sound 'preambular', while letting 'sleeping dogs lie'.[39]

However, Articles 7 and 8 can hardly be considered 'hortatory and of no operational utility', let alone the description of bad faith drafting alluded to in the quote above. Indeed, under the basic principle of treaty interpretation codified in Article 31.1 of the 1969 Vienna Convention, '*a treaty shall be interpreted in good faith in accordance with the ordinary meaning to be given to the terms of the treaty in their context and in light of its object and purpose*'.[40] In this regard, the value of these two articles is in giving meaning to the context of the treaty and in interpreting its provisions. This was confirmed by the Appellate Body in its Report in *Japan—Alcoholic Beverages*, where it stated that 'the object and purpose of the treaty are also to be taken into account in determining the meaning of its provisions', this was followed by a footnote indicating that:

> that is, the treaty's 'object and purpose' is to be referred to in determining the meaning of the 'terms of the treaty' and not as an independent basis for interpretation.[41]

Hence the objectives of Article 7 must shape the interpretation of all its other provisions. Indeed, to stress the centrality of Articles 7 and 8 to the other provisions of the Agreement, the findings of the Panel Report in *Canada—Patent Protection of Pharmaceutical Products*, while considering an issue relating to Article 30, stated:

> In the Panel's view, Article 30's very existence amounts to a recognition that the definition of patent rights contained in Article 28 would need certain adjustments. On the other hand, the three limiting conditions attached to Article 30 testify strongly that the negotiators of the Agreement did not intend Article 30 to bring about what would be equivalent to a renegotiation of the basic balance of the Agreement. Obviously, the exact scope of Article 30's authority will depend on the specific meaning given to its limiting conditions. The words of those conditions must be examined with particular care on this point. *Both the goals and the limitations stated in Articles 7 and 8.1 must obviously be borne in mind when doing so as well as those of other provisions of the TRIPS Agreement which indicate its object and purposes.*[42]

[39] ibid.

[40] Vienna Convention on the Law of Treaties (23 May 1969) 8 ILM 679 (1969). Emphasis added.

[41] WTO *Japan—Taxes on Alcoholic Beverages, Report of the Appellate Body*, 12 and fn 20 WT/DS8/AB/R; WT/DS10/AB/R; WT/DS11/AB/R (4 Oct 1996).

[42] WTO *Canada—Patent Protection of Pharmaceutical Products, Report of the Panel* WT/DS114/R (17 Mar 2000) para 7.26 [hereinafter *Canada—Patent Protection*] Emphasis added.

Clearly, this qualification of the specific meaning given to Article 30's limiting conditions in the light of Articles 7 and 8.1, underlines the importance of these articles in the TRIPS Agreement. This is contrary to the position attributed to certain developed countries (most notably the US and EU) that they are of a hortatory nature, or are only useful in those cases when the literal interpretation of the Agreement's other articles are inadequate, in other words in nullification and impairment cases.[43]

(B) Standards for Patent Protection

Part II Section 5 of the TRIPS Agreement lays down the standards on the availability, scope and use of patent rights. The section also contains specific issues of enforcement of patent rights, most notably in Article 34 on the burden of proof in process patents. In this regard, while the TRIPS Agreement does not aim at harmonizing Members' patent laws and regulations, yet its restrictions on Members' freedoms in devising their own priorities has been severely constrained. Prior to TRIPS, countries were able, according to their priorities, to determine areas of non-patentability, the nature of the rights conferred to patentees, and the duration and terms of these rights, however, following TRIPS, 'this freedom which was used by developing countries to frame their patent laws in accordance with their own objectives and interests no longer exists under the TRIPs Agreement'.[44]

Article 27 of TRIPS, as a general rule, subject to the standard tests of novelty, inventive step, and industrial application, sets as the norm, the patentability of any invention in any field of technology, with the only exclusions being those laid down by the agreement.[45] The article defines what qualifies as patentable subject matter, and accordingly, '*patents shall be available for any inventions, whether products or processes, in all fields of technology, provided that they are new, involve an inventive step and are capable of industrial application . . . patents shall be available and patent rights enjoyable without discrimination as to the place of invention, the field of technology and whether products are imported or locally produced*'. The effect of these provisions on DCs was to outlaw a number of common practices in their patent law and policy. Most significantly was the practice of excluding certain classes of products or fields of technology from patentability, chiefly pharmaceutical products and chemicals (as opposed to the patenting of pharmaceutical processes which was more

[43] See Gorlin (1999) (n 33) 16–18. See also arguments of the EC in *Canada—Patent Protection*, 51–2.

[44] South Centre, The TRIPs Agreement: A Guide for the South: The Uruguay Round Agreement on Trade-Related Intellectual Property Rights 18 (1997).

[45] Velasquez and Boulet (1999) (n 35) 21.

generally acceptable in their patent policies).[46] Similarly, the prohibition on discrimination based on whether products are imported or locally produced cast doubt on the legality of Article 5(A) of the Paris Convention, of issuing compulsory licenses on the grounds that importation does not constitute 'local working' of the patent, where according to Article 27.1 of TRIPS, importation of the product is considered 'local working'.[47] This issue was to lead to disputes between DCs and the United States as will be discussed in Part Four.

However, this broad scope of patentability is subject to exclusions detailed in paragraphs 2 and 3 of Article 27. The exclusion under Article 27.2 relate to those inventions where '*the commercial exploitation of which is necessary to protect ordre public or morality. . .*' It is noteworthy that the exclusion is based not on the nature of the invention to be excluded from patenting, but on the harmful effects of its 'commercial exploitation'. This was specifically intended as such by IC negotiators, aiming to prevent Members from excluding patentability of certain inventions on grounds of protecting '*ordre public*' or morality, while allowing others to exploit these inventions commercially within their territory.[48] Moreover, so as to tighten the noose further, some commentators have also argued that 'commercial exploitation' includes production and free distribution by the government.[49] The terms '*ordre public*' and 'morality' are not defined in the Agreement. 'Morality' is meant to be defined according to the circumstances of each country due to cultural variation.[50] In contrast, the French term, '*ordre public*' was used instead of the English translation 'public order' specifically on the insistence of the EC, where the former encompasses a narrower scope of the 'fundaments from which one cannot derogate without endangering the institution of a given society', while the English term refers more generally to public policy.[51] However, other commentators have noted that this term is still subject to definition by Members in their national laws.[52]

[46] Gorlin argues that the specific inclusion of 'products' as well as 'processes' in 'all fields of technology' was intended primarily for the benefit of the pharmaceutical industry, and that it was doubtful whether developed countries would have approved TRIPS if it did not include such broadly inclusive language. See Gorlin (1999) (n 33) 21.

[47] See PETER KOLKER, SHOULD IMPORTATION BE CONSIDERED AS WORKING? A STUDY OF ARTICLE 27 OF THE GATT TRIPS AGREEMENT (1996).

[48] JAYASHREE WATAL, INTELLECTUAL PROPERTY RIGHTS IN THE WTO AND DEVELOPING COUNTRIES 97 (2001).

[49] See Gorlin (1999) (n 33) 24, referring to a statement by a US negotiator on TRIPS.

[50] Watal (2001) (n 48) 98.

[51] Gervais (1998) (n 1) 149. See also CARLOS CORREA, INTELLECTUAL PROPERTY RIGHTS, THE WTO AND DEVELOPING COUNTRIES 62–67 (2000).

[52] INTELLECTUAL PROPERTY AND INTERNATIONAL TRADE: THE TRIPS AGREEMENT 193 (Carlos Correa and Abdulqawi Yusuf eds 1998).

Another exclusion includes '*to protect human, animal or plant life or health or to avoid serious prejudice to the environment. . . .*' This type of exclusion is similar to that found in prior GATT practice, notably in Article XX(b) of GATT, and also included in Article XIV(b) of GATS.[53] It has been argued that therefore it will also be subject to the strict and narrow interpretation that has characterized GATT/WTO panel decisions on GATT Article XX(b).[54] Finally, Article 27.2 is subject to the qualification that '*such exclusion is not made merely because the exploitation is prohibited by their law*'.

Further exclusions to patentability are given under Article 27.3. Subparagraph (a) states that Members may exclude from patentability '*diagnostic, therapeutic and surgical methods for the treatment of humans or animals*'.[55] This normally may be considered a standard basis for exclusion from patentability.[56] However, the United States had sought to exclude diagnostic and therapeutic methods at the insistence of the pharmaceutical lobby.[57] Subparagraph (b) further excludes from patentability '*plants and animals other than micro-organisms, and essentially biological processes for the production of plants or animals other than non-biological and microbiological processes*'. This exclusion is based primarily on ethical grounds. However, it does not extend to plant varieties, where it is specifically stated that '*Members shall provide for the protection of plant varieties either by patents or by an effective sui generis system or by any combination thereof.*'

Undoubtedly, these are severe limitations on the grounds for exclusions from patentability. However, in a critical reading of the wide scope of patentability in TRIPS, and from the broader view of TRIPS' Articles 7 and 8 on Principles and Objectives, the following interpretation gives a somewhat different perspective on the reality of the scope of patentability:

> The presence of these exceptions further reinforces the understanding that intellectual property rights are qualified and may be subject to competing interests that may be more important than exclusive patent rights. And the international legal norms of human rights, including protection and promotion of the human right to health, should certainly be one source for defining *ordre public* and 'morality.'[58]

[53] However, TRIPS unlike the other Agreements, adds 'avoid serious prejudice to the environment' as a basis for an exception. This is also the only provision in TRIPS to refer to damage to the environment.

[54] Watal (2001) (n 48) 97–98.

[55] However, this does not encompass devices or machines for diagnosis or therapy and surgery.

[56] Correa (2000) (n 51) 67.

[57] Gorlin (1999) (n 33) 25.

[58] Richard Elliott *TRIPS and Rights: International Human Rights Law, Access to Medicines, and the Interpretation of the WTO Agreement on Trade-Related Aspects of*

Having thus far, in an analysis of Article 27, discussed the scope of patentability, **Article 28** provides the 'Rights Conferred' to patent owners. These rights have been divided into those concerning product patents and those concerning process patents. With regard to product patents in Article 28.1(a), a patent owner shall have the exclusive right to '*prevent third parties not having the owner's consent from the acts of: making, using, offering for sale, selling, or importing for these purposes that product*'. These enumerated rights entail a considerable departure from previous international norms on patent rights as codified in the Paris Convention which largely left the issue of the rights conferred for national governments to decide upon. Those enumerated acts, rarely figuring in DC patent laws, were most common in IC legislation, and indeed, it has been pointed out that the standards in Article 28.1 reflected those from the US, Belgium, and France among others.[59] The only exception was the relatively novel introduction of the acts of 'offering for sale' and 'importing', designed to make the culpability of patent infringements easier to establish in litigation.[60]

It is the act of 'importation' however, which was to prove controversial. As alluded to earlier, a footnote to Article 28.1 states that '*this right, like all other rights conferred under this Agreement in respect of the use, sale, importation or other distribution of goods, is subject to the provisions of Article 6*'. Article 6, we are reminded, states that with regard to dispute settlement under TRIPS, none of its provisions may be used to address the issue of the exhaustion of rights, as qualified by reference to Articles 3 and 4. Hence the question is whether this implies that the right to prevent unauthorized third parties from the act of importation is an absolute right under Article 28.1, or subject to limitation by the 'international exhaustion' doctrine? At one end of the spectrum is the opinion that it is not an absolute right, but subject to the limitation.[61] At the other end, lies the opinion, more in tune with the interests of pharmaceutical MNEs, that the footnote reference to Article 6

> does not add or subtract from the substance of article 28 and the importation right . . . it would appear that the article supports the territorial principle of patents and could be used to support the principle in fora other than in TRIPs dispute settlement cases within the WTO.[62]

Intellectual Property Rights CANADIAN HIV/AIDS LEGAL NETWORK, 46 (Nov 2001) <http://www. aidslaw.ca/Maincontent/issues/cts/briefs/TRIPS-human-rights-briefPDF.pdf> (last visited 3 Mar 2006).

59 Gervais (1998) (n 1) 153–4.

60 Watal (2001) (n 48) 110.

61 Correa (2000) (n 51) 83–84.

62 Gorlin (1999) (n 33) 27. It must be noted that Dr Gorlin acted as Counsel for the Intellectual Property Committee, an MNE lobby coalition, as well as INTERPAT, an association of research-based pharmaceutical companies. Hence, the assumption of his empathy towards pharmaceutical MNE interests is well founded.

It must be noted however, that the specific inclusion of the footnote to Article 28, and the lack of any provisions specific to standards on exhaustion in TRIPS, signifies the independence provided for Members to decide on their own exhaustion regime. Hence, should a Member opt for an international exhaustion regime allowing for parallel imports, this implies a restriction on the rights conferred to patent owners under Article 28.

The rights conferred to process patents are stated in Article 28(1)(b), where patent owners shall have the exclusive rights

> to prevent third parties not having the owner's consent from the act of using the process, and from the acts of: using, offering for sale, selling, or importing for these purposes at least the product obtained directly by that process.

The significance of this right under TRIPS is that it extends protection for process patents to the products produced by that particular process. This is commensurate to a double patent; on the process, as well as on the product. Taken in conjunction with Article 34 on the reversal of the burden of proof, as will be discussed below, this entails an unprecedented strengthening of process patents.[63] The final right conferred by Article 28 is found in its paragraph 2, where 'Patent owners shall also have the right to assign, or transfer by succession, the patent and to conclude licensing contracts.'

The TRIPS Agreement can thus far be seen to have established profound requirements with regard to the scope of patentability and the rights to be accorded patent owners under the domestic laws and regulations of Members. These requirements involve severe constraints on the ability of DCs to engage in formulating their patent laws while considering their other developmental and public health objectives, in tune with their public policy priorities. Nonetheless, the Agreement attempts to create a balance in this regard by introducing in Articles 30, 31, and 32, certain exceptions to the otherwise absolute rights enjoyable by patent owners under TRIPS provisions. These articles deal respectively with: exceptions to the rights conferred; other use without authorization of the right holder; and revocation/forfeiture of patents.

Article 30 allows Members to provide exceptions to the exclusive rights granted to patentees, subject to three conditions: that they are 'limited'; that they '*do not unreasonably conflict with a normal exploitation of the patent . . .*'; and that they '*do not unreasonably prejudice the legitimate interests of the patent owner, . . .*'. In doing so, Members must also take into account '*the legitimate interests of third parties*'. The problem with the conditions in this article is that they do not set clear boundaries on what are to be

[63] See Velasquez and Boulet (1999) (n 35) 24.

considered permissible exceptions. The preliminary approach to exceptions during the TRIPS negotiations, as the EC proposed, was to create a limited list of exceptions, mainly encompassing 'rights based on prior use, acts done privately and for non-commercial purposes and acts done for experimental purposes'.[64] However, this method became troublesome to certain negotiating parties as the list of exceptions became longer as Members listed their required exceptions.[65] As a solution, the adopted language of Article 30 was taken from Article 9.2 of the Berne Convention.[66] According to Correa's comparative analysis of national legislation on exceptions to patent rights, he presents eight such exceptions that can be reasonably covered by Article 30.[67] These mainly revolve around exceptions for use not directly relating to a commercial exploitation of the patent.

Among the most contentious of issues to surround the negotiation and implementation of TRIPS was the issue of compulsory licensing. This issue, along with those of 'government use' and restrictive business practices are the subject of **Article 31**. The issue of compulsory licenses (along with parallel importation) is at the core of DC efforts to provide cheap generic medicine for their populations, as well as a means of fostering the growth of their local pharmaceutical industry. And the issue of the interpretation and feasible modifications to Article 31, along with Article 30, has been at the forefront of efforts to restore a balance to the TRIPS Agreement, particularly following the adoption of the Doha Declaration.

Compulsory licensing is an important tool for government patent policy. The right of governments to issue compulsory licenses according to their own priorities was a right recognized by international IP law prior to TRIPS, where Article 5(A) of the Paris Convention authorized States to take legislative measures to provide for compulsory licenses to prevent abusive exploitation of the rights granted by the patent, including failure to work. The grounds on which such licenses were issued varied, but in DCs they usually involved those cases of anti-competitive practices, non-working, government use, national emergencies, or other public-interest grounds. This freedom for governments to issue compulsory licenses was highly prized by DCs. Observing this principle, the TRIPS Agreement leaves Members the freedom to decide on the grounds for issuing compulsory licenses, save in three stipulated restrictions: on the grounds of lack of 'local working' (Article 27.1)—an issue that was to prove controversial as alluded

64 GATT *Draft Agreement on Trade-Related Aspects of Intellectual Property Rights Submitted by the Delegation of the European Communities to the TRIPS Negotiating Group*, 8 MTN.GNG/NG11/W/68 (29 Mar 1990).

65 Gorlin (1999) (n 33) 29–30.

66 Berne Convention for the Protection of Literary and Artistic Works (24 July 1971) 828 UNTS 221 (as revised in Paris on 24 July 1971, and amended on 28 Sept 1979).

67 Correa (2000) (n 51) 75–6.

to earlier;[68] on dependent patents (clause (l)); and in the case of semiconductor technology (clause (c)).[69] Apart from those three restrictions, Members were free to continue the prior practice, supported in this regard by Article 8 of the Agreement, which provided them with public interest and prevention of abusive practice, among others, as grounds for such action.[70]

On the other hand, IC negotiators and the pharmaceutical lobby were not content on granting DCs a free hand to decide the conditions for authorizing use without the patent owner's consent. Hence, Article 31 was encumbered by a long list of conditions that must be met for issuing a compulsory licence, and indeed this was one of the main objectives of the pharmaceutical industry in the TRIPS negotiations.[71] Hence, the *chapeau* of Article 31 states that '*Where the law of a Member allows for other use of the subject matter of a patent without the authorization of the right holder, including use by the government or third parties authorized by the government, the following provisions shall be respected.*' The rest of the article then lists eleven such conditions (clauses (a)–(j) and (l)), in addition to a waiver from two of these conditions with respect to restrictive business practices (clause (k)). [72]

The most important conditions are that authorization shall be based on the individual merits of the case (clause (a)), rather than authorizing such use for an entire category of inventions, such as pharmaceutical products.[73] Similarly, clause (b) requires that prior efforts have to be made by the proposed licensee to obtain authorization from the right holder '*on reasonable commercial terms and conditions and that such efforts have not been successful within a reasonable period of time*'. This condition however may be waived in national emergencies or other situations of extreme urgency, or in cases of public non-commercial use. Among the other conditions is adequate remuneration to the patent owner (clause (h)), and the opportunity for the judicial review of both the decision to grant the compulsory license (clause (i)) and the level of remuneration (clause (j)). Finally, under

[68] Importation can satisfy the requirement for 'working'. However, some recent developing country legislation allows the issuance of compulsory licences where patent owners do not manufacture their invention locally. This is the case in the new Brazilian industrial property law; see Decree No 9.279 (14 May 1996) Art 68(1).

[69] IIPI (2000) (n 36) 31.

[70] See UNCTAD (1996) (n 24) 34.

[71] Gorlin (1999) (n 33) 34.

[72] For a discussion of these conditions, see Watal (2001) (n 48) 321–7; SOUTH CENTRE, INTEGRATING PUBLIC HEALTH CONCERNS INTO PATENT LEGISLATION IN DEVELOPING COUNTRIES 91–107 (2000); Correa (2000) (n 51) 89–94; and Blakeney (1996) (n 28) 88–93.

[73] However, this is a go-between position between allowing categories of inventions and adopting an 'each case' approach which the US refused as it would have conflicted with its laws as well as necessitating a cumbersome bureaucratic effort on the part of governments. See Watal (2001) (n 48) 322.

the provisions of clause (k), Members are exempt from applying the conditions in clause (b) on the exertion of prior efforts to obtain the licence voluntarily, and clause (f) on predominantly supplying the local market, in cases necessary for remedying a restrictive business practice.

In the ensuing debate concerning TRIPS and public health, the most important provisions in the Agreement, in addition to Article 30, revolve around clause (f) of Article 31. The condition stipulated in clause (f) requires that '*any such use shall be authorised predominantly for the supply of the domestic market of the Member authorizing such use*'. The significance of this provision is that developing country governments are constrained in their ability to supply their domestic markets through importing from a manufacturer in another country who was granted a compulsory license by their government. It is in dealing with this constraint that this provision figures in post-Doha efforts to address access to medicine.[74]

The final of the three articles in TRIPS providing an exception to the rights enjoyable by patent owners is **Article 32** on Revocation/Forfeiture of patents. The article states, '*an opportunity for judicial review of any decision to revoke or forfeit a patent shall be available*'. This article merely requires that the revocation or forfeiture of a patent be subject to judicial review, whereas, the grounds for taking the action of revocation or forfeiture are to be found in Article 5(A) of the Paris Convention. Accordingly, importation does not constitute a forfeiture of the patent. More importantly, subparagraph (3) restricts forfeiture to those cases where compulsory licensing has not brought about a prevention of abuses, and can only be undertaken after a minimum of two years from the grant of the first compulsory licence. While IC negotiators sought to limit the grounds for revocation strictly to those that would have led to a refusal of original grant, DCs attempted to include public interest grounds.[75] The dismissal of addressing the issue was agreed, given the reliance on Article 5(A) of Paris, and those of Articles 30 and 31 in TRIPS.

Articles 33 and 34, the last two articles of Section 5, deal respectively with the term of patent protection, and the burden of proof in civil proceedings relating to process patents. **Article 33** requires the granting of a term of protection not less than 20 years from the filing date of the patent application. The length of patent term protection was never harmonized prior to TRIPS, and hence, there was a great variety of terms of protection in different national legislation, averaging 14 years. Consequently, the negotiations

[74] See Frederick M Abbott *WTO TRIPS Agreement and Its Implications for Access to Medicines in Developing Countries* COMMISSION ON INTELLECTUAL PROPERTY RIGHTS STUDY PAPER 2A (2002) <http://www.iprcommission.org/papers/pdfs/study_papers/spa2a_abbott_study.pdf> (last visited 3 Mar 2006).

[75] Gorlin (1999) (n 33) 39–40.

on this article were difficult with DCs resisting the extension of the protection period to 20 years.[76] Finally, **Article 34** requires the reversal of the burden of proof in civil proceedings in cases of process patent infringement involving identical products. Traditionally, the burden had been on the plaintiff in such cases to prove that the respondent had infringed his/her right in the patented process. However, according to Article 34.1, '*the judicial authorities shall have the authority to order the defendant to prove that the process to obtain an identical product is different from the patented process*'. However, both, or either of the following conditions is to be met: that the product obtained by the process is new, and that there is a substantial likelihood that the identical product was made by the patented process and that the owner was unable to determine the process actually used, through reasonable efforts.

(C) Other Relevant Provisions

The TRIPS Agreement contains similarly comprehensive treatment of intellectual property rights other than patents, as well as specific provisions on the control of anti-competitive practices in contractual licenses pertaining to intellectual property rights (Article 40). Furthermore, the Agreement addresses, in what is an unprecedented development in international intellectual property law, detailed provisions on the enforcement of IP rights internally and at the border.[77] The enforcement provisions of TRIPS are contained in Part III (Articles 41–61), and apart from the general obligations in Article 41, it contains sections on civil and administrative procedures and remedies; provisional measures; special requirements related to border measures; and provisions on criminal procedures.[78]

In parallel to the enforcement provisions of the TRIPS Agreement, are the provisions of Part V on dispute settlement, which achieved a stated aim of the MNEs lobbies during the TRIPS negotiations, by linking the enforcement of the TRIPS Agreement to the WTO's effective dispute settlement system.[79] **Article 64** of TRIPS states that '*the provisions of Articles XXII and XXIII of GATT 1994 as elaborated and applied by the Dispute*

[76] Gervais (1998) (n 1) 169.

[77] See Watal (2001) (n 48) 333–4. In the words of a former US Commissioner for Patents: '...TRIPS tells all countries—developed, developing and least-developed—what they must do and when and how they must do it. To the international legal scholars I have contacted, this is unprecedented in multinational treaties.' See Gerald Mossinghoff *National Obligations Under Intellectual Property Treaties: The Beginning of a True International Regime* 9 FED CIR BJ 591, 603 (2000).

[78] For a coverage of the TRIPS Enforcement provisions, see Blakeney (1996) (n 28) 123–132; Gorlin (1999) (n 33) 53–75; and Watal (2001) (n 48) 333–62.

[79] With the exception that the dispute settlement system does not address issues on Members' exhaustion regime, as stipulated in TRIPS Art 6.

Settlement Understanding shall apply to consultations and the settlement of disputes under this Agreement except as otherwise specifically provided herein'. The effects of placing TRIPS obligations under the umbrella of the WTO's newly created dispute settlement mechanism meant that DCs had to adhere to an international intellectual property regime that was linked to the international trade regime, consequently legitimizing trade retaliation against them should they not observe any of their obligations under TRIPS. To date, the record of DC dispute settlement involvement under the WTO's dispute settlement mechanism has seen them predominantly as defendants, with the vast majority of cases being initiated by the United States as complainant.[80] On the other hand, developing countries did achieve some positive gains and special treatment from the dispute settlement system. Most importantly was the outlawing of unilateral trade retaliation measures, something that they welcomed after a decade of languishing under the effects of the infamous '301' trade retaliatory process of the United States.[81] Furthermore, the Dispute Settlement Understanding contains provisions regarding the taking into account of DC interests, and most importantly for least-developed country Members, is the provision in Article 24 enjoining complainants in cases involving least-developed countries to consider their 'special situation' and to 'exercise due restraint'.[82]

Contrary to this MNE victory in linking TRIPS enforcement to the WTO dispute settlement mechanism, the Agreement contains under Part VI, a concession to developing and least-developed country Members in the form of certain transitional arrangements concerning the coming into force of their obligations under the Agreement. Under the provisions of **Article 65**, there are three particular dates with regard to the coming into effect of Members' obligations under the TRIPS Agreement. Paragraph 1 stipulates a general transitional period of one year from the coming into force of the TRIPS Agreement, after which the general obligation is for all Members to apply the Agreement, starting from 1 January 1996. However, paragraphs 2 and 3 allow DC Members, and Members in the process of transformation from a centrally planned economy into a market, free enterprise economy, a further transitional period of four years from that stipulated under paragraph 1. Hence, for these two categories of Members, their obligation to apply the Agreement begins on 1 January 2000. Excepted from this further

80 Sue Ann Mota *TRIPS—Five Years of Disputes at the WTO* 17 ARIZ J INT'L AND COMP L 533, 533–536 (2000). *See also* Watal (2001) (n 48) 66–75.

81 See AGGRESSIVE UNILATERALISM: AMERICA'S 301 TRADE POLICY AND THE WORLD TRADING SYSTEM (Jagdish Bhagwati and HT Patrick eds 1990); Timothy C Bickham *Protecting US Intellectual Property Rights Abroad with Special 301* 23 AIPLA QJ 195 (1995); and M Getlan TRIPs and the Future of Section 301: A Comparative Study in Trade Dispute Resolution 34 COLUM J TRANSNAT'L L 173 (1995).

82 *See* Blakeney (1996) (n 28) 143.

four years transitional period are Articles 3, 4, and 5, which they must apply from 1 January 1996.

Moreover, DC Members that are required under the provisions on product patents in Part II Section 5 of the Agreement to extend such protection to classes of products not previously covered by product patent protection in their domestic laws and regulations, are entitled to delay such extension for a further period of five years from the end of the transitional period for them as defined in paragraph 2. In other words, they have until 1 January 2005 to extend such protection. This last provision is of particular significance for the pharmaceutical industry, as it was the sector most commonly excluded form the grant of product patent protection in DCs. But while DCs are granted these 'grace periods' for the application of the Agreement to allow them to introduce laws and regulations that fulfil the minimum standards of TRIPS, paragraph 5 of Article 65 requires that during this period any changes in their laws, regulations and practices do not result '*in a lesser degree of consistency with the provisions of this Agreement*'.

Article 66 on the other hand addresses the transitional arrangements for least-developed Members. According to its provisions, this category of Members shall not be required to apply the provisions of TRIPS, other than Articles 3, 4, and 5, for a period of 10 years from the date of its application as defined in Article 65.1. Hence, least-developed countries have a transitional period up to 1 January 2006. Furthermore, the Agreement gives the Council for TRIPS the authority to accord extensions to this period. During the Doha Ministerial Conference, such a period was indeed agreed where '*least-developed country Members will not be obliged, with respect to pharmaceutical products, to implement or apply Sections 5 and 7 of Part II of the TRIPS Agreement or to enforce rights provided for under these Sections until 1 January 2016*'.[83]

However, during the transition period, the TRIPS Agreement instructs Members under the transitional arrangement to establish a 'mailbox' system for receiving patent applications. The *chapeau* of **Article 70.8** states that '*where a Member does not make available as of the date of entry into force of the WTO Agreement patent protection for pharmaceutical and agricultural chemical products commensurate with its obligations under Article 27, that Member shall*': and it goes on to presents three conditions, namely: that notwithstanding the provisions on transitional arrangements, provide a means by which applications for patents for such inventions can be filed; apply to these applications the criteria for patentability laid down in the Agreement, as if those criteria were being applied on the date of filing in that Member or the priority date of the application; and provide patent

[83] WTO *Ministerial Conference, Fourth Session, Doha, 9–14 November, 2001, Declaration on the TRIPS Agreement and Public Health* WT/MIN(01)/DEC/2, para 7 (20 Nov 2001).

protection in accordance with this Agreement as from the grant of the patent for the remainder of the term, as counted from the filing date (according to Article 33), for those applications that meet the criteria for protection referred to in the second condition above.

Article 70.9 created a novelty in international IP law concerning the extension of exclusive marketing rights (EMRs) to pharmaceutical and agricultural chemical products during the transitional period. It stipulates that, '*where a product is the subject of a patent application in a Member in accordance with paragraph 8(a), exclusive marketing rights shall be granted, notwithstanding the provisions of Part VI, for a period of five years after obtaining marketing approval in that Member or until a product patent is granted or rejected in that Member, whichever period is shorter, provided that, subsequent to the entry into force of the WTO Agreement, a patent application has been filed and a patent granted for that product in another Member and marketing approval obtained in such other Member*'. The question that arises therefore concerns the difference between these so-called 'exclusive marketing rights' and patents. While an EMR does not preclude others from making or using the patented invention, yet they are not allowed to market it or sell it, therefore, there seems to be no fundamental difference between them.[84] The consequent impact of the provisions of paragraphs 8 and 9 of Article 70 for DCs is that, effectively, they do not allow them to enjoy the privilege of the transitional arrangements stipulated in Part VI, with regard to the introduction of protection for pharmaceutical and agricultural chemical products. This was a major victory for pharmaceutical MNEs,[85] and a major constraining factor on DCs' ability to make use of the theoretical flexibilities and special treatment provided for in TRIPS.

Before concluding discussion of the relevant provisions of the TRIPS Agreement, it is pertinent here to mention two further provisions of the Agreement. Primarily, **Article 71.1** addresses the issue of the review and amendment of the TRIPS Agreement. The Agreement requires the Council for TRIPS to review the implementation of the Agreement after the expiration of the transitional period referred to in Article 65(2). Two years later, and on two-year intervals afterwards, the Council is also required to review the Agreement paying particular attention to '*the experience gained in its implementation*'. Furthermore, the Council may also undertake similar reviews at any other time '*in the light of any relevant new developments which might warrant modification or amendment of this Agreement*'.

84 See Watal (2001) (n 48) 118.

85 Gervais (1998) (n 1) 268–270; and Gorlin (1999) (n 33) 99–106.

Finally, mention should also be made of **Article 73** on security exceptions. According to its clause (b), nothing in the TRIPS Agreement shall be construed to prevent a member from taking any action, which it considers necessary for the protection of its essential security interests taken, inter alia, in time of war or other *emergency in international relations*. While the association of intellectual property rights, per se, to national security interests and emergencies in international relations might seem a little far-fetched, yet the challenges faced by DCs in other areas, most notably the HIV/AIDS pandemic, is such as to arguably release them from unnecessary constraints on their public policies imposed by regimes such as TRIPS.[86]

[86] The AIDS/HIV pandemic in Africa is arguably an issue of significance for the maintenance of international peace and security as evidenced by successive meeting of the Security Council on the issue. See Press Release SC/6781, United Nations, Security Council Holds Debate on Impact of AIDS on Peace and Security in Africa (10 Jan 2000).

PART TWO

'TOP-DOWN' RULE-MAKING: THE FLAWED URUGUAY ROUND NEGOTIATIONS OF THE TRIPS PHARMACEUTICAL-RELATED PROVISIONS

The history of the negotiation of the Agreement on Trade Related Aspects of Intellectual Property Rights, and the context within which its initiation and progress occurred have been the subject of numerous legal and non-legal studies.[1] In a significant number of those accounts, the discourse acknowledges that the rule-making process of the TRIPS Agreement and more notably the background to this rule-making process in terms of domestic, unilateral and bilateral developments in the area of intellectual property protection has been disproportionately influenced by the interests of industrialized countries' corporate actors.[2] Corporate interests with a stake in a high level of intellectual property safeguards encompass industries with considerable investments protected by copyright laws, trademark laws, and patent laws as well as other forms of intellectual property protection.[3] Among the most prominent industries with investments protected by patent laws is the dynamic and research intensive pharmaceutical industry.

[1] See INTELLECTUAL PROPERTY AND INTERNATIONAL TRADE: THE TRIPs AGREEMENT (Carlos M Correa and Abdulqawi A Yusuf eds 1998); DANIEL J GERVAIS, THE TRIPS AGREEMENT: DRAFTING HISTORY AND ANALYSIS (1998); JACQUES J GORLIN, AN ANALYSIS OF THE PHARMACEUTICAL-RELATED PROVISIONS OF THE WTO TRIPS (INTELLECTUAL PROPERTY) AGREEMENT (1999); GATT OR WIPO? NEW WAYS IN THE INTERNATIONAL PROTECTION OF INTELLECTUAL PROPERTY (Friedrich-Karl Beier and Gerhard Schricker eds 1989); FROM GATT TO TRIPs: THE AGREEMENT ON TRADE-RELATED ASPECTS OF INTELLECTUAL PROPERTY RIGHTS (Friedrich-Karl Beier and Gerhard Schricker eds 1996).

[2] See Susan K Sell *Multinational Corporations as Agents of Change: the Globalization of Intellectual Property Rights* PRIVATE AUTHORITY AND INTERNATIONAL AFFAIRS 169 (A Claire Cutler et al eds 1999); Susan K Sell *The Origins of a Trade-Based Approach to Intellectual Property Protection—The Role of Industry Associations* 17 SCI COMM 163 (1995).

[3] The TRIPS Agreement refers to four more classes of intellectual property rights: geographical indication, industrial designs, layout designs (topographies) of integrated circuits, and undisclosed information.

As such, the pharmaceutical industry was and continues to be at the forefront of corporate lobbying of patent laws.

These lobbying efforts by the pharmaceutical industry and particularly those of the US-based multinational pharmaceutical giants have significantly affected the course of the multilateral negotiations on intellectual property, specifically those relating to patents, during the Uruguay Round of the General Agreement on Tariffs and Trade (GATT) 1986–94.[4] On the other hand, DCs resisted the pressure to introduce IP rules, specifically patent rules, within the GATT framework. However, the ability of DCs to resist the pressure from the pharmaceutical multinational enterprises, as presented through the medium of ICs' negotiating positions and unilateral and bilateral tactics, was overwhelmed. As a result, the change in the negotiating position of DCs prior to the official launch of the Uruguay Round compared to the final result of the negotiations resulting in the TRIPS Agreement is considerable. In effect, it amounted to a capitulation by DCs to the ICs' negotiating objectives, which represented pharmaceutical MNEs interests with regard to the specifics of those patent provisions of relevance to the multinational pharmaceutical industry.

The focus of analysis in Part Two is this anomaly in the rule-making of the pharmaceutical-related patent provisions of the TRIPS Agreement. As will be argued below, the problem is in essence one of a 'top-down' exercise in the rule-making of these provisions. While the interests of pharmaceutical MNEs were largely incorporated into the final text of the TRIPS Agreement, those of DCs were gradually dismissed over the course of the negotiations. Such a usurpation of a negotiating position comes not as a result of a value re-appraisal by DCs,[5] but rather as a result of this 'top-down' pressure exerted during the rule-making process. Upon reflection, the flaws of such an approach are evident and complicate the implementation process as will be presented in Part Three, and consequently, they lead to a profusion of political and legal disputes on the relevant provisions of the Agreement as will be analysed in Part Four. Therefore, the aim of this part is to identify and analyse the causes of this 'top-down' approach to rule-making in the context of the pharmaceutical-related patent provisions of the TRIPS Uruguay Round negotiations, and the significant role played by the pharmaceutical MNEs therein.

[4] While there has been a number of studies on the role of the business sector in influencing the TRIPS negotiation as noted above, these have tended to be of a general character and not specific to one particular industry sector or to one specific category of intellectual property. It is hence an important aim of this volume, through this chapter, to focus on the specific role of the multinational research-based pharmaceutical industry in influencing the pharmaceutical-related patent provisions of TRIPS.

[5] On the contrary, the main domestic interests in DCs remain opposed to the adoption of the standards in the TRIPS pharmaceutical-related patent provisions as will be explained in Part Three of this book.

It should be noted at the outset that the dangers of falling into the trap of a one-sided 'dogmatic' treatment of the issue and 'caricaturizing' events and positions are considerable. The background of the TRIPS negotiations and the broader process of negotiating other issues within the Uruguay Round are to date perhaps the most comprehensive and complex undertaking of international economic rule-making, spanning nearly a decade of global multilateral negotiations. In such a framework, the positions of the negotiating parties, of the various affected industries and indeed of industry sub-sectors are multi-faceted. This matrix of interests is similarly anchored to a canvass of domestic, regional and global economic and political conditions that serve only to accentuate their complexity. As a precaution against these risks, this book has specifically narrowed down the focus of inquiry—limiting it to one particular issue of the negotiation of the TRIPS Agreement—that of the pharmaceutical-related patent provisions, and mainly the standards and norms on patent protection. Furthermore, an additional precaution observed, is to recognize from the outset the legitimate interests and rights of DCs in their pursuit of patent regimes and laws that stem from their developmental and public health policy priorities, as well as the interests of research-based pharmaceutical MNEs in protecting, recouping, and earning a profit on their R&D investments that amount to the raison d'être of the commercial nature of their activities.

Chapter 5 examines the position of the pharmaceutical MNEs. The first section will look at the interests of the pharmaceutical MNEs, in terms of their concerns, justifications and losses sustained due to the existing patent regime. It will also consider the specific problems faced by them with regard to the then prevailing standards and norms of patent protection.[6] Focusing on the United States, the second section will then examine the process through which the pharmaceutical MNEs were able to organize and lobby ICs to adopt their interests in their quest to address the need to overhaul the international IP regime. It will also examine the unilateral and bilateral approach adopted by the United States (particularly the 301 processes), to engage the issue with recalcitrant DCs, in parallel with the TRIPS negotiations.

Chapter 6 will then focus on the TRIPS negotiation itself, from the lead up to the Uruguay Round and covering the negotiations until their completion. It will examine the choice and utility of using GATT as a forum for IP rule-making, the aims and positions of the negotiating parties, and the progress of the specific TRIPS provisions of interest in this study, mainly those pertaining to standards on patent protection, and their progression from conception to codification.

[6] An analysis of the pre-TRIPS patent legislation in selected DCs is presented in Chapter 7 of this volume.

Chapter 5

Pharmaceutical MNEs Patent Regime Preferences

In a report published by the European Commission in 1985 on the eve of the launch of the Uruguay Round, the following observations on the nature of the pharmaceutical industry were made:

> The World pharmaceutical market in 1982 was worth US $81,500m. Most sales were in the developed market economies. The industry is both research intensive and marketing intensive. There are substantial economies of scale and large companies have a pronounced advantage. . . . A limited number of large companies dominate the world industry. Generally organised on a multinational basis, they originated in a limited number of developed countries, of which France, Germany, Japan, Switzerland, the UK and the USA are the most important. Production, like consumption, is concentrated in the advanced nations.[1]

With regard to the geographic distribution of the pharmaceutical industry, there is a wide disparity between the industry portion headquartered in ICs and those based in DCs. This study, in its treatment of the interest, concerns and mobilization efforts of the pharmaceutical industry, will be primarily concerned with that of the large pharmaceutical MNEs, ie those largely based in ICs. However, in the ongoing argument of the book, the interests and efforts of the pharmaceutical industry based in DCs represents an opposite side of the coin, and will therefore be discussed in Part Three, where it will be more appropriately treated in its reaction to the requisite implementation process of the TRIPS Agreement provisions. This chapter will therefore engage primarily in a delineation of the interests of the pharmaceutical MNE industry, followed by their mobilization efforts towards international patent law reform.

(I) PHARMACEUTICAL MNES INTERESTS

The pharmaceutical industry is a broad industry that is traditionally divided

[1] ML BURSTALL AND IAN SENIOR, THE COMMUNITY'S PHARMACEUTICAL INDUSTRY 3 (1985).

horizontally into three categories according to the extent of innovation and technology involved in production.[2] The first category, over-the-counter (OTC) drugs, are sold directly to consumers without prescriptions and contains the least research content. Thus, the main cost outlay in their production is marketing costs.[3] The second category is post-patent generic drugs available by prescription, which account for a high percentage of the pharmaceutical industry in key DCs.[4] Finally, the third category, in-patent drugs, involves the most outlay of R&D costs and is almost entirely dominated by the pharmaceutical MNEs. It is the category primarily responsible for the phenomenal growth of the industry since the 1930s.[5] We are concerned here with the producers of this last group.

(A) Justifications, Interests, and Concerns of Pharmaceutical MNEs

Pharmaceutical MNEs advocate that a strong patent protection regime serves not only their interests, but is also beneficial to the global economy at large, including the economies of DCs who would stand to benefit from an increase in innovation. This MNE position finds resonance in some accounts testifying to the economic utility of adopting a strong patent regime as advocated by the pharmaceutical MNEs.[6] Indeed, two studies published by the International Finance Corporation (IFC) in 1994 and 1995 underscored the importance that IC-based corporations place on the presence of a strong IP protection regime when considering investment in a given country.[7] Of the six industries examined, this was particularly true in

[2] OECD, The Pharmaceutical Industry: Trade Related Issues 9–10 (1985).

[3] For a history of the development of the OTC drug market, see Milton Silverman and Philip R Lee, Pills, Profits, and Politics ch 9 (1974).

[4] For an account of the generic drug industry, especially as it pertains to developing countries, see Milton Silverman, Mia Lydecker and Philip R Lee, Bad Medicine: The Prescription Drug Industry in the Third World ch 4 (1992).

[5] See OECD (1985) (n 2) 10.

[6] See Edwin Mansfield *Intellectual Property, Technology and Economic Growth* in Intellectual Property Rights in Science, Technology, and Economic Performance: International Comparisons 17–30 (Francis W Rushing and Carole Ganz Brown eds 1990). See also Richard P Rozek *Protection of Intellectual Property Rights: Research and Development Decisions and Economic Growth* in Intellectual Property Rights in Science, Technology, and Economic Performance: International Comparisons, 31–46; and R Michael Gadbaw and Timothy J Richards *Introduction* in Intellectual Property Rights: Global Consensus, Global Conflict? 1–37 (R Michael Gadbaw and Timothy J Richards eds 1988). For a different account of the economic benefit of strong patent protection, see Ch 8 below.

[7] See Edwin Mansfield *Intellectual Property Protection, Foreign Direct Investment, and Technology Transfer* Int'l Fin Corp Discussion Paper No 19 (1994) <http://www.bvindecopi.gob.pe/colec/emansfield2.pdf> (last visited 3 Mar 2006); and Edwin Mansfield *Intellectual Property Protection, Direct Investment, and Technology Transfer* Int'l Fin Corp Discussion Paper No 27 (1995) <http://www.bvindecopi.gob.pe/colec/emansfield.pdf> (last visited 3 Mar 2006).

the chemical industry, which includes pharmaceuticals.[8] Furthermore, pharmaceutical MNEs argue that the discovery of new drugs is possible due to the protection afforded by patent regimes that allow the innovating firms to recoup their R&D expenditures.[9]

Therefore, the pharmaceutical MNEs justified their position by emphasizing the value of protecting IP as an important contribution to innovation and to the economic progress of all countries including DCs. Moreover, it was the US pharmaceutical MNEs' success in projecting their image as a highly productive industry at the forefront of America's international competitiveness that gained firm support for their cause.[10] The pharmaceutical industry was awarded a highest ranking in terms of its competitiveness in a survey of thirteen US manufacturing industries examined in 1992.[11] In the most important IC market, this characterization of the pharmaceutical industry proved a strong argument to justify the protection of IP rights internationally. This was a US industry, globally competitive at a time when the US economy was under severe economic strains during the mid-1980s and facing considerable balance of payment burdens. Henceforth, the US multinational pharmaceutical industry's emphasis on securing backing for its preferences of a strong international IP regime rested more on brandishing its domestic flagship industry status as opposed to other industries similarly interested in IP protection. As Ryan argued,

> the pharmaceutical interests, unlike the copyright interests, did not advocate stronger intellectual property laws based on claims of huge piracy losses in developing countries. Instead they urged US action based on their opportunities and potential for future foreign investment and sales.[12]

In a report prepared for the US Senate by the US International Trade Commission in 1991, the protection of IP rights figured as a component of the major factors and determinants in the global competitiveness of the US and other IC pharmaceutical industries.[13]

[8] Mansfield [1994] (n 7) 2–3; and Mansfield [1995] (n 7) 3 (Table 2).

[9] *Intellectual Property and International Issues: Hearing before the Subcomm. on Intellectual Property and Judicial Administration of the House Comm. on the Judiciary* 102nd Cong 105–6 (1991) (statement of Gerald Mossinghoff, President, Pharmaceutical Manufacturers Association) [hereinafter Mossinghoff 1991 House Judiciary Statement].

[10] See US *International Trade Performance and Outlook: Competitive Position in the Automotive, Aerospace, and Chemical and Pharmaceutical Sectors: Hearing before the Subcomm. on Trade of the Comm. on Ways and Means,* 102nd Cong. 502-504 (1992) (statement of Gerald Mossinghoff, President, Pharmaceutical Manufacturers Association) [hereinafter Mossinghoff 1992 House Statement].

[11] Joseph Spiers *Productivity Looks Promising* FORTUNE (9 Mar 1992) 21.

[12] MICHAEL P RYAN, KNOWLEDGE DIPLOMACY: GLOBAL COMPETITION AND THE POLITICS OF INTELLECTUAL PROPERTY 8 (1998).

[13] US INTERNATIONAL TRADE COMMISSION, GLOBAL COMPETITIVENESS OF US ADVANCED-

The pharmaceutical MNEs' interest in a strong IP protection regime lies in their quest to protect their R&D, thus maintaining their ability to innovate and provide new drugs to the market.[14] In terms of time expended in the development of a new drug, the typical R&D outlay is claimed to be between 10 and 12 years, costing onwards of US$350 million.[15] The pharmaceutical MNE industry's R&D expenditures are among the highest of industry groups.[16] Therefore, a high standards patent protection regime is a high priority for the industry.[17] Table 5.1 below depicts the amount of R&D expenditure on drugs and medicines on selected years during the period 1976–96. Undoubtedly, the numbers represent a considerable resource allocation on the part of the pharmaceutical industry in OECD countries. While we cannot accurately estimate the amount specifically contributed by the major pharmaceutical MNEs, they are responsible for a bulk of the outlay on R&D expenditures in the industry. Indeed, Ryan claims that 93 per cent of new drug therapies are introduced by private enterprises.[18] Table 5.1 also indicates that almost consistently, the US spends the most on R&D, closely followed by the EU, with Japan lagging behind, although reducing the gap in the mid-1990s as compared to the mid-1970s.

Given this considerable expenditure on R&D and the importance of new product development to the multinational pharmaceutical industry, the protection of IP rights is a major concern for pharmaceutical MNEs. Numerous studies reported the losses sustained by the major industries, particularly US industries, due to the lack of effective protection and/or enforcement of IP rights abroad, especially in the major DCs.[19] These losses

TECHNOLOGY MANUFACTURING INDUSTRIES: PHARMACEUTICALS: REPORT TO THE COMMITTEE ON FINANCE, US SENATE, ON INVESTIGATION NO 332-302 UNDER SECTION 332(G) OF THE TARIFF ACT OF 1930, US ITC Pub No 2438 (1991) [hereinafter US ITC 1991 Report].

[14] For a discussion of pharmaceutical inventions and innovation, see PHILIP W GRUBB, PATENTS FOR CHEMICALS, PHARMACEUTICALS AND BIOTECHNOLOGY: FUNDAMENTALS OF GLOBAL LAW, PRACTICE AND STRATEGY 210–23 (1999).

[15] Ryan (1998) (n 12) 29–30.

[16] In the early 1990s, the Pharmaceutical Manufacturers' Association claimed that the average development cost of a new innovative drug was approximately US $231 million. See *Hearings on Fast Track: Intellectual Property: Hearings before the Subcomm. on Patents, Copyrights and Trademarks of the Senate Judiciary Comm.* 102nd Cong 59 (1991) (statement of Gerald Mossinghoff, President, Pharmaceutical Manufacturers Association) [hereinafter Mossinghoff 1991 Senate Statement].

[17] For an analysis of the interests of MNEs in a strong IP regime in TRIPS, using product-cycle theory and hegemonic stability theory, applied first to Anglo-American experience and then to the experience of DCs, see VanGrasstek Communication *Trade-Related Intellectual Property Rights: United States Policy, Developing Countries and the Uruguay Round* in URUGUAY ROUND: FURTHER PAPERS ON SELECTED ISSUES 80–95 (UNCTAD 1990).

[18] Ryan (1998) (n 12) 30.

[19] The most important of such studies coming at the initial phases of the Uruguay Round negotiations is US INTERNATIONAL TRADE COMMISSION, FOREIGN PROTECTION OF INTELLECTUAL PROPERTY RIGHTS AND THE EFFECT ON US INDUSTRY AND TRADE: REPORT TO THE UNITED STATES

Table 5.1: R&D Expenditures in the Area of Drugs and Medicines for Major OECD Countries and the EU 1976–96 (in millions of PPP dollars at current prices)

	1976	1980	1984	1988	1992	1996
US	1091.0	1777.0	3319.3	4906.2	7944.0	9773.0
EU[20]	1047.3	1808.0	2831.6	4777.0	7111.4	N/A
Japan	377.7	741.6	1336.1	2040.3	3422.4	4018.9
UK	252.4	495.6	789.3	1473.9	2347.4	2875.8
France	176.5	322.3	576.0	800.6	1252.8	1471.8
Germany	331.0	528.4	656.7	1090.5	1371.3	N/A
Italy	142.8	237.2	405.1	725.3	1049.0	817.5
Canada	19.2	33.9	48.5	101.9	234.0	413.2
TOTAL	3437.9	5944.0	9962.6	15915.7	24732.3	N/A

Source: *OECD, Research and Development in Industry: Expenditures and Researchers, Scientists and Engineers, 1976–97 (OECD Paris 1999): various tables.*[21]

were due not only to the exploitation of the fruits of the MNEs' R&D outlays, but were also due to the market losses suffered by the pharmaceutical MNEs. In 1985, the US-based Pharmaceutical Manufacturers Association (PMA) estimated that in only five countries (Mexico, Brazil, Argentina, South Korea, and Taiwan) its member companies lost market shares of between 30 and 70 per cent on products that should have been protected but were not.[22] Had a patent protection regime similar to those prevalent in ICs and containing the standards advocated by the pharmaceutical MNEs been in place, those member companies would have enjoyed market exclusivity for their patented products for the duration of the patent term. This problem was compounded by the fact that by the early 1990s forty per cent of total sales of the US pharmaceutical MNEs were international sales.[23] Finally, the vulnerability of the pharmaceutical industry to

TRADE REPRESENTATIVE, INVESTIGATION NO 332-245, UNDER SECTION 332 (G) OF THE TARIFF ACT OF 1930 US ITC Pub No 2065 (1988) [hereinafter US ITC 1988 Report]. See also US ITC 1991 Report (n 13); and STEPHANIE EPSTEIN AND JAMES MATTHEW JONES, INTELLECTUAL PROPERTY AT A CROSSROADS: GLOBAL PIRACY AND INTERNATIONAL COMPETITIVENESS 15–24 (1990).

[20] EU figures represents the total for the fifteen countries then comprising the EU.

[21] Figures for Germany refer to West Germany until 1990 and starting from 1991 the figure refers to the unified Germany.

[22] *Unfair Foreign Trade Practices (Part 2): Hearing before the Subcomm. on Oversight and Investigations, and the House Comm. on Energy and Commerce* 99th Cong 196 (1985) (statement of Gerald Mossinghoff, President, Pharmaceutical Manufacturers Association) [hereinafter Mossinghoff 1985 House Statement].

[23] Mossinghoff 1991 Senate Statement (n 16) 59.

piracy was underlined by the fact that the duplication of chemical compounds is a relatively straightforward task, as opposed to researching and developing it, which entailed considerable expenses.[24]

(B) Identifying the Problem Issues in International Patent Protection

From the perspective of IC business interests, particularly from that of the pharmaceutical MNEs, the problem issues of IP protection were those of regime deficiencies and general enforcement inadequacies in the protection of intellectual property.[25] This was true both at the domestic (DC) and international (WIPO) levels. While MNEs were generally well coordinated and had similar concerns about the deficiencies in the IP regimes of DCs as well as those in the international regime, there were some important differences. Such differences mainly concerned the importance attached to a particular type of intellectual property, whether pertaining to copyright, trademarks, or patents.[26] Notwithstanding these differences, certain classes of problems such as enforcement and dispute settlement were cross cutting issues of interest affecting the entire industry spectrum. This facilitated the emergence of common stances on the IP issue in addition to the important specific concerns carried forth by specialized industry lobbying groups within the IP industry lobbying armada.[27]

Before addressing the problem issues, another vital factor to bear in mind in characterizing the IP problem, as argued by MNEs, ICs, and particularly the United States, has been its strategic redefinition as a 'trade' problem in the first instance.[28] As their preferred strategy opted for a transfer of the IP agenda from WIPO to the trade-based GATT regime, MNEs sought

[24] Epstein and Jones (1990) (n 19) 16–17.

[25] US ITC 1988 Report (n 19) 1–6. An excellent review of the complaints of the ICs about inadequate protection of intellectual property is Frank Emmert *Intellectual Property in the Uruguay Round—Negotiating Strategies of the Western Industrialized Countries* 11 MICH J INT'L L 1317, 1319–44 (1990).

[26] For the perspectives of the electronics, pharmaceutical, recording, communications and chemical industries respectively on the international protection of intellectual property rights, see INTELLECTUAL PROPERTY RIGHTS AND CAPITAL FORMATION IN THE NEXT DECADE 119–59 (Charles E Walker and Mark A Bloomfield eds 1988).

[27] Two particularly powerful groups were the efforts focusing on copyright, led by the International Intellectual Property Alliance (IIPA), and the efforts focusing on patents as they affected the pharmaceutical industry, led by the Pharmaceutical Manufacturers' Association (PMA). Both these groups were US-based and led. A larger industry-wide group was the Intellectual Property Committee (IPC), also US-based and led, and played a major role in organizing non-US based industry in lobbying the GATT intellectual property negotiations.

[28] In 1987, the Vice President of IBM argued 'that intellectual property has become a trade problem is not surprising, because the source of the problem is the same as that of other trade issues. That is, nations often put domestic priorities first and only later understand that national actions favoring them can seriously erode their own international trade interests.' Kenneth W Dam *The Growing Importance of International Protection of Intellectual Property* 21 INT'L LAW 627, 630 (1987).

to dress the problem in the 'trade gown'.[29] A landmark document in international business's (including the pharmaceutical MNEs) lobbying campaign of the TRIPS negotiations was issued trilaterally by the Intellectual Property Committee of the United States, Keidanren of Japan, and the European UNICE in the summer of 1988.[30] In this document, a definition of the problem was that

> [i]nadequate and ineffective protection of intellectual property against infringements of intellectual property rights has substantially distorted international trade. If adequately and effectively protected, intellectual property promotes the expansion of international trade, investment and transfers of technology.[31]

Furthermore, in lobbying the US Congress before the Uruguay Round negotiations and throughout the course of the negotiations, business interests and especially the Pharmaceutical Manufacturers' Association sought to define and frame their testimonies during congressional hearings on trade-related issues.[32] Moreover, business interests lobbied for the introduction of reporting on IP infringement in the USTR's annual report to Congress entitled *National Trade Estimate Report on Foreign Trade Barriers*.[33] The characterization of the issue as a trade problem has therefore shifted the focus from that of DCs choosing their own IP protection regime according to their public policy priorities, to an issue of trade distortion and export losses. Commenting on the problem in DCs, the President of the Pharmaceutical Manufacturers' Association stated:

> all have significant deficiencies in intellectual property protection for pharmaceuticals, the correction of which would substantially improve the market share for US pharmaceutical companies.[33a]

[29] See *Possible New Round of Trade Negotiations: Hearings Before the Senate Comm. on Finance* 99th Cong 144, 149–52 (1986) (statement of Kenneth W Dam, Vice President, Law and External Relations, IBM Corp on behalf of the Intellectual Property Committee) [hereinafter Dam 1986 Senate Statement]. Please refer to Ch 6 for a discussion of the choice of GATT as a forum for addressing the IP problem.

[30] KEIZAI DANTAI RENGOKAI, UNICE, INTELLECTUAL PROPERTY COMMITTEE, BASIC FRAMEWORK OF GATT PROVISIONS ON INTELLECTUAL PROPERTY: STATEMENT OF VIEWS OF THE EUROPEAN, JAPANESE AND UNITED STATES BUSINESS COMMUNITIES (1988) [hereinafter Trilateral Report].

[31] ibid 11.

[32] See Mossinghoff 1985 House Statement (n 22); and *Unfair Foreign Trade Practices: Hearings Before the Subcomm. on Oversight and Investigations of the House Comm. on Energy and Commerce*, 101st Cong. (1989) (statement of Gerald Mossinghoff, President, Pharmaceutical Manufacturers Association) [hereinafter Mossinghoff 1989 House Energy and Commerce Statement].

[33] This annual report was first presented to the Senate Finance Committee and the House Ways and Means Committee in 1985. Its statutory basis lies in the Trade and Tariff Act of 1984 § 303.

[33a] Mossinghoff 1985 House Statement (n 22).

Furthermore, in a testimony to Congress the Intellectual Property Committee argued that:

> First, intellectual property is important to international competitiveness. And second, inadequate international protection of intellectual property has become a major cause of distortions in the international trading system. Under these circumstances, the IPC believes that it is both appropriate and necessary for intellectual property issues to be dealt with under international trade rules as a supplement to existing international intellectual property conventions and agreements.[34]

Three major problem areas have been pinpointed by MNEs: (1) problems of deficiency in DCs intellectual property regimes pertaining to standards and norms of protection; (2) problems associated with a lack of or ineffectiveness in enforcement, and the lack of a credible dispute resolution mechanism; and (3) problems of deficiencies in the standards codified in international intellectual property protection regimes, most importantly the Paris Convention.[35] The focus here will be on the inadequacy pertaining to standards and norms of patent protection.

In a survey of US companies conducted by the United States International Trade Commission,[36] eight specific problems were identified in the patent regimes of 54 countries comprising:

1. no patent protection;
2. patentability precluded by statute;
3. term too short;
4. early lapse;
5. compulsory licensing;
6. Paris Convention non-adherence;
7. patent claims are narrowed too much; and
8. unrealistic working requirements.

Not surprisingly, the patent laws of the DCs examined in this book,[37] suffered from most, if not all, of the eight inadequacies reported by US firms.[38] While the specific patent law provisions relating to our selected

[34] Dam 1986 Senate Statement (n 29) 146.

[35] Paris Convention for the Protection of Industrial Property 21 UNTS 305 (20 Mar 1883) [hereinafter Paris Convention].

[36] US ITC 1988 Report (n 19) 3-5—3-6.

[37] The four countries are: Argentina, Brazil, Egypt, and India. Please refer to Chapter Seven below for an examination of their patent laws.

[38] By far the worst offenders under these criteria as identified by the firms surveyed, were Brazil and India, which each figure in 7 out of eight of the individual complaints. See US ITC 1988 Report (n 19) Table 3–1.

DCs will be covered in Chapter 7 it is useful here to briefly refer to the main problems perceived by the pharmaceutical MNEs.[39]

Pharmaceutical MNEs focused their complaints on five almost identical problems to the eight identified above.[40] First was the problem associated with the absence of any patent regime in certain countries. This, however, was a limited problem affecting a limited number of countries.[41] Secondly, there was the more widespread practice of excluding certain classes of subject matter from patentability with pharmaceuticals figuring prominently in such statutory exclusions. For example, Brazil excluded pharmaceutical products and processes from patentability,[42] warranting its 'anti-pharmaceutical patent policy' as described by PMA to be 'the most egregious'.[43] Thirdly and more widespread still, was the practice of affording process protection in certain subject matter, particularly pharmaceuticals, while excluding products from patentability. Argentina, Egypt, and India were examples of countries following that practice.[44] The fourth complaint of the pharmaceutical MNEs was what they perceived as inadequacy in the term of protection.[45] This was particularly a problem given the pharmaceutical MNEs' claim that bringing a new product to market can take upwards of 12 years, and hence if the term of protection falls short of that there is effectively no protection.

Finally, the fifth complaint concerning DCs' compulsory licensing and related lapse provisions pertains primarily to the working requirements on patent holders. Pharmaceutical MNEs had two main contentions with these provisions.[46] The limited period of time within which working of the patent should occur (three years as authorized by the Paris Convention) is incongruent with the much lengthier period of time required by them to bring their products to the market, estimated at 10 years from patent grant. The

[39] See Gerald J Mossinghoff *Research-Based Pharmaceutical Companies: The Need for Improved Patent Protection Worldwide* 2 J L AND TECH 307 (1987).

[40] As outlined in Peter C Richardson *The Need for Adequate and Effective Protection of Intellectual Property: Perspectives of the Private Sector—Patents* 19 GA J INT'L AND COMP L 352, 353–54 (1989). Peter C Richardson was then Assistant General Counsel, and General Patent Counsel of Pfizer Inc.

[41] In 1989, Indonesia and Turkey were perhaps the only major examples, ibid 353.

[42] Decree No 5.772 (21 Dec 1971) Art 9(c).

[43] *USTR Identification of Priority Practices and Countries Under Super 301 and Special 301 Provisions of the Omnibus Trade and Competitiveness Act of 1988: Hearing Before the Subcomm. on Trade of the House Comm. on Ways and Means* 101st Cong 134 (1989) (statement of Gerald Mossinghoff, President, Pharmaceutical Manufacturers Association) [hereinafter Mossinghoff 1989 House Ways and Means Statement]. For PMA complaints against the patent regimes of Brazil, India and Argentina, see ibid 134–6.

[44] For Argentina, see Law No 111 (11 Oct 1864) Art 4; for Egypt, see Law No 132 (1949) art 2; and for India, see Indian Patents Act No 39 (19 Sept 1970) § 5.

[45] As an example, India provides a patent term of only five years for pharmaceutical processes. See Indian patents Act No 39 (19 Sept 1970) § 53(1)(a).

[46] Richardson (1989) (n 40) 354–5.

second contention was that economic realities militate against having production facilities in every single jurisdiction where patent protection is sought. Thus, it would be far more economically efficient for some markets to be supplied through imports. Once the problem issues had been identified, the pharmaceutical MNEs had the considerable task of resolving them in favour of their interests.

(II) MOBILIZING FOR INTERNATIONAL PATENT LAW REFORM

Having identified specific problem issues, MNEs with a significant stake in intellectual property protection, sought to overhaul the international IP regime to protect their interests globally and particularly in key DCs. A main avenue to accomplish this goal was through procuring the assistance of the key players in the global economy, particularly the United States, to engage bilaterally the major DCs accused of violating their IP rights. Second, the MNEs sought to initiate a multilateral undertaking on the subject that would guarantee them a single governing global standard for all countries.

(A) The Bilateral Approach: Lobbying the Key Player(s)

> We hope the imposition of this sanction, which is modest in comparison to the revenue losses sustained by our industry in Brazil, will impress upon Brazil the seriousness with which the United States views the unauthorized appropriation of its citizens' intellectual property.
>
> Pharmaceutical Manufacturers' Association[47]

In pursuit of their aims for international patent law reform, pharmaceutical MNEs, as well as MNEs in general, realized early on in the quest for a strong patent regime that the involvement of the US administration and Congress as allies was essential to their efforts.[48] Not only was the United States a strategic market for the vast majority of its trading partners and one they could not afford to forego, but equally, the United States was also a leader in international economic diplomacy whose domestic economic legislation had a worldwide impact. A logical first step for the concerned business sectors was to fine-tune the US legislative and policy process to conform to their objectives and then to deploy this arsenal of laws 'as

[47] See *Pharmaceutical Manufacturers' Association Statement* 2 World Intell Prop Rev (BNA) 220 (1988).

[48] Ryan (1998) (n 12) 67.

instruments of commercial warfare.'[49] Below, an overview of the most relevant US legislation in this regard is presented, followed by an analysis of how the US pharmaceutical lobby, and specifically the Pharmaceutical Manufacturers Association, potently deployed this arsenal against two key DCs, Brazil, and Argentina. Finally, while the US bilateral approach on IP matters was by far the most significant and effective during and throughout the Uruguay Round negotiations, a brief analysis of the EC's role is also discussed below.

Through a series of amendments particularly in 1988, US trade legislation integrated the protection of IP rights. Perceived unjustified acts by foreign trading partners constituted violations, which required the US Trade Representative to intervene to protect the intellectual property of its citizens. The most famous of these legislative instruments were Section 337,[50] Section 301,[51] 'Special 301',[52] and 'Super 301'.[53] While the first instrument was designed to protect US IP owners from violations in import trade, the three latter instruments were designed to induce change in the IP regimes of America's trading partners using access to the highly coveted US market as leverage.[54]

Section 337 was designed to protect US producers from:

> *unfair methods of competition* and *unfair acts* in the *importation* of articles into the United States, or in their sale by the owner, importer, consignee, or agent of either, the effect or tendency of which is to *destroy or substantially injure* an industry, *efficiently and economically operated*, in the United States, or to *prevent the establishment* of such an industry, or to restrain or monopolize trade and commerce in the United States . . .[55]

'Unfair methods of competition and unfair acts,' included violation of US-owned IP rights.[56] A previous amendment to Section 337 served to

[49] Robert C Cassidy *National Trade Policy Instruments and the GATT: A US Lawyer's Perspective* in CONFLICT AND RESOLUTION IN U.S.–EC TRADE RELATIONS 159 (Seymour J Rubin and Mark L Jones eds 1989). See also Susan K Sell *The Origins of a Trade-Based Approach to Intellectual Property Protection—The Role of Industry Associations* 17 SCI COMM 163 (1995).

[50] Tariff Act of 1930 § 337, *amended by* 19 USC § 1337 (2003).

[51] Trade Act of 1974 § 301, *amended by* 19 USC § 2411 (2003).

[52] 19 USC §§ 2242, 2212(b)(2) (2003).

[53] 19 USC § 2420 (2003).

[54] However, the initial impetus for integrating intellectual property concerns into legislation primarily dealing with trade, was initially apparent in the Caribbean Basin Economic Recovery Act and in the Generalized System of Preferences Renewal Act. *See* Mossinghoff 1985 House Statement (n 22) 194.

[55] Tariff Act of 1990 § 337(a), *amended by* Trade Act of 1974 § 341, Pub L No 93–618 (1975) (emphasis added).

[56] Between the years 1974 and 1986, more than 90 per cent of Section 337 investigations

depoliticize the process by transferring the authority to issue orders excluding the importation of foreign goods violating US IP rights from the President to the International Trade Commission,[57] and thus shielding US business from the 'whims' of the diplomatic prerogatives of the President. The MNE lobby, however, was not entirely satisfied with the process. Primarily, complainants had to show that the 'unfair method of competition' or the 'unfair acts' had the effect of destroying or substantially injuring the industry.[58] They also had to prove that they were an '*efficiently and economically operated*' industry '*in the United States*'.[59] Due to these burdensome conditions, US IP owners seeking to exclude imports of goods infringing their IP rights lobbied for an amendment. The amendment to Section 337 occurred as part of the 1988 Omnibus Trade and Competitiveness Act.[60] The amended Section 337 eliminated the injury requirement in those investigations related to statutory IP rights (ie patents, copyrights, trademark, and mask works), where it declares 'unlawful' '[*t*]*he importation into the United States, the sale for importation, or the sale within the United States after importation by the owner, importer, or consignee, of articles that—(i) infringe a valid and enforceable United States patent . . .*'.[61]

Hence, this facilitated complainant's argument limiting it to a showing of statutory IP infringement only. The 1988 amendment deleted the requirement that the industry be 'efficiently and economically' operated, and it simplified the other requirement that it be a domestic industry (reference to the old text of an industry '*in the United States*'). In the latter case, the amendment refers to the Commission as granting relief '*only if an industry in the United States, relating to the articles protected by the patent, copyright, trademark, or mask work concerned, exists or is in the process of being established*'.[62] In the following paragraph, an '*industry in the United States*' shall be considered to exist if there is: (A) significant investment in plant and equipment; (B) significant employment of labour or capital; or (C) substantial investment in its exploitation [of the IP protected article], including engineering, research and development, or licensing.[63]

initiated by the ITC were IP related. See GAO study quoted in, AS Newman *The Amendments to Section 337: Increased Protection for Intellectual Property Rights* 20 LAW AND POL'Y INT'L BUS 571(n 9) (1989).

[57] 1975 amendment in subsection (a) Pub L 93–618 substituted 'Commission' for 'President'. See Sell (1995) (n 49) 166.

[58] Tariff Act of 1930 § 337(a) 19 USC § 1337 (2003).

[59] ibid.

[60] Omnibus Trade and Competitiveness Act of 1988 Pub L No 100–418 (1988).

[61] 19 USC § 1337(a)(1)(B) (2003).

[62] 19 USC § 1337(a)(2) (2003).

[63] 19 USC § 1337(a)(3) (2003).

While US MNEs were able to protect their domestic market from import competition quite effectively after the amendments to Section 337, the lack of what they deemed adequate IP protection in overseas markets continued to create major problems for them. A different set of trade legislation was required to combat 'lax' IP protection in foreign markets. This need was fulfilled through Section 301 of the Trade Act of 1974 as amended. This instrument was designed to protect the United States from certain 'unfair trade practices' by its trading partners. It did so initially by requiring the Trade Representative to '*take all appropriate and feasible action within the power of the President*'[64] to enforce the right of the United States under any trade agreement, or to respond to any act, policy or practice of a foreign country that '*is inconsistent with the provisions of, or otherwise denies benefits to the United States under, any trade agreement*'[65] or 'is *unjustifiable* and *burdens or restricts United States commerce*'.[66] In this regard, '*unjustifiable*' was defined to include, inter alia, '*any act, policy, or practice . . . which denies . . . protection of intellectual property rights*'.[67] Furthermore, '*unreasonable*' was also defined to include, inter alia, any act, policy, or practice that denies the '*provision of adequate and effective protection of intellectual property rights . . .*'.[68] The '*appropriate and feasible action*' within the power of the President, to take in case of a violation under Section 301, included the suspension or withdrawal of concessions in a trade agreement with the country in violation under Section 301, or the imposition of duties and other such restrictions, or fees and restrictions on the imports or services of such a country respectively.[69]

It was not until the 1988 amendments to Section 301, however, that the USTR was obligated to take action with regard to a 301 complaint, thus no longer retaining discretion in deciding whether to initiate action. New powers were also introduced in the Omnibus Trade and Competitiveness Act of 1988, where under 'Special 301', the USTR was required to identify countries which deny '*adequate and effective*' protection of IP rights to American firms and to investigate their practices.[70] Furthermore, according to the new 'Super 301', the USTR was required to identify 'priority foreign countries', and to self-initiate Section 301 investigations of the practices of these so-designated countries.[71] Such identification was based on the USTR's annual *National Trade Estimate Report on Foreign Trade Barriers*.[72]

64 19 USC § 2411(a)(1)(B)(ii) (2003).
65 19 USC § 2411(a)(1)(B)(i) (2003).
66 ibid. Emphasis added.
67 19 USC § 2411(d)(4)(B) (2003).
68 19 USC § 2411(d)(3)(B)(i)(II) (2003).
69 19 USC § 2411(c)(1) (2003).
70 19 USC §§ 2242, 2212(b)(2) (2003).
71 19 USC § 2420(a) (2003).
72 This Report, required by statute under the Trade and Tariff Act of 1984 § 303, identifies and analyses acts, policies or practices that constitute significant barriers to or distortions of US exports of goods and services; property protected by trademarks, patents and copyrights exported or licensed by US citizens; and US direct investment overseas.

Mainly through the Pharmaceutical Manufacturers' Association, Section 301 was put to effective use by the US Pharmaceutical MNEs as part of their strategy to induce and coerce change in the patent regimes of certain strategic markets in DCs.[73] Indeed, as Ryan argues,

> [s]pecial 301 intellectual property policy has similarly been used for the benefit of some of the most globally competitive American industry sectors—pharmaceuticals and fine chemicals, films and music recordings, computer software—and these industry groups have shaped the USTR's diplomacy agenda for protecting intellectual property.[74]

Section 301 investigations cover a number of very interesting landmark cases relating to the US bilateral approach to international IP protection.[75] Nonetheless, the most interesting and relevant from the perspective of pharmaceutical MNEs were two cases initiated by the USTR in response to petitions filed by PMA against Brazil in 1987[76] and against Argentina in 1988.[77]

In its petition against Brazil, PMA specifically targeted the denial of patent protection not only to pharmaceutical products, but also for the processes for preparing those products.[78] The result of this denial, PMA argued, adversely affects its member companies in four ways: injury to their

[73] See Susan Sell *Intellectual Property Protection and Antitrust in the Developing World: Crisis, Coercion, and Choice* 49 INT'L ORG 315, 323–30 (1995). Sell argues that:
'In all eight cases [301 IP cases], the targeted governments agreed to improve intellectual property protection along the lines desired by the United States. Furthermore, the timing of the changes demonstrates the strong link between this exercise of US leverage and the changes in targeted states. In short, both the substance and the timing of these policies can be explained as a product of coercion.'

[74] Ryan (1998) (n 12) 85.

[75] One of the first and standard setting of the cases of the use of section 301 in IP violations was USTR, Korea: Initiation of Investigation Under Section 302; Adequacy of Korean Laws for the Protection of Intellectual Property Rights, 4 Nov 1985, USTR Pub Docket No 301–52, 50 Fed Reg at 45,883 (1985). For commentary on the Korean 301 investigation, see JH Bello and AF Holmer *Significant Recent Developments in Section 301 Unfair Trade Cases* 21 INT'L LAW 211, 221–223 (1987); and AY Park *International Trade: Agreement Between the United States and the Republic of Korea Concerning Insurance Market Access and Intellectual Property Protection in the Republic of Korea, 21 July, 1986* 28 HARVARD INT'L LJ 166 (1987). See also 2 World Intell Prop Rev (BNA) 131 (1988).

[76] Unfair Trade Practices; Brazil Patent Protection for Pharmaceuticals; Initiation of an Investigation 52 Fed Reg 28, 223 (28 July 1987).

[77] Initiation of Section 301 Investigation; Argentina's Failure To Provide Adequate and Effective Intellectual Property Protection for Pharmaceuticals 53 Fed Reg 37,668 (27 Sept 1988).

[78] Petition filed by P Trooboff, Covington and Burling, on behalf of the Pharmaceutical Manufacturers' Association, 11 June 1987, in Brazil—Pharmaceutical Patents USTR Public Docket No 301–61,1 [hereinafter PMA Brazil Petition]. The specific object of the complaint was Art 9(c) of the Brazilian Patent Law, which excludes, inter alia, pharmaceutical products and the processes for their production from patentability.

patent rights; injury to their investments in Brazil; injury to their exports from the United States and other nations to Brazil; and lost opportunities that would otherwise exist for further investment and trade with Brazil.[79] PMA estimated the losses of its member companies between 1979 and 1986 at US $160 million and projected losses under the status quo until the year 2000 amounting to US $280 million.[80] Counsel for PMA argued that such action from Brazil burdened and restricted US commerce. An accompanying legal memorandum stated that

> the 1984 amendments to the Trade Act enable the Petitioner to satisfy the unreasonable requirement of Section 301 of the Trade Act, as amended, by showing that the Brazilian system unfairly denies adequate and effective protection of intellectual property rights with respect to pharmaceutical products.[81]

On the importance of the petition from the US industry perspective, PMA argued that:

> this Petition deals directly with the capacity of United States industry to compete on a fair basis in an important market for American products. The issues raised by this Petition cannot be answered by referring to the needs of governments to develop their economy or meet the material needs of their people. Thoughtful leaders and scholars in developing nations recognize that these nations will benefit more from respect for the intellectual property rights of others than from contributing to the weakening of those rights.[82]

On the other hand, while Argentina provided patent protection for pharmaceutical processes, it did not provide protection to pharmaceutical products.[83] As such, PMA's petition against Argentina was primarily based on the absence of product protection—an absence it notes was found sufficient for a Section 301 determination of unfairness in the earlier Brazil case.[84] Moreover, PMA advanced four additional causes of complaint inherent in the Argentine patent law. Primarily, PMA's petition noted that patent

[79] ibid 2.

[80] ibid Appendix E 'Lost Sales by US Pharmaceutical Industry Resulting from Brazilian Failure to Provide Patent Protection.'

[81] ibid 12.

[82] ibid 21–2. Almost identical language appears in Petition filed by P Trooboff, Covington and Burling, on behalf of the Pharmaceutical Manufacturers' Association (10 Aug 1988) in Argentina—Pharmaceutical Patents USTR Public Docket No 301–68, 34–5 [hereinafter PMA Argentina Petition].

[83] Law No 111 Art 4 [1852–1880] ADLA 434 (11 Oct 1864).

[84] PMA Argentina Petition (n 82) 16–17.

protection for pharmaceutical processes under Argentine law was inadequate and ineffective and therefore a totally unsatisfactory substitute for product protection.[85] This result was due largely to the ineffectiveness of process protection in the pharmaceutical industry, because the end product could be developed with easily changeable processes. Secondly, innovators bore the burden of proving that the defendant infringed their pharmaceutical process patent as opposed to the defendant proving he or she did not. Third, the enforcement of patent rights suffers from weaknesses in the remedial provisions and enforcement of the patent law because there is no injunctive relief, and a financial penalty estimated when the law was enacted in 1864 has become severely devalued.[86] Finally, Article 47 of the patent law provides for the lapse of all patents if they are not worked in Argentina within two years from the year of grant, which is a provision in violation of Article 5 of the Paris Convention that mandates the passage of a minimum period of three years.[87]

Compared to the Brazil case, the estimated economic losses suffered by PMA member companies seemed to be much more severe—with sales losses of up to US$526 million between 1980 and 1987, and estimated losses reaching over US$1 billion from 1987 to 2000.[88] Given these losses, PMA sought four main remedies: the introduction of product patent protection for pharmaceutical products; the protection of trade secrets; amendment of the lapse provision of Article 47 of the Argentine patent law; and most interestingly, market exclusivity rights for 'pipeline' products that are currently subject to patent protection in countries other than Argentina.[89]

While reflecting bilateral concerns of the US pharmaceutical industry in important markets such as Brazil and Argentina, the Brazil and Argentina petitions were filed with a broader purpose in mind. As an engagement of leading DCs (particularly of Brazil) antagonistic to the regulatory position of the pharmaceutical MNEs for stronger patent protection worldwide, these two cases served to underscore the resolve of the pharmaceutical MNEs. In the words of PMA President Gerald Mossinghoff:

> Brazil is a leader of the so-called G-77 countries' effort to reduce the already minimum standards for patent protection in the Paris Convention. It has also opposed efforts to include intellectual property protection within the purview of the GATT as a trade-related issue. As a

[85] ibid 20.
[86] Law No 111 Art 53 [1852–80] ADLA 435 (11 Oct 1864).
[87] ibid 434; Multilateral Protection of Industrial Property art 5 21 UST 1583, 1592 (14 July 1967).
[88] PMA Argentina Petition (n 82) Appendix G 'Lost Sales by US Pharmaceutical Industry Resulting from Argentine Failure to Provide Patent Protection.'
[89] ibid 32.

newly industrialized nation, it is time for Brazil, the eighth largest economy in the West, to start playing by the rules of the international trading system.[90]

The pressure created by PMA in launching the Brazil Section 301 case, however, went beyond any of the other IP-related Section 301 cases because it led to the first imposition of retaliatory measures. On 21 July 1988, the US President determined that 'Brazil's failure to provide process and product patent protection for pharmaceutical products is unreasonable and burdens or restricts US commerce', and directed the USTR to hold hearings on imposing 'increased duties or other import restrictions' on some Brazilian products from a list of products accounting for US$200 million in trade.[91] On 20 October 1988 the US President issued proclamation 5885, which increased US import duties by 100 per cent *ad valorem* on articles imported and produced in Brazil to the value of US$40 million.[92] This action was terminated on 2 July 1990 pursuant to the Brazilian government's announcement of its decision to seek legislation to provide patent protection for pharmaceutical products and processes.[93] By contrast, the Argentine investigation was terminated upon the withdrawal by PMA of its petition on 23 September 1989, citing progress in bilateral consultations between the governments of the United States and Argentina.[94]

The United States clearly had a powerful statutory arsenal to tackle the issue of international IP protection. Put to effective use by the US international business sector, this arsenal was notoriously unilateralist, coercive, and in certain aspects, GATT-illegal. The European Communities submitted a GATT complaint against Section 337.[95] Subsequently, the GATT panel found it to be inconsistent with Article III(4), where it accorded procedural treatment less favourable to imported products allegedly infringing US intellectual property as compared to products of US origin.[96] Furthermore, Brazil also lodged a GATT complaint against US Section 301, but withdrew the

[90] Statement of Gerald J Mossinghoff, President, PMA in *Brazil—Pharmaceutical Patents* USTR Public Docket No 301–61 (n 78).

[91] Determination Under Section 301 of the Trade Act 53 Fed Reg 28,177 (27 July 1988). Transcripts of the hearings, which took place on 8 Sept 1988, over two sessions, are available with the author, and can be accessed from USTR Public Docket No 301–61.

[92] Proclamation No 5885, 53 Fed Reg 41,551 (20 Oct 1988).

[93] Determination to Terminate Increased Duties on Certain Articles from Brazil 55 Fed Reg 27,324 (2 July 1990).

[94] Letter from Gerald Mossinghoff, President, PMA to A Jane Bradley, Chairman, Section 301 Committee USTR in Argentina—Pharmaceutical Patents USTR Public Docket No 301–68 (n 83).

[95] See European Community 1989 Report on US Trade Barriers [IP (89) 324].

[96] See Lyn M Schlitt *Protection of Intellectual Property Rights Under Section 337 of the Tariff Act: Addressing the GATT Panel Report* 510 PLI/COMM 103 (1989).

complaint following a mutual understanding. As a leading commentator argued in the late 1980s on the state of 301 action:

> No doubt exists, however, that this program meets with a high degree of foreign resistance, risks significant damage to United States foreign policy interests, and is terribly inefficient. Moreover, gains achieved by United States negotiators are passed on at no cost to its major trade competitors in the European Communities and Japan, thus strengthening the argument for a multilateral approach.[97]

In contrast to the United States, the European Community and its Member States lagged behind in terms of the priority they accorded to the protection of IP rights. This was particularly the case with patents, as the EC was a net importer of patents vis-à-vis trademarks and copyrights of which it was a net exporter.[98] The EC was reluctant to link the IP issue to trade and introduce it as an issue in the forthcoming round of GATT negotiations, where initially, the EC adopted an approach very close to the DCs' position. Only gradually did the EC warm to the US approach of the inclusion of an agreement on IP, as will be discussed in Chapter Six below.[99] In the EC's policy document for the new round of negotiations, the Council of Minister's 'Overall Approach', the EC not only separated the treatment of counterfeit goods from that on IP, but more importantly, presented a weak statement on its objectives, stating:

> International trade increasingly depends upon an appropriate protection of intellectual property rights. . . . Such protection should guarantee an adequate return on investment devoted to developing new goods and services . . . while at the same time avoiding unreasonable barriers to trade. The New Round could contribute to the definition of a better balance between these often conflicting objectives, having due regard to ongoing work in other organisations such as WIPO. As a first step, a review of those GATT provisions which already deal with intellectual property, including in particular Articles XX and IX, should be undertaken.[100]

[97] Frederick M Abbott *Protecting First World Assets in the Third World: Intellectual Property Negotiations in the GATT Multilateral Framework* 22 VAND J TRANSNAT'L L 689, 711–12 (1989).

[98] Mogens Peter Carl *Intellectual Property Rights in the Uruguay Round: the EC Viewpoint, in* CONFLICT AND RESOLUTION IN US–EC TRADE RELATIONS 249–50 (Seymour J Rubin and Mark L Jones eds 1989).

[99] For a concise commentary on the initial EC position on IP, see HUGO PAEMEN AND ALEXANDRA BENSCH, FROM THE GATT TO THE WTO: THE EUROPEAN COMMUNITY IN THE URUGUAY ROUND 84–85 (1995).

[100] Overall Approach: New Round of Trade Negotiations in Defence of Open Multilateral Trade, EEC Doc No 7748/86, SEC (86) 840 final.

The EC had no forceful agenda for international IP protection, seeking neither at the bilateral nor at the multilateral level. In addition, the degree of business influence on EC policy-making was more limited compared to that enjoyed by business over the US policy-making process.[101] This leads us to the importance attached by the MNEs to a multilateral approach to IP protection where they sought an international lobbying campaign in favour of introducing high standards on patent protection into the new GATT round of negotiations.

(B) The Multilateral Approach: Pharmaceutical MNEs and the TRIPS Patent Negotiations

The pharmaceutical MNEs, as other international business interests, eventually realized that reliance on the bilateral approach was an unsustainable strategy. Not only were certain bilateral tactics GATT-illegal, but they were also subject to the political priorities of the government deploying them and thus unreliable in the long term. More importantly, reliance on an international regulatory framework requiring signatory parties to adhere to the standards enshrined therein guaranteed IP owners a durable and legitimate, if indirect, mechanism of protection. This was even more coveted if this framework comprised standards conforming to their preferences with an effective enforcement and dispute settlement mechanism. Therefore, a multilateral approach was preferred, and GATT as a venue was ideal in this regard.[102] However, this did not entail forfeiture of the bilateral approach, which was still advocated by a leading MNE executive as necessary to secure agreement within GATT, where bilateral pressure was a tactic to achieve the multilateral GATT strategy.[103]

United States' MNEs began a campaign to launch multilateral trade negotiations within the GATT ambit on IP, aiming to produce a multilateral code that included the 'adoption and implementation of adequate and effective rules for the protection of intellectual property'.[104] Two US business mobilization efforts were crucial in this regard: the Advisory Committee for Trade Negotiations (ACTN); and the Intellectual Property Committee (IPC). Established by statute in 1974 to provide the US President with advice on trade negotiations, the ACTN was a committee of leading executive officers from major US corporations with a stake in US and interna-

[101] See Marco Bronckers *National Trade Policy Instruments and the GATT: An EC Lawyer's Perspective* in CONFLICT AND RESOLUTION IN U.S.-EC TRADE RELATIONS 146 (Seymour J Rubin and Mark L Jones eds 1989).

[102] The choice of GATT as a venue preferred by MNEs and IC governments was briefly discussed earlier, and will be further discussed in Ch 6.

[103] Dam (1987) (n 28) 636–7.

[104] Trilateral Report (n 30) 17.

tional trade policy.[105] On the issue of IP protection and the quest by the US business community to include the issue within the GATT ambit by including it in the upcoming new round of multilateral trade negotiations, the ACTN issued in October 1985 an outline of a multilateral IP agreement to be concluded within GATT and supplied it to the US administration.[106] This was followed by a report issued by the ACTN Task Force on Intellectual Property,[107] which ultimately influenced the administration's statement on the protection of US IP abroad.[108]

In addition to the ACTN effort, one of the leading US corporate officers, Pfizer's CEO Edmund Pratt (who also served as Chair of ACTN) together with the CEO of IBM, decided in March 1986 to establish the IPC as a coalition of senior executive officers from twelve major US corporations in diverse areas of activity with a common interest in IP protection.[109] The objectives of the IPC were:[110]

- The inclusion and successful negotiation of a satisfactory arrangement for intellectual property (patents, copyrights, trade secrets and trademarks) in the new round of GATT trade negotiations;
- the development of a coherent international strategy, including bilateral negotiations, in support of intellectual property protection;
- cooperation between the US private sector and the international business community in support of improved international intellectual property protection; and
- changes in various US trade laws to improve the protection of intellectual property.

Therefore, in its quest for the successful negotiation of a GATT-based IP

[105] See 19 USC § 2155 (2001).

[106] US TRADE REPRESENTATIVE, TASK FORCE ON INTELLECTUAL PROP., SUMMARY OF PHASE I: RECOMMENDATIONS OF THE TASK FORCE ON INTELLECTUAL PROPERTY TO THE ADVISORY COMMITTEE FOR TRADE NEGOTIATIONS (1985). See also Jacques J Gorlin *The Business Community and the Uruguay Round* in INTELLECTUAL PROPERTY RIGHTS AND CAPITAL FORMATION IN THE NEXT DECADE 170–72 (Charles E Walker and Mark A Bloomfield eds 1988); and Susan K Sell *Multinational Corporations as Agents of Change: the Globalization of Intellectual Property Rights* PRIVATE AUTHORITY AND INTERNATIONAL AFFAIRS 169, 171 (A Claire Cutler et al eds 1999).

[107] US TRADE REPRESENTATIVE, ADVISORY COMMITTEE FOR TRADE NEGOTIATIONS TASK FORCE ON INTELLECTUAL PROPERTY RIGHTS, SUMMARY OF PHASE II: RECOMMENDATIONS OF THE TASK FORCE (1986).

[108] US TRADE REPRESENTATIVE, ADMINISTRATION STATEMENT ON THE PROTECTION OF US INTELLECTUAL PROPERTY ABROAD (1986), reproduced as an attachment to *Intellectual Property Rights: Hearings Before the Subcomm. on Int'l Trade of the Senate Comm. on Fin.*, 99th Cong 96–100 (1986) (statement of Harvey E Bale, Assistant USTR).

[109] See Dam 1986 Senate Statement (n 29) 146. See also Carol Bilzi *Towards an Intellectual Property Agreement in the GATT: View of the Private Sector* 19 GA J INT'L AND COMP L 343, 343–5 (1989); and Sell (1999) (n 106) 183–86.

[110] Dam 1986 Senate Statement (n 29) 149.

protection regime, the IPC sought to secure an international consensus between business interests not only in the United States but also in Europe via UNICE and Japan via Keidanren.[111] In this regard, the IPC had a number of MNEs in the pharmaceutical and chemical industries with a high stake in ensuring a strong patent protection regime for future multilateral negotiations on the issue, including Bristol-Meyers, Merck, Pfizer, Du Pont, and Monsanto. Pfizer took the lead in this group—particularly in lobbying the US Congress. Similarly, Pfizer engaged the TRIPS negotiators on the ground in Geneva where it hired a number of Geneva-based lobbyists for that purpose.[112]

Despite Pfizer's active role within the IPC, the Pharmaceutical Manufacturers Association and its associated lobbying of the US administration and Congress was the spearhead of the pharmaceutical MNEs' mobilization campaign to defining, fine-tuning, and pursuing their goals of international protection of IP rights.[113] As examined above, PMA was also active in petitioning for the initiation of 301 investigations. Resulting in a considerable advantage in its access to policy-makers and expertise in the IP area, PMA was presided over by none other than Gerald J Mossinghoff, a former US Assistant Secretary of Commerce and Commissioner of Patents. Obviously, PMA realized that the involvement of the US administration and Congress in its endeavour was crucial to the success of its efforts. Apart from the exertions of ACTN on the administration and its direct impact on the US position on international IP protection as well as the work of the IPC in lobbying the administration and in framing the US negotiating objectives through Congress,[114] PMA was the principal mobilization vehicle of US pharmaceutical MNEs in lobbying the US Congress. A direct method for performing this task was through testimony concerning the negotiations, on US national interests in the new round of multilateral trade negotiations, and its follow-up in Congressional hearings convened during the TRIPS negotiations.[115] This effort maintained pressure on the US legislature and

[111] The fruits of this cooperation was the issuance of the Trilateral Report, referred to earlier, and arguably the single most important contribution of international business to the Uruguay Round negotiations.

[112] Interview with Gerald J Mossinghoff, former President, Pharmaceutical Manufacturers Association in Washington DC (29 Aug 2002) [hereinafter Mossinghoff Interview].

[113] During the period from 1985 and until the end of the Uruguay Round and beyond, PMA representatives regularly appeared before Congress as witnesses for hearings on issues related to IP protection.

[114] *Possible New Round of Trade Negotiations: Hearings Before the Senate Comm. on Finance*, 99th Cong 144 (1986). See also *GATT: The Impact on American Industries: Hearing and Mark-up on HR 362 Before the Subcomm on Econ Policy, Trade and Env't of the House Comm. on Foreign Affairs*, 103rd Cong 44–79 (1994) (statement of Jacques Gorlin, Intellectual Property Committee).

[115] See Mossinghoff 1991 Senate Statement (n 16) 56–63; Mossinghoff 1991 House Judiciary Statement (n 9) 99–118; *Trade and Tech: Implications of the GATT Negotiations: Hearing Before the Subcomm on Tech and Competitiveness of the House Comm on Science, Space and Technology*, 102nd Cong 68–81, 91–102 (1991) (statement of Gerald Mossinghoff,

the presidential administration through constantly voicing MNEs concerns on IP issues. Pressure was also maintained through PMA's evaluation of the final TRIPS Agreement itself during congressional hearings on the results of the Uruguay Round.[116]

As referred to earlier, the IPC played a prominent and active role in engaging international business interests headquartered outside the United States, focusing its efforts mainly in Europe and Japan. Furthermore, in July 1986 the International Chamber of Commerce endorsed a similar approach favoured by US MNEs on IP protection for the Uruguay Round.[117] As to the specifics of the pharmaceutical MNEs' forward international deployment, an important role was performed by the International Federation of Pharmaceutical Manufacturers Associations (IFPMA).[118] IFPMA was important to the pharmaceutical MNEs' lobbying strategy at the international level for two main reasons. Primarily, it was a venue where discussion and agreement on specific courses of action could swiftly be dispensed across the world given its international membership, coupled with the fact that IFPMA was largely influenced by the US PMA. In the words of Gerald Mossinghoff: 'PMA had a lot to do with IFPMA policies.'[119] Second, and most conveniently, IFPMA was headquartered in Geneva and only a stone's throw away from where the TRIPS negotiations were being held in GATT. Thus, it was able to follow up on developments and provide feedback as well as engage the negotiators personally. IFPMA's then Executive Vice-President, Richard Arnold, was praised by the PMA President as having proved to be a consistent and resourceful lobbyist and a great help for the pharmaceutical industry.[120] Finally, mention should also be made of the work undertaken by the International Association for the Protection of

President, Pharmaceutical Manufacturers Association) [hereinafter Mossinghoff 1991 House Science Statement]; *Uruguay Round of Multilateral Trade Negotiations: Hearings Before the Subcomm on Trade of the House Comm on Ways and Means*, 103rd Cong 69–74 (1993) (statement of Harvey E Bale, Pharmaceutical Manufacturers Association) [hereinafter Bale 1993 House Statement].

116 See *Trade Agreements Resulting from the Uruguay Round of Multilateral Trade Negotiations: Hearings Before the House Comm on Ways and Means and its Subcomm on Trade*, 103rd Cong 559–68 (1994) (statement of Gerald Mossinghoff, President, Pharmaceutical Manufacturers Association). See also *Trade Agreements Resulting from the Uruguay Round of Multilateral Trade Negotiations: Hearings Before the House Comm on Ways and Means and its Subcomm on Trade*, 103rd Cong 134–49 (1994) (statement of Timothy Hackman, Intellectual Property Committee); and *Jobs Through Anti-Piracy: Hearing Before the Subcomm on Econ Policy, Trade and Env't of the House Comm. on Foreign Affairs*, 103rd Cong 75–81 (1994) (statement of Peter C Richardson, Pfizer, Inc).

117 See extracts of ICC statements on the TRIPS negotiations and Agreement in INTERNATIONAL CHAMBER OF COMMERCE, INTELLECTUAL PROPERTY AND INTERNATIONAL TRADE: A GUIDE TO THE URUGUAY ROUND TRIPS AGREEMENT 128–35 (1996).

118 See INTERNATIONAL FEDERATION OF PHARMACEUTICAL MANUFACTURERS ASSOCIATIONS, GATT TRIPS AND THE PHARMACEUTICAL INDUSTRY: A REVIEW (1995).

119 Mossinghoff Interview (n 112).

120 ibid.

Industrial Property (AIPPI),[121] a private association aiming towards the protection of industrial property. AIPPI was the oldest of the organizations reviewed possessing a tradition stretching as far back as the 1890s.[122] Among the key questions AIPPI members reviewed and issued resolutions on were those on 'GATT/WTO,' and on 'Enforcement of Intellectual Property Rights.'[123]

So far, we have examined the mechanism of action that the MNEs and particularly the pharmaceutical MNEs undertook to push for their international IP protection objectives at the multilateral level. These mechanisms were naturally used to push for the norms they wished to incorporate into a new regime for IP protection. With regard to the form within which these norms were to be incorporated, the IPC sought their inclusion within the GATT. The argument they presented was that IP was, after all, not a new issue to the GATT, where its Articles XX(d), IX, XII, XVIII, and III, are of relevance to patents, trademarks, and copyrights.[124] Furthermore, given that the root cause of the problem being dealt with was the 'trade-related' aspects of IP rights, it was clearly within the scope of GATT. The IPC advocated a dual pronged approach within GATT: primarily, finalizing negotiations over the anti-counterfeiting code for trademarks, and secondly, introducing IP provisions that would focus on patent and copyright infringement and

> could seek to develop and enforce substantive norms and standards . . . and . . . agreed rules of behaviour, . . . dispute settlement procedures and authority to impose trade restrictions on countries that tolerate violation of intellectual property rights.[125]

Two years later however, with the GATT mandate on IP firmly in place and negotiations underway, the IPC changed its preferred approach and opted for a GATT 'agreement' rather than an anti-counterfeit code and amendment of GATT articles.[126]

The Trilateral Report issued by the IPC, Keidanren and UNICE detailed the standards and norms championed by MNEs for adoption into an agree-

121 See Joan Clark *The Role of GATT/TRIPS, of WIPO and of AIPPI in the further Development of Intellectual Property Right Protection*, in INT'L ASSOC OF THE PROTECTION OF INDUS PROP, AIPPI AND THE DEVELOPMENT OF INDUSTRIAL PROPERTY PROTECTION 1897–1997, 481–8 (Simone Amberg and Ruth Vogt eds 1997).

122 ibid.

123 See INT'L ASSOC OF THE PROTECTION OF INDUS PROP, AIPPI CHRONICLE AND RESOLUTIONS, Questions 94, 134, 134A, 134B (Martin J Lutz ed 1999).

124 Dam 1986 Senate Statement (n 29) 152, 165.

125 ibid 153.

126 Trilateral Report (n 30) 18–19. Interestingly, this was also the approach advocated by the US delegation in the very first meeting of the negotiating group on intellectual property (Negotiating Group 11), as will be discussed in Ch 6 below.

ment. In the words of Pfizer's Vice President and General Counsel, it was the 'standard reference' for the GATT IP negotiations regarding the views of the private sector.[127] Most importantly, those standards advocated the patentability of both products and processes without discrimination as to subject matter, and a patent term of 20 years from filing.[128] On the issue of working and compulsory licensing, the Report required that there be no revocation on grounds of non-working and that a compulsory licence awarded for non-working shall be granted only to permit local manufacture. Where impractical, importation authorized by the patentee shall be deemed to satisfy the requirements for working. Finally, neither exclusive nor sole compulsory licences shall be granted, nor shall compulsory licensing provisions discriminate against particular classes of subject matter—an important requirement for the pharmaceutical industry. In the case of a compulsory licence being granted, full compensation should be due to the patentee.[129]

As will be examined below,[130] the congruence between the provisions advocated by the business community and those advanced by the main IC delegations during the negotiations on TRIPS was indicative of the influence MNEs had on shaping IC positions. Regardless, towards the latter stages of the negotiations, and as will be discussed below, the pharmaceutical MNEs began to voice discontent with certain aspects of the unfolding instrument. This mainly centred on what they considered to be overly long transition provisions for DCs and the lack of 'pipeline' protection.[131] Nonetheless, the multilateral strategy of the MNEs was by all counts successful in launching the TRIPS negotiations towards the realization of their interests. The following chapter examines the negotiation process.

[127] *Oversight of the Trade Act of 1988: Hearing Before the Senate Comm on Fin (Part 2 of 3)*, 101st Cong 34 (1989) (statement of CL Clemente, Vice President and General Counsel, Pfizer Inc on behalf of the Intellectual Property Committee).

[128] Trilateral Report (n 30) 32.

[129] ibid 32–3.

[130] The provisions advocated by the Trilateral Report on the standards for patent protection are presented in Table 6.1 below, where they are compared to the submissions of the EC, the US and Japan.

[131] *Hearings on Fast Track: Intellectual Property: Hearings Before the Subcomm on Patents, Copyrights and Trademarks of the Senate Comm on the Judiciary* 102nd Cong 172 (1991) (statement of CL Clemente, Vice President and General Counsel, Pfizer Inc). In addition, Susan Sell notes complaints by the US pharmaceutical industry with regard to the compulsory licensing provisions. See Sell (1999) (n 106) 185.

Chapter 6

The TRIPS Patent Negotiations

Thus far, we have presented the background and parallel bilateral developments to the Uruguay Round negotiations on intellectual property, and specifically as they related to patents and the interests and mobilization efforts of the pharmaceutical MNE industry. Arguably, this backdrop was dominated by the American MNEs, and the role of the US government bilaterally was pervasive in carrying forward the quest for a new global IP regime as envisioned and encouraged by the US pharmaceutical industry, among other business concerns. Hence, this chapter is able to examine the negotiations of the TRIPS patent-related provisions, placing the study in its wider context. While the role of the US government and the US pharmaceutical MNEs predominated, yet the Uruguay Round negotiations were a period of showdown, with the interests of the MNEs and ICs on the one hand clashing with those of the DCs on the other.[1] This chapter will begin by an examination of the choice and utility of GATT as a forum for rule-making in the field of intellectual property protection, and the substantive implications of such a choice. It will then focus on the progress in the specific provisions on standards and norms of patent protection from conception and through the various codification attempts up to the final negotiations on the TRIPS Agreement.

(I) GATT AS A FORUM FOR NEGOTIATIONS ON IP

(A) Background to the Choice of GATT as a Forum

One of the major debates prior to the launch and during the early phases of the Uruguay Round was the appropriateness of admitting intellectual property as an issue within the GATT framework, what a leading scholar describes as the 'GATTability of IPRs'.[2] Traditionally, IP issues were discussed within the forum of the World Intellectual Property

[1] It is important to note however, that there were significant differences in IC positions during the TRIPS negotiations, and more so in the other topics negotiated during the UR.

[2] Thomas Cottier The Prospects for Intellectual Property in GATT 28 COMMON MKT L REV 383, 392–7 (1991).

Organization.[3] The fuel in the argument of this debate was the perceived advantage to their interests that each party to the debate imagined would accrue in a rule-making effort in their preferred forum, whether it is WIPO or GATT.[4] While ICs, supported and prodded by their MNEs, strove to include IP in GATT and the upcoming multilateral trade negotiations, DCs were diametrically opposed to this inclusion, preferring WIPO as the venue for any rule-making effort.[5] In this regard, and prior to an examination of the reasoning behind each party's preferred course, there are two main events of significance in GATT and in WIPO that provide a necessary background for understanding the GATT/WIPO conundrum.

The first of these two events, occurring in GATT, focused on the work it had conducted on IP related topics in the late 1970s, focusing on counterfeit trade.[6] Armed with this work, which resulted in a draft agreement, the United States sought its adoption within GATT.[7] Those efforts, strongly opposed by DCs, led however to the first reference to an IP-related matter of direct relevance to trademarks in a GATT Ministerial Declaration, where a statement on 'Trade in Counterfeit Goods' was incorporated into the Ministerial Declaration of the 38th GATT Ministerial Session, stating that:

> [t]he CONTRACTING PARTIES instruct the Council to examine the question of counterfeit goods with a view to determining the appropriateness of *joint action in the GATT framework on the trade aspects of commercial counterfeiting* and, if such joint action is found to be appropriate, the modalities for such action, *having full regard to the competence of other international organizations*. For the purposes of such examination, the

[3] Convention Establishing the World Intellectual Property Organization (14 July 1967) 828 UNTS 3 (as amended on 28 Sept 1979).

[4] For an exposition of the public international law implications of negotiating IPRs in the GATT framework as opposed to WIPO, and the implications of GATT law and WIPO law, see Werner Meng *GATT and Intellectual Property Rights—The International Law Framework* in LIBERALIZATION OF SERVICES AND INTELLECTUAL PROPERTY IN THE URUGUAY ROUND OF GATT 57–73 (Giorgio Sacerdoti ed 1990). See also Friedl Weiss *TRIPS in Search of an Itinerary: Trade Related Intellectual Property Rights and the Uruguay Round Negotiations* in ibid 98–113.

[5] For the United States, the first official reference linking IP protection to international trade was made in January 1984 by Gerald J Mossinghoff, Commissioner of Patents. See Susan K Sell *Multinational Corporations as Agents of Change: the Globalization of Intellectual Property Rights* PRIVATE AUTHORITY AND INTERNATIONAL AFFAIRS 169, 179 (A Claire Cutler et al eds 1999).

[6] Negotiations between the United States and the European Communities had reached a draft anti-counterfeit code, see GATT *Agreement on Measures to Discourage the Importation of Counterfeit Goods* L/4817 (31 July 1979). This draft agreement was subsequently revised with the participation of other ICs, see GATT Doc L/5382 (18 Oct 1982).

[7] See MICHAEL BLAKENEY, TRADE-RELATED ASPECTS OF INTELLECTUAL PROPERTY RIGHTS: A CONCISE GUIDE TO THE TRIPS AGREEMENT 1–2 (1996).

> CONTRACTING PARTIES request the Director-General to hold consultations with the Director-General of WIPO in order to clarify the legal and institutional aspects involved.[8]

The second event, largely coinciding with the first, was the last major attempt at rule-making in the area of patents prior to the launch of the Uruguay Round, the ill-fated revision conferences of the Paris Convention, conducted under the aegis of WIPO, and held in 1980, 1981, and 1982.[9] The revision attempt failed in its purpose due to the opposed interests of DCs on the one hand, and ICs, particularly the United States, on the other.[10] The significance of these two events lie in that they signified the emergence of IP as an issue within GATT, albeit limited to the issue of trade in counterfeit goods, and at the same time, a stalemate in rule-making efforts within WIPO. In Gerald Mossinghoff's description, nothing seemed to happen in WIPO, and hence leading to a growing conviction by the US negotiators for the need to move to another venue where the US would not have an uphill struggle.[11]

From the perspective of ICs, particularly of the United States, and as strongly endorsed by their business sectors, the preference for GATT was due to a number of factors. And as with the opposite preference of DCs to maintaining the issue within WIPO and away from GATT, those factors largely informed by interests, were also cloaked in a garb of principle. Industrialized countries hence preferred the GATT route primarily due to the negotiating advantages they held vis-à-vis DCs, and as opposed to the advantages the latter held in WIPO and other similar UN-style bodies. While GATT decision-making functioned on the principle of consensus, yet the dominance of ICs in international trade, the inter-linkage of negotiations on a plethora of trade issues, and the relative insulation of GATT from Cold War politics made it a much easier task for ICs to drive the agenda. Furthermore, GATT promised to deliver more to ICs due to the potential for introducing enforcement provisions, and linking those to a dispute settlement mechanism, both of which were lacking in the Paris Convention and the WIPO structure.[12]

Apart from these advantages, ICs argued that on the basis of principle,

[8] Ministerial Declaration (29 Nov 1982) GATT BISD (29th Supp) 9 (1983). Emphasis added.

[9] The revision conferences were held in Geneva in 1980, Nairobi in 1981, and Geneva in 1982.

[10] Interview with Gerald J Mossinghoff, former President, Pharmaceutical Manufacturers Association, in Washington, DC (29 Aug 2002) [hereinafter Mossinghoff interview]. Gerald Mossinghoff was the US Representative to the Revision Conferences of the Paris Convention.

[11] ibid.

[12] See GATT *Statement by United States at Meeting of 25 March* MTN.GNG/NG11/W/2 (3 Apr 1987) 4 [hereinafter US March 1987 Statement].

the emerging problems in the area of IP were becoming increasingly trade-related, and hence GATT was an appropriate forum in which to discuss them. As the United States argued, deficiencies in the protection of intellectual property 'impair negotiated trade concessions because copied goods displace legitimate exports of products from countries where adequate and effective protection is present. Furthermore, deficiencies defeat the GATT's objective of expanding world trade and reducing distortions to such trade.'[13]

On the other hand, as expected, the major DCs opposed the inclusion of discussions on IP within GATT as they opposed the linkage of IP to other issues in trade.[14] Developing countries understood this IC preference as a back door strategy deployed to achieve the aims they failed to achieve in the Paris revision among other aims. The principle basis of their opposition was the inappropriateness of conducting IP discussions in a trade forum, when a specialized organization, WIPO, was responsible for IP, and also that IP issues cover intangible objects, while GATT was restricted to trade in tangible goods.

Despite DC opposition, ICs, and once more, particularly the US, succeeded in including the 'trade-related aspects of intellectual property rights including trade in counterfeit goods' in the Punta del Este Declaration.[15] This undoubtedly was a major victory for the US and the pharmaceutical and other MNEs. However, as will be revealed below, the 'tug-of-war' was in no way over, yet the inclusion of the topic squarely on the agenda for the new round, necessitated more effort from DCs to limit the disciplines that would be sought under it.

(B) Structure of the TRIPS Negotiations

As mandated by the Punta del Este Declaration, a 'Group of Negotiations on Goods' (GNG) was established and mandated, inter alia, to elaborate and put into effect detailed trade negotiating plans and to establish negoti-

[13] ibid 1.

[14] During the preparatory process to the Uruguay Round, both Brazil and Argentina presented proposals to the Preparatory Committee that excluded any mention of IP. See GATT *Draft Ministerial Declaration, Revision: Submission from Brazil* PREP.COM (86)W/41/Rev.1 (16 July 1986); and GATT *Draft Ministerial Declaration: Submission from Argentina* PREP.COM (86)W/49 (29 July 1986). Ultimately, it was the joint Swiss–Colombian proposal referring to IP that was adopted as the basis for the 1986 Ministerial Declaration. See GATT *Preparatory Committee Draft Ministerial Meeting, Revision* PREP.COM (86)W/47/Rev.2 (30 July 1986).

[15] A first hand account by members of the US delegation to the Punta del Este Ministerial Meeting is compiled in Diane Yu, Punta: An Oral History of the 1986 GATT Ministerial Meeting in Punta Del Este, Uruguay (Nov 1987) (unpublished manuscript, on file with the Institute of International Economic Law Georgetown University Washington, DC).

ating groups as required.[16] Fourteen such negotiating groups were established by the Group of Negotiations on Goods; with the eleventh such group entitled the Negotiating Group on Trade-Related Aspects of Intellectual Property Rights Including Trade in Counterfeit Goods (Negotiating Group on TRIPS or NG11).[17] The Group of Negotiations on Goods set an 'Initial Phase' for the negotiating process for NG11 that set out three indents on 'trade-related aspects of intellectual property rights', 'trade in counterfeit goods', and 'consideration of the relationship between the negotiations in this area and initiatives in other fora'.[18] On the trade-related indent, the GNG set out the following tasks:

> [i]dentification of relevant GATT provisions and examination of their operation on the basis of suggestions by participants for achieving the Negotiating Objectives and of factual information by the secretariat as required. Initial examination of the specific suggestions and of the procedures and techniques that might be used to implement them.[19]

Following the Initial Phase, the GNG envisioned a 'Subsequent Negotiating Process,' for the purpose of 'further examination of the specific suggestions and of the procedures and techniques that might be used to implement them,' the tabling of specific texts and their examination with a view to the 'establishment of a common negotiating basis,' and finally, leading up to 'negotiations on the basis established.'[20]

(II) NEGOTIATING THE PATENT PROVISIONS

The TRIPS negotiations can be divided into five main phases throughout the period 1987–93. While the earlier phases of the negotiations—as was true of the other negotiation issues in the Uruguay Round—were characterized by slow progress, and particularly in the Negotiating Group on TRIPS (NG 11), by a debate on the validity of admitting IP within the GATT fold, later phases of the negotiations acquired a dynamism and speed in the tabling of texts and drafts. As the process gradually moved from the early and more formal phases into a more intensive and more limited format, the role of DCs in the negotiations became less effective, while the

[16] *Punta del Este Ministerial Declaration on the Uruguay Round* MIN.DEC (20 Sept 1986) Part I Section G [hereinafter Punta del Este Declaration].

[17] GATT *Fifth Meeting of the Group of Negotiations on Goods—Record of Decisions Taken* MTN.GNG/5 (9 Feb 1987) 3.

[18] ibid 17.

[19] ibid.

[20] ibid.

influence and interests of the pharmaceutical MNEs, as espoused by the IC delegations, became more so. The following subsections will examine this process, bearing in mind that the emphasis throughout will be specifically on the negotiations over the standards and norms on patent protection, as being the most controversial in the 'tug-of-war' between DCs on the one hand, and the major ICs and the pharmaceutical MNEs on the other.

(A) Initial Phase (1987–8)

Following the Punta del Este Ministerial Meeting in October 1986, Negotiating Group 11 on TRIPS held its first meeting in Geneva in March 1987, appointing Ambassador Lars Anell of Sweden as its Chairman.[21] Apart from this opening meeting and throughout 1987, the Group held four other formal meetings.[22] The meetings were focused on the three indents stipulated by the GNG for the Initial Phase of the negotiations.[23] The general discourse of the debate in these five initial meetings of the Negotiating Group centred on a need for developing 'new rules and disciplines,' as advocated by ICs on the one hand, and the quest for limiting as much as possible the mandate of the group, as attempted by DCs, on the other. A further point of debate was the identification of existing GATT provisions relating to IP and the work of the Group.[24] Two further important undertakings in the negotiations during 1987 were the tabling of submissions from IC delegations (EC, Japan, US, Nordic Countries and Switzerland) on trade problems encountered in connection with IPRs,[25] and four suggestions by four IC delegations on achieving the negotiating objective.[26]

[21] GATT *Meeting of the Negotiating Group of 25 March 1987—Note by the Secretariat*, MTN.GNG/NG11/1 (10 Apr 1987).

[22] GATT *Meeting of the Negotiating Group of 10 June 1987—Note by the Secretariat*, MTN.GNG/NG11/2 (23 June 1987); GATT *Meeting of the Negotiating Group of 23 September 1987—Note by the Secretariat*, MTN.GNG/NG11/3 (8 Oct 1987); GATT *Meeting of the Negotiating Group of 28 October 1987—Note by the Secretariat*, MTN.GNG/NG11/4 (17 Nov 1987) [hereinafter Meeting of 28 October 1987]; GATT *Meeting of the Negotiating Group of 23-24 November 1987—Note by the Secretariat* MTN.GNG/NG11/5 (14 Dec 1987).

[23] Our interest in this discussion pertains to the first indent on trade-related aspects of intellectual property rights.

[24] See GATT *Work Undertaken in GATT Concerning Trade-Related Aspects of Intellectual Property Rights, Including Trade in Counterfeit Goods—Note by the Secretariat* MTN.GNG/NG11/W/4 (6 May 1987); and GATT *GATT Provisions Bearing on Trade-Related Aspects of Intellectual Property Rights—Note by the Secretariat*, MTN.GNG/NG11/W/6 (22 May 1987).

[25] GATT *Submissions from Participants on Trade Problems Encountered in Connection with Intellectual Property Rights*, MTN.GNG/NG11/W/7 (29 May 1987) [hereinafter Submissions from Participants], and addenda MTN.GNG/NG11/W/7/Add 1, and MTN.GNG/NG11/W/7/Add 2.

[26] GATT *Suggestion by the United States for Achieving the Negotiating Objective* MTN.GNG/NG11/W/14 (20 Oct 1987) [hereinafter US October 1987 Suggestion]; GATT

An examination of the relevant submissions from IC delegations on the trade problems encountered in connection with IPRs leads to an almost identical congruence with the problems advanced by the pharmaceutical MNEs. Furthermore, there is an almost identical listing of these problems in the different submissions, with four main items figuring most prominently: limitations of patentable subject matter such as the exclusion of pharmaceutical products from patentability; insufficient terms of patent protection; severely constraining non-voluntary or compulsory licensing provisions; and finally, inadequate enforcement provisions.[27] Nonetheless, some individual priorities and limited controversy did emerge in a largely unified IC position. Specifically, the Japanese submission contained reference to and a criticism of the US 'first to invent rule' as an 'excessive/discriminative protection of intellectual property rights'.[28] However, ICs did manage to present a largely unified and specific listing of the problems encountered by their firms in the IPR field, and were therefore beginning to set the pace for the unfolding negotiations in the Group.

This trend was further reinforced by the four submissions of the US, Switzerland, EC, and Japan, for achieving the negotiating objective. The United States presented its vision on the negotiations during the very first formal meeting of the Negotiating Group, emphasizing the inadequacy of existing GATT provisions on trade-related aspects of IP protection. The delegation of the European Communities also joined in this criticism.[29] The US presented the need to develop new norms and standards to be embodied in an '*Agreement* on protection and enforcement of intellectual property rights.'[30] Furthermore, in its later submission, the US identified the outcome of the work of the group as an '*Agreement on Trade-Related Aspects of Intellectual Property Rights*.'[31] As such, from the outset, the US delegation emphasized its aim of negotiating a new agreement, rather than amending the GATT, or even acting outside of the GATT framework as advocated by DCs.

The essential points revealed in the submissions included a unanimous desire for a dispute settlement mechanism linked to GATT, a more stringent enforcement mechanism at the domestic level, and as a concession to DCs,

Suggestion by Switzerland for Achieving the Negotiating Objective MTN.GNG/NG11/W/15 (26 Oct 1987) [hereinafter Swiss October 1987 Suggestion]; GATT *Guidelines Proposed by the European Community for the Negotiations on Trade-Related Aspects of Intellectual Property Rights* MTN.GNG/NG11/W/16 (20 Nov 1987) [hereinafter EC Proposed Guidelines]; and GATT, *Suggestion by Japan for Achieving the Negotiating Objective* MTN.GNG/NG11/W/17 (23 Nov 1987) [hereinafter Japan November 1987 Suggestion].

27 ibid.

28 'Submission by Japan,' in Submissions from Participants (n 25) 15.

29 EC Proposed Guidelines (n 26) 1.

30 US March 1987 Statement (n 12) 4. Emphasis added.

31 US October 1987 Suggestion (n 26) 3. Emphasis added.

the inclusion of technical assistance provisions. Furthermore, the US and Japanese submissions included specific norms on standards of patent protection that national laws should be required to achieve.[32] These included, mainly, that the requirements for patentability are novelty, non-obviousness, and utility or capability of industrial application.[33] While the US proposal referred to a minimum term of patent protection of 20 years from filing or 17 from grant, the Japanese referred to a term of at least 15 years.[34] The US and Japanese proposals diverged however with regard to standards pertaining to compulsory licensing, where the US sought that as a general stance, compulsory licences should not be available, and if they were, that they be issued on a case-by-case basis as adopted in the final TRIPS Agreement.[35] On the other hand, the Japanese submission recommended that compulsory licensing be subject to the rules of the Paris Convention,[36] and hence significantly lower standards to those advocated by the US. More significantly however, in the Japanese submission, was the proposal of a waiver whereby countries may exclude from patentability 'inventions as are contrary to public safety or health, or to the maintenance of public order or morality',[37] a similar text of which appears in the final TRIPS Agreement (Article 27). The other two submissions by Switzerland and the EC referred to the need to create an institutional structure, and indeed in the more precise language of the Swiss proposal, 'a body within GATT',[38] emerging later as the WTO's TRIPS Council.

A reading of the four submissions by the ICs therefore reveals that they already introduced the main points that were to figure in the final TRIPS Agreement specifically with regard to patents. This therefore leads to a realization that very early on during the negotiations, the ICs submitted the vision they sought, and arguably, at the risk of oversimplifying the contentious process as will be revealed below, they proceeded to extract their preferred norms and standards from reluctant yet gradually acceding DCs.

On the other hand, some DC delegations adopted a proactive policy of offering suggestions during this Initial Phase of the negotiations. Most notably Brazil presented a proposal relating to the second indent of the Initial Phase of the negotiations focusing on trade in counterfeit goods, suggesting that participants sign up to the Madrid Agreement for the

[32] The similar approach opted for under the EC submission, was the 'transposition' within GATT of rules that enjoy wide international recognition.

[33] US October 1987 Suggestion (n 26) 7; and Japan November 1987 Suggestion (n 26) 6.

[34] ibid.

[35] US October 1987 Suggestion (n 26) 7.

[36] Japan November 1987 Suggestion (n 26) 6.

[37] ibid.

[38] Swiss October 1987 Suggestion (n 26).

Repression of False or Deceptive Indications of Source on Goods.[39] These proposals however did not extend to the first indent on trade-related aspects, as the active policy of the DCs was to exclude its treatment from GATT purview. Indeed, DC delegations considered proposals presented by some IC delegations, particularly the US proposal, to be outside the mandate of the Group,[40] where

> it was not the job of the Group to establish a new system for the protection of intellectual property rights in GATT. These were matters for WIPO and were extensively under consideration in the various parts of WIPO's current activities.[41]

Furthermore, they argued that:

> [t]he protection of intellectual property was primarily designed to serve other social goals. An intellectual property right was a contract between the intellectual property owner and the society providing the protection, under which the intellectual property owner had not only rights but also obligations. The US suggestion, dealt with the rights and would entail a weakening of measures to protect the public interest against abusive uses of monopoly rights in intellectual property.[42]

Discussions continued during 1988, with the Negotiating Group holding six further official meetings, discussing the proposals to date, as well as those further submissions presented by some delegations during 1988.[43]

[39] GATT *The Madrid Agreement for the Repression of False or Deceptive Indications of Source on Goods—Suggestion by Brazil* MTN.GNG/NG11/W/11 (9 July 1987). See also Mexico's communication of its newly promulgated decree pertaining to trade in counterfeit goods, in GATT Decree Prohibiting the Importing of Goods Illegally Bearing Marks Registered in Mexico—Communication from Mexico MTN.GNG/NG11/W/10 (30 June 1987).

[40] The practice followed by the GATT Secretariat in the notes of the meetings of NG11 was not to ascribe positions taken to any particular group, but rather, to use the more generic term of 'some delegations,' or 'some participants,' that can refer to any class of participants. Nonetheless, it may be inferred that some of these positions are representative of DC positions while others are representative of IC positions.

[41] Meeting of 28 October 1987 (n 22) para 11.

[42] ibid para 12.

[43] GATT *Meeting of the Negotiating Group of 29 February—3 March 1988—Note by the Secretariat* MTN.GNG/NG11/6 (8 Apr 1988); GATT *Meeting of Negotiating Group of 16-19 May 1988—Note by the Secretariat* MTN.GNG/NG11/7 (21 June 1988); GATT *Meeting of the Negotiating Group of 5-8 July 1988—Note by the Secretariat*, MTN.GNG/NG11/8 (29 Aug 1988) [hereinafter Meeting of 5–8 July 1988]; GATT *Meeting of the Negotiating Group of 12-14 September 1988—Note by the Secretariat* MTN.GNG/NG11/9 (13 Oct 1988); GATT *Meeting of the Negotiating Group of 17-21 October 1988—Note by the Secretariat* MTN.GNG/NG11/10 (30 Nov 1988); and GATT *Meeting of the Negotiating Group of 14-15 November 1988—Note by the Secretariat* MTN.GNG/NG11/11 (1 Dec 1988).

The new proposals were submitted by the delegations of the Nordic countries,[44,45] the European Communities,[46] as well as revisions to the Japanese[47] and US proposals,[48] and finally, the only DC submission thus far, by Brazil.[49] IC submissions to the Group continued to further refine and develop their proposals while drawing closer to a common position. In this regard, the second EC submission presented in July 1988, largely echoed by the Japanese revised submission two months later, covered the patentability criteria; coverage of patent rights and exception thereof—largely on public interest grounds but subject to judicial review; a patent term of twenty years from filing; and rules on compulsory licensing.[50] Table 6.1 below compares the standards on patent protection as advocated in the EC and Japanese submissions, the revised US submission of October 1988, in addition to the standards of the Trilateral Report of IPC-Keidanren-UNICE.

While IC delegations were submitting revised drafts containing more detailed standards on patent protection—as in other IP areas—in late 1988, DC delegations were still preoccupied with what they considered to be exercises beyond the mandate of the Group as laid down in the Punta del Este Declaration.[51] DC delegations strove to substantiate their claims that the Group's mandate was being exceeded by IC submissions, and that an alternative approach was required. One of the few, perhaps only, substantial attempts in this by DCs during 1988 came yet again from Brazil. In its submission of October 1988, Brazil presented that negotiations in the group should focus not only on the first indent on 'trade-related' aspects of IPRs, but should also bear in mind the ultimate objective of the Uruguay Round, the promotion of 'growth and development', hence

[44] GATT *Suggestion by the Nordic Countries for Achieving the Negotiating Objective* MTN.GNG/NG11/W/22 (12 Feb 1988).

[45] GATT *Communication by the Nordic Countries* MTN.GNG/NG11/W/29 (20 Oct 1988).

[46] GATT *Guidelines and Objectives Proposed by the European Community for the Negotiations on Trade Related Aspects of Substantive Standards of Intellectual Property Rights* MTN.GNG/NG11/W/26 (7 July 1988) [hereinafter Second EC Submission].

[47] GATT *Submission by Japan—Addendum* MTN.GNG/NG11/W/17/Add.1 (23 Sept 1988) [hereinafter Revised Japanese Submission].

[48] GATT *Suggestion by the United States for Achieving the Negotiating Objective—Revision* MTN.GNG/NG11/W/14/Rev.1 (17 Oct 1988) [hereinafter Revised US Submission].

[49] GATT *Submission from Brazil* MTN.GNG/NG11/W/30 (31 Oct 1988).

[50] Second EC Submission (n 46) 5–6; and Revised Japanese Submission (n 47) 2–3.

[51] See GATT *Statement by Thailand at the Meeting of 12-14 September 1988* MTN.GNG/NG11/W/27 (21 Sept 1988) [hereinafter Thai 1988 Statement]; GATT *Statement Made by the Delegation of Mexico at the Meeting of 17, 18 and 21 October 1988* MTN.GNG/NG11/W/28 (19 Oct 1988) [hereinafter Mexican 1988 Statement]; and GATT *Submission from Brazil* MTN.GNG/NG11/W/30 (31 Oct 1988) [hereinafter Brazil 1988 Submission]. See also Meeting of 5–8 July 1988 (n 43) para 29, where participants argued that the second EC submission 'dealt with matters that fell outside the Negotiating Objective of the Group.'

Table 6.1: Comparison of Patent Standards Advocated in 1988 Submissions of the EC, Japan, US, and the Trilateral Report (IPC–Keidanren–UNICE)

	IPC–Keidanren–UNICE Submission (June 1988)	**Second EC Submission (July 1988)**	**Revised Japanese Submission (September 1988)**	**Revised US Submisison (October 1988)**
Rights Conferred	The right to exclude others from the manufacture, use or sale of the patented invention and, in the case of a patented process, the ability to exclude other from the use or sale of the direct product thereof.	Prevent third parties not having the proprietor's consent from making, offering, putting on the market or using . . . or importing or stocking the product for these purposes For processes, the right to prevent others not having proprietor's consent from using, or importing or stocking for these purposes the product obtained directly by that process.	Prevent third parties not having owner's consent from: In case of a product—manufacturing, using, assigning, leasing or importing the product, and acts of displaying, for the purpose of assignment or lease, the product; in case of a process—acts of using the process; in case of a process for the manufacture of a product—using the process, using, assigning, leasing or importing the product directly manufactured by the process, displaying, for the purpose of assignment or lease, the product directly manufactured by the process.	Exclude others from the manufacture, use or sale. In the case of a process, the right to exclude other from importation, use or sale of at least the direct product thereof.

Table 6.1: Continued

	IPC–Keidanren–UNICE Submission (June 1988)	**Second EC Submission (July 1988)**	**Revised Japanese Submission (September 1988)**	**Revised US Submisison (October 1988)**
Exceptions to Rights Conferred	No reference.	Private acts, non-commercial purposes and experimental use.	No reference.	No reference.
Criteria for Patentability	New, industrially applicable and unobvious devices, products and processes without discrimination as to subject matter.	Products or processes. Industrial application, new, and involve an inventive step.	Inventions of products or processes. Industrially applicable, novel, and involve an inventive step.	All products and processes that are new, useful and unobvious.[52]
Exceptions to Patentability	No reference.	Contrary to '*ordre public*'[53] or morality. Plant or animal varieties or essentially biological processes for the production of plants or animals, excluding microbiological processes.	Inventions contrary to public order, morality or public health, and of inventions of substances manufactured through nuclear transformation.	No reference.
Patent Term Compulsory	20 years from filing. Granted on grounds of	20 years from filing. Subject to review by a	20 years from filing. Subject to judicial	20 years from filing. Subject to judicial

[52] The US paper notes that the terms 'useful' and 'unobvious' encompass or are synonymous with the terms 'capable of industrial application' and 'inventive step.' See Revised US Submission (n 48) 3.
[53] This was the first reference to the '*ordre public*' exception, as discussed in Chapter 4 of this volume.

Licences	non-working only to permit local manufacture. When justified factors make it impractical to carry out the invention locally, importation authorized by patentee should be deemed to satisfy local working. No exclusivity. No discrimination against particular classes of subject matter. Full compensation to patentee.	court of law, where granting is sought on grounds of insufficiency of exploitation, for dependent patents, official licences, or use in the public interest.	review where granting is sought on grounds of failure to work or insufficient working, or in respect of dependent patents, or in the public interest.	review and non-exclusive. Solely to address, only during its existence, a declared national emergency). or to remedy an adjudicated violation of antitrust laws. May also be used non-exclusively by a government for governmental purposes.
Possibility of Patent Forfeiture	No revocation on grounds of non-working.	No reference.	Forfeiture subject to judicial review.	No revocation on grounds of non-wokring.

> the originality of the Group's work lies . . . in the need to keep in view both the trade-related and developmental aspects of IPRs, distinguishing it from more legal discussions being held in other fora.[54]

Gauged in such terms, Brazil thus submitted that the Group's work should focus on three questions. Primarily 'access to technology,' and how it is affected by rigid and excessive protection of IPRs, arguing that discussions in the Group were skewed in favour of owners of IPRs.[55] Second, the question of the 'use of IPRs,' and how its abuse can lead to restrictions and distortions in international trade. Finally, the question of how to deal with the risk that a rigid system of IPR protection implies for international trade.

Two particular points are noteworthy about this initial phase of the negotiations. Primarily, DC delegations were largely engaged in a defensive posture, arguing against what was almost the fait accompli of the eventual introduction of some form of rules on IP. As such, this defensive posture, with the exception of Brazil's important yet limited intervention, could be claimed to have worked against their interests in the latter stages of the negotiations, as they declined to shape the evolving rules in their initial stages. Second, it is important to observe the high degree of coincidence between the provisions sought in the Trilateral Report, and those of the three other IC submissions, as reflected in Table 6.1. The initial stage was thus largely favourable to the interests of the MNEs.

(B) Mid-Term Review (December 1988–April 1989)

The Montreal Ministerial Meeting of December 1988 was intended to act as a mid-term review of the progress achieved in the various issues of negotiation in the multilateral trade negotiations, then scheduled to complete in 1990.[56] In the area of intellectual property, the mid-term review was considered by some commentators as an opportunity for the major ICs to reach consensus on the framework for an IP agreement and for commitments on specific substantive standards.[57] The Montreal Ministerial however ended in a stalemate due mainly to differences over the negotiations on agriculture and intellectual property, and to a lesser extent on textiles and safeguards.[58] Consequently, the Trade Negotiations Committee

[54] Brazil 1988 submission (n 51) para 6. [55] ibid para 15.

[56] For discussion of the proposed submission by the Negotiating Group on TRIPS, see GATT *Meeting of Negotiating Group of 14-15 November 1988—Note by the Secretariat* MTN.GNG/NG11/11 (1 Dec 1988).

[57] THE GATT URUGUAY ROUND: A NEGOTIATING HISTORY (1986-1992), VOLUME II: COMMENTARY, 2268 (Terence P Stewart ed 1993).

[58] See GATT *Trade Negotiations Committee Meeting at Ministerial Level—Montreal, December 1988* MTN.TNC/7(MIN) (9 Dec 1988), where the TNC requests GATT Director-General to conduct high level consultations on the four issues.

(TNC) decided to hold a meeting at the level of high officials in Geneva in April 1989, until which time it hoped further consultations and the efforts of the GATT Director-General would facilitate agreement.[59]

The stalemate in the negotiations over intellectual property was due to the inability of the participants to agree on a unified basis for further negotiations, where the Negotiating Group submitted, in addition to the Chairman's elements, three further proposals by different participants for the consideration of Ministers at the Montreal Meeting.[60] The Chairman's elements contained the common factors in the purview of the Group to date, which were of a general nature and with limited substantive content. His elements contained references to the application of GATT principles, general need for enforcement, 'the specification of reference points regarding the availability, scope and use of IPRs', and the need for a multilateral dispute settlement mechanism that would multilateralize settlement of disputes rather than the use of national trade policy instruments—a clear reference to US 301 practices.[61] The Chairman's elements also included reference for the need to facilitate the flow of technology, transitional arrangements and technical cooperation in favour of DCs—in sum, the least controversial and mainly agreed upon elements in the negotiations to date. The three further proposed elements involved more controversial views and were presented to reflect the thinking of particular groupings of delegations, with the first set of elements being consistent with DC thinking and the later two sets presenting IC priorities.

The main gist of the first elements proposed by some participants—and reflecting the views of DCs—advocated that WIPO was the venue for setting standards and norms for IP protection, and that consequently GATT should stay clear of undertaking such discussions.[62] Furthermore, it also expressed caution that possible enforcement provisions should not become in themselves barriers to legitimate trade. On the other hand, the second and third proposed elements presenting views consistent with US and EC positions, referred explicitly to the need for adequate substantive standards and norms on the availability, scope and use of IPRs—whether they be derived from international conventions, or where these prove inadequate, from suitable national legislation.[63] The latter proposed elements also encompassed a quest for strong enforcement measures, both internally and at the border, as well as a dispute settlement mechanism.[64]

Final agreement was made possible, and a pronouncement on 'Trade-Related Aspects of Intellectual Property Rights, Including Trade in

[59] ibid.
[60] ibid 21–4.
[61] ibid 21.
[62] ibid 22, paras A.1–A.4.
[63] ibid 22–3, paras B.1(a), and C.2(c).
[64] ibid 22–3, paras B.1(b), B.1(c), C.2(b), and C.2(d).

Counterfeit Goods' was adopted by the time of the TNC meeting in Geneva in April 1989.[65] In this TNC Decision, five key issues were agreed upon as the basis for continued negotiations.[66] Most significantly, they included reference to the provision of adequate standards and principles concerning the availability, scope and use of trade-related intellectual property rights; the provision of effective and appropriate means for enforcement (taking into account differences in national legal systems); the multilateral settlement of disputes; and the institution of transitional arrangements to guarantee the broadest participation possible. While these references tended to be more in tune with the position of ICs, especially with regard to the provision of standards and enforcement, yet the text also included two concessions to developing countries. Primarily, that the outcome of the negotiations is not prejudged, and that the negotiations are without prejudice to the views of participants concerning the institutional aspects of the implementation.[67] Secondly and most importantly, that consideration will be given to the underlying public policy objectives of participants' national systems for IP protection, including developmental and technological objectives.[68]

(C) Resumption of Negotiations (Mid-1989–Early 1990)

Following the decision adopted by the TNC in its April 1989 meeting (particularly paragraph 4 on IP therein), where it set the basis for continued negotiations in the area of IP, as in other areas of the Uruguay Round, the negotiations began to take a more structured approach. This trend was apparent in the resumed negotiations from mid-1989, where the Negotiating Group began to tackle specific issues in its discussions and in the submissions of participants. The work of the Group was divided into item I on 'trade-related aspects of intellectual property rights,' and item II on 'trade in counterfeit goods.' The former included the five issues of: (1) 'basic principles' of the GATT and of IP conventions and their applicability to the work of the Group; (2) 'standards and principles' on the availability, scope and use of trade-related intellectual property rights; (3) 'enforcement' of intellectual property rights both internally and at the border; (4) 'dispute settlement' provisions; and (5) 'transitional arrangements' for implementing agreed upon provisions.[69]

[65] GATT *Mid-Term Meeting* MTN.TNC/11 (21 Apr 1989) [hereinafter Mid-Term Meeting].

[66] ibid 21, para 4.

[67] ibid para 3.

[68] ibid para 5.

[69] For initial comments by participants on each of these issues, see GATT *Meeting of Negotiating Group of 11-12 May 1989* MTN.GNG/NG11/12 (13 June 1989) paras 8–16.

During the period July 1989 to February 1990, the Negotiating Group on TRIPS officially convened four times to discuss the agenda item on the 'provision of adequate standards and principles concerning the availability, scope and use of trade-related intellectual property rights'.[70] Discussions were based on new submissions on the issue presented by a substantial number of IC delegations,[71] with the exception of the United States and the European Communities who had made earlier submissions covering the issue. The submission of IC delegations on the topic again focused on the distortions that the inadequate protection of intellectual property—as reflected in standards and norms of protection—have on international trade and even on the nullification and impairment of rights under GATT.[72] These inadequacies, they argued, were present both at the international level, such as deficiencies in the Paris Convention standards on patent protection, as well as in national laws on IP protection. As such, IC proposals would oblige participants to incorporate defined and agreed upon minimum standards into their national legislation.[73]

It is noteworthy that during this phase of the negotiations, DCs began to actively present submissions that sought to voice their interest and concerns.[74] Indeed, a reading of the DC submissions reflects in large part their concern at the pace and seemingly growing consensus among IC delegations on the introduction of a comprehensive IP regime within GATT. The Indian paper was the most detailed of the DC submissions, and while

[70] GATT *Meeting of Negotiating Group of 12–14 July 1989* MTN.GNG/NG11/14 (12 Sept 1989) [hereinafter Meeting of 12–14 July 1989]; GATT *Meeting of Negotiating Group of 30 October—2 November 1989* MTN.GNG/NG11/16 (4 Dec 1989); GATT *Meeting of Negotiating Group of 11, 12 and 14 December 1989* MTN.GNG/NG11/17 (23 Jan 1990); and GATT *Meeting of Negotiating Group of 5–6 February 1990* MTN.GNG/NG11/18 (27 Feb 1990).

[71] GATT *Standards and Norms for Negotiations on Trade-Related Aspects of Intellectual Property Rights—Communication from Australia* MTN.GNG/NG11/W/35 (10 July 1989) [hereinafter Australia Submission]; GATT *Proposal by the Nordic Countries for the Negotiations on Standards and Principles for Trade-Related Aspects of Intellectual Property Rights* MTN.GNG/NG11/W/36 (10 July 1989); GATT *Standards and Principles Concerning the Availability, Scope and Use of Trade-Related Intellectual Property Rights—Communication from Switzerland* MTN.GNG/NG11/W/38 (11 July 1989) [hereinafter Swiss Submission]; GATT *Standards and Principles for Negotiations on Trade-Related Aspects of Intellectual Property Rights—Communication from New Zealand* MTN.GNG/NG11/W/46 (24 Oct 1989); GATT *Standards for Trade-Related Intellectual Property Rights—Submission from Canada* MTN.GNG/NG11/W/47 (25 Oct 1989); GATT *Standards for Trade-Related Intellectual Property Rights—Submission from Hong Kong* MTN.GNG/NG11/W/51 (29 Nov 1989); GATT *Submission by Japan—Addendum—Patents: Non-Voluntary Licenses,* MTN.GNG/NG11/W/17/Add.3 (8 Dec 1989); and GATT *Trade-Related Intellectual Property Rights—Submission by Austria* MTN.GNG/NG11/W/55 (8 Dec 1989).

[72] See Swiss submission (n 71) 1

[73] See ibid 2; and Australia submission (n 71) 1–2.

[74] See GATT *Standards and Principles Concerning the Availability, Scope and Use of Trade-Related Intellectual Property Rights—Communication from India* MTN.GNG/NG11/W/37 (10 July 1989) [hereinafter India 1989 Submission]; GATT *Guidelines for Negotiations that*

it engaged in a discussion of appropriate standards and norms of patent protection, suitable for DCs, yet it clearly stated that this discussion was solely as a reply to the IC submissions, and that India maintained that such pronouncements on standards and norms should not be engaged in within the GATT framework.

The protection of intellectual property rights has no direct or significant relationship to international trade. It is because substantive issues of intellectual property rights are not germane to international trade that GATT itself has played only a peripheral role in this area and the international community has established other specialized agencies to deal with them. It would therefore not be appropriate to establish within the framework of the General Agreement on Tariffs and Trade any new rules and disciplines pertaining to standards and principles concerning the availability, scope, and use of intellectual property rights.[75]

The Brazilian submission, similarly, was concerned with a proper delineation of the subject matter of the negotiations, and argued that it necessitated a clearer understanding on the relation between intellectual property and trade, hence it was not an exercise in legislating on IP protection per se—an activity to be carried out within WIPO.[76] India's submission on the standards and principles pertaining to patent protection was the most detailed presented by a DC delegation thus far during the negotiations, and contained a well-argued substantive analysis of the basis of its pronouncements.[77] In fact, India's submitted standards and principles on patent protection reflected those provisions in the Indian Patent Act.[78] With regard to specific advocated standards on patent protection, the most noticeable point raised in two DC submissions, those of India and Peru, was the exclusion of pharmaceutical products from patent protection.[79]

In their submissions, DCs emphasized paragraph 5 of the TNC Decision of April 1989, that consideration will be given to the underlying public policy objectives of participants' national systems for IP protection, includ-

Strike a Balance Between Intellectual Property Rights and Development Objectives—Communication from Peru MTN.GNG/NG11/W/45 (27 Oct 1989) [hereinafter Peru 1989 Submission]; GATT *Standards and Enforcement of Intellectual Property Rights—Communication from the Republic of Korea* MTN.GNG/NG11/W/48 (26 Oct 1989) [hereinafter Korea 1989 Submission]; GATT *Communication from Brazil* MTN.GNG/NG11/W/57 (11 Dec 1989) [hereinafter Brazil 1989 Submission]; GATT *Communication from Mexico* MTN.GNG/NG11/W/60 (22 Jan 1990); and GATT *Communication from Chile* MTN.GNG/NG11/W/61 (22 Jan 1990) [hereinafter Chile 1990 Submission].

75 India 1989 Submission (n 74) 19–20.

76 Brazil 1989 Submission (n 74) 1–3. See also Chile 1990 Submission (n 74) 1.

77 India 1989 Submission (n 74) 3–13.

78 Patents Act No 39 (19 Sept 1970). An analysis of the provisions of the Indian Act, together with the patent laws of Argentina, Brazil, and Egypt, will be presented in Ch 7 below.

79 India 1989 Submission (n 74) 8; and Peru 1989 Submission (n 74) 2. Noticeably, the Brazil submission was silent on the topic of the patentability of pharmaceutical products, and

ing developmental and technological objectives.[80] Accordingly, DCs underscored the freedom of countries to attune their patent and IP regimes, more generally, to their own developmental and specific conditions, hence a balance was to be struck between public policy objectives on the one hand, and the duties and obligations of patent owners and the private rights of patent holders on the other.[81] This also included specific measures to rectify the restrictive and anti-competitive practices that sometimes arise from the patent monopoly.

Finally, mention should be made of an important communication from Bangladesh on behalf of the least-developed countries concerning special treatment to be accorded to these countries, whether in granting them the right to adopt necessary 'measures and policies' domestically, requiring GATT Contracting Parties to consider the vital interests of these countries when considering remedial measures, and the provision of technical assistance in the preparation of domestic regulations relating to this field.[82]

(D) The Draft Texts

The period from early 1990 and until December 1991 witnessed the submission of a number of draft texts. The first batch or series of texts were submitted during the period March–June 1990, from four IC delegations,[83] and a fifth from a group of DC delegations.[84] The second series, prepared in anticipation of the scheduled conclusion of the Uruguay Round in Brussels in December 1990, was a series of draft texts prepared by the Chairman of the Negotiating Group, Ambassador Lars Anell.[85] The third

it must be borne in mind that the Brazil submission was after the PMA-initiated 301 action against Brazil. Also importantly, Korea specifically admits pharmaceutical products within the subject matter for patent protection. See Korea 1989 Submission (n 74) 2.

80 Mid-Term Meeting (n 65) para 5.

81 See Korea 1989 Submission (n 74) 1; Peru 1989 Submission (n 74) 1–2; Brazil 1989 Submission (n 74) 1–3; and India 1989 Submission (n 74) paras 2–4.

82 GATT *Proposals on Behalf of the Least-Developed Countries—Communication from Bangladesh* MTN.GNG/NG11/W/50 (17 Nov 1989).

83 GATT *Draft Agreement on Trade-Related Aspects of Intellectual Property Rights—Communication from the European Communities* MTN.GNG/NG11/W/68 (29 Mar 1990); GATT *Draft Agreement on the Trade-Related Aspects of Intellectual Property Rights—Communication from the United States* MTN.GNG/NG11/W/70 (11 May 1990) [hereinafter US Draft Text]; GATT *Draft Amendment to the General Agreement on Tariffs and Trade on the Protection of Trade-Related Intellectual Property Rights—Communication from Switzerland* MTN.GNG/NG11/W/73 (14 May 1990) and MTN.GNG/NG11/W/73/Corr.1 (14 June 1990); and GATT *Main Elements of a Legal Text for TRIPS—Communication from Japan* MTN.GNG/NG11/W/74 (15 May 1990) [hereinafter Japan Draft Text].

84 GATT *Communication from Argentina, Brazil, Chile, China, Colombia, Cuba, Egypt, India, Nigeria, Peru, Tanzania and Uruguay* MTN.GNG/NG11/W/71 (14 May 1990) [hereinafter DC Draft Text].

85 GATT *Status of Work in the Negotiating Group—Chairman's Report to the GNG* MTN.GNG/NG11/W/76 (23 July 1990). The Chairman's draft was revised in October 1990, and three further revisions were presented on 20, 22 and 23 Nov 1990.

was the submission of the Draft Final Act Embodying the Results of the Uruguay Round of Multilateral Trade Negotiations, at the Brussels Ministerial in December 1990, which contained the draft text on intellectual property as reflected in the Chairman's draft of 22 November 1990.[86] Finally, what was to be known as the Dunkel Draft, as prepared by the GATT Director-General Arthur Dunkel, was submitted a year later in December 1991.[87]

The standards on patent protection presented in the IC submitted draft texts (especially the EC, US and Japan drafts) mainly reiterated the same positions they had presented in their 1988 submissions,[88] with a few differences. Table 6.2 below identifies those differences. To a large extent, the IC drafts coincided on the major issues pertaining particularly to: the criteria for patentability, with the exception of the issue of the first-to-file versus the first-to-invent, where the latter system was championed by the US but opposed by the EC and Japan; exceptions to patentability; rights conferred and exceptions thereto; term of protection; and the issue of compulsory licensing. An interesting development however, was to be found in the US draft, concerning transitional protection for patents.[89] This provision concerning 'Exclusive Marketing Rights' as it came to be incorporated in the TRIPS Agreement, required Contracting Parties to provide transitional protection for products embodying subject matter deemed to be unpatentable under their then present patent laws, in situations where three conditions hold: that the subject matter to which the product relates will become patentable after the entry into force of the Agreement; a patent has been issued by another Contracting Party prior to the entry into force of the proposed draft; and finally, that the product has not been marketed in the territory of the Contracting Party providing such transitional protection. Clearly, this situation fits well the needs of the pharmaceutical industry, where under numerous jurisdictions pharmaceutical products were excluded from patentability.

With regard to the proposed instrument of the agreement in the draft texts submitted by the ICs, three formats were presented. Primarily, the Japanese proposed an Agreement setting out the objectives, and referring particularly to the principles of national treatment, most favoured nation, and transparency.[90] This was to be supplemented by an Annex comprising a section on standards for the protection of the various IPRs, and another

[86] GATT *Draft Final Act Embodying the Results of the Uruguay Round of Multilateral Trade Negotiations* MTN.TNC/W/35/Rev.1 (3 Dec 1990).

[87] GATT *Draft Final Act Embodying the Results of the Uruguay Round of Multilateral Trade Negotiations* MTN.TNC/W/FA (20 Dec 1991).

[88] Please refer to Table 6.1 above.

[89] US Draft Text (n 83) Art 26.

[90] Japan Draft Text (n 83) 2–4.

Table 6.2: Main Differences on Standards of Patent Protection Compared to the 1988 Submissions[91]

	EC Draft	US Draft	Japan Draft
Criteria for Patentability	*Article 23*: Same language. But specifically requires patents to be available according to the first to file principle.[92]	*Article 23*: Same language.	*Paragraph 4(2)*: Same language.
Exceptions to Patentability	*Article 23*: Same language, however it now required Contracting Parties to provide for the protection of plant varieties by patents and/or an effective *sui generis* system.	No reference, as in 1988 submission.	*Paragraph 4(3)*: Same language.
Rights Conferred and Exceptions	*Article 24*: Adds 'prior use' as a ground for limited exceptions to the exclusive rights conferred.	*Article 24*: Same language.	*Paragraph 4(1)*: Same language.
Possibility of Patent/Forfeiture Revocation	*Article 24*: Specifically prohibits revocation of patents on grounds of non-working.	*Article 24*: Revocation only on grounds that patent does not meet patentability criteria in Art 23 above.	*Paragraph 4(5)*: Allows for forfeiture of patent—although the conditions for it are deliberately narrow and vague.

[91] Reference to articles and paragraphs are to the respective submitted draft texts.
[92] Japan Draft Text (n 83) 2–4.

Table 6.2: Continued

	EC Draft	US Draft	Japan Draft
Term of Protection	*Article 25*: Adds that 20 years from filing is a minimum period, and encourages extension of term.	*Article 25*: Adds that 20 years from filing is a minimum period, and encourages extention of term.	*Paragraph 4(4)*: Adds the option of either 20 years from filing or the filing date of the earliest application invoked in the said application. Also encourages extension of term.
Compulsory Licenses	*Article 26*: More narrow provisions on Compulsory Licensing than the 1988 Submission. Except in cases of a manifest national emergency, a licence can only be issued after unsuccessful efforts to negotiate a voluntary licence. They may not be issued for non-working or insufficiency of working, if it is justified by existence of legal, technical or commercial reasons.	*Article 27*: Very similar conditions as stipulated in 1988 submission. With the explicit addition that a compulsory license is the sole limitation on a patent owner's exclusive rights.	*Paragraph 4(5)*: May only be granted— after a refusal to grant a voluntary licence in accordance with normal commercial practice—on grounds of national security, failure to work or insufficiency of exploitation after the expiration of a period of four years from filing or three years from grant (unless there are legitimate reasons), and also with regard to inter-dependent patents.
Process Protection	*EC Article 24(4); US Article 24(3); Japan Paragraph 4(1)*: Stipulate for the reversal of the burden of proof from the claimant to the defendant in cases involving process patent infringement.		

on enforcement.[93] The second structure was presented by Switzerland, which proposed an amendment to GATT in the form of introducing a Part V to the General Agreement, which will include the articles of the entire proposed agreement on the protection of trade-related intellectual property rights. Finally, the third model, presented in both submissions of the United States and the European Communities, also advocated an amendment of GATT through the introduction of a single new article with all the provisions on IP attached to it in the form of an annex.[94]

By contrast, the DC submission was divided into two parts on 'Intellectual Property and International Trade,' and on 'Standards and Principles Concerning the Availability, Scope and Use of Intellectual Property Rights.'[95] The first part, to be treated through a clarification of GATT provisions, addressed only the problems associated with counterfeit and pirated goods, defined as pertaining to trademark infringement and copyright violation, respectively.[96] Hence, the first part does not address patents. The second part, designed as a separate agreement, addresses the question of the standards of protection to be accorded to the various IPRs, including patents. It is important to note however that this second part was intended for implementation, as stipulated in its Article 22 in the 'relevant international organization'[97]—that is WIPO.

Nonetheless, the competence issue aside, DCs were willing to present their views on what they regarded as suitable for incorporation in a feasible international instrument on standards for IP protection, including patents. Once more, the premise of the DC draft was on the public policy objectives, including 'the needs for economic, social and technological development . . . particularly in sectors of special public concern, such as health, nutrition, agriculture and national security.'[98] With regard to the specific standards on patent protection advocated, these included the right of parties to exclude from patentability 'certain kinds of products or processes . . . , provided that such exclusion applies equally to inventions by nationals and foreigners'.[99] Hence, pharmaceutical products can be excluded as a category, subject only to the principle of national treatment.

[93] ibid 5–15. However, the Japanese text did not include any elaboration on the enforcement provisions.

[94] The EC submission proposed the introduction of Art IX (bis) in specific, to the General Agreement.

[95] DC Draft Text (n 84).

[96] See ibid 3, fn 1.

[97] ibid 13. For an authoritative explanation on the part of one of the sponsors of the DC submission, citing both parts as separate, with Part I capable of being implemented within the GATT framework, whereas Part II, which was not trade-related, ought to be lodged outside the GATT framework, see GATT *Meeting of the Negotiating Group of 14–16 May 1990—Note by the Secretariat* MTN.GNG/NG11/21 (22 June 1990) para 27.

[98] DC Draft Text (n 84) Part II, Art 1(1).

[99] ibid Art 4(2).

With regard to the duration of protection, that was to be left as a matter for national legislation to determine.[100] More interestingly, the DC draft enumerated not only the 'rights of the patent owner,' but equally, 'obligations on the patent owner'—an issue that was less explicitly treated in the IC submissions. The most important of these obligations was none other than the obligation to work the patented invention domestically within time limits fixed by national legislation, and subject to sanctions.[101] Finally, the draft stipulates for a significantly more open licensing regime as compared to the IC drafts, specifically with regard to food and medicine.[102]

Following this spate of delegation submissions, and in view of the approach of the then scheduled conclusion of the Uruguay Round anticipated for December 1990, the Chairman of NG11 proceeded to compile draft texts, produced under his responsibility 'in the hope that it will assist the further work of the Group and does not commit any participant'.[103] The Chairman submitted a total of five such drafts during the period July–November 1990.[104] The July draft, submitted to the Group of Negotiations on Goods, included two approaches, 'A' and 'B', representing the different substantive perspectives of the IC and DC delegations respectively. In addition, the former advocated a single agreement, and the latter, two separate agreements, as outlined earlier. The text was revised by the chair in October, with the major difference being the introduction of the 'minimum requirements' philosophy of TRIPS, where parties to the proposed agreement would be bound at a minimum by the standards contained therein, while not being precluded from adopting higher standards should they desire, provided there is no contravention of the agreement.[105] The latter three revisions in November 1990 of the Chairman's draft contained only minor changes. Finally, the penultimate Chairman's draft of 22 November 1990, was presented to the Brussels Ministerial as part of the Draft Final Act. It contained both settled issues, but more importantly, disputed language, particularly the fundamental issue of the application of the draft agreement into GATT. Four days after the launch of the Brussels Ministerial however, the negotiations came to a halt over failure to resolve the problems over agriculture, and were dissolved on 7 December 1990.

To restart the negotiations, including on IP, the Chairman of the Trade Negotiations Committee, GATT Director General Arthur Dunkel, outlined in his proposal of February 1991, that delegations be given an opportunity

[100] ibid Art 4(3). [101] ibid Art 5(2)(iii). [102] ibid Art 6.

[103] GATT *Status of Work in the Negotiating Group—Chairman's Report to the GNG* MTN.GNG/NG11/W/76 (23 July 1990) 1 [hereinafter Chairman July 1990 draft].

[104] The drafts were issued on 23 July, 1 Oct, 20 Nov, 22 Nov, and 23 Nov 1990.

[105] For commentary on this revision, see Stewart (ed) Vol II (1993) (n 57) 2274–5.

> to consider the present state of the negotiations in this area [IP], taking into account the work done in Brussels, and to identify any areas in which technical work could usefully be undertaken at this stage.[106]

This phase of the negotiations, dominated by the overarching politics on agriculture, arguably marked the commencement of real bargaining diplomacy over the Round's issues as a whole. Arthur Dunkel, aware of the dangers that this deadlock posed, pressed for a continuation of the technical discussions within seven negotiating groups, instead of the original fifteen—one of which was still devoted to the trade-related aspects of intellectual property rights, and remained under the chairmanship of Ambassador Lars Anell. The Negotiating Group on TRIPS, as it now became formally known, held its first meeting in June 1991.[107]

During this initial meeting, and in subsequent meetings of the restarted negotiations on TRIPS, DCs criticized the Brussels draft for continuing to ignore their preoccupations, particularly pertaining to this 'drive towards uniformity of IPR regimes', which was in conflict with the special needs of DCs.[108] Most importantly, some DC delegations noted that 'transitional arrangements' were not sufficient to address the developmental concerns raised.[109] However, limited progress was being achieved, with three main issues being before the TRIPS negotiators at that stage: a proposal by Korea on international transfer of technology as it related to disputes arising therein as a result of anti-competitive practices;[110] consultations on the questions raised by Article 73 of the Draft Final Act, concerning the extent to which parties would be obliged to apply the new obligations on TRIPS to existing intellectual property;[111] and issues of dispute settlement.[112]

Nonetheless, the politics involved in the rule-making undertaking of the Uruguay Round came to bear at this stage of the negotiations. In his 'stocktaking' on the UR negotiations at that stage, the Chairman of the Trade Negotiations Committee, Arthur Dunkel, emphasized three basic decisions that would have to be made in the rule-making effort in TRIPS.[113]

[106] GATT *Programme of Work: Proposal by the Chairman at Official Level*, para 41, MTN.TNC/W/69 (26 Feb 1991).

[107] GATT, *Meeting of Negotiating Group of 27 and 28 June 1991—Note by the Secretariat* MTN.GNG/TRIPS/1 (25 July 1991) para 41.

[108] ibid para 3.

[109] ibid.

[110] GATT *Proposal for the Establishment of Dispute Prevention System in Respect of Transfer of Technologies—Communication from the Republic of Korea* MTN.GNG/TRIPS/W/1 (12 July 1991).

[111] GATT *Meeting of the Negotiating Group of 16 and 20 September 1991—Note by the Secretariat* MTN.GNG/TRIPS/2 (7 Oct 1991) para 7.

[112] ibid para 8.

[113] GATT *Stocktaking of the Uruguay Round Negotiations by the Chairman of the Trade Negotiations Committee at Official Level* MTN.TNC/W/89 (7 Nov 1991) para 13.

Primarily, the level of protection must be adequate; secondly, requiring an effective multilateral dispute settlement mechanism and a commitment to use it as the means of settling disputes on TRIPS matters. Most importantly however was the third decision that Dunkel asserted was at stake, particularly with regard to countries importers of technology (mainly DCs), which is that the commitments in the area of TRIPS 'will have to be viewed in the context of the overall results of the Round.'[114] Undoubtedly, the most authoritative acknowledgment that DCs might not/will not be getting what they negotiated for in the area of TRIPS.

(E) The Final TRIPS Negotiations

The Dunkel Draft of December 1991 served as the negotiating text on TRIPS during the remainder of the Uruguay Round negotiations.[115] However, it becomes increasingly difficult, at this stage, to disentangle the preoccupation of the negotiating delegations from across the various issues being negotiated, so as for them to focus on one particular issue such as TRIPS. This, the nature of the single undertaking in GATT negotiations, proves a mixed blessing characteristic of deal-making across the various issues under negotiation. Developing countries, and especially India and Egypt, among others, with a well developed textile manufacturing base were concerned in this latter stage of the Uruguay Round with negotiations on textiles. Similarly, the IC delegations were also concerned with negotiations on agriculture, services and market access.[116] As such, various preset completion dates for the Round were discarded along the tortuous road of final negotiations.[117] In addition, an important parallel set of regional economic negotiations were being undertaken between the United States, Canada, and Mexico, to create NAFTA, with significant negotiations on intellectual property rights.

[114] ibid.

[115] For a thorough comparison of the Dunkel draft with the Final Act Embodying the Results of the Uruguay Round, see THE GATT URUGUAY ROUND: A NEGOTIATING HISTORY (1986-1994), VOLUME IV, THE END GAME (Terence P Stewart ed 1993) annex I. For a further work comparing the Brussels draft, the Dunkel draft, and the Final Act, see DANIEL J GERVAIS, THE TRIPS AGREEMENT: DRAFTING HISTORY AND ANALYSIS (1998).

[116] For an analysis of the final stages of the Uruguay Round negotiations across the various issues, see Stewart (ed) Vol IV (1993) (n 115).

[117] The Trade Negotiations Committee set in January 1992 a targeted completion date of 15 April 1992, but it was discarded as the impasse over agriculture continued. In late 1992, Arthur Dunkel called for a final agreement by March 1993, coinciding with the US negotiating deadline for Fast-Track authority. Furthermore, the leaders of the US, UK and EC called for a January 1993 completion. Yet again, these targeted dates were overrun. Finally, the US administration secured from Congress renewal of Fast-Track negotiating authority in June 1993, to conclude the Round by 15 Dec 1993 and to sign by 16 Apr 1994.

Nonetheless, during the period from the issuance of the Dunkel draft and until the conclusion of the Uruguay Round, significant concerns with regard to the TRIPS text were voiced. Discontent was stemming not only from DCs, most notably India, but more profoundly from the pharmaceutical MNEs that sought further amendments in the Dunkel draft upwards to suit their particular interests, supported by the newly-elected Clinton administration.

The US pharmaceutical MNEs were content with the Dunkel draft as the basis for an IP agreement within GATT. Indeed, that draft had incorporated the main concerns they had raised during the lead up and early stages of the Uruguay Round. In the words of Pfizer's Senior Vice President:

> [t]he Dunkel text on TRIPS goes a long way in providing the type of international intellectual property protection that the IPC, three successive Administrations and the US Congress have been seeking together in the GATT for over the last seven years. As a general rule, the text contains high standards of protection and enforcement, has a multilateral dispute resolution mechanism and *limits many of the exceptions and derogations from the standards of protection that had been a concern for the IPC.*[118]

However, this satisfaction with the Dunkel text was not absolute. The MNEs still had an axe to grind with regard to two main contentious issues. These issues, in addition to raising them during numerous testimonies before the US Congress,[119] were voiced directly to the United States Trade Representative.[120] The first concerned what they deemed to be overly long transition periods for DCs in the Dunkel text. Specifically, they attacked Article 65 of the Dunkel text, allowing DCs a five-year transition period to bring their disciplines into conformity with TRIPS standards, arguing that DCs, most of whom already had the prerequisite institutional infrastructure

118 *Uruguay Round of Multilateral Trade Negotiations: Hearings before the Subcomm on Trade of the House Comm on Ways and Means* 103rd Cong 65 (1993) (statement of CL Clemente, Vice President and General Counsel, Pfizer Inc) [hereinafter Clemente 1993 Senate Statement]. Emphasis added.

119 See US *International Trade Performance and Outlook: Competitive Position in the Automotive, Aerospace, and Chemical and Pharmaceutical Sectors: Hearing before the Subcomm on Trade of the Comm on Ways and Means* 102nd Cong 509 (1992) (statement of Gerald Mossinghoff, President, Pharmaceutical Manufacturers Association); US *International Trade Performance and Outlook: Competitive Position in the Automotive, Aerospace, and Chemical and Pharmaceutical Sectors: Hearings before the Subcomm on Trade of the House Comm on Ways and Means* 102nd Cong 525 (1992) (statement of Robert Neimeth, Pfizer Inc); Clemente 1993 Senate Statement (n 118); and *Uruguay Round of Multilateral Trade Negotiations: Hearing before the Senate Comm on Finance* 103rd Cong 97–9 (1993) (statement of Edmund Pratt Jr, President Emeritus, Pfizer Inc) [hereinafter Pratt 1993 Statement].

120 Letter from the Intellectual Property Committee, to the Honourable Michael Kantor, United States Trade Representative (11 Mar 1993) (on file with author).

to provide adequate IP protection, should only be allowed an additional year as a transition period.[121] Furthermore, with regard to paragraph 4 of the article, they requested its deletion on the grounds that there should be no differentiation among industrial sectors with respect to transition arrangements.[122] The second issue concerned the absence of so-called 'pipeline' protection, mainly benefiting pharmaceutical products, in the Dunkel text. MNEs sought in the introduction of such a provision, that countries that would be introducing pharmaceutical and chemical patent protection for the first time, would be required to grant protection for a pharmaceutical product patented in another country protection for the remaining life of the patent, provided that it had not already been marketed in that country.[123]

In pressing for these revisions to the Dunkel text, MNEs utilized the US administration's need to seek renewal for its trade negotiating authority, which expired in March 1993. Given this need, lobbying the US Senate resulted in the renewal of fast-track negotiating authority, with the requirement that the 'overarching goal' in the IP area is for an agreement that provided adequate protection for all forms of IPRs.[124] As such, on 22 November 1993, less than a month before the conclusion of the Round, the US formally requested five major changes to the TRIPS text, two of which are of direct relevance.[125] Primarily, the US proposed a one-year transition period, as opposed to five years, with respect to DCs, for commitments pertaining to enforcement and criminal procedures, with an option for an additional one year extension. Second, it requested Exclusive Marketing Rights covering pharmaceutical products, notwithstanding the transition provisions.[126]

On the other hand, by that late stage of the Uruguay Round, DCs had largely acquiesced into the Dunkel text on TRIPS. A number of the major DCs had initiated reform of their IP regimes to bring them into conformity with the standards established in the Dunkel text on TRIPS.[127] The renegade remained India. Due to pressure from local industries, and in exchange for a reduction in the transition period, India pressed for changes in the TRIPS text, mainly the exclusion, inter alia, of any form of 'pipeline'

[121] ibid. Thus a total of two years prior to the application of the agreements' provisions.
[122] ibid. This was particularly important to the pharmaceutical industry as that paragraph granted certain countries an additional waiver of five years for the extension of product patent protection to classes of products (including pharmaceutical products) that were previously not patentable under their patent laws.
[123] Pratt 1993 Senate Statement (n 119) 98. This provision was secured in NAFTA. See North American Free Trade Agreement 1993, Can–Mex–US (17 Dec 1992) 32 ILM 289, Art 1709 (4),
[124] See Stewart (ed) Vol IV (1993) (n 115) 516.
[125] Referred to in ibid 524.
[126] ibid.
[127] While clearly, no single factor can be attributed to cause this shift, yet undoubtedly, the US 301 process was a significant factor.

protection, and for language that would not consider importation as 'working,' particularly with regard to compulsory licensing considerations.[128] While, the language for 'pipeline' protection advocated by the pharmaceutical MNEs, incorporated in NAFTA, did not ultimately figure in the TRIPS Agreement, yet India preferred not to open the Dunkel text for further revisions lest it induce further changes contrary to its interest.

An assessment of the results of the negotiations on TRIPS, especially as they affected DCs, was prepared by the GATT Secretariat towards the end of the Uruguay Round.[129] This assessment noted that, in addition to the Agreement establishing transition arrangements, it also provided members with the possibility to

> limit the scope of rights within certain limits, including to grant compulsory licenses under certain conditions . . . and recognizes the right of countries to adopt measures consistent with its provisions to protect public health and nutrition, and to promote the public interest in sectors of vital importance.[130]

What this assessment however fails to account for is the impact that the Agreement would have on the public policy priorities that DCs continuously had argued for during the TRIPS negotiations. The TRIPS Agreement, in almost all aspects, was a victory for the pharmaceutical MNEs. While DCs managed to secure transition arrangements, as their chief gain, yet the terms of the provisions, particularly on standards and norms on patent protection could be said to have confirmed their worst fears as they fought against the inclusion of IP in GATT before the launch of the Uruguay Round.

[128] For a critical analysis of the Dunkel Draft and the final provisions of TRIPS, see GATT AGREEMENT OR DUNKEL DRAFT TREATY: ITS IMPACT ON AGRICULTURE INDUSTRY, TRIPS AND TRIMS AND DRUG INDUSTRY (D Bhorali ed 1994); and GATT: CRITICAL ANALYSIS OF GENERAL AGREEMENTS ON TARIFFS AND TRADE (Ajay Kulshreshtha, Kamla Trivedi and Ravindra Kumar eds 1994).

[129] GATT *An Analysis of the Proposed Uruguay Round Agreement, with Particular Emphasis on Aspects of Interest to Developing Economies* MTN.TNC/W/122 (29 Nov 1993).

[130] ibid 80.

PART THREE

IMPACT OF TRIPS IMPLEMENTATION ON DEVELOPING COUNTRY LAW AND POLICY

The analysis in this book has thus far examined the negotiating process of the TRIPS Agreement as an exercise in 'top-down' rule-making, where the interests of the pharmaceutical MNEs championed over those of DCs and their stakeholders. At the end of this process, the TRIPS Agreement was established as an international legal instrument binding on members of the newly created World Trade Organization, where its Article 1 required them to give effect to its provisions within their legal systems. The TRIPS Agreement entailed obligations binding on its members that required implementation into their domestic legal system. Part Three analyses this process of implementation of the TRIPS pharmaceutical-related provisions and the required changes brought about in DCs' patent legislation. In so doing, it focuses on the perception by DC governments and their domestic stakeholders of the TRIPS implementation process. The examination reveals that there was a high degree of opposition within DCs to what was perceived as negative and impedimentary effects of implementing the pharmaceutical-related TRIPS provisions. On the other hand, considerable IC and pharmaceutical MNE pressure was exerted during this phase to safeguard their respective interests in carrying forward this implementation process. While this part generally considers the case of four DCs (Argentina, Brazil, Egypt and India), it will devote a particular focus on the implementation process in the case of Egypt.

Chapter 7 below examines DC patent law prior to TRIPS. It was the result of a dissatisfaction with the level of patent protection accorded in DCs and a disapproval of the international patent protection system that the pharmaceutical MNEs pressed for a regime overhaul. The chapter will therefore examine patent law provisions, primarily those relating to the pharmaceutical industry in the four DCs identified above. Chapter 8 will then consider the different perspectives on this process of implementation. The perspectives examined are those of DC governments and their domestic stakeholders; that of the pharmaceutical MNEs; those of the ICs, focusing on the US perspective; and finally, the perspective of key international organizations including that of the WTO. Having established the general concerns and positions of the various stakeholders involved in the TRIPS implementation process, Chapter 9 will then offer a more detailed analysis of the implementation process as it transpired in the case of Egypt. The value of this exercise is in its ability to emphasize an example of the key issues and problems raised by the different stakeholders, and the pressures exerted by them in this process of legislative implementation in a major DC. Finally, Chapter 10 brings our analysis back to an examination of DC patent legislation following their amendments to bring them into conformity with TRIPS obligations.

Chapter 7

Status of DC Law Pre-TRIPS Implementation

Patent laws prior to the implementation of TRIPS-compliant legislation varied across different jurisdictions.[1] Nonetheless, certain common themes can be witnessed in the various patent or industrial property laws of DCs.[2] In this chapter, an overview of specific standards prevalent in the patent or industrial property laws across selected DCs (Egypt, Argentina, Brazil, and India) prior to TRIPS is presented.[3] These countries have been consistently identified by the multinational pharmaceutical industry from the 1980s onwards, as possessing sub-standard and/or inadequate patent protection legislation.

By far the oldest patent legislation in force before TRIPS among those of the four DCs examined was that of Argentina enacted in 1864.[4] The patent law of Egypt was enacted in 1949,[5] India issued its Patents Act in 1970,[6] and Brazil issued its Industrial Property law in 1971.[7] In addition to the legislative enactments for protection of patents and industrial property,

[1] One of the early undertakings of the negotiating group on intellectual property during the Uruguay Round (Negotiating Group 11), was to request WIPO to prepare a memorandum on the various standards adopted on intellectual property. See GATT *Existence, Scope and Form of Generally Internationally Accepted and Applied Standards/Norms for the Protection of Intellectual Property: Note Prepared by the International Bureau of WIPO* MTN.GNG/NG11/W/24 (5 May 1988), Part I on patents [hereinafter WIPO IP Law Study]. For a thorough and more recent comparative review of patent law and practice in different jurisdictions, see WORLD PATENT LAW AND PRACTICE Vols 2 and 2A (JW Baxter et al eds 2001).

[2] For a recent review of the patent situation in Developing Countries, specifically as it relates to pharmaceuticals, see PHILIP W GRUBB, PATENTS FOR CHEMICALS, PHARMACEUTICALS AND BIOTECHNOLOGY: FUNDAMENTALS OF GLOBAL LAW, PRACTICE AND STRATEGY ch 3 (1999).

[3] For an excellent, although dated, study of patent laws prevalent prior to TRIPS, see STEPHEN P LADAS, PATENTS, TRADEMARKS, AND RELATED RIGHTS: NATIONAL AND INTERNATIONAL PROTECTION Vol I, ch 12 (1975). For a comparative study on the situation in Asian and Pacific countries, see WIPO, THE SITUATION OF INDUSTRIAL PROPERTY IN THE COUNTRIES OF ASIA AND THE PACIFIC 3–59 (1984). For a comparative study on the situation in African countries, see WIPO, THE SITUATION OF INDUSTRIAL PROPERTY IN THE COUNTRIES OF AFRICA 5–79 (1987).

[4] Law No 111 on Patents of Invention (11 Oct 1864). For a brief exposition of the development of intellectual property protection in Latin America and the role of private initiatives therein, with emphasis on Argentina and Brazil, see AIPPI AND THE DEVELOPMENT OF INDUSTRIAL PROPERTY PROTECTION 1897-1997, 355–368 (AIPPI ed 1997).

[5] Patent and Designs Act No 132 of 1949 [hereinafter Egypt 1949 Patent Act].

[6] Patents Act No 39 of 1970 [hereinafter India Patents Act 1970].

[7] Decree No 5.772 on Code of Industrial Property (21 Dec 1971).

Argentina, Brazil, and Egypt have guarantees to the protection of the rights of inventors over their inventions specifically articulated in their constitutions. Argentina's Constitution under Article 17, guarantees every author or inventor the exclusive ownership of his work, invention or discovery for the term granted him by law.[8] Brazil's Constitution assures inventors of a temporary privilege in the use of their inventions and the protection of their industrial creations.[9] On the other hand, Egypt's Constitution is less specific, where what is guaranteed is the freedom of scientific research and literary, artistic and cultural invention and the provision of necessary means for its realization.[10]

In analysing the pre-TRIPS standards in the selected jurisdictions, we will emphasize certain aspects of their patent legislation. The principal provisions of interest addressed below are: patentability requirements and exclusions from patentability; scope of exclusive rights conferred; and finally provisions on compulsory licensing and working requirements. These will be treated accordingly.

(I) GENERAL PROVISIONS

(A) Patentability Requirements and Exclusions from Patentability

The requirements for patentability in the patent laws of DCs was an aspect that did not generate much criticism as it was fairly standardized across different jurisdictions. Traditionally, the requirements for patentability of an invention comprised the three conditions of novelty, capability of industrial application, and the presence of an inventive step.[11] The patentability requirements as laid down in the laws of Argentina (Article 3), Brazil (Article 6), Egypt (Article 1), and India (section 2(j)) are only explicit with regard to the two requirements of 'novelty' and 'industrial application' or 'utility', while the third requirement of an 'inventive step' figured less prominently. India's Act, nonetheless, mentions by implication the need for the invention to involve an inventive step so that it's grant may not be opposed (section 25(1)(e)),[12] or consequently revoked on petition (section 64(1)(f)).

By contrast, the statutory exclusion from patentability in the patent legislation of the four DCs examined here was among the most contentious aspects of their pre-TRIPS patent regimes. While patents, in general, were available to cover most fields of invention, yet the most significant feature in DCs' patent legislation was the exclusion of chemical and pharmaceuti-

[8] ARG CONST (22 Aug 1994) Art 17.

[9] BRAZ CONST (5 Oct 1988) Art 5, item xxix.

[10] EGYPT CONST (11 Sept 1971) Art 49.

[11] See Ladas (1975) (n 3) 286–7.

[12] Applies to process patents only.

cal products, and in some instances processes, from patentability.[13] In 1988, 49 countries mostly DCs but also including a few ICs,[14] excluded pharmaceutical products from patentability, and a further 10 also excluded pharmaceutical processes from protection.[15] Brazil's industrial property code (Article 9(c)) stipulated that '*food and chemical-pharmaceutical substances, matter, admixtures or products and medicaments of any kind, as well as the respective process for obtaining or modifying them*' were not patentable. On the other hand, the laws of Argentina (Article 4), Egypt (Article 2), and India (section 5) excluded pharmaceutical compositions or substances from patentability but allowed for the patenting of methods or processes of manufacture of pharmaceutical products.

(B) Scope of Rights Conferred

With regard to the scope of exclusive rights conferred by a patent, as described in Chapter 4 of this book, this defines the rights that the patentee enjoys in relation to her patented invention which she can exclude others from.[16] The most thorough description of the conferred rights is laid down in the Patent Act of India. Section 48(2) of the Indian Act, stipulates that a patent shall confer upon the patentee the exclusive right to make, use, exercise, sell or distribute the article or substance subject of the patent, whereas in the case of a patent for a method or process of manufacture, the enumerated rights cover the use or exercise of the method or process. On the other hand, the legislation of Argentina, Brazil and Egypt are much more concise in their description of the rights conferred, but not necessarily in the intended coverage of those rights. The laws of both Argentina (Article 1) and Egypt (Article 10) prescribe an exclusive right for the patentee of working the invention while that of Egypt adds working '*by all means*'. Finally, Brazil's code in its Article 5, guarantees to authors the 'ownership and exclusive use' of their inventions, hence it is the only legislation that employs the word 'use', although there appears to be no implied difference in this regard. On the other hand, the contentious element in this

13 In addition to Grubb (1999) (n 2) a good survey of the status of pharmaceutical protection in ten major developing countries can be found in TB Lewis *Patent Protection for the Pharmaceutical Industry: A Survey of the Patent Laws of Various Countries* 30 INT'L LAW 835, 856–65 (1996). See also L-N McLeland and J Herbert O'Toole *Patent Systems in Less Developed Countries: the Cases of India and the Andean Pact Countries* 2 J L AND TECH 229, 244–48 (1987). For a comparative evaluation of the exclusion of pharmaceutical products and processes from patentability across different jurisdictions, see Ladas (1975) (n 3) 309–12.

14 Finland, Iceland, Monaco, Norway, Portugal, Spain. In Australia and New Zealand, the Commissioner of Patents could refuse to grant a patent where the product is a mere mixture of known ingredients. In Canada, patents were denied pharmaceutical products unless produced by processes also claimed.

15 WIPO IP Law Study (note 1) annex II.

16 For a discussion of this aspect of patent law, see Ladas (1975) (n 3) 392–402.

aspect of DC legislation was the duration which patentees were allowed to enjoy such conferred rights over their inventions.

There were two important points to bear in mind with regard to the duration of the patent term: primarily, the length of time or the duration of the patent term, and second, the point from which the patent term is calculated.[17] Argentina's patent term duration under its law proves to be the exception of the laws examined. Article 5 of Argentina's patent law grants a patent for five, ten, or fifteen years 'according to the merit of the invention and wish of the applicant', counted from the date of the patent grant. Furthermore, foreign patents are limited to a maximum term of protection of ten years, or until the expiration of the original foreign patent, whichever is shorter. By contrast, the duration under the legislation of Brazil (Article 24) and Egypt (Article 12) extended to 15 years from the date of filing of the application.[18] India's Patent Act (section 53(1)(b)) granted a general patent term of 14 years from the date of the patent.[19] However, both Egypt and India's legislation on patent term duration had important exceptions affecting the pharmaceutical industry. Article 12 of the Egyptian law limited the patent term duration for chemical methods or processes of manufacture that produce food or medical substances to a maximum of ten years with no possibility of renewal. Similarly, section 53(1)(a) of the Indian Patents Act set the term of patents granted in respect of processes capable of producing substances intended, or capable of being used, as food or medicine or drugs, to five years from the date of the sealing of the patent, or seven years from the date of filing, whichever period was shorter.

(II) COMPULSORY LICENSING AND WORKING REQUIREMENTS

Among the more controversial features of pre-TRIPS DCs' patent laws from the perspective of the pharmaceutical MNEs and ICs were their provisions on compulsory licences and working requirements.[20] One particular ground for issuing compulsory licences; issuance based on grounds of non-working of the invention, in whatever manner non-working was defined, was strongly contested by the pharmaceutical industry as was covered earlier. With regard to compulsory licensing, the legislation of Argentina and India set opposite ends of the continuum. Argentina's patent law had

[17] For details on the duration of patents across different jurisdictions in 1988, see WIPO IP Law Study (n 1) annex VI. See also Ladas (1975) (n 3) 386–89.

[18] Under certain conditions, the Egyptian patent law augured the possibility of a renewal of up to five years following the end of the specified patent term. See Egypt 1949 Patent Act, art 12.

[19] India's patent act defines the 'date' of the patent as that on which the complete specification was filed. See India Patents Act 1970, § 45(1).

[20] See Ladas (1975) (n 3) 423–36.

no provisions on compulsory licences even though it addressed the issue of non-working, as will be discussed. On the other hand, India's Patents Act had a highly elaborate system of standards on compulsory licences, where the key concept of the '*reasonable requirements of the public*', affected both 'public interest' and 'nonworking' grounds. As such, India's provisions in this area will be discussed separately below.

With regard to issuing a compulsory licence on grounds of non-working, the *chapeau* of Article 33 of Brazil's law obliged the patentee who failed to initiate the exploitation of the patent '*in an effective manner in the Country*' within three years immediately following its issuance, or who discontinued such exploitation for more than one year, to grant a licence to any third party that requested it.[21] Furthermore, paragraph 1 of the same article stipulated that for reasons of public interest, a special non-exclusive compulsory licence may be granted for the exploitation of the patented invention '*when it is not being exploited or when, although it is being "effectively" exploited, such exploitation does not meet the demands of the market*'. And finally, paragraph 2 of the same article did not recognize importation as exploitation in an effective manner. Similarly, Article 30 of Egypt's law allowed the grant of a compulsory licence if the invention was not being worked within three years from the date of the patent grant.[22] Alternatively, if the patentee was unable to work the patent on a reasonable commercial scale to cope with the needs of the country, it allowed the grant of a compulsory licence '*to any person applying therefore and to whom the patentee previously refused to license his working rights or claimed exorbitant conditions*'.

Argentina, Brazil, and Egypt provided for further action other than issuing compulsory licences in cases of non-working of the patent. Article 47 of Argentina's law stipulated that '*valid patents granted shall lapse when two years have expired from their date of issue without working the invention which forms their subject; when the working is interrupted for a like space of time, except in case of "force majeure"*. . . .' Likewise, Brazil's legislation under Article 49 held a patent to have lapsed when the invention had not been exploited in an 'effective manner'[23] in Brazil within four years of the date of issue of the patent, or five years from the date of the issue of the patent when a licence had been granted, or when the exploitation of the patented invention had been discontinued for more than two consecutive years. Finally, Article 36 of the Egyptian law similarly allowed for a third party to apply for the cancellation of a patent '*if the invention is not*

[21] This provisions is however subject to a *force majeure* amnesty.

[22] This provision is also subject to a *force majeure* extension under Art 31, extending a grace period of up to two years for the patentee to adequately work the invention.

[23] 'Effective manner' is defined in Art 52.

worked in Egypt within a period of two years following the date of grant of a compulsory license'.

By contrast, India's Patent Act contained numerous provisions on compulsory licences and 'licenses of right.'[24] Section 84(1) stipulated that after the expiration of three years from the sealing of a patent, any person may apply for the grant of a compulsory licence '*alleging that the reasonable requirements of the public with respect to the patented invention have not been satisfied or that the patented invention is not available to the public at a reasonable price* . . .' Additionally, section 86(1) allowed the Central Government to apply for an order that a given patent be endorsed '*license of right*' for the same reasons as specified in section 84(1) above. Furthermore, and of particular interest to the pharmaceutical industry, section 87(1)(b) contained specific provisions for inventions claiming, inter alia, substances intended for use or capable of being used as food, medicine or drug (the class of inventions referred to in section 5), where these patents would be endorsed as '*license of right*' three years after the date of the patent sealing. Moreover, further action was stipulated under section 89(1), where two years after a compulsory licence had been granted in respect of a patent or the grant of a licence when that patent had been designated as '*license of right*', the Central Government or any person interested could have applied for an order '*revoking the patent on the ground that the reasonable requirements of the public with respect to the patented invention have not been satisfied or that the patented invention is not available to the public at a reasonable price*'.

Finally, section 90 of the Indian Act provided an important piece of the puzzle when it defined when the '*reasonable requirements of the public*' shall be deemed not to have been satisfied.[25] It is fair to say that this definition was so wide that it was almost assured for an interested party to find a basis under which to claim that the reasonable requirements of the public had not been satisfied. Under section 90(c) the '*reasonable requirements of the public*' shall be deemed not to have been satisfied '*if the patented invention is not being worked in India on a commercial scale to an adequate extent or is not being so worked to the fullest extent that is reasonably practicable*'. Apart from that, there were four other classes of conditions stipulated under sections 90(a), (b), (d), and (e), where the reasonable requirements would not have been met. Two of these conditions are inter-

[24] The difference between a compulsory licence and a 'license of right' was that while applicants for compulsory licences were required by law to demonstrate that the '*reasonable requirements of the public*' had not been met, or that the patented invention was not available to the public at a reasonable price, once a patent had been designated '*license of right*,' no such demonstration was required and any interested party had the right to apply for the licence. See D Moitra and S Ravirdran *India Patent Law and Practice* in 92–2 DIGEST OF INTELLECTUAL PROPERTY LAWS OF THE WORLD 12 (Lester Nelson ed 1992).

[25] This definition applies to §§ 84, 86, and 89.

esting in underlying the width of coverage of this form of exception to protection under the Indian Patents Act. Section 90(a)(iii) would consider the reasonable requirements test as unmet if '*a market for the export of the patented article manufactured in India is not being supplied or developed*'. Likewise, section 90(d) would also have considered it unmet, '*if the demand for the patented article in India is being met to a substantial extent by importation from abroad* . . .', hence an announcement that importation is not considered working.[26] The breadth of these exceptions had prompted a commentator to describe India's Act as possibly the 'worst patent law in the world . . . where not only are patents ineffective against importation, they are actually invalidated if the patentee imports the patented products'.[27] But this last concern with importation was also present in the Brazilian legislation as analysed above.

[26] This is similar to Art 33(2) of Brazil's industrial property code.
[27] Grubb (1999) (n 2) 36.

Chapter 8

Perspectives on TRIPS Implementation

The signing of the TRIPS Agreement ended a specific and quite difficult stage in the Agreement's history, its negotiation phase. A new phase began during the 1990s where implementation of the standards of protection as enshrined in TRIPS was to take effect into the domestic legal systems of WTO members. Some changes in patent laws had already been introduced prior to the signing of TRIPS, but for practical purposes they may be considered part and parcel of the drafting and legislative implementation phase that was set in motion by TRIPS. This phase proved no less problematic than the negotiation phase, particularly with regard to the pharmaceutical-related standards of protection, and exposed yet again the rift between the interests of DCs and their domestic stakeholders on the one hand, and the pharmaceutical MNEs and ICs on the other.[1] This chapter will deal with the different perspectives on the implementation of the TRIPS pharmaceutical-related provisions and the resistance exhibited by DCs and their stakeholders in this endeavour. It will analyse its causes, and equally, the concerns raised and pressures exerted by the pharmaceutical MNEs and ICs, particularly the United States, in deriving implementation.

Four particular perspectives are important and will be reviewed here. Primarily, there is the perspective of DC governments and stakeholders. The second perspective is that of the pharmaceutical MNEs seeking to protect their proprietary pharmaceutical products worldwide and secure their global markets. The third perspective is that of ICs seeking high standards of patent protection and the upholding of the TRIPS regime for the benefit of their powerful economic actors, the pharmaceutical MNEs and other IP-reliant industries. Finally, the fourth perspective covers the role performed by key international organizations in aiding and supporting TRIPS implementation in DCs, including that of the World Trade Organization, the World Intellectual Property Organization, UNCTAD, and the World Bank.

[1] See Frederick M Abbott *The WTO TRIPS Agreement and Global Economic Development* 72 CHI-KENT L REV 385 (1996), predicting that DCs will continue to resist changes to their IP legislation, and when they do make changes, they will be slow to enforce them in favour of foreign enterprises. On a piece arguing how DCs will push back, in the case that ICs push too hard and too fast for TRIPS implementation, see JH Reichman *Enforcing the Enforcement Procedures of the TRIPS Agreement* 37 VA J INT'L L 335 (1997).

(I) PERSPECTIVES OF DCS AND THEIR STAKEHOLDERS

Developing countries' governments and their domestic stakeholders perceived certain impedimentary and other negative impacts on their interests that would result from the implementation of the TRIPS pharmaceutical-related provisions. Two levels of problems were perceived to constitute such effects. Primarily, concerns of a more general nature over the effects of the TRIPS rule-making process were harboured by DC governments and stakeholders and hence negatively affected the implementation process as a whole. These concerns were linked to perceived constraints on DCs' ability to pursue public policy priorities in their economic and social development paths.[2] Two such concerns will be discussed below. The second level of problems is comprised of more specific concerns in implementing certain provisions of the TRIPS Agreement. Further analysis of specific issues as they arose during the legislative implementation process in the case of Egypt will also be discussed in Chapter 9 below.

Prior to this treatment however, a word of caution is due, where it is important to note that to describe the reaction to TRIPS implementation in DCs as exclusively negative is inaccurate and a distortion of a complex situation. There are elements within DCs that view TRIPS implementation positively as a means of modernizing economic regulatory structures and enabling the local pharmaceutical industry and the public health service to function in a more competitive as opposed to a sheltered environment.[3] Furthermore, there are also DC stakeholders that have interests interwoven with those of the pharmaceutical MNEs.[4]

(A) Concerns over the Effects of the TRIPS Rule-Making Process

The first concern related to TRIPS implementation being hampered and delayed in DCs particularly in the cases of Egypt[5] and India[6] was the

[2] Among the more important areas of public policy affected by IPRs identified in a World Bank study are policies relating to market structure. See WORLD BANK, INTENSIFYING ACTIONS AGAINST HIV/AIDS IN AFRICA: RESPONDING TO A DEVELOPMENT CRISIS 35–8 (2000).

[3] See DUNCAN MATTHEWS, GLOBALISING INTELLECTUAL PROPERTY RIGHTS: THE TRIPS AGREEMENT 113 (2002).

[4] Most notably local legal counsel retained by the pharmaceutical MNEs and other local lobbyists.

[5] Egypt's new IP law, covering patents, was promulgated in June 2002. *See* Law on the Protection of Intellectual Property Rights, No 82 of 2002 (2 June 2002) [hereinafter Egypt 2002 IP Law].

[6] India modified its patent law to bring it into conformity with the EMR requirements and mailbox provisions in 1999. See Patents (Amendment) Act 1999, No 17 of 1999 (26 Mar 1999) [hereinafter India Patents (Amendment) Act 1999]. For a brief discussion on the opposition to patent law reform in India post-TRIPS, see Suresh Koshy *The Effects of TRIPS on Indian Patent Law: A Pharmaceutical Industry Perspective* 1 B U J SCI AND TECH L 4, 8 (1995).

perceived coercive nature of how the TRIPS standards were brought about. The resentment harboured by DCs at the nature of the TRIPS negotiations was not conducive to a trouble-free implementation process within these countries. Implementing the pharmaceutical-related provisions of TRIPS was thus akin to an exercise in swallowing bitter medicine. This was also fuelled by further coercive efforts by the pharmaceutical MNEs and ICs, particularly the United States, in seeking implementation. As Finger and Schuler present, 'the process by which these obligations were taken on has not helped to build the domestic politics to implement them.'[7] A perception of the standards as largely favouring foreign stakeholders, the pharmaceutical MNEs, and requiring legislation more in tune with the needs of ICs[8] complicated efforts at reaching a 'national consensus' on implementation and did not provide a sense of ownership of the ensuing legislation.[9] Therefore, the mere perception of a lack of volition and of coercion was counterproductive from the very beginning.[10] As summed up in the case of Argentina,

> [e]ven if a stronger regime is theoretically better for Argentina in the long term, the current coercive activity of the US drug industry to enact Argentine legislation results in democratic instability and its effectiveness is severely limited by Argentine resistance.[11]

Furthermore, an Indian commentator argued that

> as soon as the GATT treaty [*sic*] is signed, our Parliament will be

[7] J Michael Finger and Philip Schuler *Implementation of Uruguay Round Commitments: The Development Challenge* WORLD BANK WORLD POLICY RESEARCH WORKING PAPER NO 2215, 5 (1999)<http://www-wds.worldbank.org/servlet/WDS/ContentServer/WDS/ib/2001/02/10/000094946_01013005324822/Rendered/PDF/multi-page.pdf> (last visited 6 Mar 2006).

[8] See Patricia M Smith *A Long and Winding Road: TRIPS and the Evolution of an International Competition Framework* 2 J INT'L ECON L 435 (1999), arguing that Anglo-American conceptions of IP having dominated international IP standards and were forced on DCs without regard to their own notions of IP. See also Michelle McGrath *The Patent Provisions in TRIPs: Protecting Reasonable Remuneration for Services Rendered—or the Latest Development in Western Colonialism?* 7 EUR INTELL PROP REV 398 (1996).

[9] Primo Braga and Fink underscore the importance of the need to develop a 'national consensus' in implementing TRIPS obligations. See Carlos A Primo Braga and Carsten Fink *Reforming Intellectual Property Rights Regimes: Challenges for Developing Countries* 1 J INT'L ECON L 537 (1998). For an important point made with regard to the lack of a sense of 'ownership' of the UR results on the part of DCs and LDCs and how that affected the view of implementation as imperially imposed, see Finger and Schuler (1999) (n 7) 3–5, 24.

[10] On DCs' resistance to TRIPS implementation, see JH Reichman and David Lange *Bargaining Around the TRIPS Agreement: the Case for Ongoing Public-Private Initiatives to Facilitate Worldwide Intellectual Property Transactions* 9 DUKE J COMP AND INT'L L 11, fns 20–22 (1998); Abbott (1996) (n 1); and Reichman (1997) (n 1).

[11] WS Vicente *Questionable Victory for Coerced Argentine Pharmaceutical Patent Legislation* 19 UPA J INT'L ECON L 1101, 1104 (1998).

> compelled to pass legislation on matters that go against the letter and spirit of our Constitution and our national interest. . . .[12]

Moreover, a former Permanent Representative of Egypt to the WTO argued that business influence on the IC delegations was largely felt in their TRIPS negotiation agenda and that consequently its impact, once implemented into DC legislation, is to serve that agenda.[13] This saga also caught media attention in DCs where national newspapers printed headlines and articles antagonistic of TRIPS and its impact on their national economies and directly linking its implementation to external IC and MNE pressures, alluding to the theme of economic neo-imperialism.[14]

The second concern, to an extent related to the problem of coercion to enact implementing legislation was the perceived lack of concrete evidence on the economic benefits of implementing the TRIPS pharmaceutical-related provisions in DCs.[15] There exists from the perspective of DC stakeholders, mixed evidence even on the long-term benefits of these provisions.[16] Indeed, there emerged research that presented negative

[12] Harendra Deva Goswami *Dunkel Draft—We Protest Why?* in GATT AGREEMENT OR DUNKEL DRAFT TREATY: ITS IMPACT ON AGRICULTURE INDUSTRY, TRIPS AND TRIMS AND DRUG INDUSTRY 88 (D Bhorali ed 1994).

[13] Interview with Dr Mounir Zahran, former Permanent Representative of Egypt to the WTO, in Cairo (27 Apr 2003).

[14] See *Foreign Pressures on Egypt to Implement 'GATT' Immediately* AL-AHRAM (30 Sept 2002); *Foreign Companies Exert Pressure on National Companies* AL-AHRAM (30 Nov 2002); *Foreign Plot to control the Drug and Cement Industries* AL-AHRAM (3 Dec 2002). Similar sentiments were expressed in the Indian Media. See HEINZ REDWOOD, NEW HORIZONS IN INDIA: THE CONSEQUENCES OF PHARMACEUTICAL PATENT PROTECTION 45–6 (1994).

[15] For a critique of the economic and other justifications of the ICs' advocacy for a strong IP regime, see JEROME H REICHMAN, IMPLICATIONS OF THE DRAFT TRIPS AGREEMENT FOR DEVELOPING COUNTRIES AS COMPETITORS IN AN INTEGRATED WORLD MARKET 1–2 (1993). For a discussion of divergences in the concept, economics, and functions of IPRs, see Weiss in LIBERALIZATION OF SERVICES AND INTELLECTUAL PROPERTY IN THE URUGUAY ROUND OF GATT 91–8 (Sacerdoti ed 1990). For an economic study showing the lack of a link between development and inventiveness and patenting, particularly with regard to the pharmaceutical sector, see PM Challu *The Consequences of Pharmaceutical Product Patenting* 15 WORLD COMP 65 (1991). On the reverse argument, or on a 're-thinking' of the advantages of IP Protection, see Thomas Cottier *The Prospects for Intellectual Property in GATT* 28 COMMON MKT L REV 383, 390 (1991). For a general discussion of IP in the differing perspectives of DCs and ICs, see PR de Almeida *The Political Economy of Intellectual Property Protection: Technological Protectionism and Transfer of Revenue Among Nations* 10 INT'L J TECH MGMT 214 (1995); Alan V Deardorff *Should Patent Protection Be Extended to All Countries?* in THE WORLD TRADING SYSTEM: CRITICAL PERSPECTIVES ON THE WORLD ECONOMY, VOL IV, THE URUGUAY ROUND AND BEYOND (Robert Howse eds 1998); and Alan S Gutterman *The North–South Debate Regarding the Protection of Intellectual Property Rights* 28 WAKE FOREST L REV 89, 118–24 (1993).

[16] On North-South divergent perspectives on IPRs, see Abdulqawi A Yusuf in INTELLECTUAL PROPERTY AND INTERNATIONAL TRADE: THE TRIPS AGREEMENT 4–6 (Carlos Correa and Abdulqawi A Yusuf eds 1998). On why patent moves may harm Third World, see C RAGHAVAN, RECOLONISATION: GATT, THE URUGUAY ROUND AND THE THIRD WORLD 122–5

evidence on TRIPS implementation.[17] Most notably, a study conducted by the Federation of Egyptian Industries in 2002 concluded that the effect of TRIPS implementation would result in the demise of the local Egyptian pharmaceutical industry in a period of five to fifteen years.[18] Some studies point out that such evidence will not be possible to ascertain until sufficient practice in implementation takes place, and enough empirical studies generated on the issue.[19] Even on the specific issue of an R&D upsurge in the pharmaceutical industry, evidence was not conclusive on the effect of patent protection therein.[20] In summary, it has been pointed out that:

> [i]t may still be too early to tell in this case, where the economic impact of the TRIPs agreement is only just beginning to be felt. Developing new drugs takes significant amounts of time as well as money, and though strengthening IPRs makes developing country markets more attractive, these long lags mean that the 'demand-pull' effect of the TRIPs agreement on pharmaceutical R&D may take many years to become fully visible.[21]

Apart from the impact of the TRIPS pharmaceutical-related provisions on R&D spending in DCs, the argument that those provisions will stimulate and attract Foreign Direct Investment (FDI) is equally inconclusive.[22]

(1990). On the question of whether an IP system benefits DCs written from an African perspective, see Umesh Kumar, An Introduction to the African Industrial Property System 318–43 (1993). For a good concise bibliography on the pros and cons of DCs adoption of a patent system, see A Samuel Oddi *The International Patent System and Third World Development: Reality or Myth?* 1987 Duke LJ 831, FN 4 (1987).

[17] On the argument that US efforts to harmonize IP law may fail to serve the best interests of DCs and NICs and the international community, see Silverstein in International Trade and Intellectual Property: The Search for a Balanced System 155–71 (George R Stewart, Myra J Tawfik and Maureen Irish eds 1994) 155–71.

[18] Federation of Egyptian Industries (2002).

[19] See Keith E Maskus, Intellectual Property Rights in the Global Economy 7, 143–170 (2000).

[20] See G Velasquez and P Boulet *Globalization and Access to Drugs: Perspectives on the WTO/TRIPS Agreement* Report to the World Health Organization, 82 (1999) <http://www.who.int/medicines/library/dap/who-dap-98-9-rev/who-dap-98-9.htm> (last visited 7 Feb 2002); and Maskus (2000) (n 19) 42–44. On evidence that pharmaceutical MNEs were unlikely to increase their R&D in India as a result of the introduction of TRIPS standards, see Jean O Lanjouw *The Introduction of Pharmaceutical Product Patents in India: 'Heartless Exploitation of the Poor and Suffering'?* Yale University Economic Growth Center Discussion Paper No 775, 32–33 (1997). However, other studies expected more general beneficial effects of higher standards of IP protection for transfer of technology to DCs. See Matthews (2002) (n 3) 110.

[21] Jean O Lanjouw and Iain Cockburn *Do Patents Matter?: Empirical Evidence After GATT* NBER Working Paper Series No 7495, 29 (2000).

[22] See Carlos A Primo Braga and Carsten Fink *The Relationship Between Intellectual Property Rights and Foreign Direct Investment* 9 Duke J Comp and Int'l L 163, 181 (1998); Abbott (1996) (n 1) 391; and Karin Timmermans and Togi Hutadjulu The TRIPS Agreement and Pharmaceuticals: Report of an ASEAN Workshop on the TRIPs Agreement and its Impact on Pharmaceuticals 23–4 (2000).

In a WIPO-commissioned study, the author presented that given that the primary aim of the TRIPS Agreement was trade facilitation,[23] it therefore does not have the propensity to stimulate private investment, and that to work towards that aim an even higher degree of protection should be sought, what he refers to as 'investment-oriented protection'.[24] But even with regard to trade facilitation, the weight of evidence is not conclusive with regard to a positive perception of TRIPS.[25]

Undoubtedly, the impact TRIPS implementation has is contingent on the particular environment of the economy in question, what Frederick Abbott refers to as its 'context-sensitive' characteristic.[26] In addition, the impact on some stakeholders within the economy will be more profound than for others, therefore complicating further efforts to arrive at concrete evidence on the net benefit or cost of strengthened IPR protection. Even advocates of the benefits entailed in TRIPS implementation argue that 'in different degrees, most developing countries will face the powerful tension between private gains derived from non-robust systems and the potential gains to the overall economy from robust protection.'[27] It is in this regard that in one of the United States' technical assistance programs to Egypt, through its Agency for International Development (USAID), a cost-benefit analysis study on the impact of TRIPS implementation on the Egyptian economy was planned.[28] Beyond doubt such a study would have contributed to a reduction in the mood of uncertainty concerning the benefits and/or costs of implementation. Unfortunately, the study did not proceed due to USAID not completing this part of the project.[29]

(B) Concerns over Specific TRIPS Implications

Apart from the macro concerns discussed above, there were more specific problems attached to the implementation of certain TRIPS provisions cited by DC stakeholders as constituting negative and/or impedimentary effects.

[23] The TRIPS Preamble states the desire '*to reduce distortions and impediments to international trade....*'

[24] Robert M Sherwood *The TRIPS Agreement: Implications for Developing Countries* 37 IDEA J L AND TECH 491, 495 (1997).

[25] See Carsten Fink and Carlos A Primo Braga *How Stronger Protection of Intellectual Property Rights Affects International Trade Flows* WORLD BANK POLICY RESEARCH WORKING PAPER NO 2051, 12–13 (1999).

[26] Frederick M Abbott *The Enduring Enigma of TRIPS: A Challenge for the World Economic System* 1 J INT'L ECON L 497, 497–8 (1998). Vicente elaborates on the suitability of different IP regimes to countries at different stages of development and with different characteristics. See Vicente (1998) (n 11) 1116–20.

[27] Sherwood (1997) (n 24) 493.

[28] Interview with Ms Jaleen Moroney, Chief of Party, Technical Assistance for Intellectual Property Rights in Egypt (TIPRE) USAID Project, in Cairo (23 Apr 2003) [hereinafter Moroney Interview].

[29] ibid.

These included those related to the extension of patent protection to all fields of technology including pharmaceuticals (TRIPS Article 27); the extension of the patent protection period to 20 years (TRIPS Article 33); limited exceptions to rights conferred by a patent and restrictions on compulsory licenses (TRIPS Article 31); the inclusion of protection for undisclosed information (TRIPS Article 39); and the reversal of the burden of proof (TRIPS Article 34). Indeed, most of these perceived negative provisions in the TRIPS Agreement were mentioned by the Egyptian Minister of State for Scientific Research as representing pressures that needed to be positively engaged with by stakeholders for a rational handling of TRIPS.[30] Furthermore, the grant of exclusive marketing rights (TRIPS Article 70.9), largely negated the hoped for advantage to DC domestic stakeholders, and was hence also perceived as a negative aspect in TRIPS implementation. The effects of the implementation of these TRIPS provisions was perceived in DCs to result most importantly in: (1) an expected increase in the price of pharmaceutical products; (2) financial and administrative burdens directly arising from implementation; and (3) the increasing domination of the pharmaceutical market by the pharmaceutical MNEs at the expense of the local pharmaceutical manufacturers.

The issue of an expected increase in the price of pharmaceutical products following the implementation of TRIPS provisions in DCs has been and continues to be an issue of considerable concern.[31] This concern related to the direct effect an expected increase would have on DCs' health policies and the welfare of their populations, and in that regard, such concerns were echoed by the World Health Organization.[32] Indeed, the pre-TRIPS patent policies of a large number of DCs have consciously adopted the exclusion of pharmaceutical products from patenting in view of the strategic nature of this product to public welfare.[33] Under TRIPS, the legal monopoly conferred by a patent would lead to an increase in prices given the lack of competition from generic producers. In the case of Egypt, a study estimated that following the introduction of pharmaceutical product patenting in 2005, price increases in the order of 500–600 per cent over the prices of non-patented products were to be expected.[34] In India, the expected

[30] Dr Moufid Shehab, Minister of Higher Education and of State for Scientific Research, Address at the Annual Conference on Intellectual Property, Faculty of Laws, Cairo University 15 (17 Feb 2003) (transcript on file with author) [hereinafter Shehab 2003 Address].

[31] See Carlos Correa INTELLECTUAL PROPERTY RIGHTS, THE WTO AND DEVELOPING COUNTRIES 35 (2000); Matthews (2002) (n 3) 113–16; and Maskus (2000) (n 19) 159–67.

[32] See Frederick M Abbott *TRIPS in Seattle: the Not-So-Surprising Failure and the Future of the TRIPS Agenda* 18 BERKELEY J INT'L L 165, 171 (2000).

[33] See Matthews (2002) (n 3) 114.

[34] AZZA EL SHINAWY ET AL, THE IMPACT OF GATT/TRIPS AGREEMENT ON THE EGYPTIAN PHARMACEUTICAL SECTOR 8 (1997).

increase was calculated to be between 2000 and 3000 per cent.[35] Furthermore, the chairman of the health committee of Egypt's lower house of parliament, in addition to warning of the impending increase in price anticipated once pharmaceutical product patenting is introduced in 2005, added that there will be a gradual decrease in the share of the local Egyptian pharmaceutical companies in the Egyptian pharmaceuticals market.[36]

Another perceived threat is the problem of market domination by the pharmaceutical MNEs. In this regard, it should be noted that a number of DCs, including Brazil, that geared their patent policy to exclude the patenting of certain products such as pharmaceuticals, did so in order to afford protection to their domestic industries.[37] The threat of market domination by the pharmaceutical MNEs has been perceived as resulting from price and product quality competition where the MNEs due to their economies of scale and higher quality control have an advantage over local pharmaceutical industries. This would be further exacerbated in the long-term due to the MNEs' significantly larger R&D base, an advantage in product innovation and hence through patenting, of a monopoly on new pharmaceutical products.[38] It has also been pointed out that local pharmaceutical firms might be wary of innovating around patented pharmaceutical products, as they stand to risk litigation by the pharmaceutical MNEs and thus entailing significant costs.[39]

A third specific concern perceived on the part of DCs and their stakeholders revolved around the added financial and administrative burdens of implementation, and ultimately a disruption of prior practice in the patent field.[40] In the words of a leading commentator on the TRIPS Agreement,

> [t]he broad coverage and complexity of areas to be addressed and the generality or ambiguity of some provisions create difficulties for implementation as well as increased costs of administration. External demands for changes outside and beyond the framework and obligations set forth by the Agreement have not completely ceased.[41]

[35] Martin J Adelman and Sonia Baldia *Prospects and Limits of the Patent Provision in the TRIPS Agreement: The Case of India* 29 VAND J TRANSNAT'L L 507, 531 (1996).

[36] Interview with Dr Hamdy El Sayed, Head of the Egyptian Medical Union and Chairman, Health Committee, People's Assembly, Cairo (6 Apr 2004) [hereinafter El Sayed Interview].

[37] Rana Gosain and Henry Sherrill *The Effects of GATT/TRIPs on Brazil's Patent Legislation* PAT WORLD 24, 24 (May 1995).

[38] See RAOUF HAMED, MUSTAQBAL SINA'AT AL-DAWAA FI MISR WAL MANTEQA AL-ARABIYA [FUTURE OF THE DRUG INDUSTRY IN EGYPT AND THE ARAB REGION] 35–6 (1997).

[39] El Sayed Interview (n 36).

[40] UNCTAD, THE TRIPS AGREEMENT AND DEVELOPING COUNTRIES 19–20, 36–7 (1996).

[41] Carlos Correa *Implementation of the TRIPS Agreement in Latin America and the Caribbean* 19 EUR INTELL PROP REV 435, 443 (1997).

These added burdens include implementation costs from administrative changes and upgrades including the provision of new technical capabilities and the training of staff, new judicial procedures, and customs regulations.[42] Such costs would be even higher in those countries, particularly LDCs, where a patent regime was to be established anew.[43] In the case of the four DCs examined in Chapter 7 above, the situation was not as severe, given that a patent office and administrative procedures had already been established for many decades. Nonetheless, the expected increase in the volume of patent applications, and the admission of new subject matter areas for patenting,[44] created new demands on their patent system, not least the training of new patent examiners.[45]

In light of the above effects of TRIPS implementation perceived by DCs and their stakeholders, it is not surprising that a level of opposition to TRIPS implementation existed. This led to calls by DCs during the lead up to the ill-fated 1999 Seattle Ministerial Conference for negotiating rules that would take into account their interests in re-working a balance in the TRIPS Agreement.[46] Furthermore, DCs also requested extensions of TRIPS implementation deadlines or a moratorium on dispute settlement against them as they sought to bring their regimes into compliance.[47] However, DCs were to face considerable pressure from pharmaceutical MNEs and ICs for prompt implementation of TRIPS.

(II) PERSPECTIVE OF THE PHARMACEUTICAL MNES

An appreciation of the perspective of the pharmaceutical MNEs with regard to the implementation of TRIPS necessitates a view that encompasses and continues from their strategy during the negotiation of the TRIPS Agreement itself. The MNEs were not only interested in the implementation of TRIPS per se, but were pursuing their interest in IP regimes that would protect their interests as best as possible. Accordingly, they sought to move beyond TRIPS towards higher standards of patent protection.[48] The implementation phase presented another opportunity to achieve

[42] ibid. See also Sherwood (1997) (n 24) 518–20, 524–5.

[43] UNCTAD (1996) (n 40) 36.

[44] Specifically, pharmaceutical product patenting.

[45] In a World Bank study, the importance of developing a new cadre of examiners is deemed a high priority and a costly task, prompting a recommendation for international cooperation on the issue. See World Bank (2000) (n 2) 43–4.

[46] See Abbott (2000) (n 32) 167.

[47] ibid 169.

[48] On the concern of MNEs with regard to the transition term in TRIPS and the lack of pipeline protection, see Gerald J Mossinghoff and Thomas Bombelles *The Importance of Intellectual Property Protection to the American Research-Intensive Pharmaceutical Industry* 31 COL J WORLD BUS 38, 44 (1996).

this aim.[49] However, this strategy was differentiated according to the market at hand and the degree to which they perceived violations to their IP interests therein. While Argentina and India maintained the highest priority for the pharmaceutical MNEs during the implementation phase of TRIPS in the latter 1990s, Brazil and Egypt were a near second in terms of the urgency of action sought in raising the standards of their patent regimes.[50]

As discussed earlier, pharmaceutical MNEs were translating their influence through the mechanisms afforded them by their home countries. In this regard once more, the United States was to prove predominantly the most important IC, home to the largest pharmaceutical MNEs. With the Pharmaceutical Research and Manufacturers of America (PhRMA) spearheading the efforts of the US-based pharmaceutical MNEs, it was a pursuit of further gains, which from its perspective partly failed to materialize in the final TRIPS Agreement due to the presence of transitional periods and the lack of pipeline protection. In seeking US government support, it presented that

> PhRMA and its member companies nonetheless supported Congressional approval of the Uruguay Round on the understanding that the US government will continue its policy of pursuing bilateral improvements to the terms of intellectual property protection with our foreign trading partners.[51]

[49] Reichman noted how MNEs were interested in IP regimes that closely mirrored those of the ICs. See JH Reichman *Securing Compliance with the TRIPS Agreement After US v India* 1 J INT'L ECON L 585, 590–2 (1998).

[50] In its Special 301 submissions to the USTR, PhRMA continuously advocated the placement of India under the 'Priority Foreign Country' designation during the period 1995–1999, Argentina was similarly placed for the period 1996–1999, and as for Egypt, it was mainly placed on the 'Priority Watch Country' designation for the same period. See *Submission of the Pharmaceutical Research Manufacturers of America for the 1995 'Special 301' Report on Intellectual Property Protection* (13 Feb 1995) (on file at the USTR Reading Room, and copy on file with author) [hereinafter PhRMA 1995 301 Submission]; *Submission of the Pharmaceutical Research Manufacturers of America for the 1996 'Special 301' Report on Intellectual Property Barriers* (20 Feb 1996) (on file at the USTR Reading Room, and copy on file with author) [hereinafter PhRMA 1996 301 Submission]; *Submission of the Pharmaceutical Research Manufacturers of America for the 1997 'Special 301' Report on Intellectual Property Barriers* (18 Feb 1997) (on file with the USTR Reading Room, and copy on file with author) [hereinafter PhRMA 1997 301 Submission]; *Submission of the Pharmaceutical Research Manufacturers of America for the 1998 'Special 301' Report on Intellectual Property Barriers* (23 Feb 1998) (on file at the USTR Reading Room, and copy on file with author) [hereinafter PhRMA 1998 301 Submission]; *and Submission of the Pharmaceutical Research Manufacturers of America for the 1999 'Special 301' Report on Intellectual Property Barriers* (16 Feb 1999) (on file at the USTR Reading Room, and copy on file with author) [hereinafter PhRMA 1999 301 Submission].

[51] Mossinghoff and Bombelles (1996) (n 48) 44.

Sell also noted that two main IP lobby groups, the Intellectual Property Committee (IPC) and the International Intellectual Property Alliance (IIPA), articulated post-TRIPS strategies that centred around the intervention of the US government on their behalf.[52]

In this regard, a main US government mechanism open for MNE influence continued to be the Special 301 process. This tool was used by the US in seeking not only to implement TRIPS, but in numerous cases continue towards TRIPS-plus provisions.[53] This was in contrast to the pronouncements made during the Uruguay Round negotiations on TRIPS, where promises of a cessation of bilateral pressures in the arena of IP diplomacy were made. This use was naturally encouraged by the pharmaceutical MNEs:

> For Special 301 to be useful in these countries [DCs], we believe that there has to be increased pressure from the US Government to put a halt to product patent theft, which represents expropriation of the private property of US citizens. We hope that USTR will not hesitate to exert such pressure this year, and seek finally to bring these countries to account for the patent theft which they so brazenly have allowed.[54]

The pharmaceutical MNEs, apart from seeking the influence of their ICs in exerting pressure on DCs, as well as lobbying the government agencies and other bodies involved in patent law reform in DCs, also engaged in creative techniques to achieve their aims. In this regard, capitalizing on a wave of religious resurgence in Middle Eastern societies, a very interesting tool deployed in Egypt has been to seek the intervention of religious scholars to tell their fellow Egyptians that it is 'un-Islamic to copy other's work.'[55] This went further, with Egypt's highest Islamic religious authority, the Mufti, issuing a decree against piracy in 2002.[56] Such a technique, and apart from the independence of other bodies in stating independent opinions on an increasingly captivating issue in Egypt, undoubtedly reveals the resourcefulness of the pharmaceutical MNEs and supporters of higher patent protection standards, in mobilizing all possible sources of support.

Whatever mechanism or tool the pharmaceutical MNEs deployed, certain clear objectives were pursued. The major pharmaceutical MNEs, acting through PhRMA, outlined three macro challenges to their global

[52] Susan K Sell *Industry Strategies for Intellectual Property and Trade: The Quest for TRIPS, and Post-TRIPS Strategies* 10 CARDOZO J INT'L AND COMP L 79, 101 (2002).

[53] On TRIPS-plus, see Reichman and Lange (1998) (n 10) fns 17–19 and accompanying text.

[54] Letter from Harvey E Bale, Senior Vice President, PhRMA, to Irving Williamson, Office of the USTR (20 Feb 1996) (on file with author) [hereinafter Bale Letter].

[55] Abeer Allam *Seeking Investment, Egypt Tries Patent Laws* NY TIMES (4 Oct 2002).

[56] ibid.

interests and communicated them to the USTR.[57] Primarily, PhRMA complained of the continuing ability of certain countries, mainly India, Argentina, and in a latter stage, South Africa, to 'hold out against adopting adequate and effective patent protection for pharmaceutical products.'[58] Secondly, it was concerned that even in those countries that had proceeded with adopting legislation that protected pharmaceutical product patents, they still lacked adequate enforcement of those codes, and failed to implement other provisions agreed in either bilateral or plurilateral agreements with the US and other countries, such as pipeline protection.[59] This second concern voiced by PhRMA related to their disconcertment with countries refusing to adopt TRIPS-plus provisions. Finally, the third concern related to countries that have attempted to limit or de-value patent protection for pharmaceutical products by means other than direct denial of patent protection, including import barriers, high tariff rates, and delays in drug registration.[60] Pharmaceutical MNEs also identified more specific concerns. Among these was the transitional period where MNEs sought a speedier implementation of TRIPS.[61] Hence their desire to work for accelerated implementation of TRIPS in key emerging markets.[62] Another specific concern which the MNEs failed to resolve in the final TRIPS Agreement but which they vociferously fought for in post-TRIPS patent regime reforms was the lack of pipeline protection, an issue that was to spring up in their evaluation of the situation in Egypt.

(III) PERSPECTIVES OF THE ICS

While ICs largely perceived the TRIPS negotiations as having successfully covered their major concerns with regard to IP protection, and specifically patent protection, the challenge at hand then became implementing TRIPS and its standards into domestic IP legislation. In contrast to the perspective of DCs and their stakeholders, ICs were keen to proceed with an expedited implementation of TRIPS.[63] Moreover, in so doing, there was an attempt to

[57] See Bale Letter (n 54); and Letter from Shannon S Herzfeld, Senior Vice President, PhRMA, to Sybia Harrison, Special Assistant to the Section 301 Committee USTR (23 Feb 1998) (on file with author) [hereinafter Herzfeld Letter].

[58] Argentina and India in particular have figured prominently in this regard. On Argentina, see PhRMA 1996 301 Submission (n 50). On India, see PhRMA 1999 301 Submission (n 50).

[59] Herzfeld Letter (n 57).

[60] ibid.

[61] PhRMA particularly criticized the decision by India to make use of the transitional period for introducing pharmaceutical product patent protection. See PhRMA 1995 301 Submission (n 50).

[62] Mossinghoff and Bombelles (1996), (n 48), 39 and 44.

[63] On IC pressure for TRIPS implementation, see WTO *General Council, Preparations for the 1999 Ministerial Conference, EC Approach to Trade-Related Aspects of Intellectual*

move beyond what was accomplished in TRIPS, and thus include TRIPS-plus provisions in newly drafted DC legislation. ICs promised a vision of the effects of TRIPS implementation different from that perceived by DC stakeholders. Not only was TRIPS implementation conducive to the promotion of global trade, but more pertinently, it was presented as necessary for the economic development efforts of DCs.[64] Visions of development aside, the ICs spurred in large part by the pharmaceutical MNEs, were also willing to engage in lobbying tactics and economic pressures on DCs for implementation and in certain cases the enactment of TRIPS-plus provisions. The United States Congress pressed in its legislation implementing the results of the Uruguay Round that US foreign policy objectives in the intellectual property arena should be:

> to accelerate the implementation of the Agreement on Trade-Related Aspects of Intellectual Property Rights. . . . [And] to seek enactment and effective implementation by foreign countries to protect and enforce intellectual property rights that supplement and strengthen the standards of the Agreement on Trade-Related Aspects of Intellectual Property Rights and the North American Free Trade Agreement in particular. . . .[65]

Therefore, three particular objectives can be discerned to reveal what were predominant US concerns and purposes in this implementation phase. Primarily, it was the basic concern with ensuring compliance with TRIPS implementation. Secondly, to ensure that compliance and implementation are effectuated in an accelerated manner regardless of the existence of the transitional periods.[66] Third, a concern with the implementation of standards that went beyond those enshrined in TRIPS towards TRIPS-plus provisions.

Having identified these objectives, ICs and particularly the United States, can be seen to engage in three particular tools for achieving these objectives. These tools comprised: (1) the lobbying of DC governments and recourse to

Property Rights in the New Round, Communication from the European Communities WT/GC/W/193 (2 June 1999); and WTO *General Council, Preparations for the 1999 Ministerial Conference, Proposal on Trade-Related Aspects of Intellectual Property Rights, Communication from Japan* WT/GC/W/242 (6 July 1999).

[64] See Shanker A Singham *Competition Policy and the Stimulation of Innovation: TRIPS and the Interface Between Competition and Patent Protection in the Pharmaceutical Industry* 26 BERK J INT'L L 363 (2000); and Sherwood (1997) (n 24) 496–510. On the MNE claims that TRIPS implementation will not lead to higher prices of medicine, see Mossinghoff and Bombelles (1996) (n 48) 47.

[65] Uruguay Round Agreements Act of 1994, Title III § 315, Pub L No 103–465 (1994).

[66] In its 1999 Special 301 Report, the USTR stated that 'ensuring that developing countries come into full compliance with the Agreement before the end of these transition periods is one of this Administration's highest priorities with respect to intellectual property rights.' See USTR 1999 Special 301 Report, 4 (30 Apr 1999).

economic pressure such as the use of the Special 301 mechanism in the case of the United States;[67] (2) use of the TRIPS Council review mechanism and in more extreme cases the WTO dispute settlement mechanism;[68] and (3) the provision of technical assistance to DCs in their TRIPS implementation efforts.[69]

In engaging in bilateral lobbying and pressure, the United States issued a number of reports that identified problem countries and those issues of concern. A key report in this regard is the *National Trade Estimate Report on Foreign Trade Barriers*.[70] Similarly, another report, reflecting US administration action on trading partners' lack of IP protection, is the Special 301 report.[71] Both these reports indicate the main areas of concern in the United States with DCs IP regimes, and are hence invaluable in shedding light on those concerns.[72] Furthermore, the Special 301 report with its country designations on its various lists, is indicative of the extent of the pressure being exerted by the United States on certain DCs, and as discussed earlier, was designed to initiate action against countries engaging in unfair trading practices. Table 8.1 below lists the Special 301 designations of selected DCs (including Argentina, Brazil, Egypt and India) during the period 1995–2002.

A second tool, put to effective use by the ICs was the WTO's review of implementing legislation of members.[73] This proved to be among the more useful provisions of TRIPS from the perspective of ICs' interests in seeking and monitoring implementation of the Agreement. Accordingly, TRIPS Article 63.2 on transparency states that '*Members shall notify the laws and regulations referred to in paragraph 1 to the Council for TRIPS in order to assist that Council in its review of the operation of this Agreement.*'[74] Upon

[67] In 1999, the USTR announced that beginning December 1999, it would launch a comprehensive review of how DC members of the WTO have implemented TRIPS. See ibid 4.

[68] The use of the WTO Dispute Settlement mechanism, transforming the TRIPS issue into its dispute phase, will be treated in Ch 11.

[69] Drahos also notes that the United States was keen to negotiate bilateral treaties with certain DCs to incorporate TRIPS-plus provisions. See Peter Drahos *Trade-Offs and Trade Linkages: TRIPs in a Negotiating Context* QUAKER UNITED NATIONS OFFICE—GENEVA OCCASIONAL PAPER NO 1, 7 (2000).

[70] This annual report was first presented to the Senate Finance Committee and the House Ways and Means Committee in 1985. Its statutory basis lies in the Trade and Tariff Act of 1984 § 303.

[71] The 'Special 301' provisions of the Trade Act of 1974, as amended, require the USTR to identify foreign countries that deny adequate and effective protection of IPRs or fair and equitable market access for US persons that rely on IP protection. See 19 USC §§ 2242, 2212(b)(2) (2003).

[72] It should be noted here that these reports were not primarily geared to an analysis of TRIPS implementation in DCs, but rather approached the issue within the general overview of IP regimes in those countries and how they might adversely affect US interests.

[73] See JAYASHREE WATAL INTELLECTUAL PROPERTY RIGHTS IN THE WTO AND DEVELOPING COUNTRIES 53–57 (2001).

[74] The TRIPS Council spelt out in greater detail a 'basic procedure' for the notification of

Table 8.1: USTR Special 301 Designation of Selected DCs (1995–2002)

	Priority Foreign Country	**Priority Watch List**	**Watch List**
2002	Ukraine	Argentina, Brazil, Egypt, India	
2001	Ukraine	Argentina, Egypt, India	Brazil
2000	None	Argentina, Egypt India	Brazil
1999	None	Argentina, Egypt, India	Brazil
1998	Paraguay	Argentina, Egypt, India	
1997	None	Argentina, Egypt, India	Brazil
1996	China	Argentina, India	Brazil, Egypt
1995	None	Brazil, India	Argentina, Egypt

this notification, the TRIPS Council would engage in a review of the national implementing legislation of each member following a basic procedure in this regard adopted by the Council in May 1996 ahead of its first review session in July 1996 and slightly modified at subsequent review meetings.[75] The review entails the submission of questions by members on the notified laws and regulations of the member under review, the latter in turn submitting responses to these questions as well as presenting an introductory statement and making oral responses to the Council at its review

implementing legislation under Art 63.2. See WTO, *TRIPS Council, Procedures for Notification of, and Possible Establishment of a Common Register of, National Laws and Regulations Under Article 63.2* IP/C/2 (30 Nov 1995).

[75] The basic procedures for the review of national implementing legislation are laid out in WTO *TRIPS Council, Minutes of Meeting Held on 9 May 1996* IP/C/M/7 (13 June 1996) para 6. For a summary of the modified procedures, see WTO *TRIPS Council, Procedures for the Notification and Review of Legislation, Note by the Secretariat* JOB(99)/6928 (18 Nov 1999).

meeting.[76] This mechanism became a main tool whereby ICs could not only effectively monitor DCs implementation efforts, but more importantly, to exert pressure on them to adopt new IP legislation in conformity with their TRIPS obligations. A closer look at this mechanism as it covered Egypt's legislation is presented in the following chapter.

A third strategy adopted by ICs in carrying forward their TRIPS implementation objectives has been the provision of technical assistance to DCs in support of the implementation of the latter's TRIPS obligations. It should be noted of course that the provision of technical assistance, apart from being an auxiliary tool for IC strategy, was itself an obligation bearing upon them by virtue of TRIPS Article 67. In the provision of assistance by ICs, it has been noted that the EC has taken the lead due in part to a larger resource base for technical cooperation activities compared to that of the United States.[77] While this is arguably the case as an overall approach, however, US assistance has nonetheless been targeted strategically at certain countries, and has been deployed as a component of its official development assistance programmes. Most notably, in the case of Egypt, significant technical assistance in the IPR area has been carried out through USAID, as will be examined further below. This assistance has been targeted as much as possible to assist in the creation of an IPR regime that subscribes to IC visions.

(IV) OTHER PERSPECTIVES

A fourth perspective pertinent to the issue of TRIPS implementation by DCs is that of the relevant international organizations. The WTO as the 'home-institution' of the TRIPS Agreement had a direct role to perform in this process.[78] WIPO with its heritage and expertise in international IP issues had an equally important role in TRIPS implementation. Finally, other international organizations concerned with issues of economic development including the World Bank, UNCTAD and the UNDP, also had important contribution to make in this regard. The role these organizations were called to perform focused on the provision of assistance to DCs in their efforts to implement TRIPS.

The WTO through its TRIPS Council performed the important function of monitoring and ensuring compliance with TRIPS.[79] As discussed above,

[76] ibid. For an overview of the TRIPS Council review process, see Adrian Otten *Implementation of the TRIPS Agreement and Prospects for its Further Development* 1 J INT'L ECON L 523, 524–6 (1998).

[77] Matthews (2002) (n 3) 121.

[78] See Adrian Otten (1998) (n 76).

[79] The WTO has a number of mechanisms to review TRIPS implementation, including the Trade Policy Review Mechanism covering review of different legislation, including IP. Second, the Council for TRIPS, pursuant to TRIPS Arts 63 and 68 has been entrusted with the task of ensuring the proper operation of the Agreement. See Watal (2001) (n 73) 50–1.

this function was partly carried out through the review process of implementing legislation. Another no less important aspect of this function is to offer DC and particularly LDC members required assistance in this legislative reform process. It is in this regard that the role of the constellation of relevant international organizations is important and complementary to TRIPS implementation. Given the novelty of the standards mandated by TRIPS for implementation into DC IP legislation, and indeed the novelty of the area of IP protection for a number of LDCs, assistance from these international organizations was essential. It has been argued that especially with regard to sub-Saharan African countries, the implementation of TRIPS is largely a function of the willingness of the WTO in specific to engage in the provision of technical assistance to these countries.[80] In this endeavour, four broad areas were identified, namely: (1) supporting the IP reform efforts; (2) implementing reforms and building IP institutions; (3) enhancing the environment under which IPRs operate; and (4) increasing the understanding of the social and economic effects of IP protection.[81]

WIPO had a lead role to perform.[82] Traditionally, it has performed advisory roles for its members including the drafting of model IP legislation.[83] Being the oldest institution in the IP arena, WIPO had the necessary technical expertise and resources that the WTO lacked in the provision of technical assistance for DCs. As early as 1995 these resources were brought into action when the WIPO General Assembly called for arrangements to be able to respond to requests from DCs for technical and legal assistance relating to TRIPS.[84] It also commissioned studies on the implications of TRIPS on DCs.[85] This activity performed by WIPO can also be seen as an institutional re-definition of its role in the aftermath of the TRIPS Agreement that gave the pre-eminent role in international IP legislation to the WTO. Given this focus in WIPO's post-TRIPS role, a Cooperation Agreement was launched by the WTO and WIPO in January 1996, instituting joint technical assistance initiatives relating to the TRIPS Agreement for the benefit of DCs.[86] Furthermore, a joint WIPO–WTO initiative was

[80] Frederick S Ringo *The Trade-Related Aspects of Intellectual Property Rights Agreement in the GATT and Legal Implications for Sub-Saharan Africa: Prospective Policy Issues for the World Trade Organization* 28 J WORLD TRADE 120, 122 (1994).

[81] Braga and Fink (1998) (n 9) 552–3.

[82] See Richard Wilder in Velasquez and Boulet (1999) (n 20) 69–70.

[83] See WORLD INTELLECTUAL PROPERTY ORGANIZATION AND UNITED NATIONS ECONOMIC COMMISSION FOR AFRICA, MODEL LAW FOR ENGLISH-SPEAKING AFRICAN COUNTRIES ON PATENTS (1978).

[84] WIPO General Assembly Doc WO/GA/XVI/7 (3 Oct 1995) para 24, item 9.

[85] See Sherwood (1997) (n 24).

[86] World Intellectual Property Organization-World Trade Organization: Agreement between the WIPO and the WTO (22 Dec 1995) art 4, 35 ILM 754 (entered into force 1 Jan 1996).

launched in July 1998 to provide assistance to DCs for meeting their January 2000 TRIPS implementation deadline, and covered assistance in preparing legislation, training, institution-building, and modernizing IP systems and enforcement.[87] A similar program was initiated in June 2001 specifically targeting LDCs.[88]

Similarly, the World Bank and UNCTAD have undertaken to initiate studies and projects of assistance to DCs undertaking reforms in their IPR regimes. In this regard, two studies were carried out by UNCTAD for Egypt and India, while a project was pursued for Brazil by the World Bank.[89] Assistance aside, the UNDP was critical of the implications of the TRIPS Agreement in certain aspects of development policy. The UNDP 1999 Human Development Report was particularly critical of the negotiating process of TRIPS, presenting that there was 'far too little participation from many developing countries now feeling the impact of their conditions.'[90] This criticism was to gradually rise in the context of the access to medicines debate, where other international organizations, most notably the World Health Organization, joined in expressing concern about the effects of TRIPS on DCs. This will be discussed in Part Four below.

These technical assistance programs initiated by the various international organizations were important in providing necessary support for DCs. Nonetheless, a worrying aspect was the extent to which such assistance was subject to the influence of the pharmaceutical MNEs and IC interests. Commentators have noted that pressure was exerted by MNEs and certain ICs on WIPO, WHO, and UNCTAD to limit their advice to that seeking to model DCs' legislation on those of ICs thus foregoing some of the important flexibilities inherent in TRIPS.[91] Moreover, it has also been noted that some US business lobbies are opposed to the provision of technical assistance to DCs, viewing it as a possible weakening of the required pressure that should be brought to bear on DCs for TRIPS implementation.[92]

[87] See WTO Press Release 108, WTO and WIPO Join Forces to Help Developing Countries Meet Year-2000 Commitments on Intellectual Property (21 July 1998). See also Otten (1998) (n 76) 529–530.

[88] See WTO Press Release 231, WIPO and WTO Launch New Initiative to Help World's Poorest Countries (14 June 2001).

[89] See Finger and Schuler (1999) (n 7) 20–1, 48 and 51.

[90] United Nations Development Program, 1999 Human Development Report 67–76 (2000).

[91] Reichman refers to MNEs' 'bullying' of these organizations. See Reichman (1998) (n 49)592.

[92] Matthews (2002) (n 3) 121.

Chapter 9

TRIPS Implementation Process: The Case of Egypt

Chapter 8 analysed the perspective of the various stakeholders involved in TRIPS Implementation in DCs. In this chapter, the analysis is taken one step further into the process of legislative implementation, the act of law making at the domestic level,[1] and the ensuing product of this implementation, the new patent legislation. In so doing, the focus will be on the implementation process in Egypt.[2] It is important to note that each country's experience in implementing its TRIPS obligations and reforming its patent-related legislation is unique.[3] Nonetheless, the analysis carried out in Chapter 7 on pre-TRIPS patent regimes underlined the commonality of key aspects in DCs' domestic patent legislation. By extension, in the various domestic legislative reform efforts common issues were at stake. Therefore, the focus here on the implementation process in Egypt, while bound in its Egyptian context, can be viewed as indicative of the important issues relating to the implementation process as they arose in DCs.

There is no 'magical moment' where the implementation of TRIPS can be said to have begun. While clearly there are cut-off dates required by TRIPS, yet the reform of patent law in DCs began at different points in time, and these were efforts designed ultimately to bring their legislation into conformity with the evolving higher standards advocated in TRIPS. Table 9.1 below lists the main cut-off dates for the implementation of the different pharmaceutical-related TRIPS provisions, and the corresponding action undertaken by Egypt to comply with its obligations.

[1] For an elaboration on how law making at the domestic level figures in our analysis of rule making at the international level, please refer to Ch 2.

[2] For a discussion of the debate emerging in Egypt on legislative implementation of TRIPS as it related to the pharmaceutical industry, see Nermien Al-Ali *The Egyptian Pharmaceutical Industry After TRIPS—A Practitioners' View* 26 FORDHAM INT'L LJ 274, 295–305 (2003).

[3] For a concise summary of particular nations' implementation of TRIPS, see FM Scherer *The Pharmaceutical Industry and World Intellectual Property Standards* 53 VAND L R 2245 (2000). For an interesting table examining the various implementation steps taken by DCs—particularly with regard to signing on to the conventions, and more importantly USTR and TABD action and views thereon, see Carlos A Primo Braga and Carsten Fink *Trade-Related Intellectual Property Rights: From Marrakech to Seattle* in THE WORLD TRADE ORGANIZATION MILLENNIUM ROUND: FREE TRADE IN THE TWENTY-FIRST CENTURY 184 (Klaus Gunter Deutsch and Bernhard Speyer eds 2001).

Table 9.1: Main Requirements for Implementing the Pharmaceutical-Related TRIPS Provisions and Corresponding Action in Egypt

TRIPS Provision	**Date of Entry Into Force**	**Egypt Action**
Article 70.8 (Mailbox)	1 Jan 1995	Egyptian Patent Office identified as government agency in charge of receiving patent applications. Notified to the WTO on 20 September 1995.[4] Regulated in Article 43 of the new IP law issued in 2002.[5]
Article 70.9 (EMRs)	1 Jan 1995	Egyptian Patent Office identified as the government agency responsible for issuing the certificate of exclusive marketing rights, and the conditions for this issuance laid out in Prime Ministerial Decree No 547 for the year 2000, and notified to the WTO on 20 April 2000.[6] Regulated in Article 44 of the new IP law issued in 2002.
Article 3 (Accord National Treatment to WTO Members, subject to the exceptions provided in Paris); Article 4 (Accord MFN treatment and notification under para d); Article 5.	1 Jan 1996	Extends NT and MFN treatment with respect to copyright and related rights. Notified to the WTO on 30 October 1997, and notes that similar announcement with regard to other IPRs will follow.[7] Regulated in Article 4 of the new IP law issued in June 2002.

[4] WTO *TRIPS Council, Notification of Laws and Regulations Under Article 63.2 of the Agreement, Egypt* IP/N/1/EGY/1 (21 Sept 1995).

[5] Law on the Protection of Intellectual Property Rights No 82 of 2002 (2 June 2002) [hereinafter Egypt 2002 IP Law].

[6] WTO *TRIPS Council, Notification of Laws and Regulations Under Article 63.2 of the Agreement, Egypt, Addendum* IP/N/1/EGY/1/Add.1 (8 May 2000).

[7] WTO *TRIPS Council, Notification of Laws and Regulations Under Article 63.2 of the Agreement, Egypt* IP/N/1/EGY/2 (6 Nov 1997).

TRIPS Provision	Date of Entry Into Force	Egypt Action
Articles 27–34 (Standards on patent protection).	1 Jan 2000	Regulated in Book One, Part I of the new IP law issued in June 2002.
Article 39 (Standards on the protection of undisclosed information).	1 Jan 2000	First regulated through a Prime Ministerial decree, concerning the data exclusivity of chemical agricultural and pharmaceutical products submitted for marketing approvals.[8] Regulated in Book One, Part III of the new IP law issued in June 2002.
Article 65.4 (Permission to delay product patent protection for areas of technology not so protectable on the general date of application of TRIPS).	1 Jan 2005	Egypt opts to delay the introduction of product patent protection for pharmaceutical products until 1 January 2005, as stipulated in Article 2 of the presidential decree issuing the new Egyptian IP law.

In this chapter, we cover the main issues that arose during Egypt's legislative implementation exercise, and the role of the different stakeholders in seeking their interests in this process. Initially, the concerns and pressures exerted by the pharmaceutical MNEs and the United States will be discussed. This will be followed by a discussion of the review of Egypt's IP legislation in the WTO. The third section will then be devoted to the evolution of Egypt's draft IP legislation through its various drafting phases, and the bureaucratic and other rivalries occurring. However, throughout this exposition, the efforts of the various stakeholders transfixed on four main issues that run throughout the analysis below. These issues are: (1) Egypt's delay in implementing its obligations beyond the fixed deadlines; (2) the question of whether Egypt would avail itself of the Article 65.4 mandated transitional period for providing patent protection for pharmaceutical products; (3) implementing the 'mailbox' and EMRs provisions; and (4) the problematic issue of the protection of undisclosed information.

8 Prime Ministerial Decree No 2211 for the year 2000 (25 Nov 2000).

(I) IC AND MNE CONCERNS AND PRESSURE ON EGYPT

(A) Concerns of the Pharmaceutical MNEs

Pharmaceutical MNEs operating through PhRMA placed Egypt under the 'priority watch country' classification in their recommendation for Special 301 action by the USTR.[9] The most problematic issue PhRMA had with the patent regime of Egypt was its continuing delay in adopting TRIPS-compliant legislation. PhRMA noted that the legislation in force, the 1949 law, had specific discriminatory aspects against pharmaceuticals.[10] These discriminatory aspects revolved around the lack of product patent protection for pharmaceuticals, and what it considered a very short period of process patent protection, which given the long period between grant of patent and commercialization of the product due to regulatory review, made the protection period virtually meaningless.[11]

On the other hand, the pharmaceutical MNEs also recognized that Egypt was in the process of drafting a new law to bring it into conformity with TRIPS. Given the importance of the drafting phase, they were quite eager to comment on and exert pressure during the drafting process. The pharmaceutical MNEs, through their local representatives in Egypt, were able to understand the evolving debate surrounding implementation, and identify the problem issues.[12] Similarly, commentary was forthcoming from local legal experts retained by the pharmaceutical MNEs.[13] In this regard, counsel were retained, particularly by PhRMA Egypt, and were also consulted by USAID IP assistance programs on the draft law, conducting a thorough survey of problematic issues in the draft law from the perspective of the pharmaceutical lobby.[14]

[9] See *Submission of the Pharmaceutical Research Manufacturers of America for the 1995 'Special 301' Report on Intellectual Property Protection* (13 Feb 1995) (on file at the USTR Reading Room, and copy on file with author) [hereinafter PhRMA 1995 301 Submission]; *Submission of the Pharmaceutical Research Manufacturers of America for the 1997 'Special 301' Report on Intellectual Property Barriers* (18 Feb 1997) (on file with the USTR Reading Room, and copy on file with author) [hereinafter PhRMA 1997 301 Submission]; *Submission of the Pharmaceutical Research Manufacturers of America for the 1998 'Special 301' Report on Intellectual Property Barriers* (23 Feb 1998) (on file at the USTR Reading Room, and copy on file with author) [hereinafter PhRMA 1998 301 Submission]; and *Submission of the Pharmaceutical Research Manufacturers of America for the 1999 'Special 301' Report on Intellectual Property Barriers* (16 Feb 1999) (on file at the USTR Reading Room, and copy on file with author) [hereinafter PhRMA 1999 301 Submission].

[10] PhRMA 1995 Special 301 Submission (n 9); and PhRMA 1999 301 Submission (n 9).

[11] PhRMA 1995 Special 301 Submission (n 9).

[12] Interview with Dr Ahmed El Hakim, Director of External Affairs and Health Policy, Pfizer-Egypt, in Cairo (15 Jan 2003).

[13] On the role of local agents of the pharmaceutical MNEs in providing information on the status of patent protection in DCs, see DUNCAN MATTHEWS, GLOBALISING INTELLECTUAL PROPERTY RIGHTS: THE TRIPS AGREEMENT 92 (2002).

[14] Interview with Mr Karim El Helaly, Attorney, Zaki Hashem and Partners Law Office,

While the pharmaceutical MNEs acknowledged that 'most of the substantive provisions [of the new IP law] are positive and reflect the standards established by TRIPs,' yet they noted important undecided issues.[15] Four critical issues or problems were identified by the MNEs. Primarily, the length of the transitional period for product patent protection that Egypt was going to undertake and whether it was going to opt for the full period authorized by TRIPS. Second, whether it was going to opt for a provision on pipeline protection.[16] Both issues reflecting TRIPS-plus provisions. The MNEs made direct recourse to the US government in seeking favourable action by Egypt on these issues. PhRMA proceeded to 'urge the US Government to continue its work on the issue with the Egyptian authorities to achieve a short transition period and pipeline protection.'[17]

The third problem identified by the MNEs concerned the institution of the grant of EMRs. This became particularly important when the US pharmaceutical MNE, Eli Lilly, requested the Egyptian Ministry of Health (MoH) to issue an EMR in Egypt for its proprietary pharmaceutical product Zyprexa.[18] The MoH declined the request citing the lack of any legislation on the issue.[19] Although much delayed, the EMR issue was eventually resolved as will be discussed below. The fourth problem concerned the issue of undisclosed information. As will be discussed below, controversy emerged between the pharmaceutical MNEs and the Ministry of Health on this issue. The issue became notorious when local producers sought marketing approval for generic versions of Pfizer's Viagra—the Viagra war as it became known in Egypt—prompting a plea from Pfizer going all the way up to the Egyptian President.[20]

(B) US Concerns and Pressure

As early as 1995, the USTR in its Special 301 Report, expressed its serious concern about the lack of effective patent protection in Egypt under its patent law of 1949.[21] Criticism was mainly directed at the lack of product patent protection for pharmaceutical products and what the US viewed as

Cairo, in Cairo (15 Jan 2003). See also Karim El Helaly, Significant Problems in the Egyptian IPR Code (2000–3) (unpublished manuscript, on file with author).

[15] ibid.

[16] PhRMA 1998 301 Submission (n 9).

[17] ibid.

[18] Interview with Dr Mustafa El Hadary, Former Head of Drug Policies, Egyptian Ministry of Health, in Cairo (11 May 2003) [hereinafter El Hadary Interview].

[19] ibid.

[20] Letter from Mohand Sidi Said, Vice President—Pfizer Inc to HE Mohamed Hosni Mubarak, President of Egypt (29 Mar 2001) (on file with author).

[21] USTR 1995 Special 301 Report, 10 (29 Apr 1995).

overly broad compulsory licensing provisions.[22] The 1949 law allowed the issuance of a compulsory licence on the basis of non-working within a period of three years following grant.[23] The US complained that contrary to the stipulations of the Stockholm Act of the Paris Convention, Egypt did not provide for the alternative period of four years from the date of filing.[24] A further criticism concerned the fact that a patent could be forfeited in the case of continued non-working two years following the issuance of the first compulsory licence.[25] These concerns were compounded by dissatisfaction with an inadequate patent term of 15 years.[26] Criticisms of the 1949 law aside, in a post-TRIPS environment, the United States was more concerned about the delay in the enactment of a new patent law implementing Egypt's obligations under TRIPS. This complaint became more insistent as Egypt neared its mandated implementation date of 1 January 2000, and went beyond it.[27] This was reflected in the elevation of Egypt's 'Special 301' designation under the 'watch list' in 1995 and 1996 unto the 'priority watch list' during the period 1997–2002.[28] The United States lobbied the Egyptian government to work more closely with right holders to ensure effective enforcement of existing laws and to expedite the conformity of its patent regime with international obligations.[29] Initially, intense pressure was exerted to persuade Egypt to forego the transitional period for instituting pharmaceutical product patent protection.[30] This issue was raised in a USAID commissioned report proposing that 'Egypt should be persuaded to eschew the 10-year delay in effectiveness for product patents available under the GATT,' and that 'at most a 5-year delay, and then only after prompt adoption of the law, should be considered acceptable. . . .'[31]

[22] ibid 10; and USTR 1998 Special 301 Report, 11 (1 May 1998). Similar language is to be found in the 1996 and 1997 Reports, and was repeated later in the 2001 Report when the draft IP law was not yet enacted. See also USTR 1995 National Trade Estimate Report on Foreign Trade Barriers—Egypt, 4 (on file with author) [hereinafter 1995 NTE Report—Egypt].

[23] Patent and Designs Act No 132 of 1949, Art 30 [hereinafter Egypt 1949 Patent Act].

[24] 1995 NTE Report—Egypt (n 22) 4.

[25] ibid.

[26] USTR 1999 Special 301 Report, 12 (30 Apr 1999).

[27] USTR 1998 Special 301 Report, 11 (1 May 1998); USTR 1999 Special 301 Report, 12 (30 Apr 1999); and USTR 2002 Special 301 Report, 20 (3 May 2002). See also USTR 1997 National Trade Estimate Report on Foreign Trade Barriers—Egypt, 90–1 (on file with author).

[28] See USTR 1995 Special 301 Report (29 Apr 1995); USTR 1996 Special 301 Report (3 May 1996); USTR 1997 Special 301 Report (30 Apr 1997); USTR 1998 Special 301 Report (1 May 1998); USTR 1999 Special 301 Report (30 Apr 1999); USTR 2000 Special 301 Report (28 Apr 2000); USTR 2001 Special 301 Report (27 Apr 2001); and USTR 2002 Special 301 Report (3 May 2002).

[29] USTR 1999 Special 301 Report, 12 (30 Apr 1999).

[30] USTR 1999 National Trade Estimate Report on Foreign Trade Barriers—Egypt, 96 (on file with author).

[31] NATHAN ASSOCIATES INC, FINAL REPORT TO USAID: PRICE AND MARKET LIBERALIZATION IN EGYPT, VOL 2: PHARMACEUTICAL INDUSTRY 16 (1995).

However, despite this pressure, Egypt opted to make full use of its TRIPS privilege in delaying product patent protection of pharmaceuticals until 1 January 2005.[32]

Three further concerns were raised by the United States with regard to Egypt's patent regime and its TRIPS implementation. Primarily, Egypt had considerably delayed implementing a mechanism to grant exclusive marketing rights (EMRs) and when a decree was enacted to regulate their grant,[33] the US noted that the decree had not yet been implemented.[34] The background to this was the incident involving Eli Lilly discussed above. The second concern related to a specific provision in Egypt's draft IP law that would require patent applications for pharmaceutical products to be examined and approved by the Ministry of Health before a patent grant is issued,[35] hence violating TRIPS Article 27 that required no discrimination in the granting of patent rights among the various fields of technology. The third concern raised by the US involved the issue of undisclosed information and the protection of confidential test data pertaining to pharmaceutical products. In 2001 in particular, the US referred to reports that certain generic manufacturers were granted marketing approval in Egypt based on confidential test data submitted by the proprietary drug companies, hence claiming a violation of TRIPS Article 39, and Egypt's own Decree No 2211.[36] However, based on the action of the Government of Egypt in this matter, the US alluded to progress in the following year's report.[37] These three concerns will be further addressed below.

One of the main avenues open for the United States to influence TRIPS implementation in Egypt has been through the provision of technical assistance. The mandate of one of the programs of USAID in Egypt entitled 'Strengthening Intellectual Property Rights in Egypt' (SIPRE), was to aid the Egyptian government in its efforts to draft the new IP law.[38] This role was carried over into a second USAID project, 'Technical Assistance for Intellectual Property Rights in Egypt' (TIPRE).[39] Indeed, active commentary

32 Presidential Decree issuing Law No 82 of 2002, Art 2(b).

33 Prime Ministerial Decree No 547 for the year 2000 (8 Mar 2000).

34 USTR 2001 National Trade Estimate Report on Foreign Trade Barriers—Egypt, 94 (on file with author). See also USTR 2000 Special 301 Report, 15 (28 Apr 2000).

35 USTR 2001 Special 301 Report, 18 (27 Apr 2001); and USTR 2002 Special 301 Report, 20 (3 May 2002).

36 See USTR 2001 Special 301 Report, 18 (27 Apr 2001). This issue will be further examined below.

37 USTR 2002 Special 301 Report, 20 (3 May 2002).

38 Interview with Ms Jaleen Moroney, Chief of Party, Technical Assistance for Intellectual Property Rights in Egypt (TIPRE) USAID Project, in Cairo (23 Apr 2003) [hereinafter Moroney Interview].

39 Ms Jaleen Moroney, Chief of Party of the TIPRE Project, maintained that the mandate of TIPRE, with regard to the drafting exercise of the new law, was more a passive role consisting primarily of responding to queries from the Egyptian side, rather than actively engaging in the drafting exercise. ibid.

on the draft law was forthcoming from the US and its USAID-funded programs during the parliamentary discussions both in the Shura Council and in the People's Assembly.[40] Commentary on the draft law was provided to the Academy of Scientific Research, among other agencies.[41] In the words of Dr Fayez from the National Research Centre of Egypt, USAID was 'showering the government with reports that reflected US and MNE interests, as well as convening experts drawn from US universities in workshops organized around the issue, with a line of argumentation attuned to their interests.'[42]

An example of this 'targeted' technical assistance was a book published in Egypt in English and in Arabic by the USAID projects that covered the principles and practice of intellectual property, written exclusively by former US Patent and Trademark Office (PTO) officials.[43] This book was aimed to fill a gap in the literature available in Egypt on IPR issues. However, in its treatment of IPRs and economic development and public interest, the book offers a one-sided view of the matter congruent with that of the US and the right holders, dismissing wholesale, arguments that are critical of the utility of TRIPS patent standards in a DC context, and as discussed earlier in the book.[44]

(II) TRIPS COUNCIL REVIEW OF EGYPT'S LEGISLATION

The review session on Egypt's IP legislation, originally scheduled for late autumn 2000, was held in June 2001,[45] where the Egyptian Minister of Higher Education and of State for Scientific Research presented a statement before the TRIPS Council and responded to questions posed by Council members.[46] Egypt's review process involved the posing of a total of 239 questions exclusively by IC delegations (Canada, EC, Japan, Switzerland, and the United States) from as early as 1998, but mainly during the period September 2000 until November 2002. By far the largest number of questions was posed by the United States followed by the European

[40] Interview with Dr Mohamed Bahaa El-Din Fayez, National Research Centre, Cairo, in Cairo (5 May 2003) [hereinafter Fayez Interview].

[41] Specifically, TIPRE provided comments on the draft law to the Academy of Scientific Research on 22 Oct 2001, 26 Dec 2001, and 7 Jan 2002.

[42] Fayez Interview (n 40).

[43] INTELLECTUAL PROPERTY: PRINCIPLES AND PRACTICE (Jaleen Moroney ed 2003).

[44] ibid 8–16.

[45] WTO *TRIPS Council, Procedures for the Notification and Review of Legislation, Note by the Secretariat* JOB(99)/6928 (18 Nov 1999); and WTO *TRIPS Council, Members Whose Legislation is Scheduled to be Reviewed in 2001, Note by the Chairman* JOB(01)/4 (30 Jan 2001).

[46] Interview with HE Dr Moufid Shehab, Minister of Higher Education and of State for Scientific Research, in Cairo (4 May 2003) [hereinafter Shehab Interview].

Communities. This procedure was viewed by Dr Bahaa El-Din Fayez of the National Research Centre in Egypt, who was involved in drafting Egypt's responses, as one of the more visible instances of IC pressure on Egypt's TRIPS implementation.[47] Table 9.2 below offers a breakdown of the questions posed by date and by the IC delegation posing them. Reflecting the concerns of the ICs, these questions were intended as a thorough review of the IP regime of Egypt, as was carried out with other WTO members, and were concomitant with the discussion and drafting phase of Egypt's new IP legislation.

Table 9.2: Questions Posed by WTO Members on Egypt's IPR Regime[48]

	Until October 2001	October 2001–March 2002	March 2002–November 2002
Canada	3 Questions[49]	None	None
EC	60 Questions[50]	9 Questions[51]	None
Japan	1 Question[52]	None	None
Switzerland	11 Questions[53] 3 Questions[54]	None	None
United States	6 Questions[55] 45 Questions[56] 46 Questions[57] 7 Questions[58]	None	48 Questions[59]

[47] Fayez Interview (n 40).

[48] These questions were primarily posed within the context of the TRIPS Art 63.2 Review of Legislation, but also included questions posed within the context of the Implementation of TRIPS Art 70.

[49] WTO *TRIPS Council, Review of Legislation, Questions Posed by Canada* IP/C/W/261 (9 May 2001), and addendum IP/C/W/261/Add.1 (13 June 2001). Egypt's response in WTO *TRIPS Council, Review of Legislation, Responses from Egypt to questions posed by Canada and Switzerland, Addendum*, IP/C/W/278/Add.3 (29 Nov 2001).

[50] WTO *TRIPS Council, Review of Legislation, Questions Posed by the European Communities and their member States* IP/C/W/274 (12 June 2001). Egypt's response in WTO *TRIPS Council, Review of Legislation, Responses from Egypt to questions posed by the European Communities and their member States, Addendum* IP/C/W/278/Add.1 (14 Nov 2001).

[51] WTO *TRIPS Council, Review of Legislation, Follow-up Questions Posed by the European Communities and their member States to Egypt, Addendum* IP/C/W/274/Add.2 (8 Mar 2002). Egypt's response on file with author.

[52] WTO *TRIPS Council, Review of Legislation, Questions Posed by Japan* IP/C/W/258 (27 Apr 2001). Egypt's response in WTO *TRIPS Council, Review of Legislation, Responses from*

While the sum of these questions proved to be a thorough and exhaustive article-by-article examination of TRIPS implementation in Egypt, a pattern of questions repeated in different IC questionnaires point to specific concerns in the area of the implementation of pharmaceutical-related protection. In this regard, particular attention will be devoted to three specific areas of concern: (1) implementation of TRIPS Articles 70.8 and 70.9 concerning the mailbox provision and EMRs; (2) compulsory licensing; and (3) the protection of undisclosed information.

The United States posed specific questions to Egypt, among other DCs, concerning the implementation of Articles 70.8 and 70.9 that were to enter into force for all WTO members on 1 January 1995.[60] Primarily, the US questions dealt with the availability and procedure for implementing the mailbox provision of TRIPS Article 70.8. While Egypt had notified the details of the agency responsible for the receipt of patent applications for inventions in the field of pharmaceutical and agricultural chemical products (the Patent Office, affiliated to the Academy of Scientific Research),[61] the US query related to the legal basis for the filing and future handling of such applications in Egyptian legislation. Of greater concern to IC interests

Egypt to the questions posed by Japan, Switzerland and the United States IP/C/W/278 (12 June 2001). Question relates only to copyrights.

[53] WTO *TRIPS Council, Review of Legislation, Questions Posed by Switzerland* IP/C/W/263 (14 May 2001). Egypt's response in IP/C/W/278 (n 52) and IP/C/W/278/Add.3 (n 49).

[54] WTO *TRIPS Council, Review of Legislation, Follow-up Questions Posed by Switzerland, Addendum* IP/C/W/263/Add.1 (28 Aug 2001). Egypt's response in WTO *TRIPS Council, Review of Legislation, Responses from Egypt to follow-up questions posed by Switzerland and the United States* IP/C/W/278/Add.2 (14 Nov 2001).

[55] WTO *TRIPS Council, Implementation of Articles 70.8 and 70.9, Questions Posed by the United States* IP/C/W/113 (26 Oct 1998). Egypt's response in WTO *TRIPS Council, Implementation of Article 70.8 and 70.9* IP/C/W/136 (10 Mar 1999).

[56] WTO *TRIPS Council, Review of Legislation, Questions Posed by the United States* IP/C/W/215 (3 Oct 2000). Egypt's response in IP/C/W/278 (n 52).

[57] WTO *TRIPS Council, Review of Legislation, Questions Posed by the United States* IP/C/W/268 (31 May 2001). Egypt's response on file with author.

[58] WTO *TRIPS Council, Review of Legislation, Follow-up Questions Posed by the United States, Addendum* IP/C/W/268/Add.2 (5 July 2001). Egypt's response in IP/C/W/278/Add.2 (n 54).

[59] These last batch of US questions were unavailable to the author, but were referred to by Dr Mohamed Bahaa El-Din Fayez of the National Research Centre, Cairo Egypt. Fayez Interview (n 40).

[60] See (n 55). Similar concerns regarding the implementation of paragraphs 70.8 and 70.9 were also expressed by the European Communities and Japan. See WTO *TRIPS Council, Minutes of Meeting Held on 17 September 1998* IP/C/M/20 (15 Oct 1998) paras 12–13. The questions posed on the implementation of Arts 70.8 and 70.9 were technically separate from the review process of DCs IP legislation.

[61] IP/N/1/EGY/1 (n 4). By the time the US had posed these questions, at the end of 1998, the Egyptian Patent Office had received 439 patent applications relating to pharmaceutical or agricultural chemical products that have been dealt with in the mailbox system. See IP/C/W/136 (n 55).

however was the issue of the granting of EMRs as provided for under TRIPS Article 70.9. The US questions stressed a concern with the lack of legal or administrative arrangements for the issuance of EMRs. This concern, as expressed in the aforementioned questions, preceded and in a sense anticipated the Eli Lilly dispute mentioned above. The US pressure generated prompted the issuance in 2000 of a Prime Ministerial decree organizing the granting of EMRs.[62]

Secondly, both the European Communities and the United States posed questions concerning the regulation of compulsory licensing under proposed Egyptian legislation. Two of these questions requested a clarification concerning the availability of such licenses and the conditions that must be respected in issuing them.[63] Other questions dealt with more specific issues. In relation to TRIPS Article 31(b), the EC requested a definition of the 'efforts' that a proposed user should engage in to obtain authorization on reasonable commercial terms from the right-holder prior to an authorization for a compulsory licence, and equally, the definition of the 'reasonable period of time' that such efforts must be subject to.[64] Moreover, the EC also enquired about how authorization for a compulsory licence shall be 'predominantly for the supply of the domestic market'.[65] The United States directed its specific enquiries on how the safeguards in TRIPS Article 31(l) concerning authorization for the compulsory licensing of a related patent would be implemented in Egypt.[66] Egypt's response to these questions made specific reference to the provisions of the draft Egyptian IP law and how it was compliant with TRIPS Article 31.[67]

Finally, a third important cluster of questions posed by the EC, the US and Switzerland concerned the protection of undisclosed information. As will be discussed below, the protection of undisclosed information was to prove one of the more contentious issues during the drafting of the Egyptian IP legislation. DCs viewed such protection particularly as it related to the protection of test and other data submitted for the marketing approval of pharmaceutical or agricultural chemical products (TRIPS Article 39.3), to be another attempt by ICs and the pharmaceutical MNEs to reduce competition from local pharmaceutical industries, over and above the constraints imposed under the TRIPS patent provisions.[68] Both the United States and

[62] Prime Ministerial Decree No 547 for the year 2000 (8 Mar 2000).

[63] IP/C/W/274 (n 50) at Egypt Question no 35; and IP/C/W/268 (n 57) at Egypt Question no 29.

[64] IP/C/W/274 (n 50) at Egypt Question 36.

[65] ibid.

[66] IP/C/W/215 (n 56) at Egypt Question 26.

[67] IP/C/W/278 (n 52); IP/C/W/278/Add.1 (n 50); and Egypt's Response to the Revised Questions Posed by the United States (on file with author).

[68] Fayez Interview (n 42). See also Frederick M Abbott *The TRIPS Agreement, Access to Medicines and the WTO Doha Ministerial Conference* Quaker United Nations Office—Geneva, Occasional Paper No 7, 29–30 (2001).

Switzerland in their questions conveyed apprehension on the lack of specific mention of the protection of submitted test data against reliance on such data in granting marketing approval for subsequent applications for equivalent generic products.[69] This issue remains controversial. Another important aspect of IC questions in this regard concerned matters of definition, where the EC asked how did Egyptian draft legislation propose to define 'protection of data against unfair commercial use,' in addition to a question concerning the time period for such protection.[70] Egypt was to include a definition of such a term in Articles 58 and 59 of its new Patent Law.

(III) DRAFTING THE NEW EGYPTIAN IP LAW

A presidential decree on 20 March 1995 approved Egypt's accession to the World Trade Organization and its adherence to the Final Act Embodying the Results of the Uruguay Round of Multilateral Trade Negotiations and its Schedule of Commitments, effective from 1 January 1995.[71] While Egypt's international commitments for implementation of TRIPS had different cut-off dates, as indicated in Table 9.1 above, a law in conformity with TRIPS should have been in place by 1 January 2000.[72] However, it was only in June 2002, that a presidential decree promulgated Law No 82/2002 on the Protection of Intellectual Property Rights.[73] This section will examine the drafting process of the new IP law through its various stages and will examine the major contentious pharmaceutical-related issues that have arisen during this implementation process.

(A) Drafting at the Executive Branch

During 1996, Egypt had made commitments to its chief economic partner, the United States, to submit a draft of a suitable new patent law to parliament during its 1996 session.[74] However, it was not before the year 2000 that a new IPR law was approved by the cabinet, and submitted to parliament for approval in early 2001. In June 2001, an Egyptian delegation presented the new draft law to the TRIPS Council in Geneva.[75] With

[69] US in IP/C/W/268/Add.2 (n 58) Question 7; and Switzerland in IP/C/W/263/Add.1 (n 54) Additional Response to Question 9.

[70] IP/C/W/274/Add.2 (n 51) Follow-up Question to Question 46; and IP/C/W/274 (n 50) Question 44.

[71] Presidential Decree No 72 for 1995 (20 Mar 1995).

[72] With the exception of the waivers stipulated under TRIPS Art 65.4, relating inter alia to pharmaceutical product patenting, as Egypt decided to avail itself of it.

[73] Egypt 2002 IP Law.

[74] USTR 1996 National Trade Estimate Report on Foreign Trade Barriers—Egypt, 4 (on file with author).

[75] Please refer to Section II above.

further modifications, the law was not approved until June 2002. During this intervening period, and from the inception of its initial draft, the law passed through a number of executive committees and legislative committees in both houses of Egypt's legislative body. This process was contingent on the constitutional directives of each country and hence with an inherent specificity to each.[76] Yet in moving beyond these specificities, an image may be discerned concerning the degree of resistance and/or support TRIPS implementation experienced as reflected in this law making exercise.

Of two possible methods, Egypt opted for the drafting of a new single IP law to encompass all the different categories of IP, rather than modifying its pre-existing IP laws.[77] An initial draft of the law was prepared by the Ministry of State for Scientific Research, being the ministry with chief responsibility for the patent and undisclosed information provisions of the draft law, and presented in June 1999 to the Ministry of Justice where a special committee was formed, comprising the membership of the various pertinent ministries to undertake the task of preparing a draft to be presented to the Council of Ministers.[78] It becomes apparent at this stage of the draft laws' history that a rivalry was emerging over the patent provisions between the Ministry of Health on the one hand, and other ministries, chiefly the Ministry of State for Scientific Research, on the other.[79] A former senior Ministry of Health official who was involved in the drafting process noted that initially, the draft law reflected a bias towards Research and Development interests.[80] This however, as he qualified, was ameliorated following a meeting between the Minister of Health and the chair of the Special Committee at the Ministry of Justice in 2000.

The draft then proceeded for examination at the level of the Council of Ministers. It was approved in principle on 6 June 2000, pending its review by a Ministerial Committee that included, inter alia, the Ministers of Economy and Foreign Trade, Health and Population, Supply and Internal

[76] In this regard, we are cautioned that '...*the national legal system can have a profound impact on the extent to which the international obligations are faithfully followed. Among the critical issues here are the status of the international obligation in domestic law, and the structure of the domestic judicial system that enforces domestic law.*' See IMPLEMENTING THE URUGUAY ROUND 5 (John Jackson and Alan Sykes eds 1997).

[77] El Hadary Interview (n 18). Moreover, Dr Fayez noted that the eventual division of the new law into 'Books' each dealing with a particular type of IP, was consciously emulated from the French IP regime, Fayez Interview (n 40).

[78] The Ministry of Justice's special committee was headed by Counsellor Serry Siam, Assistant Minister of Justice for Legislative Affairs, established by Decision No 5 on 3 Nov 1999, with a mandate for the final preparation of a draft IP law, based on the input from the various relevant ministries, to be presented to the Cabinet of Ministers. See Dr Moufid Shehab, Minister of Higher Education and of State for Scientific Research Address at the Conference on Intellectual Property and its Effects on Development in Egypt, 12 (21 Jan 2002) (transcript on file with author) [hereinafter Shehab 2002 Address].

[79] El Hadary Interview (n 18).

[80] ibid.

Trade, Industry, and Military Production.[81] During this phase of the consideration of the draft, input was sought not only from the various ministries and legal experts appointed to the committee,[82] but equally from certain interested NGOs, representing the various domestic stakeholders.[83] Having performed its mandate throughout the summer and early autumn of 2000, the Committee presented the results to the Council of Ministers on 4 October 2000, and once more on 4 January 2001.[84]

(B) Drafting at the Legislative Branch

Following this stage of consideration within the cabinet, the draft law was passed from the executive towards the legislative branch. The upper house of parliament, the Shura Council, received the draft for examination in February 2001, where it was reviewed first by an ad hoc joint committee comprising the membership of the relevant committees and then by the Council's plenary.[85] The draft law was approved within the Council following modifications agreed to by the relevant ministers.[86] In April 2001, the draft proceeded to its final legislative stage at the lower house of parliament, the People's Assembly. At the Assembly, it was put under the agenda of the Committee on Education and Scientific Research in view of the fact that the cabinet member in charge of the draft law was the Minister of Higher Education and Scientific Research.[87] It was mainly during the 2001/2002 parliamentary session that intensive deliberations occurred over the draft law, within a joint committee representing the committees on constitutional and legislative affairs, economic affairs, industry, energy, agriculture and irrigation, culture, information, and tourism.[88] Finally, the draft law was approved by the People's Assembly and promulgated by the President on 2 June 2002. Its executive regulations were released in August 2003.[89]

This process of legislative implementation was characterized by a thorough debate of the issues involved, prompting a senior participant in the

[81] Interview with Dr Fawzy Al-Rifaey, President of the Academy of Scientific Research and Technology, in Cairo (4 May 2003).

[82] The legal experts serving on the committee included Professor Hossam Al-Saghir and Dr Mohamed Hossam Loutfi. It also included experts from the public research community, most notably Dr Mohamed Bahaa El-Din Fayez from the National Research Centre, and Dr Raouf Hamed from the National Organization for Drug Control and Research.

[83] Submissions received included those from the Egyptian Society for the Protection of Intellectual Property, the Association of Egyptian Inventors and Innovators, and the Federation of Egyptian Industries. The author wishes to thank Dr Fawzy Al- Rifaey for making this information available.

[84] Shehab 2002 Address (n 78) 13.

[85] ibid.

[86] ibid.

[87] Fayez Interview (n 40).

[88] Shehab 2002 Address (n 78) 13–14.

[89] Prime Ministerial Decree No 1366 for 2003 (16 Aug 2003).

process to describe it as one of the most democratic and open of the debates of the Egyptian Parliament.[90] Key domestic stakeholders attempted to push their particular interests, in addition to foreign stakeholders, namely the pharmaceutical MNEs and the leading IC, the United States. Moreover, the debate transfixed at points on particular issues that served to highlight the contested nature of the implementation process.

Throughout the drafting process, the Ministry of Health, conscious of the implications TRIPS implementation was likely to have on the pharmaceutical sector, lobbied for two main demands. Primarily, it sought a provision giving it, rather than the Patent Office, the right to examine patent applications pertaining to pharmaceutical products, given its chief concern in balancing the application with public health priorities.[91] As alluded to above, this demand was brought to the attention of the USAID-funded SIPRE Project, which advised the Egyptian government against it, cautioning that Egypt should not undertake such a step.[92] This demand, argued SIPRE, would have entailed breaches of Paris Convention Article 12(1), and TRIPS Articles 27.1, 41, and 62.[93] Eventually, a watered down version was adopted in the promulgated law in its Article 17, wherein the Patent Office is obliged to send to the Ministry of Health, inter alia, copies of patent applications with a health value, with the Minister of Health having the right to object to the patent grant.

The second demand by the MoH was a provision establishing a fund for medicines, to ameliorate the consequences of an expected rise in the prices of pharmaceutical products.[94] Such a fund was to be established in Article 18 of the new law, to be regulated by a presidential decree, and put under the direction of the Minister of Health. It must be acknowledged that placement of such a provision in the midst of an IP law is ambiguous, where the establishment of a fund for medicines has no connection to the protection of IP. Nonetheless, its inclusion reinforces the prevailing mood among legislators—or at least of one party among them—that the impact of the new IP law, in implementing TRIPS standards, would have the effect of substantially increasing the prices of pharmaceutical products. Legislating for the establishment of the fund was therefore deemed a regulatory provision to address this 'side-effect'.

While the demands put forth by the MoH offers a glimpse into the stakes involved in TRIPS implementation by different government agencies, the

[90] Fayez Interview (n 40).

[91] El Hadary Interview (n 18).

[92] Legal Issues Regarding Proposal to Transfer Patent Examination of Pharmaceutical Patent Applications to the Ministry of Health and Population, Memorandum prepared by Judy Winegar Goans USAID SIPRE Project (13 Jan 2001) (on file with author).

[93] ibid.

[94] El Hadary Interview (n 18).

parliamentary debate was also fuelled and followed from within by the interests of the local pharmaceutical manufacturers. Two very influential parliamentarians played centre stage in this debate. In the Shura Council, Dr Tharwat Bassily, Chairman of Amoun Co, a major local pharmaceutical company, acted as deputy chairman of the Health Committee. Also in the Shura Council, Dr Galal Ghorab, Chairman of the Holding Company for Pharmaceuticals and Chemicals, and acting as the Chairman of the Health Committee, whom we alluded to earlier in his success in opposing pressure to forgo the transitional period, proved a vociferous defender of the interests of the local pharmaceutical companies. Finally, in the People's Assembly, Dr Hamdy El Sayed, Head of the Medical Union, and chairman of the Health Committee maintains strong criticism of TRIPS and of its implementation in Egypt. Indeed, these parliamentarians and local pharmaceutical magnates were described by one commentator as presenting one pole of the debate on implementation counterpoised to the individuals representing the pharmaceutical MNE interests, Roshdy and El Hakim, of Pfizer.[95]

(C) Contentious Issues

Particular issues arose pertaining to TRIPS implementation in the Egyptian context that would prove contentious, not only during the drafting of the law, but similarly, following its promulgation. Three particular issues are worth emphasizing in this regard: (1) the debate concerning whether or not to make use of the extension period stipulated by TRIPS Article 65.4; (2) the establishment of a mailbox system and issuance of EMRs as stipulated by TRIPS Articles 70.8 and 70.9; and (3) the implementation of the provisions on undisclosed information of TRIPS Article 39.

The debate on whether or not Egypt should avail itself of the extension period for applying product patent protection to pharmaceuticals pursuant to TRIPS Article 65.4 raged as early as 1999, and was viewed by some analysts as one of the main reasons for the delay in promulgating the new IP law.[96] Apart from the pressure exerted in this regard by the United States, the pharmaceutical MNEs lobbied the Egyptian government to forgo this extension, and alluded to possible additional investment as an enticement.[97] The MNEs and the United States had persuaded the Egyptian Patent Office (EPO) and the Minister of Health to forego this transitional period. Indeed, there were some voices within the government as well as among Egyptian legal experts that deemed the extension to be of minimal

[95] ibid.

[96] Al-Ali (2003) (n 2) 295.

[97] According to Dr El Hadary and Dr Fayez, the offers were made by Pfizer, Eli Lilly and MSD. El Hadary Interview (n 18); and Fayez Interview (n 40).

real value,[98] due to the countervailing nature of EMRs that would have provided MNEs with a monopoly over their new pharmaceutical products in any case. One such attempt was made through the auspices of the Egyptian Foreign Ministry to convene local Egyptian specialists to study a possible deal with the ICs, mainly the US, on a possible early implementation of product patent protection for pharmaceuticals.[99] This was vehemently opposed by Dr Galal Ghorab, chairman of the Holding Company for Pharmaceuticals and Chemicals (the umbrella grouping of public sector companies in that field), and acting chairman of the Upper House of Parliament's Health Committee.[100] Ultimately, a decision was made by the government to make full use of the waiver until 1 January 2005.

On another requirement, concerning the implementation of TRIPS Articles 70.8 and 70.9, Egypt's commitments were to come into effect as of 1 January 1995. Egypt was more forthright in implementing Article 70.8 mailbox commitment, although still going beyond its deadline. In September 1995, its mission to the WTO notified the TRIPS Council that the 'Egyptian Patent Office affiliated to the Academy of Scientific Research is the agency in charge of receiving patent applications for inventions in the field of pharmaceutical and agricultural chemical products.'[101] However, this notification still lacked precise information, prompting the United States through its WTO Mission, to pose questions to Egypt to clarify its implementation of Articles 70.8 and 70.9.[102] As previously discussed, these questions pointed to the vacuum in Egyptian legislation concerning pharmaceutical and agricultural chemical protection.

These questions also alluded to the lack of information concerning the agency authorized to issue EMRs as stipulated in Article 70.9.[103] The defensive posture of Egypt's replies to increasing US pressure, as well as pressure from the EC for implementation of Article 70.9, relied mainly on general remarks about the commitment of the Egyptian Patent Office to TRIPS provisions. Reference was also made to specific articles in the draft IP law, then under consideration by the legislative committee of the Cabinet.[104] However, a critical juncture was reached in 1999, when the US

[98] One such legal expert is Dr Hossam Loutfi, who commended the path taken by Jordan in this regard where it reached a deal with the MNEs. Interview with Dr Hossam Loutfi, Attorney at Law, in Cairo (6 May 2003).

[99] Interview with Dr Raouf Hamed, National Organization for Drug Control and Research, in Cairo (3 May 2003).

[100] See Al-Ali (2003) (n 2) 295–6.

[101] IP/N/1/EGY/1 (n 4).

[102] These questions were simultaneously posed to Argentina, Egypt, Paraguay and Uruguay. See IP/C/W/113 (n 55). Please refer to Ch 8 above.

[103] ibid.

[104] Egypt's replies to the questions posed by the US delegation concerning the implementation of Art 70 are contained in IP/C/W/136 (n 55).

pharmaceutical MNE, Eli Lilly, requested the MoH to issue it with an EMR for its product, Zyprexa.[105] The MoH declined the request citing that while there might be international obligations for Egypt under TRIPS, yet there was as of yet no Egyptian legislation in this regard.[106] Following intense lobbying by the pharmaceutical MNEs and the United States,[107] it was not until March 2000 that Egypt issued a Prime Ministerial decree to fulfil its commitments for issuing EMRs.[108] The Decree stipulated that the Egyptian Patent Office would have the power to issue certificates of exclusive marketing rights, as stipulated under TRIPS Article 70.9. This was later codified in the new IP law in its Articles 43 and 44.[109]

Finally, the third contentious issue to arise during TRIPS implementation in Egypt concerned provisions on undisclosed information. While this issue involved an element of the TRIPS Agreement not relating to standards on patent protection, yet its significance to the pharmaceutical industry was considerable. A battle ensued between the MoH and the pharmaceutical MNEs over whether generic producers, in seeking marketing approval for a generic product, could rely on test data submitted earlier for an equivalent proprietary product, and whether this would constitute 'unfair commercial use'. This became notorious as it involved Pfizer's Viagra, where local producers began production of generic versions, and were accused by Pfizer of breaching its 'data exclusivity' presented for marketing approval.[110] The MoH, El Hadary argued, believed that the information in its possession, if used by others to seek marketing approval for their products, would not represent a case of 'unfair commercial use.'[111] Ultimately, the new law defined a period of protection of five years from the date of submission of the information to the competent government authority, or until it is no longer confidential, whichever comes first.[112] This was considered by Dr Fayez of the National Research Centre to constitute a TRIPS-plus provision in Egypt's new law, as he pointed out that Article 39.3 of TRIPS did not specify a particular time period for such protection.[113]

The examination above reveals that the implementation process in Egypt was characterized by considerable discussions and contention among the different stakeholders. The involvement of the pharmaceutical MNEs and ICs, most notably the United States, in this process in Egypt was quite visi-

[105] El Hadary Interview (n 18).

[106] ibid.

[107] ibid.

[108] Prime Ministerial Decree No 547 for the year 2000 (8 Mar 2000).

[109] For an account on certain peculiarities in the text of these Articles, see Al-Ali (n 2)300–301.

[110] El Hadary Interview (n 18). See also Abeer Allam *Seeking Investment, Egypt Tries Patent Laws* NY TIMES (4 Oct 2002).

[111] El Hadary Interview (n 18).

[112] Egypt 2002 IP Law, Art 56.

[113] Fayez Interview (n 40)

ble through direct pressure, lobbying, and in the case of the US, through the provision of targeted technical assistance. On the other hand, not all DC domestic stakeholders viewed TRIPS implementation negatively. Indeed, in Egypt some quarters view positive gains both to their direct interests and more generally to the economic interest of Egypt.[114] Similarly, some quarters in DCs, including Egypt, have found it in their interests to exaggerate the negative and impedimentary impact of TRIPS implementation on the pharmaceutical and health sectors. This tendency was referred to by Egypt's Minister of Higher Education and Scientific Research, prompting him to argue that an examination of TRIPS and its implications ought to occur within more balanced light, without being seen as purely representing 'evil.'[115] Nonetheless, there emerged a strong resistance in Egypt to implementing the TRIPS standards of patent protection as they related to pharmaceuticals. The fact of Egypt's eventual adoption of those standards did not decrease this opposition, and it is expected that such opposition will flare once again in the aftermath of the introduction of pharmaceutical product patenting in 2005.[116] In the following chapter, an examination of the new post-TRIPS patent legislation in Egypt is compared to those of other DCs.

[114] See Rehab El-Bakry *Crushed Hopes* BUS TODAY EGYPT (Cairo) (Apr 2003). See also *Huquq Al-Milkeya Al-Fikreya wa Sira'a Al-Aqweyaa wal Du'afaa* [Intellectual Property Rights and the Struggle of the Strong and the Weak] AL-AHRAM AL-IQTISADI (Cairo) (14 Apr 2003) 44–49.
[115] See Dr Moufid Shehab Minister of Higher Education and of State for Scientific Research, Address at the Annual Conference on Intellectual Property, Faculty of Laws, Cairo University, 23 (17 Feb 2003) (transcript on file with author) [hereinafter Shehab 2003 Address].
[116] Interview with Dr Hamdy El Sayed, Head of the Egyptian Medical Union and Chairman, Health Committee, People's Assembly, Cairo (6 Apr 2004) [hereinafter El Sayed Interview].

Chapter 10

Status of DC Law Post-TRIPS Implementation

Despite the considerable resistance, discussed earlier, to the implementation of the TRIPS patent standards into the domestic legislation of Egypt, as was the case in other DCs, these standards were eventually adopted. After all, these were obligations that members of the WTO were required to comply with in an international agreement binding upon them. In Chapter 7, the more contentious aspects of the pre-TRIPS patent legislation of Argentina, Brazil, Egypt, and India were compared. Extending this comparative analysis, we consider here the set of legislation of these same DCs after the fact; in other words, their post-TRIPS legislation. The focus in this appraisal of post-TRIPS patent legislation will be on three aspects, namely: (1) transitional provisions including specific provisions on pharmaceutical product patenting; (2) general provisions, including patentability requirements and exclusions from patentabilty, as well as rights conferred and exceptions thereto; and (3) compulsory licensing and working requirements.

According to TRIPS Article 1.1, members are required to give effect to the provisions of the Agreement according to the appropriate method of implementation within their own legal system and practice. Under TRIPS Article 65.2 DCs were granted a five-year transitional period to apply TRIPS provisions. By 1 January 2000, DCs were expected to be in full compliance with TRIPS. However, Article 65.4 provided DCs that were required to extend product patent protection to areas of technology that were not so protectable in their territory on the general date of TRIPS application (including most importantly pharmaceutical products), a further transitional period of five years to do so ending on 31 December 2004. However, notwithstanding either of these transitional periods, DCs were required to provide a mailbox system for pharmaceutical product patent applications and the issuance of exclusive marketing rights according to the stipulations of paragraphs 8 and 9 of Article 70.

(I) TRANSITIONAL PROVISIONS

Transitional periods were to apply equally to Argentina, Brazil, Egypt, and India, as with other DCs. However, the response of the four countries varied with that of Argentina and Brazil in particular being quite different from those of Egypt and India. Both Argentina and Brazil proceeded to implement their patent laws well in advance of the 1 January 2000 deadline of compliance with TRIPS standards. This is primarily attributable to intense PhRMA and US pressure.[1] Argentina's new law was initially released and entered into force on 23 October 1995, but modified and re-issued in March 1996.[2] Brazil's new law was issued in May 1996 and entered into force on 15 May 1997.[3] On the other hand, Egypt and India enacted new TRIPS-compliant legislation in June 2002, thus going beyond the TRIPS mandated transitional period. Egypt issued its new law in June 2002,[4] and India issued a major amendment to its Patents Act 1970 in the same month.[5]

More significant still was the variance between the four countries regarding the date on which patent protection would be extended to pharmaceutical products. Both Egypt and India opted to make full use of their TRIPS Article 65.4 privilege, delaying patent protection to pharmaceutical products until 1 January 2005. In repealing its old patent law, Egypt exempted from this repeal and until 1 January 2005 provisions concerning the exclusion from patentability of chemical products relating to food or medicine.[6] India's Patent (Amendment) Act 2002 maintained the exclusion of pharmaceutical products from patentability, and required a further amendment to the Act that would institute such protection effective 1 January 2005.[7] On the other hand, Argentina excluded pharmaceutical products from patent protection for a period of five years from the date of publication of the law, rather than the 10-year period allowed under TRIPS Article 65.4.[8] Finally, Brazil's 1996 industrial property law did not differentiate with regard to the extension of patent protection to pharmaceutical products where similar to

[1] In the case of Argentina, see Kimberley A Czub *Argentina's Emerging Standard of Intellectual Property Protection: A Case Study of the Underlying Conflicts Between Developing Countries, TRIPS Standards, and the United States* 33 CASE WESTERN RESERVE J INT'L L 191, 191–201 (2001). In the case of Brazil, see Naomi A Bass *Implications of the TRIPS Agreement for Developing Countries: Pharmaceutical Patent Laws in Brazil and South Africa in the 21st Century* 34 GEO WASH INT'L L REV 191, 206–10 (2002).

[2] Law No 24.481 on Patents and Utility Models (as amended by Law No 24.572) (20 Mar 1996) [hereinafter Argentina 1996 Patent Law].

[3] Law No 9.279 to Regulate Rights and Obligations Relating to Industrial Property (14 May 1996) [hereinafter Brazil 1996 IP Law].

[4] Law on the Protection of Intellectual Property Rights No 82 of 2002 (2 June 2002) [hereinafter Egypt 2002 IP Law].

[5] Patents (Amendment) Act No 38 of 2002 (25 June 2002) [hereinafter India Patents (Amendment) Act 2002].

[6] Presidential Decree issuing Law No 82 of 2002, Art 2(b).

[7] Consultations on this revision is currently ongoing in India. See Ministry of Commerce and Industry, Department of Industrial Policy and Promotion, *Interactive Session on Amendments to the Patents Act, 1970—Background Note*, available at <http://www.patentoffice. nic.in/ipr/patent/ int_session.pdf (last visited 22 Mar 2004).

[8] Argentina 1996 Patent Law Art 100.

all other subject matter they became patentable on the entry into force of the law on 15 May 1997. Therefore, Brazil opted to forego its TRIPS Article 65.4 privilege.[9]

Given their decision to make use of their option to delay the introduction of patent protection for pharmaceutical products, Argentina, Egypt, and India had the corresponding obligation to apply TRIPS Article 70 provisions concerning the introduction of a mailbox system and a system to issue EMRs. Brazil on the other hand, given its admission of pharmaceutical product patenting without a transitional period had no obligation in this regard. Egypt's enactment of provisions setting a mailbox system and issuing EMRs was covered in the previous chapter. The common thread across Argentina, Egypt and India with regard to the mailbox and EMRs commitments is that they were only forthcoming following the exertion of US pressure. As reviewed in the earlier chapter, Egypt issued a decree to regulate the grant of EMRs belatedly in 2000 following US intervention. In the case of India, its delay in implementing these provisions was the subject of two WTO dispute settlement cases initiated by the US and the EC.[10] Eventually, India in 1999, amended section 5 of its Patents Act on the exclusion of pharmaceutical products from patenting through the insertion of a new sub-clause that effectuates the receipt of applications into the mailbox.[11] Furthermore, this amendment introduced a new 'Chapter IVA' into India's legislation that regulated the examination of applications for the grant of EMRs.[12] Finally, Argentina's new law instituted a mailbox system through a provision allowing the receipt of patent applications for pharmaceutical products, which could only be granted at the entry into effect of pharmaceutical product patenting five years following the publication of the law.[13] This provision however, failed to establish a system for the grant of EMRs, and consequently, Argentina's failure to comply with TRIPS in this regard was a cause that initiated a request for consultations by the United States under the WTO DSU mechanism.[14]

[9] This was despite considerable domestic opposition. See *Brazil's Lower House Passes Bill to Protect Intellectual Property* 13 Int'l Trade Rep (BNA) (17 Apr 1996).

[10] The India WTO disputes will be discussed in Chapter 11.

[11] India Patents (Amendment) Act 1999 § 2, amending § 5 of the Patents Act 1970.

[12] India Patents (Amendment) Act 1999 § 3, inserting a new Chapter IVA into the Patents Act 1970.

[13] Argentina 1996 Patent Law Art 101.

[14] On the US–Argentina consultations, please refer to Ch 11.

(II) GENERAL PROVISIONS

(A) Patentability Requirements and Exclusions from Patentability

With regard to patentability requirements, there were noticeable changes in the post-TRIPS legislation concerning the criteria for patentability. The three key criteria, namely: novelty, inventive step, and industrial application, have been explicitly referred to in the laws of Argentina (Article 4), Brazil (Article 8), Egypt (Article 1), and India.[15] Moreover, their post-TRIPS legislation proceeded to exhaustively define these terms. In the case of the laws of Argentina (Article 6) and Brazil (Article 10), they list for the first time subject matter that would not be considered an invention.[16]

The most significant changes however, concerned the earlier exclusions from patentability. As reviewed earlier, the exclusion of pharmaceutical products from patentability was prevalent in the patent laws of these four DCs and was a key issue during the TRIPS negotiations. The situation changed drastically under the new legislation. Argentina under Article 1 of its new patent law specified that protection would be available to '*inventions of all kinds in all areas of production*'. Apart from the deferment of pharmaceutical product patenting as examined above, the only exclusions from patentability were enumerated in Article 7 reflecting the exclusions from patentability specified in TRIPS Articles 27.2 and 27.3. These included inventions the exploitation of which is to be prevented in the interest of public good or morality and to protect human and animal life and the environment, as well as all biological and genetic material existing in nature or derived from it. Likewise, Brazil considerably narrowed the exclusions from patentability under its new industrial property law. Under Article 18 (III) of Brazil's legislation, the exclusions were similar to those in Article 7 of Argentina's law with the addition of substances or products of any kind resulting from the transformation of the atomic nucleus. Therefore, the earlier exclusions from patentability of pharmaceutical products in the case of Argentina, and of both pharmaceutical products and processes in the case of Brazil, were repealed.

Egypt's new patent law unifies exclusions from patentability under Article 2 comprising exclusions similar to those of Argentina and Brazil. On the other hand, India maintained the exclusions from patentability in its Patents Act 1970, namely those relating to the exclusion from patentability

15 India Patents (Amendment) Act 2002 § 3(f), amending § 2 of the Patents Act 1970.

16 India's Patent Act 1970 § 3, already referred to what were not to be considered inventions, but these were further refined in the Patents (Amendment) Act 2002 § 4. Egypt's law on the other hand does not make reference specifically to what are not to be considered inventions, but includes them under the general category of exclusions from patentability, see Egypt 2002 IP Law Art 2.

of an invention relating to atomic energy,[17] and substances intended for use, or capable of being used as food or as medicine or drug.[18] Contrary to Argentina and Brazil, but similar to Egypt, India therefore opted to make full use of its transitional period under TRIPS Article 65.4.

(B) Rights Conferred and Exceptions

The standards on the rights conferred by a patent were listed under TRIPS Article 28. The post-TRIPS patent legislation of Argentina, Brazil and India closely follow the wording of this TRIPS article. Brazil and India offer the patent owner the right to exclude others not having his consent from the acts of manufacturing, using, offering for sale, selling or importing the product or the process subject of the patent.[19] Argentina's law in Article 8, offers such exclusive rights to patents on products, however for patents on processes it only offers protection against third parties' 'use' of the process. These rights were considerably more detailed than those existing in the pre-TRIPS patent laws of Argentina and Brazil that were more succinct extending only to the general terms of 'working' or 'use'. In this respect, Article 10 of Egypt's new law does not modify the spirit of its old legislation maintaining that a patent shall confer on its owner '*the right to prevent a third party from exploiting the invention by any means*'. Arguably such wording confers wider rights to patent owners where the use of the words '*by any means*' encompasses all possible use, subject of course to the statutory exceptions stipulated in that same article.

Elaborations on rights conferred to patentees in post-TRIPS legislation, were similarly matched by elaborations in exceptions to rights conferred in the laws of Argentina (Article 36), Brazil (Article 43), and Egypt (Article 10), while India had already encompassed those elaborations in its 1970 Patent Act (sections 47 and 49). These exceptions include research or academic activities, private non-commercial use, the preparation of a medicine in accordance with a medical prescription in individual cases, and the temporary transit in the territory of a vehicle encompassing a patented invention. Moreover, Brazil under Article 45, and Egypt under Article 10 (2) make exceptions to prior use. More interestingly, the laws of Argentina (Article 36(c)) and Egypt (Article 10) both explicitly confirm a regime of international exhaustion, where they allow for parallel importation by third parties as an exception to the rights conferred by a patent.

[17] India Patents Act 1970 § 4.

[18] ibid § 5.

[19] Brazil 1996 IP Law Art 42; and India Patents (Amendment) Act 2002 § 25, amending § 48 of the Patents Act 1970.

Finally, it must be mentioned that the patent term, being one of the main criticisms against DC patent laws in the pre-TRIPS era, was mandated according to TRIPS Article 33 to be for a minimum period of 20 years from the date of filing. As such, the laws of the four DCs considered here all subscribed to a patent term of twenty years from filing.[20]

(III) COMPULSORY LICENSING AND WORKING REQUIREMENTS

The post-TRIPS patent laws of the four DCs under review have undergone significant changes with regard to compulsory licensing and working provisions compared to the situation prior to TRIPS. In the case of Argentina, the post-TRIPS law under its Chapter VIII, introduced for the first time provisions on compulsory licences which concept did not exist in the old law. Another major change has been the cancellation in India's new act of the pre-TRIPS concept of 'licences of right.' Furthermore, the grounds for issuing compulsory licences, while not limited under TRIPS provisions, have been spelt out in more detail in post-TRIPS DC legislation. Ultimately, these laws came to resemble more closely the provisions set under TRIPS Article 31 concerning the conditions that must be met in issuing a compulsory license. The provisions on compulsory licences in the laws of Argentina, Brazil, and Egypt exhibit more common characteristics. On the other hand, as noted with regard to its pre-TRIPS patent law, the compulsory licensing provisions in India's law maintained their special characteristic vis-à-vis those of the three other DCs.

The most common grounds for issuing a compulsory licence in the new patent laws of the four DCs included: (1) lack of working or exploitation; (2) emergency situations or national security considerations; and (3) as pertains dependent or related patents. With regard to lack or insufficiency of working, the post-TRIPS legislation followed the conditions set out in Article 5A of the Paris Convention. Accordingly, a compulsory licence based on non-working or insufficiency of working can only be issued following the passage of three years from the grant of the patent or four years from the date of filing, and is subject to '*force majeure*' exceptions to the benefit of the patent holder. Argentina, as discussed above, included such provisions in its new law for the first time.[21] Brazil, Egypt, and India rephrased their provisions on this ground of issuing a compulsory licence,

[20] Argentina 1996 Patent Law art 35; Brazil 1996 IP Law Art 40; Egypt 2002 IP Law Art 9; and India Patents (Amendment) Act 2002 § 27(a), amending § 53(1) of the Patents Act 1970. India's act provides a retroactive effect on patents which have not expired on the date of entry into force of the Patents (Amendment) Act 2002 to make use of this 20-year patent term from their date of filing.

[21] Argentina 1996 Patent Law Art 43.

but the specifics remained largely unchanged.[22] However, in allowing the issuance on grounds of interruption of working, Egypt's new law reduces the time period of interruption after which such a license may be issued, from two years as was the case in the old law to one year.[23]

More importantly, the four laws differ on the question of what constituted working or exploitation. Argentina's law does not define what is meant by exploitation. Brazil and Egypt define it as manufacturing of the patented product or use of the patented product within their respective territories.[24] This definition was controversial in view of TRIPS Article 27.1 that prohibits discrimination as to whether products are imported or locally produced. This issue was taken up by the United States in its request for consultations with Brazil under the DSU, as will be discussed in Part Four of this book. India does not explicitly define working under its amended patents act. However, under another ground for issuing a compulsory licensing, namely that of the 'reasonable requirements of the public' not being met, it states that these reasonable requirements would not have been met '*if the working of the patented invention in the territory of India . . . is being prevented or hindered by the importation from abroad of the patented article . . .* '[25] Therefore, this must also be considered an indirect definition of working as local manufacturing.

Another important ground for issuing compulsory licences included emergencies, national security, situations of extreme urgency, and public interest.[26] Most notably, the four laws examined make reference to health issues as a basis for this grant. Specifically, Brazil issued a Decree regulating compulsory licences that explicitly included under the remit of public interest facts related to public health.[27] Likewise, India also includes public health crises relating to AIDS, HIV, tuberculosis, malaria or other epidemics, under this remit.[28] Other grounds cited include compulsory licences for dependent or related patents.[29] Argentina (Article 44), Brazil (Article 68), and Egypt (Article 23(5)), also allow issuance of a compulsory licence to remedy anti-competitive practices. Furthermore, Argentina (Article 42) and Egypt (Article 23(3)) include refusal to deal, in other words refusal to issue a voluntary licence on reasonable terms, as a ground for issuing a compulsory licence.

22 Brazil 1996 IP Law Art 68(1); Egypt 2002 IP Law Art 23(4); and India Patents (Amendment) Act 2002 § 39, amending § 84(1)(c) of the Patents Act 1970.

23 Egypt 2002 IP Law Art 23(4).

24 Brazil 1996 IP Law Art 68(1)(I); and Egypt 2002 IP Law Art 23(4).

25 India Patents (Amendment) Act 2002 § 39, amending § 84(7)(e) of the Patents Act 1970.

26 Argentina 1996 Patent Law Art 45; Brazil 1996 IP Law Art 71; Egypt 2002 IP Law Art 23(1); and India Patents (Amendment) Act 2002 § 39, amending § 92 of the Patents Act 1970.

27 Decree No 3.201 on Patents (Compulsory Licenses) (6 Oct 1999) Art 2(2).

28 India Patents (Amendment) Act 2002 § 39, amending § 92(3) of the Patents Act 1970.

29 Argentina 1996 Patent Law Art 46; Brazil 1996 IP Law Art 70; Egypt 2002 IP Law Art 23(6); and India Patents (Amendment) Act 2002 § 39, amending § 91 of the Patents Act 1970.

Egypt's new law is unique in singling out a particular product, medicines, where the Minister of Health may request a compulsory licence if, inter alia, the quantity of a certain medicine fails to adequately meet the national need, if it is offered at a prohibitive price, or if it relates to critical cases.[30] While this might be interpreted as a violation of TRIPS Article 27.1 prohibition on discrimination as to field of technology, so far its legality under TRIPS has not been challenged. Finally, the provisions on compulsory licenses in India's amended patents act, as mentioned earlier, maintained the wide stipulation that allows the issuance of a compulsory licence on the grounds that the '*reasonable requirements of the public with respect to the patented invention have not been satisfied. . . .*'[31] This provision is consistent with TRIPS, as the latter does not limit the grounds for issuing a compulsory licence.

While TRIPS does not regulate the grounds for issuing compulsory licensing, however, it sets in its Article 31 specific conditions that must be met in issuing such licences. The legislation of the four DCs examined comply with such conditions. These conditions include the duty on the applicant for a compulsory licence to engage in negotiations with the right holder prior to seeking such a licence.[32] Equally, the right holder is entitled to reasonable remuneration in case of the issuance of a compulsory licence.[33] The applicant for a compulsory licence must also prove that he has an interest in seeking such a licence, and that he possesses the economic and technical ability to work the patented invention.[34] Furthermore, the license must be non-exclusive and non-assignable.[35] Another important condition is that the decision regarding the grant of the compulsory licence and the remuneration accorded the right holder, must be subject to review.[36] Finally, an important condition mentioned in TRIPS Article 31, is that compulsory licences must be considered on an individual basis. Both Argentina (Article 47(b)) and Egypt (Article 24(1)) make explicit reference to this condition. On the other hand, Brazil (Article 73(6)) makes a reference to this condition only within the context of the remuneration to be accorded the right holder, while India does not make reference to this condi-

30 Egypt 2002 IP Law Art 23(2).

31 India Patents (Amendment) Act 2002 § 39, amending § 84(1)(a) of the Patents Act 1970.

32 Argentina 1996 Patent Lawarts 42 and 47(c); Brazil 1996 IP Law Art 73; Egypt 2002 IP Law Art 24(2); and India Patents Act 1970 § 84(6)(iv).

33 Argentina 1996 Patent Law Arts 43 and 47(h); Brazil 1996 IP Law Art 73; Egypt 2002 IP Law Art 24(8); and India Patents Act 1970 § 90(1)(i).

34 Argentina 1996 Patent Law Art 50; Brazil 1996 IP Law Art 68(2); Egypt 2002 IP Law Art 24(4); and India Patents Act 1970 §§ 84(6)(ii) and 84(6)(iii).

35 Argentina 1996 Patent Law Arts 47(e) and 47(f); Brazil 1996 IP Law Arts 72 and 74(3); Egypt 2002 IP Law Art 24(7); and India Patents Act 1970 §§ 90(1)(iv) and 90(1)(v).

36 Argentina 1996 Patent Law Art 48; Brazil 1996 IP Law Art 73(8); Egypt 2002 IP Law Art 24(3); and India Patents Act 1970 § 87.

tion in its amended legislation. Clearly, and as authorized by TRIPS, some of these conditions can be waived in certain circumstances, most notably in emergency situations, in the case of non-working, or to remedy anti-competitive practices.

PART FOUR

RETORTING FROM THE 'BOTTOM-UP': DISPUTES AND CHALLENGES OVER THE IMPLEMENTATION AND INTERPRETATION OF THE TRIPS PHARMACEUTICAL-RELATED PROVISIONS

The two earlier phases of the TRIPS pharmaceutical-related patent regime examined in this book, namely its negotiation and domestic implementation phases, leads us into the phase examined here. This phase is characterized by disputes and challenges over the implementation and interpretation of the TRIPS pharmaceutical-related patent provisions. The implementation of TRIPS, and the TRIPS-legality of DC actions within this phase were subject to contention between DCs, their domestic stakeholders, and global civil society on the one hand, and the ICs and the pharmaceutical MNEs on the other. This contention ultimately represented a new phase in the saga pitting, essentially, DC and pharmaceutical MNE interests at odds with each other. It is argued that this continued ailment to the TRIPS regime, as revealed by the analysis in the following chapters, not only reinforces the notion of 'top-down' rule-making of the TRIPS Agreement, but more significantly reveals continuing resistance to the IC and pharmaceutical MNEs agenda on the standards contained therein.[1] The result is hence a process of 'bottom-up' retorting action not only by DCs, but also by an increasingly effective global civil society movement. Developing countries and their stakeholders whose interests were subordinated during the rule-making phase, were now trying to salvage what they considered a bare minimum of interests, specifically in their drive to devise public health policies in the face of major health crises.

[1] See SUSAN K SELL, POWER AND IDEAS: NORTH-SOUTH POLITICS OF INTELLECTUAL PROPERTY AND ANTITRUST (1998), where she argues that 'power' may bring about a coercive change in rules, yet that does not necessarily entail a change of 'idea' or conviction.

As discussed in Part Three, once the TRIPS Agreement entered into force, the efforts of ICs, and particularly the United States spurred by its pharmaceutical MNEs, were directed at seeking its expedited implementation. There was euphoria among pharmaceutical MNEs and other IP owners that they had achieved significant progress in their global IPR objectives. Ultimately, DCs would succumb to IC pressures for TRIPS implementation, including adopting TRIPS-plus provisions where necessary,[2] the 'rule of law' as they deemed it, was well nigh.[3] There existed a perception that the confrontation over international patent protection was largely settled with the signing of TRIPS. What remained to be done in DCs was 'to catalyse the transition from top-down to bottom-up intellectual property law reform', which it was argued, could be achieved through external pressure by the WTO, the USTR, and private foreign investors.[4]

This perception proved to be mistaken, or at least partially so. While DCs were undergoing legislative reform in their intellectual property regimes to synchronize it with TRIPS minimum standards, this process was far from trouble-free, and was accompanied by considerable IC pressure.[5] Commenting on this new realization, Jacques Gorlin, a leading lobbyist for the Pharmaceutical MNEs presented that:

> the mistake that we made was that we expected countries, by virtue of their membership in the WTO and by virtue of the fact that they had accepted the TRIPS Agreement, to change their laws to meet their obligations under TRIPS. We did not envisage that a large number of countries would not meet their international obligations. While many countries have done much work in trying to meet the standards and in changing their laws, a good number, including developed countries have not.[6]

[2] On the negative effects of IC pressure for the adoption of TRIPS-plus provisions, see Matthew Stilwell and Catherine Monagle *Review of TRIPs Agreement Under Article 71.1* SOUTH CENTRE TRADE-RELATED AGENDA, DEVELOPMENT AND EQUITY OCCASIONAL PAPER NO 3, 10 (Dec 2000).

[3] See JH Reichman and D Lange *Bargaining Around the TRIPS Agreement: The Case for Ongoing Public-Private Initiatives to Facilitate Worldwide Intellectual Property Transactions* 9 Duke J Comp and Int'l L 11 (1998) 13–14.

[4] Ronald JT Corbett *Protecting and Enforcing Intellectual Property Rights in Developing Countries* 35 Int'l Lawyer 1083 (2001) 1103. See also Charles S Levy *Implementing TRIPS—A Test of Political Will* 31 Law and Pol'y Int'l Bus 789 (2000) 793–95, where he argues that bringing implementation and compliance with TRIPS can be achieved through selective litigation and diplomatic pressure.

[5] This pressure, accompanied with the threat of economic sanctions in some cases, eg with South Africa, was tantamount to a reneging of IC promises as part of the Uruguay Round negotiations, and contradictory to the spirit of the TRIPS Agreement. See also Frederick M Abbott *The TRIPS Agreement, Access to Medicines and the WTO Doha Ministerial Conference*, QUAKER UNITED NATIONS OFFICE—GENEVA, OCCASIONAL PAPER NO 7, 24 (2001).

[6] Jacques J Gorlin US *Industries, Trade Associations, and Intellectual Property Lawmaking* 10 Cardozo J Int'l and Comp L 5 (2002) 10. See also Levy (2000) (n 4) 790–2.

This resistance did not only pertain to TRIPS implementation, but more significantly to important divergences over the interpretation of certain TRIPS provisions that would question the legitimacy not only of TRIPS, but of the WTO system itself. This divergence accompanied by continued IC pressure, it is argued, has led to retorting action by DCs and global civil society. As Professor Reichman warned, if DCs were pushed too hard with incautious litigation and other intimidatory tactics, they 'may invoke a number of de facto safeguard clauses buried in Articles 7 and 8 of the TRIPS Agreement, which once called into play, could then produce unexpected results.'[7] As will be discussed below, this warning was well placed.

Part Four examines this retorting action by DCs and global civil society in three specific frameworks. Primarily, Chapter 11 looks at the actions taken within the WTO Understanding on the Settlement of Disputes (DSU) mechanism. This framework reveals the roots of discontent with TRIPS implementation, particularly its pharmaceutical-related provisions, by DCs and their stakeholders. It also sheds light on the pressure being exerted by ICs, particularly the US, in seeking a thorough implementation of TRIPS provisions. Finally, it reveals the growing divergence between both camps in the interpretation of those provisions. The second framework, in Chapter 12, examines disputes at the bilateral level, involving two specific DC cases, Brazil and South Africa. Both countries, faced by an HIV/AIDS pandemic, devised legislative measures and adopted public policies that threatened pharmaceutical MNE interests, and whose legality under TRIPS was put into question by ICs. The retorting action pursued in this framework, and taken within the context of global pandemics and the rise of the access to medicine debate, was to prove a turning point in the international discourse on patent protection. It provides the clearest examples of effective retorting action by DCs and global civil society against the TRIPS patent regime, as interpreted by pharmaceutical MNEs and IC governments. The third framework, in Chapter 13, examines the multilateral level, within the political organs of the WTO. It focuses on action taken by DCs to engage debate at the cradle of the TRIPS regime on public health policies, and its position vis-à-vis IC pressure and IC interpretations of TRIPS. Table 10.1 below offers a conceptual summary of the three frameworks examined.

As a final remark, it should be noted that in the examination of the three frameworks of retorting action, attention will be placed on the particular mechanisms of this action. Naturally, the framework already reveals partly their nature, whether they be legislative measures (or lack thereof), protest action, or diplomatic prerogatives, among others. In this regard, Reichman and Lange specified four classifications of how they

[7] JH Reichman *Securing Compliance with the TRIPS Agreement After* US *v India* 1 JIEL 585 (1998) 598.

Table 10.1: Summary of Selected Disputes and Challenges Involving DCs and NGOs on TRIPS Regime

	WTO DSU Action	**Bilateral Level Action**	**WTO Action**
India	Action by US and EC, on Indian violation of TRIPS Article 70 provisions.		Major role in leading DC action.
Argentina	Action by US, on claimed violations of various TRIPS provisions.		
Brazil	Reciprocal action with US on violations of TRIPS provisions relating to local working.	Threat of CL against MNEs, and pressure for local working. Challenge to US IP policy.	Major role in leading DC action.
South Africa		Major confrontation over Medicines Amendment Act. MNEs initiate legal action. US and EC threaten sanctions.	
DCs in Concert			Brought Public Health as an issue for discussion in TRIPS Council. Success in issuing the Doha Declaration.
NGOs	Criticism of US action towards Argentina and Brazil.	Major role in Africa dispute. Important role in Brazil dispute. Challenging MNEs, and pressuring US.	Important role in initiating the climate that led the way to WTO action.

perceive DCs are resisting the implementation of TRIPS, namely; through exploiting normative ambiguities, countervailing regulatory measures, enforcement procedures, and uncertain effects of safeguard provisions.[8] This classification, while undoubtedly useful, pertains however to a narrower set of circumstances than this present context. The retorting actions examined below pertain to the rules and to the politics of the TRIPS Agreement, and thus go into issues of its interpretation, including its compatibility with the larger corpus of international legal norms. More pragmatically, they also relate to the interests of the different stakeholders in the debate.

[8] Reichman and Lange (1998) (n 3) 19–45.

Chapter 11

Disputes under the WTO DSU Mechanism

The inclusion of a credible dispute settlement mechanism within the ambit of the WTO that covered disputes arising under the TRIPS Agreement was a profound victory for the MNEs and ICs.[1] Through such a mechanism, ICs were able to bring forth effective legal action against DCs that were seen as violating the TRIPS Agreement.[2] Previously, we alluded to how the ICs were able to make use of the WTO dispute settlement mechanism as a tool to guarantee compliance and implementation of the TRIPS Agreement by DCs.[3] As such, it can be clearly perceived as a tool of rights enforcement by ICs towards DCs.[4] However, an equally valid characterization of the rise of disputes at the level of the WTO, more pertinent to our present context, is an attempt to understand them as conveying resistance by DCs against the imposition of the TRIPS regime. It is thus considered for its

1 For a review of how the DSU would relate to the TRIPS Agreement, see Rochelle Cooper Dreyfuss and Andreas F Lowenfeld *Two Achievements of the Uruguay Round: Putting TRIPS and Dispute Settlement Together* 37 Va J Int'l L 275 (1997). For a comment on this work from a PhRMA perspective, see Judith H Bello *Some Practical Observations About WTO Settlement of Intellectual Property Disputes* 37 Va J Int'l L 357 (1997). See also RJ Gutowski *The Marriage of Intellectual Property and International Trade in the TRIPs Agreement: Strange Bedfellows or a Match Made in Heaven?* 47 Buff L R 713 (1999).

2 The significance of the new WTO dispute settlement mechanism lies in its set procedures and specific stages akin to a formal judicial proceeding. This, compared to the dispute system existing within GATT previously, was described by Celso Lafer, Brazil's former Permanent Representative to the WTO and Chairman of its Dispute Settlement Body, as a 'thickening of legality.' See Sigrid Dormer *Dispute Settlement and New Developments Within the Framework of TRIPS—An Interim Review* 31 IIC 1 (2000) 26 ff.

3 On WTO disputes involving the TRIPS Agreement, see JAYASHREE WATAL, INTELLECTUAL PROPERTY RIGHTS IN THE WTO AND DEVELOPING COUNTRIES (2001) 58–85; DUNCAN MATTHEWS, GLOBALISING INTELLECTUAL PROPERTY RIGHTS: THE TRIPs AGREEMENT (2002) 87–105; SUSAN K SELL, PRIVATE POWER, PUBLIC LAW: THE GLOBALIZATION OF INTELLECTUAL PROPERTY RIGHTS (2003) 129–138; Matthijs Geuze and Hannu Wager *WTO Dispute Settlement Practice Relating to the TRIPS Agreement* 2 JIEL 347 (1999); Dormer (2000) (n 2); Sue Ann Mota *TRIPS—Five Years of Disputes at the WTO* 17 Ariz J Int'l and Comp L 533 (2000); Daniel J Gervais *The TRIPS Agreement After Seattle: Implementation and Dispute Settlement Issues* 3 J Intell Prop Rights 509 (2000); and Jose Felgueroso *TRIPS and the Dispute Settlement Understanding: The First Six Years* 30 AIPLA QJ 165 (2002).

4 Nonetheless, the majority of disputes under TRIPS occurred among ICs. See John E Giust *Noncompliance with TRIPS by Developed and Developing Countries: Is TRIPS Working?* 8 Ind Int'l and Comp L Rev 69 (1997) 80–91.

Table 11.1: Selected WTO Requests for Consultations Relating to TRIPS Patent Provisions Involving Developing Countries

	Case No	Date	Against	Brought By	Title	Status
1.	DS 36	6 May 1996	Pakistan		US Pakistan—Patent protection for pharmaceutical and agricultural chemical products.	Mutually Agreed Solution.
2.	DS 50	2 July 1996	India	US	India—Patent protection for pharmaceutical and agricultural chemical products.	Appellate Body Report Adopted.
3.	DS 79	28 April 1997	India	EC	Patent protection for pharmaceutical and agricultural chemical products.	Panel Report Adopted.
4.	DS 171	6 May 1999	Argentina	US	Patent protection for pharmaceutical products.	Mutually Agreed Solution.
5.	DS 196	30 May 2000	Argentina	US	Certain measures on the protection of patents and test data.	Mutually Agreed Solution.
6.	DS 199	30 May 2000	Brazil	US	Measures affecting patent protection.	Mutually Agreed Solution.
7.	DS 224	31 January	US	Brazil	US Patents Code	Mutually Agreed Solution.

Source: Information gathered from the WTO website.[5]

value in shedding light on the nature of DC retorting action and the nature of the issues disputed in the Agreement.

As listed in Table 11.1 above, there have been seven requests for consultations involving DCs under the DSU arising under the TRIPS Agreement,

[5] <http://www.wto.org/english/tratop_e/dispu_e/dispu_subjects_index_e.htm#bkmk 138> (last visited 6 Mar 2006).

which relate to patent protection, and are of direct interest to the pharmaceutical industry.

Of these seven cases, five were brought by the United States, one by the European Communities, and the final case brought by Brazil. This underlines the central role the United States was undertaking in safeguarding the TRIPS regime.[6] On the other hand, the defendants were essentially large DCs that had been at the forefront of opposition during the TRIPS negotiations. They were also considered by the pharmaceutical MNEs as important markets, and whose domestic pharmaceutical industries were perceived as potential competitors. These DC defendants included, in addition to Pakistan, India twice as defendant, Argentina twice as defendant, and finally one request for consultation with Brazil. Of the six cases against DCs, four were settled prior to the panel stage through mutually agreed solutions. On the other hand, the India cases proceeded to the stage where a panel report was adopted in each of the complaints brought by the US[7] and by the EC,[8] and an Appellate Body report was adopted in the case brought by the US.[9]

The possibilities for WTO disputes being brought against DCs under TRIPS were limited in its first few years due to the fact that most DCs had transitional periods up to five years, and the existence of a moratorium on non-violation complaints (TRIPS Article 64.2).[10] As such, the legal substance of these requests for consultations and disputes revolved around those specific provisions that DCs were required to come into compliance with, notwithstanding the transitional arrangements of Part VI of the agreement. The most important substantive issues raised included the absence of formal procedures setting up the so-called 'mail-box' system for receiving patent applications pertaining to pharmaceutical and agricultural chemical products during the transitional phase, and the absence of a procedure to issue exclusive marketing rights to such products. As will be reviewed below, these were the issues at stake in the India disputes. Furthermore, the absence of exclusive marketing rights, and the ad interim weakening in Argentina's legislation of protection for undisclosed information, a violation of TRIPS Article 65.5, inter alia, were among the issues raised in the

[6] See Sell (2003) (n 3) 129.

[7] WTO *India—Patent Protection for Pharmaceutical and Agricultural Chemical Products, Report of the Panel* WT/DS50/R (5 Sept 1997), [hereinafter India—US Panel Report].

[8] WTO *India—Patent Protection for Pharmaceutical and Agricultural Chemical Products: Complaint by the European Communities and their Member States, Report of the Panel* WT/DS79/R (24 Aug 1998), [hereinafter India—EC Panel Report].

[9] WTO *India—Patent Protection for Pharmaceutical and Agricultural Chemical Products, Report of the Appellate Body* WT/DS50/AB/R (19 Dec 1997), [hereinafter India—Appellate Body Report].

[10] See Gervais (2000) (n 3) 510–11. See also Matthew Stilwell and Elizabeth Tuerk *Non-Violation Complaints and the TRIPs Agreement: Some Considerations for WTO Members* SOUTH CENTRE TRADE-RELATED AGENDA, DEVELOPMENT AND EQUITY OCCASIONAL PAPER NO 1 (Dec 2000).

request for consultations lodged with Argentina. Finally, the important issue concerning a 'local working' requirement for patents that can only be satisfied by local production, and not through importation, was at the heart of the request for consultations lodged by the US to Brazil. The cases against India, Argentina and Brazil are discussed below.

(I) INDIA DISPUTES

The India disputes with the US and the EC emphasized the centrality of pharmaceutical patent issues within disputes emanating from the TRIPS patent regime. They also stressed the concerns of the pharmaceutical MNEs. In 1995, the US claimed that due to lax patent protection in India, the estimated annual losses to its pharmaceutical industry was US $450 million.[11] These losses to the US in the case of India were alluded to directly by the Pharmaceutical Research Manufacturers of America (PhRMA) to the USTR.[12] Throughout the period 1995–9, PhRMA recommended that India be designated as a 'Priority Foreign Country' in the USTR's Special 301 designations.[13] Describing it as 'one of the world's worst offenders of patent rights', PhRMA argued that

> the Indian patent system was the most direct motivation for US efforts in the Uruguay Round negotiations relating to patents, and the negotiators of the TRIPS Agreement fully expected that India's implementation of its TRIPS obligations would produce the most dramatic level of reform.[14]

[11] USTR 1995 National Trade Estimate Report on Foreign Trade Barriers—India, 4 (on file with author).

[12] *Letter from Harvey E Bale, Jr, Senior Vice President, PhRMA to Charlene Barshefsky, USTR* (2 May 1997), available as Annex 3 in India—US Panel Report (n 7) 72. See also Matthews (2002) (n 3) 96–98.

[13] *Submission of the Pharmaceutical Research Manufacturers of America for the 1995 'Special 301' Report on Intellectual Property Protection* (13 Feb 1995) (on file at the USTR Reading Room, and copy on file with author) [hereinafter PhRMA 1995 301 Submission]; *Submission of the Pharmaceutical Research Manufacturers of America for the 1996 'Special 301' Report on Intellectual Property Barriers* (20 Feb 1996) (on file at the USTR Reading Room, and copy on file with author) [hereinafter PhRMA 1996 301 Submission]; *Submission of the Pharmaceutical Research Manufacturers of America for the 1997 'Special 301' Report on Intellectual Property Barriers* (18 Feb 1997) (on file with the USTR Reading Room, and copy on file with author) [hereinafter PhRMA 1997 301 Submission]; *Submission of the Pharmaceutical Research Manufacturers of America for the 1998 'Special 301' Report on Intellectual Property Barriers* (23 Feb 1998) (on file at the USTR Reading Room, and copy on file with author) [hereinafter PhRMA 1998 301 Submission]; and *Submission of the Pharmaceutical Research Manufacturers of America for the 1999 'Special 301' Report on Intellectual Property Barriers* (16 Feb 1999) (on file at the USTR Reading Room, and copy on file with author) [hereinafter PhRMA 1999 301 Submission].

[14] PhRMA 1999 301 Submission, 8.

Similarly, the European Communities, in their request to join consultations between the US and India stressed that 'the European pharmaceutical and agro-chemical industry has an important export interest in the Indian market.'[15] This concern and pressure naturally led the US and EC to initiate the WTO cases against India. Matthews also notes the important role played by the European Federation of Pharmaceutical Industry Associations (EFPIA) and its complaints to the EC about India, instituting the EC case against India.[16]

The United States filed a request for consultations with India on 2 July 1996,

> regarding the absence in India of either patent protection for pharmaceutical and agricultural chemical products or *formal systems* that permit the filing of patent applications for pharmaceutical and agricultural chemical products and that provide exclusive marketing rights in such products.[17]

The United States argued that India's laws did not provide systems conforming to TRIPS Articles 70.8 and 70.9, regarding the filing and examination of patent applications and the grant of exclusive marketing rights.[18] As the consultations failed to resolve the dispute, a panel was constituted by the Dispute Settlement Body on 20 November 1996.[19] In almost identical language, and on the same grounds, the EC requested consultations with India on 28 April 1997,[20] and a panel was also constituted in this case on 16 October 1997.[21]

15 WTO *India—Patent Protection for Pharmaceutical and Agricultural Chemical Products, Request to Join Consultations, Communication from the European Communities* WT/DS50/2 (22 July 1996).

16 Matthews (2002) (n 3) 97. See also *Letter from Alan Hesketh, Manager, Global Intellectual Property, Glaxo Wellcome Plc, to Bernhard Janssen, European Commission*, available as Annex 4 in India-EC Panel Report (n 8) 83.

17 WTO *India—Patent Protection for Pharmaceutical and Agricultural Chemical Products, Request for Consultations by the United States* WT/DS50/1 (9 July 1996). Emphasis added.

18 ibid.

19 WTO *India—Patent Protection for Pharmaceutical and Agricultural Chemical Products, Request for the Establishment of a Panel by the United States* WT/DS50/4 (8 Nov 1996); and WTO *India—Patent Protection for Pharmaceutical and Agricultural Chemical Products, Constitution of the Panel Established at the Request of the United States* WT/DS50/5 (5 Feb 1997).

20 WTO *India—Patent Protection for Pharmaceutical and Agricultural Chemical Products, Request for Consultations by the European Communities* WT/DS79/1 (6 May 1997).

21 WTO *India—Patent Protection for Pharmaceutical and Agricultural Chemical Products, Request for the Establishment of a Panel by the EC* WT/DS79/2 (15 Sept 1997); and WTO *India—Patent Protection for Pharmaceutical and Agricultural Chemical Products, Constitution of the Panel Established at the Request of the European Communities* WT/DS79/3 (27 Nov 1997).

The thrust of the US and EC claims against India, as largely upheld in the Panel Reports and the Appellate Body Report,[22] revolved around India's failure to establish a legally sound basis in its legal system for the receipt of 'mailbox' applications, and the grant of exclusive marketing rights thereon. Such a system should have been in place effective from 1 January 1995. On 31 December 1994, the President of India promulgated the Patents (Amendment) Ordinance 1994 to amend the Patents Act 1970, to provide a means within its folds, to allow for the implementation of TRIPS Articles 70.8 and 70.9.[23] The Ordinance, which came into effect on 1 January 1995, was issued under powers enjoyed by the President to legislate when Parliament was not in session, and under the presence of circumstances requiring immediate action.[24] Nonetheless, the Ordinance expired on 26 March 1995, six weeks following the reassembly of Parliament, as constitutionally mandated. During the same month, a Patents (Amendment) Bill, with the aim of providing permanent legislative effect to the substance of the Ordinance, was introduced, but failed to pass prior to the dissolution of Parliament on 10 May 1996.[25] As such, almost a year and a half after its obligations to implement TRIPS Articles 70.8 and 70.9, India had no legislative instrument that did so.

Notwithstanding this failure to enact legislation, India claimed that it was not in violation of its TRIPS Articles 70.8 and 70.9 obligations. Indeed, India presented that since April 1995, it had a mechanism in place whereby through administrative arrangements, its Patent Office was under instructions to receive applications filed under the so-called 'mailbox' provision of Article 70.8(a).[26] It presented that 'it is essentially for the Member itself to determine the methodology by which it sets out the mailbox system in terms of its municipal laws'.[27] On the other hand, India acknowledged that there was no legislation nor administrative procedures for the fulfilment of Article 70.9 obligations concerning the granting of exclusive marketing rights, however, it added that it had not received any request for such a grant, and therefore no breach of its obligations had ensued. India argued that Article 70.9 obliges members to provide EMRs only after the events specified in that provision have occurred, and there is nothing in the arti-

[22] For commentary on the substantive issues of the India disputes, see Geuze and Wager (1999) (n 3) 349–70; Dormer (2000) (n 2) 14–22; David K Tomar *A Look into the WTO Pharmaceutical Patent Dispute Between the United States and India* 17 Wisc Int'l LJ 579 (1999); JH Reichman *Securing Compliance with the TRIPS Agreement After* US *v India* 1 JIEL 585 (1998) 594–7; and Charles Macdonald-Brown and Leon Ferera *First WTO Decision on TRIPS: India—Patent Protection for Pharmaceutical and Agricultural Chemical Products* 20 EIPR 69 (1998).

[23] India-US Panel Report (n 7) 2–3.

[24] India Const (26 Nov 1949) Art 123(1).

[25] India-US Panel Report (n 7) 3.

[26] ibid 3, and further at para 5.4, 43–4.

[27] India—Appellate Body Report (n 9) para 9. India stated that until 15 Feb 1997, it had received 1,339 applications for pharmaceutical and agricultural chemical products under that mechanism.

cle's provisions to necessitate a system for such a grant to be generally available before the events listed in Article 70.9 have occurred.[28]

As was expected, the Panel in the US complaint held on 5 September 1997 that India had not complied with its obligations under Article 70.8(a) to establish a 'mailbox' system for applications for product patents regarding pharmaceutical and agricultural chemical inventions during the transitional period.[29] The Panel also held that India had not complied with its obligations under Article 70.9 concerning a system for the grant of EMRs.[30] Subsequent to an appeal by India, the Appellate Body on 19 December 1997 upheld the Panel's conclusions.[31] In August 1998, the Panel in the EC complaint held along identical lines.[32] India was now required to bring its patent regime into compliance. Eventually, the US and India agreed on a 15-month period ending in April 1999, whereby India implements the recommendations of the DSB and brings its laws into compliance. The EC also agreed with India on the same deadline. In March 1999, India issued the Patents (Amendment) Act, 1999, bringing its patent law into compliance with regard to the 'mailbox' provision and the EMR grant system, with retroactive effect from 1 January 1995.[33]

The United States and the MNEs were therefore jubilant with the results of the disputes. USTR Barshefsky considered it an important and significant victory for US firms, adding that DCs must understand that 'there is no free ride under TRIPs'.[34] The IC–MNE alliance was successful due to what the former General Counsel to the USTR and Executive Vice President of PhRMA described as the close coordination that takes place between private parties and the USTR-led inter-agency government team in the various steps of the dispute.[35] Despite this important case, with its legal outcome in favour of MNEs interests in implementation of TRIPS through WTO DSU enforcement action,[36] yet a closer examination reveals a trend of resistance. The disputes concerned issues arising under the Indian Government's failure to uphold its TRIPS obligations, an interpretation of which could be deemed to reflect bottom up retorting action from a major DC. India's recalcitrant posture on this issue was arguably a harbinger of a possible trend among DCs, where in the words of Professor Reichman:

28 See India—Appellate Body Report (n 9) para 10.

29 India-US Panel Report (n 7) para 6.1.

30 ibid.

31 India—Appellate Body Report (n 9) para 97.

32 India-EC Panel Report (n 8) para 9.1.

33 Patents (Amendment) Act 1999, No 17 of 1999 (26 Mar 1999).

34 Quoted in *WTO Appellate Body Upholds Drug Patent Ruling Against India* 15 Int'l Trade Rep (BNA) (7 Jan 1998).

35 Bello (1997) (n 1) 360.

36 However, it has been argued that the approach adopted by the Appellate Body in rejecting the Panel's 'legitimate expectations' test, limits that victory, and is beneficial to DC interests. See Reichman (1998) (n 22) 594–7.

> The developing countries' efforts to limit the impact of the TRIPS Agreement have begun to manifest themselves in a number of different forums. At one extreme, the government of India chose to postpone implementing the 'mailbox' and 'pipeline' [sic] rules applicable to patents, despite the contrary advice of its own legal advisors.[37]

Indeed, in its arguments before the Appellate Body, India argued that patent protection for pharmaceutical and agricultural chemical products is the most sensitive TRIPS issue in many DCs. It further proposed that as such, presenting legislative changes to implement Article 70.9 is contrary to the spirit of the TRIPS transitional arrangements, with the consequence that the transitional arrangements would allow DCs to postpone legislative changes in all fields of technology except in the most sensitive ones.[38] Both the US and EC responded by seeking to buttress the impartiality of the TRIPS regime, an attempt to diffuse it of the tension arising over its pharmaceutical-related provisions. The US argued that

> under the TRIPS Agreement, the *quid pro quo* for taking advantage of the extended transition period for granting product patents for pharmaceutical and agricultural chemical inventions was the grant of exclusive marketing rights.[39]

More specifically, the failure by India's government to pass the requisite legislative amendments in 1995 reveals a clear hostility in the Indian parliament towards TRIPS mandated changes.[40] Indeed, the 1995 Amendment Act was rejected by the communist and the right-wing Bharatiya Janta Party (BJP), the latter of which was to form the government in 1997.[41] This led to a tug of war between India's executive and legislative branches. But even in the proposed 1995 amendments based on the 1994 Ordinance, specific provisions reveal continued manoeuvres of resistance. Among its provisions, PhRMA cited problematic issues where the burden of the enforcement of the EMR was with the patent holder rather than through enforcement by the State.[42] Furthermore, it also included a section that subjects the EMR grants to the compulsory licenses regime of the 1970 Patents Act, again enraging the MNEs.[43]

[37] Reichman (1998) (n 22) 593.
[38] India—Appellate Body Report (n 9) para 12.
[39] ibid paras 21 and 27.
[40] On opposition in India to the patent law reform required by TRIPS, see Suresh Koshy *The Effects of TRIPS on Indian Patent Law: A Pharmaceutical Industry Perspective* 1 Boston Univ J Sci and Tech L 1 (1995) 36–7.
[41] See *India Will Appeal WTO Panel Ruling on Drug, Agricultural Chemical Patents* 14 Int'l Trade Rep (BNA) (24 Sept 1997).
[42] PhRMA 1997 301 Submission, 6.
[43] Patents (Amendment) Ordinance No 13 of 1994 (31 Dec 1994) § 24C. See also Koshy (1995) (n 40) 42.

It could be argued that these issues were largely to be expected as commonplace in a process of legislative IP reform. Indeed, the UK's Commission on Intellectual Property Rights noted during a visit to India that

> although there had been widespread opposition to the introduction of patent protection on products, rather than processes, there was now general acceptance that this was necessary, if not wholly desirable.[44]

However, as presented, the conduct of the Indian legislature and the government itself, revealed a tendency to oppose as much as possible a measure mandated under TRIPS. In the final analysis, the India Disputes concerned provisions under TRIPS that India was supposed to come into compliance with on 1 January 1995, it took until March 1999 for the final legislative effect to do so was undertaken, and considerable exertion of effort by ICs under the WTO DSU mechanism.

(II) ARGENTINA CONSULTATIONS

Within the span of a little over one year, the United States initiated two requests for consultations with Argentina under the WTO DSU system, on 6 May 1999, and 30 May 2000.[45] Under the first request, the US raised two issues. Primarily, the absence in Argentina of either patent protection for pharmaceutical products or an effective system for providing exclusive marketing rights in such products, hence an Article 70.9 type complaint. Second, Argentina's failure to ensure that changes in its IP regime, do not result in a lesser degree of consistency with TRIPS provisions, according to TRIPS Article 65. The US pointed out that Argentina provided a 10-year term of protection against unfair commercial use for undisclosed test data or other data submitted for marketing approval for agricultural chemical products, but that since August 1998, that protection was no longer effective, hence resulting in a lesser degree of consistency with the provisions of TRIPS Article 39.3.[46] Under the second request in May 2000, the US significantly increased the scope of issues it sought to engage in with Argentina. Most

[44] Commission on Intellectual Property Rights (CIPR) *Report on Visit to India: 29th–31st August 2001* (on file with author).

[45] WTO *Argentina—Patent Protection for Pharmaceuticals and Test Data Protection for Agricultural Chemicals, Request for Consultations by the United States* WT/DS171/1 (10 May 1999), [hereinafter First Argentina Request]; and WTO *Argentina—Certain Measures on the Protection of Patents and Test Data, Request for Consultations by the United States* WT/DS196/1 (6 June 2000), [hereinafter Second Argentina Request].

[46] See First Argentina Request (n 45).

importantly, these supplemental issues included: failure to protect against unfair commercial use of undisclosed test or other data for market approval of pharmaceutical products; denial of certain exclusive rights for patents including the right of importation; and failure to provide certain safeguards for the granting of compulsory licences.[47] In total, the US held that Argentina was in violation of TRIPS Articles 27, 28, 31, 34, 39, 50, 62, 65, and 70.

The action pursued by the USTR with regard to Argentina was in response to the urgings of the US pharmaceutical MNEs. Following the Uruguay Round, PhRMA had consistently identified Argentina as a 'Priority Foreign Country' for consideration under Special 301.[48] Nonetheless, and possibly in view of the Argentine financial crisis, an understanding was reached between the US and Argentina in June 2002 on all matters raised in the two requests for consultations.[49] Under the terms of their agreement, most importantly, Argentina agreed to enact a TRIPS-consistent EMR mechanism.[50] On the other hand, with regard to the protection of test data (TRIPS Article 39.3), both parties maintained their respective positions, and maintained that should future complaints arise, they would be referred once again to the DSU.[51]

Argentina has traditionally been a thorn in the side of the US pharmaceutical industry and the efforts of the USTR since the 1980s, where it was at the forefront of opposition to the inclusion of a high protectionist IP regime in the Uruguay Round negotiations. Indeed, as covered in Chapter 5, Argentina was targeted by the US pharmaceutical industry acting through PMA and by the USTR, for 301 action in parallel with the Uruguay Round negotiations.[52] Moreover, following the conclusion of the Uruguay Round, Argentina was subjected to intense US pressure inciting it to enact highly protectionist laws on patent protection and the protection of undisclosed test data.[53] In numerous instances, the Argentine patent law enacted in 1996, contained TRIPS-plus provisions, most notably a reduction to five years of the TRIPS mandated 10-year transitional period for the introduction of patent protection for pharmaceutical products.[54] In the face of

[47] See Second Argentina Request (n 45).

[48] See PhRMA 1995 301 Submission; PhRMA 1996 301 Submission; PhRMA 1997 301 Submission; PhRMA 1998 301 Submission; PhRMA 1999 301 Submission.

[49] WTO *Argentina—Certain Measures on the Protection of Patents and Test Data, Notification of Mutually Agreed Solution* WT/DS196/4 (20 June 2002).

[50] ibid para 2.

[51] ibid para 9.

[52] See also Kimberly Czub *Argentina's Emerging Standard of Intellectual Property Protection: A Case Study of the Underlying Conflicts Between Developing Countries, TRIPS Standards, and the United States* 33 CASE W RES J INT'L L 191 (2001) 193–5.

[53] See Wendy S Vicente *Questionable Victory for Coerced Argentine Pharmaceutical Patent Legislation* 19 UNI PENN J INT'L ECON L 1101 (1998) 1106–1109.

[54] Law No 24.481 on Patents and Utility Models (as amended by Law No 24.572) (20 Mar 1996) Art 100. See also *Argentina Approves New Patent Law After Extended Government Debate* 13 Int'l Trade Rep (BNA) 515 (27 Mar 1996).

earlier Argentine recalcitrance to enact changes in its laws demanded by the pharmaceutical MNEs and the USTR, the United States announced sanctions on Argentina's GSP benefits covering US $260 million.[55]

The DSU request for consultations initiated by the United States should therefore be seen in the light of this background, as an extension of continued US pressure on Argentine legislation. As with the case of the India disputes, a significant constituency within Argentina was at odds with the required changes to the patent regime, particularly those TRIPS-plus provisions, being imposed by the United States. In the case of Argentina, an acute struggle had ensued between the administration of President Menem and the Argentine Congress, where patent and related legislation was delayed due to presidential vetoes and overriding legislative amendments.[56] Considerable resentment was also expressed by government and Congress alike in response to US sanctions.[57]

(III) BRAZIL CONSULTATIONS

The last in the series of WTO request for consultations with a DC over TRIPS patent provisions covered here was that requested from Brazil by the United States on 30 May 2000.[58] The United States presented that under the local working requirement of Brazil's 1996 industrial property law (Article 68), a patent shall be subject to compulsory licensing if its subject matter is not worked in Brazil. This was problematic, the US added, as the law defines failure to work as '*failure to manufacture or incomplete manufacture of the product*', or failure to make full use of the patented process.[59] The US considered this as inconsistent with TRIPS Articles 27 and 28, and Article III of GATT 1994. US Pharmaceutical MNEs spurred and fully supported US action in this regard, holding the local working requirement as a direct violation of TRIPS Article 27.1.[60]

The US action was therefore premised on two causes. Primarily, the US presented that Article 68 of Brazil's industrial property law, violates TRIPS Article 27.1, where the latter prohibits discrimination regarding

[55] US *to Cut Argentine GSP Benefits for Failure to Provide Patent Protection* 14 Int'l Trade Rep (BNA) 106 (22 Jan 1997).

[56] See *Argentine Congressional Delegates Defend Law Passed by Legislature* 13 Int'l Trade Rep (BNA) (28 Feb 1996); and *Argentine President Says He'll Try to Reopen Patent Law Discussions* 13 Int'l Trade Rep (BNA) (8 May 1996). See also Czub (2001) (n 52) 195–7.

[57] See *Argentine Executives, Politicians Blast Sanctions Under Consideration by US* 14 Int'l Trade Rep (BNA) (15 Jan 1997).

[58] WTO *Brazil—Measures Affecting Patent Protection, Request for Consultations by the United States* WT/DS199/1 (8 June 2000).

[59] ibid.

[60] PhRMA 1999 301 Submission.

the availability of patents and the enjoyment of patent rights regardless of whether products are imported or locally produced.[61] Secondly, the US pointed out that Article 68 of Brazil's law stipulates that in cases involving exploitation of the patent through importation, third parties would be allowed to import either the patented product or the product obtained from the patented process (Article 68.4). This, the US claimed, violated TRIPS Article 28.1 that grants patent owners, inter alia, the exclusive right of importation. The first cause of complaint was the more substantial, and was given attention in academic discussions that questioned the US reading by arguing that in incorporating Article 5A of the Paris Convention, as well as in provisions relating to exceptions to rights conferred (TRIPS Articles 30 and 31), the TRIPS Agreement therefore allowed local working provisions similar to those of Brazil's Article 68.[62] Still other opinion was supportive of the US view, arguing that interpretation of TRIPS Article 27.1 does in fact lead to the conclusion that there should be no discrimination between imported and locally produced goods.[63]

However, following two consultation sessions, the US requested the establishment of a panel to consider the dispute on 8 January, 2001.[64] While Brazil blocked the first request for the formation of the panel on 19 January, 2001,[65] and following a few months of stalemate, both parties notified the DSB of a mutually agreed solution.[66] That solution comprised creating a consultative mechanism whereby Brazil would hold prior talks with the US, should it deem it necessary to apply Article 68 to grant a compulsory licence on patents held by US companies.[67] In this eventuality, there has therefore been no pronouncement by a WTO panel on the legality of local working under TRIPS.

Contrary to the prior DSU actions discussed above, the Brazil consultations proved to be puzzling. As will be discussed in the following chapter,

[61] WTO *Brazil—Measures Affecting Patent Protection, Request for the Establishment of a Panel by the United States* WT/DS199/3 (9 Jan 2001) [hereinafter US-Brazil Panel Request].

[62] See Matthew Stilwell and Catherine Monagle *Review of TRIPs Agreement Under Article 71.1* SOUTH CENTRE TRADE-RELATED AGENDA, DEVELOPMENT AND EQUITY OCCASIONAL PAPER NO 3, para 33 (Dec 2000); Carlos Correa *Intellectual Property Rights and the Use of Compulsory Licenses: Options for Developing Countries* SOUTH CENTRE TRADE-RELATED AGENDA, DEVELOPMENT AND EQUITY WORKING PAPER NO 5, 9 (Oct 1999). See also Paul Champ and Amir Attaran *Patent Rights and Local Working Under the WTO TRIPS Agreement: An Analysis of the U.S.–Brazil Patent Dispute* 27 Yale J Int'l L 365 (2002) 367–8.

[63] PETER L KOLKER, SHOULD IMPORTATION BE CONSIDERED AS WORKING? A STUDY OF ARTICLE 27 OF THE GATT TRIPS AGREEMENT (1996).

[64] US-Brazil Panel Request (n 61).

[65] *Brazil Blocks US Panel Request on Brazilian Patent Law Provisions* 18 Int'l Trade Rep (BNA) 142 (25 Jan 2001).

[66] WTO *Brazil—Measures Affecting Patent Protection, Notification of Mutually Agreed Solution* WT/DS199/4 (19 July 2001).

[67] ibid. The US however reserved its right to initiate future action under the DSU on this matter.

this puzzle can ultimately be understood from the context within which it emerged, as being more political than legal in nature. Suffice to say at this stage that this action against Brazil broke the sequence of trouble-free IC action against DCs under the WTO DSU mechanism.

Chapter 12

Disputes at the Domestic and Bilateral Levels

While the disputes and requests for consultations at the WTO level within the folds of its DSU mechanism could be seen as a process whereby ICs, particularly the United States, spurred on by their pharmaceutical MNEs, sought a rigorous implementation of TRIPS, the stage was now set for a qualitatively very different scenario with regards to the TRIPS regime. Contiguous to these WTO disputes and requests for consultations, DCs, supported by NGOs, were starting to voice resentment at the constraints imposed upon them by certain of the provisions of the TRIPS Agreement and their interpretations, to address issues of public health and access to medicines. In this chapter, two specific challenges will be discussed for their ability to reveal this qualitative shift. These challenges arose with regard to situations in Brazil and in South Africa.[1] While other DCs grappled with similar efforts of pursuing public health policies unhindered by IC and MNE pressures, yet the cases of Brazil and South Africa proved more contentious.

Both the Brazil and South Africa cases related directly to DC government action in pursuit of policies addressing the public health needs of their respective populations, and the concomitant debate concerning the TRIPS legality of these measures.[2] However it is important to clarify at the outset an important difference between the two cases, as will be further discussed. In the case of Brazil, the main retorting action arose from the policies of the Brazilian government. On the other hand, in the case of South Africa, while the South African government initiated a policy conscious of public health concerns and HIV/AIDS, yet the defence of this action and the retortion against pharmaceutical and ICs pressure was significantly spearheaded by a

[1] For a commentary on the significance of these two cases, see Naomi A Bass *Implications of the TRIPS Agreement for Developing Countries: Pharmaceutical Patent Laws in Brazil and South Africa in the 21st Century* 34 Geo Wash Int'l L Rev 191 (2002).

[2] These debates on TRIPS-legality, and specifically in the context of South Africa revolved about a certain interpretation of the Agreement, and has been characterized by a leading commentator as a 'most disturbing example of the abuse of the TRIPS Agreement....' See Frederick M Abbott *WTO TRIPS Agreement and Its Implications for Access to Medicines in Developing Countries* COMMISSION ON INTELLECTUAL PROPERTY RIGHTS STUDY PAPER 2A, 52 (2002) <http://www.iprcommission.org/papers/pdfs/study_papers/sp2a_abbott_study.pdf> (last visited 3 Mar 2006).

dynamic domestic and global NGO community. Prior to the discussion of the two country cases however, it is appropriate to examine the problem of access to medicines, and the position of the various stakeholders on the implications of the TRIPS patent regime therein.

(I) ADDRESSING THE ACCESS TO MEDICINE DILEMMA

As was reviewed in Part Three, the implementation of the TRIPS patent provisions in DCs spurred resistance with regard to the implications on public health policy, and particularly on the affordability of medicines. These sentiments were indeed voiced as far back as during the negotiation of TRIPS.[3] Further resentment was also fuelled by interpretations of TRIPS that went beyond the minimum standards of the Agreement. However, with the onslaught of global pandemics, particularly HIV/AIDS, DCs were faced with an urgent situation. The World Health Organization (WHO) reported that 50 per cent of DC populations lack access to essential medicines, and that 50–90 per cent of drugs in DCs are paid for out of pocket, thus severely disadvantaging the poor.[4] Access to affordable medicines, particularly anti-retrovirals (ARVs) for the treatment of HIV/AIDS became imperative. As a consequence of product patenting being gradually introduced as mandated by TRIPS, prices were increasingly beyond the ability of DCs and the vast majority of their populations to afford. Possible avenues for achieving affordability included compulsory licences, in effect disrupting the patent-owner's monopoly and hence reducing prices through competition, and through parallel imports of either the proprietary medicine in markets where it is marketed at a lower price, or of generic versions of the drugs usually selling at a lower price than its brand name equivalent. Other possibilities included requiring the patent holder to manufacture the drug domestically, hence achieving a degree of cost saving relative to imports, a strategy that was adopted by Brazil.

Compulsory licensing, legal under TRIPS Article 31,[5] has been commended by different scholars and organizations as useful for DCs, particularly in the context of affordable access to medicines. Their importance has also been stressed given that DCs facing strengthened IPRs under TRIPS standards lacked the mechanisms that have traditionally balanced

[3] Please refer to Part Two of this book.

[4] See World Health Organization *Essential Drugs and Medicines Policy* <http://www.who.int/medicines> (last visited 7 Mar 2002).

[5] For a discussion of the legality of adopting compulsory licences within the TRIPS context to address public health needs, see Frederick M Abbott *The TRIPS—Legality of Measures Taken to Address Public Health Crises: A Synopsis* 7 Widener L Symp J 71 (2001) 73–7; and Carlos Correa *Public Health and Patent Legislation in Developing Countries* 3 Tul J Tech and IP 1 (2001) 43–51.

their side effects in ICs, mainly competition laws and consumer protection.[6] The grounds upon which such licences may be issued have not been restricted by TRIPS, and may include public interest, public health, non-working and inadequate supply.[7] However, despite various exhortations by independent scholars and some organizations for DCs to use compulsory licensing, as they constituted TRIPS-legal measure,[8] yet DCs have traditionally been reluctant to do so. This reluctance has been attributed to fear of adverse effects on FDI, initial threats from the US and EU, and the lack of sufficient administrative procedures to process such an issuance.[9] Moreover, TRIPS does impose a constraint in its Article 31(f), where it stipulates that a compulsory license shall be predominantly for the supply of the domestic market of the country issuing it. This adversely impacts countries with insufficient capacity for pharmaceutical production, mainly least developed countries.[10]

Parallel imports offer another means for DCs to address the problem of access to medicine. There has been extensive debate concerning their TRIPS-legality, and more importantly, the economic desirability of parallel imports.[11] Most notably, the United States and Switzerland have been arguing that while TRIPS Article 6 excludes the initiation of DSU action on the question of parallel imports, yet that did not imply their legality, which they believed was denied under Article 28.[12] This interpretation was championed by the pharmaceutical MNEs.[13] However, this question was settled by the Doha Declaration, which acknowledged the right of each WTO

[6] Carlos Correa *Intellectual Property Rights and the Use of Compulsory Licenses: Options for Developing Countries* South Centre Trade-Related Agenda, Development and Equity Working Paper No 5, 1 (Oct 1999).

[7] ibid 11–14.

[8] See James Love *Compulsory Licensing: Models for State Practice in Developing Countries, Access to Medicine and Compliance with the WTO TRIPS Accord*, Paper Prepared for the United Nations Development Programme (21 Jan 2001) <http://www.cptech.org/ip/health/cl/ recommendedstatepractice.html> (last visited 18 Mar 2006).

[9] Frederick M Abbott *The TRIPS Agreement, Access to Medicines and the WTO Doha Ministerial Conference* Quaker United Nations Office—Geneva, Occasional Paper No 7, 11 (2001).

[10] See Abbott (2002) (n 2) 3.

[11] See Frederick M Abbott *First Report (Final) to the Committee on International Trade Law of the International Law Association on the Subject of Parallel Importation* 1 J Int'l Econ L 607 (1998); Harvey E Bale Jr *The Conflicts Between Parallel Trade and Product Access and Innovation: The Case of Pharmaceuticals* 1 J Int'l Econ L 637 (1998); See Keith E Maskus *Parallel Imports in Pharmaceuticals: Implications for Competition and Prices in Developing Countries* WIPO Studies on Intellectual Property (2001) <http://www.wipo.int/about-ip/en/studies/pdf/ ssa_maskus_pi.pdf> (last visited 18 Mar 2006); and Stefan Szymanski *International Exhaustion: A Review of the Economic Issues*, Paper Prepared for the Intellectual Property Institute (Feb 1999) (on file with author).

[12] Please refer to Ch 13 below.

[13] See Frederick Abbott (2001) (n 5) 78.

member to freely establish its own exhaustion regime.[14] Notwithstanding the legality of parallel imports, ICs have questioned its value in the specific context of access to medicines given that it might blunt the effectiveness of policies aiming for differential pricing, and the US added the concern with threats to public health of difficulties in monitoring quality of imports.[15]

These policies offered possible avenues for DCs, in their quest for affordable medicines, to counter the negative effects of high levels of patent protection as mandated by TRIPS. However, the pharmaceutical MNEs supported by the United States, contended that patents were not the problem in securing access to medicines in DCs. Harvey Bale of IFPMA, argued that access to medicine is not a one-dimensional issue related to price, and that the price effects of patent changes is almost nil or insignificant.[16] Moreover, the International Intellectual Property Institute (IIPI), in a report to WIPO, also repeated the MNEs argument that neither patents nor TRIPS are the problem with access to medicine, but rather the issue concerns the need for proper financing.[17] IIPI proceeds to recommend tiered pricing arrangements and a prohibition on parallel importation.[18] PhRMA also argued against the use of parallel imports.[19] Moreover, Professor Abbott lists statements from IFPMA spokespersons and from the USTR that echo the same line, and refutes their argument that price was not the predominant concern in securing affordable access to medicines.[20] IFPMA also attacked the use of compulsory licences, arguing that issues of safety were raised, that governments tend to use it as an industrial policy rather than as a pro-consumer tool, and that its use in a specific area, such as HIV/AIDS medicines, will mean less research funding for that area.[21]

More constraining to DCs options however, apart from the viewpoints expressed by pharmaceutical MNEs above, has been the practice by the

[14] WTO *Ministerial Conference, Fourth Session, Doha, 9–14 November, 2001, Declaration on the TRIPS Agreement and Public Health* WT/MIN(01)/DEC/2 (20 Nov 2001) para 5(d), [hereinafter Doha Declaration].

[15] See Abbot (2001) (n 9) 21–2. See also discussion in Ch 13 below.

[16] Harvey E Bale *Globalization: Pharmaceuticals and Vaccines* in G Velasquez and P Boulet *Globalization and Access to Drugs: Perspectives on the WTO/TRIPS Agreement* Report to the World Health Organization, 89 (1999) <http://www.who.int/medicinedocs/collect/edmweb/pdf/whozip35e.pdf> (last visited 3 Mar 2006). See also IFPMA *Intellectual Property: Patents and Pharmaceuticals* IFPMA ISSUE PAPER (Feb 1997) (on file with author).

[17] International Intellectual Property Institute (IIPI) *Patent Protection and Access to HIV/AIDS Pharmaceuticals in Sub-Saharan Africa* Report Prepared for the World Intellectual Property Organization, 20–23, 52–54 (2000) <http://www.wipo.int/about-ip/en/studies/pdf/iipi_hiv.pdf> (last visited 6 Mar 2006).

[18] ibid 57.

[19] See PhRMA *Frequently Asked Questions, available at* <http://world.phrma.org/faq> (last visited 9 Feb 2002).

[20] Abbott (2001) (n 9) 36–41.

[21] See Karin Timmermans and Togi Hutadjulu THE TRIPS AGREEMENT AND PHARMACEUTICALS: REPORT OF AN ASEAN WORKSHOP ON THE TRIPS AGREEMENT AND ITS IMPACT ON PHARMACEUTICALS 13 (2000).

United States of pursuing TRIPS-plus policies. In fact, US trade law authorizes the USTR to bring trade pressure on other countries on IP issues, concerning an '*unreasonable*' act, policy or practice, even when it is '*not necessarily in violation of, or inconsistent with, the international legal rights of the United States. . .*'[22] Ralph Nader and James Love, in a 1999 letter to Vice President Gore, quote a US PTO official as follows:

> The fact that [the current US] view is not reflected in the TRIPs agreement, in the multilateral context, is fully acknowledged. In our bilateral discussions, we continue to regard the TRIPs agreement as an agreement that established minimum standards for protection and, in certain situations, we may, and often do, ask for commitments that go beyond those found in the TRIPs agreement.[23]

However, on the other side of the divide, supportive of unhindered access to medicines in DCs, has been the global NGO community. Their role has been particularly prominent in this issue starting from the second half of the 1990s.[24] A leading NGO, Médicins Sans Frontières (MSF), summed up the prerogative of the 'Campaign for Access to Essential Medicines' when it called, in the wake of the Seattle Ministerial, for the need to balance protection of IPRs with assuring individuals access to medicine.[25] This particular campaign was formed by MSF, Consumer Project on Technology (CPT), and Health Action International (HAI), and eventually managed to gain the support of the UNDP, the WHO, and the World Bank.[26] Specifically, NGO campaigners have been among the earliest advocates for the use of TRIPS Article 31 compulsory licensing provisions to tackle the problem of access to medicines in DCs.[27]

The effects of NGO campaigning, the breadth of its participants, and their success in countering MNEs' and ICs' pressure, led them to have a profound impact in addressing the access to medicine dilemma. Their influence as well as the role of DCs in resisting MNE and IC pressure is examined below in the two cases of Brazil and South Africa.

[22] 19 USC § 2411 (d)(3) (2003).

[23] Letter from Ralph Nader and James Love, to Vice President Albert Gore (8 Apr 1999) <http://www.cptech.org/ip/health/sa/2gore.html> (last visited 6 Mar 2006).

[24] See SUSAN K SELL, PRIVATE POWER, PUBLIC LAW: THE GLOBALIZATION OF INTELLECTUAL PROPERTY RIGHTS (2003) 146–50.

[25] See Médecins Sans Frontières website <http://www.accessmed=msf.org/prod/publications.asp?scntid=2282001556195&contenttype=PARA&> (last visited 6 Mar 2006)

[26] See Susan K Sell *Post-TRIPS Developments: The Tension Between Commercial and Social Agendas in the Context of Intellectual Property* 14 Florida J Int'l L 193 (2002) 210–12.

[27] Ellen 't Hoen *TRIPS, Pharmaceutical Patents, and Access to Essential Medicines: A Long Way From Seattle to Doha* 3 Chi J Int'l L 27 (2002) 33–4.

(II) BRAZIL'S AIDS TREATMENT PROGRAMME

With an HIV-infected population estimated at 580,000 people, Brazil has been a model in the fight against the disease.[28] A major factor in this feat has been an impressive drug-distribution programme, started in 1992, where the Brazilian Government seeks to manufacture ARVs, and to distribute them to patients free of charge.[29] By 2001, Brazil was already manufacturing eight of the twelve AIDS medications it was distributing to HIV positive patients.[30] Through this policy, it has managed to cut the number of AIDS-related deaths by about 50 per cent in four years.[31] This policy is affordable due to the Government's policy of manufacturing generic ARVs and hence significantly reducing costs, saving the Government an estimated US $422 million in hospital treatment over four 32rs.[32] As an indicator, it was reported that the prices of AIDS drugs manufactured solely by pharmaceutical MNEs dropped by only 9 per cent during the period 1996–2000, whereas for those medicines that compete with the Government manufactured generics, the prices plummeted by 72 per cent.[33] Consequently, in 2000, the annual cost of a typical dose of ARVs in Brazil was US $4,162, compared with US $12,000–$15,000 in the United States.[34]

(A) Pressure on Brazil's Policy

Given this policy of affording ARVs to its AIDS programme, pressure was building within Brazil for achieving flexibility in the provision of less costly generic medicines.[35] One avenue was to ensure availability through the ability to issue compulsory licences for patented products. As such, on 6 October 1999, a Presidential Decree was issued regulating the implementation of Article 71 of its patent law, to permit compulsory licensing for non-commercial public use in cases of national emergency or public interest including those related to public health.[36] PhRMA was incensed by this decree. In its 1999 US NTE submission, it attacked the decree as stipulat-

[28] Stephen Buckley *Brazil Becomes Model in Fight Against AIDS* WASHINGTON POST (17 Sept 2000) A22.

[29] ibid.

[30] Miriam Jordan *Brazil May Flout Trade Laws to Keep AIDS Drugs Free* WALL STREET JOURNAL (12 Feb 2001).

[31] Mark Harrington *Brazil: What Went Right? The Global Challenge to Treatment and the Issue of Compulsory Licensing*, Paper Presented to the 10th National Meeting of People Living with HIV and AIDS, Rio de Janeiro (3 Nov 2000) 7 <http://www.aidsinfonyc.org/tag/activism/brazil.html> (last visited 6 Mar 2006).

[32] ibid. [33] See Stephen Buckley (n 28). [34] ibid.

[35] Brazil's Health Ministry reported in 2001 that unless it was able to reduce its reliance on expensive imported drugs, it estimated that spending on AIDS medicines will rise five-fold to US $1.7 billion by 2005. See Miriam Jordan (n 30).

[36] Patents (Compulsory Licenses) Decree No 3.201 (6 Oct 1999) Art 2(2).

ing the granting of compulsory licences in 'broadly defined situations of national emergency', the absence of any dialogue with industry prior to its publication, and apparent inconsistency with TRIPS obligations.[37] This issue was reportedly taken up by US Secretary of Commerce Daley in a February 2000 visit to Brazil.[38]

However, the main conflict with the United States was to come from Article 68 of Brazil's industrial property law concerning its local working provision.[39] As discussed in the earlier chapter, the US requested consultations with Brazil under the WTO's DSU mechanism on this issue, and it was noted that the politics within which it was enmeshed outweighed in significance the legal issues at stake. Indeed, it is noteworthy that as Brazil issued its new industrial property law in 1996, the pharmaceutical MNEs and the US government were quite satisfied with its provisions. PhRMA applauded this legislation stating that 'Brazil's improved patent protection regime will now serve as a positive example for the developing countries in Latin America and worldwide with inadequate patent protection.'[40] Yet Article 68's local working requirement was part of that very same legislation.[41] It is therefore clear that the timing of this dispute as it arose in May 2000 was important.

The US action came at the heels of the Presidential Decree, and the aggressive policy pursued by Brazil towards the pharmaceutical MNEs in seeking to guarantee an affordable supply of antiretroviral drugs. PhRMA applied pressure on the USTR to take action, arguably aimed not specifically at rescinding that particular provision, but more as a means of applying brakes to what they perceived as an increasingly vociferous Brazilian stance. Indeed, this action came at a time when the pharmaceutical MNEs were embroiled in their fight in South Africa, as will be discussed further below. The MNEs were hence on the defensive and worried about their position vis-à-vis the global access to medicines debate, and the increasing

37 *Submission of the Pharmaceutical Research Manufacturers of America for the 1999 National Trade Estimate Report on Foreign Trade Barriers* (3 Dec 1999) (on file with author).

38 Marcio Aith *Patents Law Can Generate Conflict with US* FOLHA DE SAO PAOLO (12 Feb 2000) translated and available at: <http://www.essentialdrugs.org/edrug/archive200002/msg00067.php> (last visited 12 Mar 2006).

39 For a review of the Brazil-US conflict, see Bass (2002) (n 1) 206–210; and Paul Champ and Amir Attaran *Patent Rights and Local Working Under the WTO TRIPS Agreement: An Analysis of the US-Brazil Patent Dispute* 27 Yale J Int'l L 365 (2002) 380–390.

40 *Submission of the Pharmaceutical Research Manufacturers of America for the 1995 'Special 301' Report on Intellectual Property Protection* (13 Feb 1995) (on file at the USTR Reading Room, and copy on file with author) [hereinafter PhRMA 1995 301 Submission].

41 While the US placed Brazil on its Special 301 'Watch List' in 1996 and 1997, yet in the 1998 301 Report there was no mention whatsoever of Brazil. It is only in the 1999 301 Report that Brazil is back on the 'Watch List,' and focus is placed on the local working provision. See USTR, 1996 Special 301 Report, 5 (3 May 1996); USTR 1997 Special 301 Report, 11 (30 Apr 1997); USTR 1999 Special 301 Report, 17 (30 Apr 1999).

tendency by afflicted DCs to seek means of acquiring less costly medicines. In fact, they had sufficient reason to be worried.

(B) Countering US Pressure

Brazil countered the pressure of the US WTO action, with an even more aggressive stance. In the words of one US official, Brazil followed the strategy that 'the best defence is a good offence'.[42] Most importantly, Brazil succeeded in placing the focus on its successful AIDS programme as being endangered by US action, and that action being spurred by pharmaceutical MNEs.[43] This claim was supported by NGOs. In February 2001, both Act Up and MSF called on the US to withdraw its WTO case against Brazil, where MSF argued that this challenge 'might handicap the successful Brazilian AIDS programme, which is largely based on Brazil's ability to manufacture affordable treatment'.[44] Indeed, the United States was forced to make statements on a number of occasions to defend itself from this charge, arguing that it was not aimed at Brazil's public health policies, but rather on the narrow issues of law comprising what it deemed to be a discriminatory Brazilian patent law provision.[45] Moreover, Brazil engaged in other retorting actions directed at US and MNE pressure, and in pursuit of its public health priorities.

Primarily, Brazil countered US pressure, by action within the WTO itself. In parallel with the US request for the establishment of a panel in the US–Brazil dispute over Article 68, Brazil initiated its own WTO DSU action against the United States over alleged discriminatory provisions in its patent law.[46] Premised on very similar grounds to the US complaint, Brazil argued that Articles 204 and 209 of Title 35, US Patent Code, contained a local working requirement that, inter alia, violated the non-discrimination principle under Article 27.1 and 28.1 of TRIPS.[47] The significance of this action was to present the US as engaging in double standards, accusing Brazil of

[42] US *Responds to Criticisms of Brazilian Patent Complaint* 18 Int'l Trade Rep (BNA) 238 (8 Feb 2001).

[43] Stephen Buckley *US, Brazil Clash Over AIDS Drugs* WASHINGTON POST (6 Feb 2001) A01. On the role of PhRMA in the Brazil case, see Sell (2003) (n 24) 136–8.

[44] US *Responds to Criticisms of Brazilian Patent Complaint* 18 Int'l Trade Rep (BNA) 238 (8 Feb 2001).

[45] See USTR 2001 Special 301 Report, 10 (27 Apr 2001); and Statement of the US Embassy in Brasilia (2 Feb 2001) reported in Reuters *Brazil May Defy US and Make More AIDS Drugs* NY TIMES (2 Feb 2001).

[46] WTO *United States—US Patents Code, Request for Consultations by Brazil* WT/DS224/1 (7 Feb 2001).

[47] ibid. See also *Brazil Seeks Consultations in WTO On US 'Local Working' Patent Rules* 18 Int'l Trade Rep (BNA) 239 (8 Feb 2001). The specific provisions deal with regulating patenting of subject matter arrived at through US government funded research.

discriminatory action that it practices within its own patent regime. Furthermore, it can also be seen as a means of exerting pressure on the US within the WTO, this was after all the first time that the United States was being presented before the DSU mechanism by a DC over alleged patent law violations. Ultimately the US relented and in a face-saving formula, reached a mutually agreed solution with Brazil where the latter also dropped its WTO complaint against the US.[48] This US decision came at the time when the TRIPS Council had begun its discussions on public health issues, and on the day of the opening of the UN special session on AIDS. This created an environment in which the US felt it politically expedient to drop its action against Brazil.

Moreover, Brazil also adopted international policies that were to prove quite troubling for the US and the pharmaceutical MNEs. It led DCs for action within international organizations, particularly the World Health Organization and the Commission on Human Rights, calling for access to medicines and priority for public health over narrower definitions of TRIPS and IC policy constraints.[49] This ultimately paved the way for action within the WTO on TRIPS and public health as will be discussed below. Another international policy pursued by Brazil, was its cooperation programmes with DCs over the HIV/AIDS pandemic, and specifically those aspects encouraging access to medicine.[50] A cooperation programme was started with South Africa.[51] In this regard, South Africa's health minister visited Far-Manguinhos, the leading Brazilian state-owned generic producer, in 2000 to review the Brazilian model, and Barbados, Chile, and Kenya were expected to begin importing small quantities of Brazil's low-cost generics for pilot studies.[52] Paulo Teixeira, National Coordinator of Brazil's AIDS programme sought an international mechanism with international organizations and other DCs that would provide a database of worldwide medicine prices, however, he noted that there were difficulties with the proposal.[53]

(C) Tackling the Pharmaceutical MNEs

On a second front, the pharmaceutical MNEs were also given their share of Brazil's retorting action. As necessitated by a need to push the prices of

[48] See Press Release 01-46, USTR United States and Brazil Agree to Use Newly Created Consultative Mechanism to Promote Cooperation on HIV/AIDS and Address WTO Patent Dispute (25 June 2001) (on file with author).
[49] Please refer to Ch 13 below.
[50] See 't Hoen (2002) (n 27) 32.
[51] See Stephen Buckley (n 28).
[52] Miriam Jordan (n 30).
[53] See Andrew Downie *AIDS Drugs Offered Free in Brazil* CHRISTIAN SCIENCE MONITOR (6 Dec 2000).

AIDS medications down, the Brazilian Government was engaged in negotiations with the pharmaceutical MNEs. This policy, while being met by resistance from the side of the MNEs and ultimately the US Government as discussed above, was successful from the Brazilian perspective. However, more cost cuts were needed, particularly in those instances involving imported patented proprietary medicines. The head of Brazil's AIDS programme warned that the need to import more expensive drugs could render the national AIDS programme unsustainable.[54] In February 2001, Brazil threatened to begin producing two antiretroviral drugs, Efavirenz and Nelfinavir, by June if the producing companies MSD and Roche respectively, did not cut their prices on these imported medicines.[55] Indeed, Far-Manguinhos imported a batch of Efavirenz from India for research purposes, a move severely criticized by MSD that threatened to take legal action against the laboratory.[56] Negotiations with the companies still did not produce the price cuts Brazil considered adequate.

As such, on 22 August 2001, Brazil's Ministry of Health announced that it was in the process of issuing a compulsory licence for the drug Viracept, the proprietary name for Nelfinavir, produced by the Swiss pharmaceutical MNE Roche,[57] following its failure to lower the price of the medicinal product sufficiently.[58] Earlier, Roche had offered a discount of 13 per cent, but Brazil rejected it as insufficient.[59] The Government argued that it spends US $88 million a year on that particular drug, representing 28 per cent of its entire AIDS budget.[60] On the other hand, Brazil announced that its negotiations with MSD over price reductions on the drug Efavirenz had been successful with an offer of a 70 per cent reduction in the price of the drug.[61] The announcement by Brazil that it was in the process of issuing the compulsory licence took the pharmaceutical industry by surprise. Indeed, the day following the announcement, Roche stated that it was 'extremely surprised to hear the news of this government announcement'.[62] This was the closest any developing country had reached in carrying out a threat of

[54] Miriam Jordan (n 30).

[55] Reuters (n 45); and Stephen Buckley (n 28).

[56] See news story at <http://dailynews.yahoo.com/h/po/20010326/co/brazil_aids_drug_dispute_courtbound_1.html> (last visited 8 Jul 2003).

[57] While Viracept is sold in Brazil by Roche, the patent is owned by the US pharmaceutical MNE Pfizer.

[58] Press Release, Ministry of Health, Brasilia 'Ministry of Health Announces Compulsory Licensing of Nelfinavir Patent' (22 Aug 2001) <http://lists.essential.org/pipermail/ip-health/2001-August/001755.html> (last visited 12 Mar 2006) [hereinafter Brazilian MoH Press Release].

[59] Jennifer L Rich and Melody Petersen *Brazil Will Defy Patent on AIDS Drug Made by Roche* NY TIMES (23 Aug 2001).

[60] ibid.

[61] Brazilian MoH Press Release (n 58).

[62] *Brazil Will Not Break AIDS Drug Patent; Government, Roche Strike Deal on Price* 18 Int'l Trade Rep (BNA) 1396 (6 Sept 2001).

compulsory licensing of a pharmaceutical MNEs' patent, despite the rhetoric of many years concerning the access to medicines debate. As such, and one week later, Roche acceded to Brazil's demand, and reduced its price on Viracept by a further 40 per cent, and announced it was to begin manufacturing the drug in Brazil in early 2002.[63]

This scenario with Roche was arguably a turning point for the relation between MNEs and DC governments, and particularly in the case of Brazil. The issue was no longer focused on TRIPS legality of actions, MNEs could no longer have the unimpeded recourse they once had to effectuating IC pressure on DCs. Their use of a broadly interpreted TRIPS to suit their interests was no longer viable. Indeed, the Roche scenario was not the end. Having achieved significant reductions on the prices of Nelfinavir and Efavirenz, Brazil was to turn its attention on another ARV, Lopinavir, produced by the US pharmaceutical MNE Abbott Laboratories.[64] Moreover, two years later, in 2003 and following the Doha WTO Ministerial with its Doha Declaration on Public Health, Brazil was still engaging in negotiations with MSD, Roche, and Abbott over further price cuts on those same ARVs, with threats of compulsory licensing and parallel importation.

The Brazilian Government was therefore successful in maintaining its AIDS treatment program, as it managed to counter US pressure, and to persuade pharmaceutical MNEs to effectuate considerable price reductions and engage in local production. This success, was also possible due to considerable support from NGOs in assisting Brazil's policies.[65] However, it was in the case of South Africa, where NGO action proved most effective.

(III) SOUTH AFRICA'S MEDICINES AMENDMENT ACT

With a population exceeding 43 million, South Africa has an HIV/AIDS epidemic of devastating proportions. One in five of its adult population is infected with HIV.[66] Every single day, 1,600 South Africans contract HIV, the highest contracting rate in the world.[67] As a consequence of this situation, on 12 December 1997, President Nelson Mandela signed the

[63] ibid.

[64] *Government to Struggle with Abbott* O GLOBO (Sao Paulo 5 Sept 2001), translated and available at <http://lists.essential.org/pipermail/ip-health/2001-September/001804.html> (last visited 12 Mar 2006).

[65] See Oxfam *Drug Companies vs Brazil: The Threat to Public Health* OXFAM POLICY PAPER (May 2001) <http://www.oxfam.org.uk/what_we_do/issues/health/downloads/drugcomp_brazil.rtf> (last visited 12 Mar 2006).

[66] IIPI (2000) (n 17) 93.

[67] George Will *AIDS Crushes a Continent* NEWSWEEK (10 Jan 2000) 64.

Medicines and Related Substances Control Amendment Act.[68] The Act encompassed three specific provisions of interest. The first and most contentious amendment introduced section 15C to the Medicines and Related Substance Control Act.[69] It endowed the Minister of Health with the power to '*prescribe conditions for the supply of more affordable medicines in certain circumstances so as to protect the health of the public, . . .*' including allowing what amounts to the parallel importation of medicines and prescribing registration procedures for them.[70] Secondly, section 22F was introduced, instituting a mandatory generic substitution obligation on pharmacists to dispense cheaper generic equivalents unless specifically instructed otherwise by the prescription or by the patient. Finally, the Amendment Act also introduced section 22G which contains price regulations on medicines with the aim of achieving a more transparent system. The essence of the Amendment Act was therefore to enable the Minister of Health to seek the lowest cost medicines available primarily through parallel importation and generic substitution where applicable, and finally a transparent pricing mechanism to carry out the first two goals.[71]

What followed the issuance of the Amendment Act was to prove a decisive chapter in the saga of the TRIPS Agreement. The pressure that was to be generated by the pharmaceutical MNEs and ICs, particularly the US government, was to cast a shadow on the legitimacy of the TRIPS regime as interpreted by them. More importantly, the unprecedented response by activists from global civil society as represented by NGOs, was to change the dynamic on TRIPS and access to medicines in the context of public health. Below, pharmaceutical MNE and IC pressures on South Africa are examined, followed by a presentation of the court action undertaken by the pharmaceutical MNEs against the Government of South Africa. Undoubtedly the efforts of the South African Government were important in resisting this pressure, as it was involved in national and international negotiations that resulted in the withdrawal of the lawsuit in April 2001.[72] However, it is argued here that this success was made possible as a result of NGOs' retorting action, as will be discussed below.

[68] Medicines and Related Substances Control Amendment Act No 90 (1997) <http://www.info.gov.za/gazette/acts/1997/a90-97.pdf> (last visited 12 Mar 2006) [hereinafter Medicines Amendment Act].

[69] Medicines and Related Substances Control Act No 101 (1965) [hereinafter Principal Act].

[70] Section 15C Medicines Amendment Act. Emphasis added.

[71] For commentary on the South African legislation and case, see Abbott (2002) (n 2) 51–54; 't Hoen (2002) (n 27) 30–1; Duane Nash *South Africa's Medicines and Related Substances Control Amendment Act of 1997* 15 Berkeley Tech L J 485 (2000); and Bass (2002) (n 1) 210–15.

[72] See Commission on Intellectual Property Rights (CIPR) The South African Drugs Case, para 17, <http://www.iprcommission.org/documents%5CS%20Africa.doc> (last visited 9 Mar 2002).

(A) Pharmaceutical MNEs and IC Pressures

Pharmaceutical MNEs viewed the Amendment Act as a threat to their market dominance interests in South Africa and in the global market for the treatment of pandemic diseases, primarily but not necessarily limited to HIV/AIDS.[73] The concerns of the MNEs related to the fact that the Amendment Act would authorize parallel importation of medicines, and potentially of allowing the compulsory licensing of MNEs' pharmaceutical products to perform the objectives of the Act.[74] But more significantly, and in placing the specific example of South Africa, as with that of Brazil, in its wider context amidst a global HIV/AIDS pandemic, the MNEs feared that the Amendment Act might prove to be the tip of the iceberg, and if they would acquiesce now, this would send a signal that would open the flood-gates with other DCs seeking to follow in South Africa's footsteps. As PhRMA presented to the US government:

> the apparent intent of the Government of South Africa is to not only to defend its diminishment of the effectiveness of patent protection in South Africa, but to urge other countries to similarly weaken patent protection for pharmaceutical products. Such a posture is plainly antagonistic to the concept of effective patent protection for pharmaceuticals, and is likely to give rise to a substantial diminishment of the effectiveness in protection not only in South Africa but elsewhere.[75]

The MNEs were therefore before a litmus test compounded by the rise of a formidable new adversary in the form of NGO campaigning stirring a global public outcry against their actions.[76] Against this backdrop, the MNEs mobilized their resources to defeat the Amendment Act. At one level, MNEs promoted the thesis that in the fight against the HIV/AIDS pandemic in sub-Saharan Africa, patents were not the problem, but rather, it was poor infrastructure and the absence of sufficient international assistance that denied sufficient access to medicines. Harvey Bale of the International Federation of Pharmaceutical Manufacturers Associations (IFPMA) argued that

[73] For information on the different drugs used in the care of HIV/AIDS patients, including ARVs, see Joint UNICEF, UNAIDS Secretariat, WHO/HTP, and MSF Project *Sources and Prices of Selected Drugs and Diagnostics for People Living with HIV/AIDS* (May 2002) <http://www. who.int/hiv/topics/arv/en/who_edm_par_2002.pdf> (last visited 12 Mar 2006).

[74] On pharmaceutical MNEs fears of the consequences of the Amendment Act, see Nash (2000) (n 71) 499–500.

[75] PhRMA 1999 301 Submission.

[76] Oxfam adopted a scathing offensive against the pharmaceutical MNEs embodied in its 'Cut the Cost' campaign. See Oxfam *South Africa v the Drug Giants: A Challenge to Affordable Medicines* OXFAM POLICY PAPER (Feb 2001) <http://www.oxfam.org.uk/what_we_do/issues/health/drugcomp_sa.htm> (last visited 12 Mar 2006). See further below on the role of NGO action.

> [t]he cost of drugs to patients in Africa is determined principally by distribution, infrastructure, training and other factors. . . . Patents do not, in fact, have an influence on access to drugs, which the population in developing countries actually consumes.[77]

Moreover, allowing parallel imports, notwithstanding the illegality of doing so according to their interpretation of TRIPS, would entail the hazards of bringing in suspect quality medicine, made worse by the absence of efficient regulatory agencies in these countries.[78] Advocacy aside, and given the imminent threat of parallel imports, certain pharmaceutical MNEs operating in South Africa, mainly GSK, Warner Lambert and Pfizer, engaged in tactical market measures to consolidate their hold on the supply and distribution channels to pre-empt competition from parallel imports and generics.[79] Their efforts however were thwarted by the South African Competition Tribunal. Yet another tactic employed by the pharmaceutical MNEs, mainly to counter the public outcry, was to engage in a campaign to offer medicines at reduced prices, and in some instances as donations.[80]

Most significantly, pharmaceutical MNEs sought the intervention of their home country governments to exert pressure on the South African government. The IC intervention came primarily from the United States, and to a lesser extent form the European Union.[81] And finally, the MNEs, acting primarily through their industry association in South Africa, the Pharmaceutical Manufacturers' Association (PMA) sought to challenge the legality of the Amendments Act in the South African court system. Below, we first consider IC pressure on South Africa, and then discuss the pharmaceutical MNEs' lawsuit against the South African government.

Following the Amendment Act's signature, and in its 1998 'Special 301' submission to the USTR, PhRMA derided the impact of the Amendment Act on South Africa's once relatively modern patent law that provided full product patent protection for pharmaceuticals.[82] Arguing that the Amendment Act would allow the Health Minister to abrogate all pharmaceutical patents in South Africa, it also presented that its Article 15C(b)

[77] Harvey E Bale Jr 'AIDS in Africa' (24 Feb 2000) (on file with author).

[78] *See* Nash (2000) (n 71) 499.

[79] Reported in posting of Zackie Achmat, Zackie@pixie.co.za to IP-Health@lists.essential.org (31 Aug 2000) <http://lists.essential.org/pipermail/ip-health/2000-August/000425.html> (last visited 16 Mar 2006).

[80] These efforts were accelerated after the initiation of the lawsuit. See Rachel L Swarns *AIDS Drug Battle Deepens in Africa* NY TIMES (8 Mar 2001). See also Bass (2002) (n 76) 213.

[81] Switzerland, as a home country to a leading pharmaceutical industry also intervened with the South African government.

[82] PhRMA 1998 301 Submission.

violated TRIPS Article 28.[83] Advising the USTR to designate it a 'Priority Foreign Country' PhRMA added that

> South Africa has become a 'test case' for those who oppose the US Government's long-standing commitment to improve the terms of protection for all forms of American intellectual property, including pharmaceutical patents . . . a direct challenge to the improvements in intellectual property protection represented by the Uruguay Round.[84]

Similar complaints by European pharmaceutical MNEs were addressed to the European Commission, where they claimed the Amendment Act was in violation of South Africa's TRIPS Articles 27 and 28 commitments.[85]

Responding to industry urgings, the USTR announced on 1 May 1998, that it placed South Africa on its Special 301 'Watch List'.[86] In its review of South Africa, the USTR urged it to 'make clear in regulations or legislation that the powers granted in the Medicines Act are consistent with its international obligations and to clarify what actions may be taken pursuant to that Act and under what circumstances'.[87] The 1999 Special 301 review also maintained South Africa's designation.[88] The reasoning of the USTR review of the Amendment Act echoed that of the PhRMA submission, namely that it conferred too broad an authority to the Minister of Health to potentially abrogate patent rights. There was no specific mention of any articles of TRIPS, implying the USTR was once more seeking TRIPS-plus provisions. As one observer contends, the USTR believed it has the right to demand South Africa to comply with 'U.S.-defined TRIPS-plus provisions.'[89] In an attributed letter from the US Ambassador in South Africa to Dr Abe Nkomo of the South African Parliament's portfolio committee on Health dated 4 October 1997, the US expressed its opposition to parallel imports of patented products anywhere in the world, and added that

> they are illegal in the United States, both as an infringement of patent rights and, because in the case of medicines, our Food and Drug Administration (FDA) believes it cannot adequately monitor quality.[90]

[83] ibid.

[84] ibid.

[85] See Letter from Ambassador Erwan Fouere, Head of European Commission Delegation in South Africa to Dr O Shisana, Director General, Department of Health, Pretoria (25 Nov 1997) <http://www.cptech.org/ip/health/eu/foure.html> (last visited 14 Feb 2001) [hereinafter Fouere Letter].

[86] USTR 1998 Special 301 Report, 21–22 (1 May 1998).

[87] ibid.

[88] USTR 1999 Special 301 Report, 24 (30 Apr 1999).

[89] Abbott (2002) (n 2) 52.

[90] Consumer Project on Technology (CPT) *Time-Line of Disputes Over Compulsory Licensing and Parallel Importation in South Africa* <http://www.cptech.org/ip/health/sa/sa-timeline.txt> (last visited 14 Jan 2004).

While the USTR and other executive agencies of the US Government were exerting pressure on South Africa, the US House of Representatives entered into the foray by threatening to cut aid appropriations to South Africa. Indeed, on 21 October 1998 it enacted legislation that withheld emergency aid to South Africa pending a report from the Secretary of State on the steps being taken by the US Government with the South African Government to get it to repeal, suspend or terminate section 15C of the Amendment Act.[91] The State Department responded on 5 February, 1999 that all relevant US Government agencies were engaged

> in an assiduous, concerted campaign to persuade the Government of South Africa (SAG) to withdraw or modify the provisions of Article 15(c) that we believe are inconsistent with South Africa's obligations and commitments under the WTO Agreement on Trade-Related Aspects of Intellectual Property Rights (TRIPS).[92]

Pressure was also exercised by the European Commission at the outset of the dispute. In March 1998, Sir Leon Brittan, Vice-President of the European Commission wrote Vice President Thabu M'Beki to express the concern of the European Commission.[93] However, the European position was not whole-hearted, particularly the European Parliament, was opposed to the action by the pharmaceutical MNEs, and issued a resolution in March 2001 supporting DCs rights to take measures to address access to medicines as long as they were TRIPS-compliant.[94] Moreover, at the end of 2000, the European Commission was paying special attention to its policy with regard to major communicable diseases.[95] As such, a significant shift from its initial position as stated by Sir Leon Brittan led the EC away from its support of the pharmaceutical MNE action in South Africa.[96]

[91] Omnibus Consolidated and Emergency Supplemental Appropriations Act, Pub L No 105–277, 112 Stat 2681 (1999).

[92] United States Department of State 'US Government Efforts to Negotiate the Repeal, Termination or Withdrawal of Article 15(c) of the South African Medicines and Related Substances Act of 1965' <http://www.cptech.org/ip/health/sa/stdept-feb51999.html> (last visited 19 Jan 2004).

[93] Letter from Sir Leon Brittan, Vice-President of the European Commission to Thabu M'Beki, Vice President of South Africa (23 Mar 1998) <http://www.cptech.org/ip/health/eu/brittan.html> (last visited 14 Jan 2004).

[94] European Parliament 'Access to Medicines for AIDS Patients in the Third World' Res No B5-0182/2001 (15 Mar 2001).

[95] EC Communication 'Accelerated Action Targeted at Major Communicable Diseases Within the Context of Poverty Reduction' COM (2000) 585 (20 Sept 2000).

[96] See IIPI (2000) (n 17) 18–19.

(B) Lawsuit Against the Government of South Africa[97]

On 18 February 1998, the Pharmaceutical Manufacturers' Association of South Africa (PMA), and 40 pharmaceutical companies,[98] filed a notice of motion with the High Court of South Africa, commencing the lawsuit against President Nelson Mandela and nine other South African officials, including the Minister of Health and the Registrar of Patents.[99] In the motion, the applicants primarily requested the court to issue an interim interdict suspending the application of the Amendment Act pending the final outcome of the case.[100] It was argued that the mere fact of initiating legal proceedings and the ensuing suspension of the Amendment Act served the strategy adopted by the pharmaceutical industry seeking to delay the application of the Act.[101] This they hoped would buy time while pressure was being exerted on South Africa by IC home countries.

The essence of the ongoing debate concerning public health issues and access to medicines centered on varying interpretations of TRIPS provisions. However, the TRIPS Agreement was arguably tangential to the specifics of the South African court case. The only mention of TRIPS in the PMA notice of motion came with regard to the new section 15C, based on TRIPS Article 27, discrimination as to the field of technology. PMA claimed that this section discriminated with respect to the enjoyment of rights in a specific field, that of pharmaceuticals, and hence was in conflict with Article 27 of TRIPS, an international agreement binding on the Republic of South Africa, and was consequently in violation of section 44(4) of the Constitution.[102] However, in its complaint to the USTR, PhRMA posited that the Amendment Act also violated TRIPS Article 28, where it interpreted that particular article to outlaw parallel imports as a violation of the exclusive rights of the patent owner.[103]

The pharmaceutical industry alleged repeated violations of the South African Constitution.[104] Most importantly, PMA et al submitted that

[97] A good review of the South African lawsuit can be found in CIPR (n 72).

[98] Reduced later to 39 companies as a result of the merger between Glaxo Wellcome and Smithkline Beecham forming Glaxo Smithkline (GSK). The applicants represented essentially a who's who of the global pharmaceutical MNEs, including Bayer, BMS, Boehringer-Ingelheim, Eli Lilly, GSK, Hoechst, MSD, Novartis, Rhone-Poulenc, Roche, and Warner Lambert. Noticeably, Pfizer was missing from the roster of applicants.

[99] *Pharmaceutical Manufacturers' Association of South Africa et al v Nelson Mandela, President of the Republic of South Africa, et al* Case No 4183/98 (Transvaal Provincial Division, filed 18 Feb 1998).

[100] Notice of Motion Case No 4183, section 1. <http://www.cptech.org/ip/health/sa/ pharmasuit.html> (last visited 12 Mar 2006).

[101] See Abbott (2002) (n 2) 54.

[102] ibid para 2.4.

[103] PhRMA 1998 301 Submission.

[104] S AFR CONST (Act 108 1996).

section 15C endowed the Minister of Health with too broad an authority to determine 'prescribed conditions' for the supply of 'more affordable medicines' in 'certain circumstances.'[105] This, they argued, lacked setting out policy considerations or any guidelines that would limit the Minister's authority and power, in violation of Articles 43 and 44 of the Constitution.[106] In addition, this same section they argued

> enables and authorises the Fourth Respondent [Health Minister]: in conflict with Sections 43 and 44 of the Constitution, to '*determine*' the extent to which rights under a patent granted in the Republic shall apply irrespective of the provisions of the Patents Act, No 57 of 1978.[107]

Furthermore, they presented that the section enables and authorizes the Health Minister to deprive pharmaceutical producers of their intellectual property rights, or to expropriate such property without any compensation, again in violation of Article 25 of the Constitution.[108]

To place the claims of the pharmaceutical MNEs in perspective, Professor Abbott points out that the contentious section of the Amendment Act was actually based on a WIPO Committee of Experts draft for a Patent Harmonization Treaty (later known as the Patent Law Treaty), and embodied in WIPO model patent laws recommended to DCs.[109] Protracted negotiations followed between the parties to the dispute, including at one point an announcement by PMA in September 2000 that it was 'suspending' the lawsuit as the South African Health Minister promised to return the Amendment Act to Parliament for amendment in early 2000.[110] However the lawsuit resumed in May 2000, but it was ultimately withdrawn in April 2001.

(C) NGOs' Retorting Action

In the case of Brazil, as discussed above, retorting action by the government proved the decisive factor. In the case of South Africa however, while acknowledging action undertaken by the government, yet it was ultimately the NGOs that are to be credited with the main action to reverse IC and MNE pressure on South Africa. In so doing, they also contributed to the success of the worldwide access to medicines campaign unimpeded by TRIPS constraints as interpreted by ICs and the MNEs. In this endeavour, NGOs pursued three specific strategies. Primarily, they engaged in a public

[105] Notice of Motion Case No 4183 (n 100) para 2.1.
[106] ibid.
[107] ibid para 2.2. Emphasis in original.
[108] ibid para 2.3.
[109] Abbott (2002) (n 2) 53–54.
[110] *Drug Companies Suspend Lawsuit Against South African License Law* 16 Int'l Trade Rep (BNA) 1490 (15 Sept 2000).

relations campaign to bring about pressure on IC governments, most notably on the US Government, as well as publicizing the policies and pressures adopted by the pharmaceutical MNEs. Second, NGOs, particularly the South African NGO Treatment Action Campaign (TAC), exerted pressure on the South African Government so as not to yield to IC and MNE pressure. Third, NGOs were successful in being admitted as *amicus curiae* in the lawsuit brought by the pharmaceutical MNEs against the Government, and were able through this platform, to significantly alter the course of the South Africa case.

In pursuing their first strategy, NGOs realized that the strength of the pharmaceutical MNEs lied in their access to the US policy process, specifically their direct access to the USTR. As such, these NGOs, particularly the US-based AIDS group ACT UP, in collaboration with Ralph Nader's Consumer Project on Technology (CPT) headed by James Love, adopted a strategy targeting the USTR and the White House.[111] In so doing, they capitalized on Al Gore's presidential campaign. Pressure on the White House and the USTR intensified, with demonstrations against Al Gore organized, and a deluge of letters and petitions. On 8 April 1999, Ralph Nader and James Love wrote to Vice President Gore expressing their

> outrage that you have used your office to pressure the South African government to repeal its statutory authority for providing for compulsory licensing of patents for essential medicines,

adding that

> you have engaged in an astonishing array of bullying tactics to prevent South Africa from implementing policies, legal under the rules of the WTO, that are designed to expand access to HIV/AIDS drugs.[112]

Another open letter was also sent to Al Gore signed by 307 public health experts and concerned persons attacking his stance on the South Africa case, and linking this stance with his presidential campaign.[113] Similarly, action was also taken to the US Congress, where NGO activists presented their argument and attacked US policy.[114]

[111] See Susan K Sell *Industry Strategies for Intellectual Property and Trade: The Quest for TRIPS, and Post-TRIPS Strategies* 10 Cardozo J Int'l and Comp L 79 (2002) 152.

[112] Letter from Ralph Nader and James Love to Vice President Albert Gore (8 Apr 1999) <http://www.cptech.org/ip/health/sa/2gore.html> (last visited 12 Mar 2006).

[113] See Consumer Project on Technology (CPT) *Open Letter to Vice President Al Gore* (1 Aug 1999) <http://www.cptech.org/ip/ health/sa/goresignon.html> (last visited 12 Mar 2006).

[114] See Statement by James Love Before the Subcommittee on Criminal Justice, Human Resources and Drug Policy, Committee on Government Reform 'What is the United States' Role in Combating the Global HIV/AIDS Epidemic?' (22 July 1999) <http://www.cptech.org/ip/health/sa/ mica-test.txt> (last visited 12 Mar 2006).

Ultimately this pressure, and particularly activists' disruption of the Gore campaign, brought about a change in his policy and consequently in that of the US Government. This was most notably established in the announcement of the joint understanding between South Africa and the United States on 17 September 1999.[115] In it, both governments refer to the resolution of their differences, stating that in implementing the provisions of the Medicines Act that permit parallel importation and compulsory licensing, South Africa will honour its obligations under TRIPS.[116] Further changes in US policy came during the Seattle Ministerial when the USTR announced that in conjunction with the Health and Human Services Secretary, they intended to develop a cooperative approach on 'health-related intellectual property matters to ensure that the application of US trade law related to intellectual property remains sufficiently flexible to respond to legitimate public health crisis.'[117] In the same statement, the USTR announced the removal of South Africa from the Special 301 'Watch List'. Ultimately, in May 2000, President Clinton issued an executive order stating that the US would not seek the revocation or revision of any IP law or policy of sub-Saharan African countries relating to HIV/AIDS as long as that law is consistent with TRIPS.[118]

While the Bush administration maintained the policy adopted under Clinton's executive order, yet NGO pressure continued with the new Bush Administration. In March 2001, as the litigation in South Africa was proceeding, Health Gap Coalition wrote President Bush calling him to denounce the lawsuit, and clearly state his support for South Africa's right to use legal measures to make access to affordable medications a reality.[119] Across the Atlantic, this strategy was also being adopted by groups such as MSF, engaging in writing to the European Commission to change its policy and support rather than pressure South Africa.[120] Equally, Oxfam's UK arm was active in publicizing the South African case and in commenting on

[115] Department of Trade and Industry, South Africa 'Joint Understanding Between the Governments of South Africa and the United States of America' (17 Sept 1999) <http://www.polity.org.za/html/govdocs/pr/1999/pr0917b.html> (last visited 19 Jan 2004).

[116] ibid.

[117] Press Release 99–97, USTR The Protection of Intellectual Property and Health Policy (1 Dec 1999) (on file with author).

[118] Executive Order 13,155, 65 Fed Reg 30, 521 (10 May 2000).

[119] Letter from Asia Russell Health GAP Coalition to President George Bush (1 Mar 2001) available in posting of Asia Russell, asia@CritPath.org to IP-Health@lists.essential.org (1 Mar 2001) <http://lists.essential.org/pipermail/ip-health/2001-March/000967.html> (last visited 16 Dec 2003).

[120] See MSF *Open Letter to Pascal Lamy Re South Africa* (12 Feb 2001) <http://lists.essential.org/pipermail/ip-health/2001-February/000889.html> (last visited 23 June 2003). In this letter, MSF asks Commissioner Lamy to withdraw a letter sent earlier by his predecessor Sir Leon Brittan to the South African Government pressuring it to repeal the Medicines Amendment Act.

developments relating to the case.[121] Oxfam notably criticized the US loan offer for South Africa to purchase US-made ARVs, calling it a 'debt that tomorrow's AIDS orphans will be forced to pay.'[122]

On a second front, NGOs, and particularly the South African based Treatment Action Campaign (TAC), exerted pressure on the South African Government so that it would not relent to IC and MNE pressures. The Government was concerned about the situation and was particularly eager to avoid the lawsuit as it sought to salvage its international economic image with investors. In this regard, following the commencement of the lawsuit in 1998, it announced that section 15C would only be used for parallel imports and not for compulsory licensing.[123] This was reported to have prompted major tensions between the health and trade ministries.[124] To counter this tendency, NGOs engaged in a strategy to force the Government's hand, principally through engaging in efforts to procure cheaper ARVs mainly from Thailand and Brazil, while distributing them for free. In a highly publicized move, Zackie Achmat, Chair of TAC, imported a batch of Biozole, a generic version of Pfizer's Fluconazole, and proceeded to hand himself in to the authorities, as a gesture of challenge to allow for parallel imports, prompting an attack on TAC from the government's Medicines Control Council.[125] Later, and following the withdrawal of the case, TAC joined forces with MSF in procuring parallel imports of ARVs from Brazil starting from January 2002.[126]

Apart from seeking parallel imports, NGOs also orchestrated a drive to seek compulsory licences. This came following the February 2001 announcement by the Indian pharmaceutical company Cipla of its offer to sell its triple-drug AIDS treatment to DCs for $1,200 wholesale, $600 to governments, and $350 to NGOs (MSF).[127] Cipla, in conjunction with MSF applied to the South African Government to grant them a compulsory

[121] See Oxfam (n 76); and Oxfam *Update on South African Court Case* OXFAM POLICY PAPER (Apr 2001) <http://www.intermonoxfam.org/cms/HTML/espanol/454/TRIPS_South_Africa_Update.pdf> (last visited 22 Mar 2006).

[122] Press Release, Oxfam (21 July 2000), available in posting of James Love, love@cptech.org to IP-Health@lists.essential.org (23 July 2000) <http://lists.essential.org/pipermail/ip-health/2000-july/000392.html> (last visited 22 Mar 2006)

[123] Posting of James Love, love@cptech.org *Report on Court Case Over South Africa Medicines Act* (4 Mar 2001) <http://lists.essential.org/pipermail/ip-health/2001-March/000978. html> (last visited 22 Mar 2006).

[124] Nick Mathiason *South Africa Fights AIDS Drug Apartheid* OBSERVER (London 14 Jan 2001).

[125] See Press Statement, Treatment Action Campaign (TAC) The Medicines Control Council: Protecting Pfizer of Protecting Patients? (20 Oct 2000) <http://lists.essential.org/ pipermail/ip-health/2000-october/000573.html> (last visited 22 Feb 2004).

[126] Frederick M Abbott *The Doha Declaration on the TRIPS Agreement and Public Health: Lighting A Dark Corner at the WTO*, 5 J Int'l Econ L 469 (2002) 478.

[127] Susan Sell notes that this offer was reached mainly thanks to the efforts of James Love. See Sell (2003) (n 24) 156.

licence to manufacture ARV drugs patented by Pharmaceutical MNEs on the grounds that they were not being sold at affordable prices.[128] While NGOs were less than satisfied by the posture of the South African Government,[129] yet it was their actions there that were in large part responsible for the worldwide public pressure mounting against the pharmaceutical industry, and its IC backers.

Finally, NGOs also focused their attention on the PMA-initiated lawsuit. Apart from organizing demonstrations, and circulating letters targeting the pharmaceutical MNEs for initiating the lawsuit, a major victory for the NGOs was the acceptance by the High Court of South Africa of TAC's request to join the proceedings as amicus curiae, despite attempts by PMA to block their application.[130] The Treatment Action Campaign emphasized in its submissions, evidence about pharmaceutical MNEs pricing practices, cost of drug development, and the public role in supporting drug development.[131] The effect of this intervention by TAC, as with the greater efforts of the NGOs, can be largely credited for ultimately causing the PMA and the pharmaceutical MNEs to withdraw their court action on 19 April 2001. In a joint press release with MSF and Oxfam, Zackie Achmat of TAC called their feat a 'triumph of David over Goliath,' and the statement added that the outcome signalled a dramatic shift in the balance of power between DCs and drug companies.[132]

The results of NGO action were crystal clear in the case of South Africa. Combined with retorting action by the Brazilian Government, it appeared that a new discourse was emerging concerning the TRIPS Agreement, and between its different stakeholders. As Ellen 't Hoen of MSF noted, two important effects of the South Africa case, and we might add of the Brazil case, was that first, interpretations and flexibilities within TRIPS and their use for public health purposes needed clarification so DCs can use them without threats, and secondly, that ICs that exerted pressure to help their MNEs, could no longer do so without repercussions at home.[133]

[128] Sell (2002) (n 26) 214.

[129] NGOs were particularly frustrated by the unwillingness of the Government to declare AIDS a national emergency, thus prompting measures to enact regulatory flexibilities to confront the disease. See Jon Jeter *South Africa Resists Call for AIDS 'Emergency'* WASHINGTON POST (15 Mar 2001).

[130] See Joint Press Release, COSATU, TAC, MSF, Oxfam and CPT High Court Accepts the Right of People with HIV to be Heard (6 Mar 2001) <http://lists.essential.org/pipermail/ip-health/2001-March/000980.html> (last visited 22 Feb 2004).

[131] See Affidavit of James Love (filed 10 Apr 2001) <http://www.cptech.org/ip/health/sa/loveaffidavit/> (last visited 19 Jan 2004).

[132] Joint Press Release, MSF, Oxfam, and TAC Drug Companies in South Africa Capitulate Under Barrage of Public Pressure (19 Apr 2001) <http://lists.essential.org/pipermail/ip-health/2001-April/001230.html> (last visited 22 Feb 2004).

[133] 't Hoen (2002) (n 27) 31.

Chapter 13

Challenges at the WTO'S Political Organs

'. . . Lighting a dark corner at the WTO.'[1]

The third framework of retorting action against the TRIPS regime, action within the political organs of the WTO, derives from the same context as that of the Brazil and South Africa cases, mainly the issue of access to medicine and the public health implications of TRIPS. It can therefore be seen as an extension of this effort. Indeed, Brazil with its experience in battling with the US and the MNEs, as discussed earlier, has been at the forefront of DC action at the WTO.[2] It must be noted nonetheless, that the third framework signalled a qualitatively significant development. Not only was action now carried out multilaterally by DCs acting in concert, as differentiated from earlier retorting action involving individual DCs, but more significantly, this was action taken at the cradle of the TRIPS regime. It was within the political process of GATT (Uruguay Round) that TRIPS was conceived, the WTO's legal mechanisms that nurtured its implementation, and it was now back to the political organs of the WTO that DCs had chosen to pursue their action.

(I) GENESIS OF WTO ACTION

The action undertaken by DCs in the WTO aimed at upholding their freedom to devise necessary public health policies unhindered by TRIPS patent provisions, and interpretations thereof by ICs, and the consequent pressure they were subject to, essentially from the United States. WTO action however did not emerge spontaneously. Indeed, apart from the context of the Brazil and South Africa cases alluded to above, the issue of access to

[1] Frederick M Abbott *The Doha Declaration on the TRIPS Agreement and Public Health: Lighting A Dark Corner at the WTO* 5 J Int'l Econ L 469 (2002) 469.

[2] For example, Professor Abbott noted that negotiations over the content of the key paragraph 4 of the Doha Declaration was undertaken by the Brazilian and US delegations as the central actors. See Abbott (20020 (n 1) 488. This in no way negates the contributions of other DCs, notably Zimbabwe on behalf of the African Group, in spearheading the WTO action. NGO action was also undeniably critical and especially valuable in diluting IC opposition.

medicine in the face of global pandemics, and the public health implications of the TRIPS Agreement had become a prominent fixture in international affairs. As such, WTO action was preceded by multilateral action in other relevant international organizations.

Developing countries focused on those organizations whose work had significant relevance to aspects of TRIPS, mainly health and human rights issues. The World Health Organization and the United Nations Commission on Human Rights (CHR) were therefore leading venues in this task.[3] In May 1999, the World Health Assembly (WHA) unanimously adopted a resolution calling upon Member States to ensure equitable access to essential medicines and to '*explore and review their options under international agreements, including trade agreements, to safeguard access to essential drugs*'.[4] This resolution was opposed by the pharmaceutical MNEs that viewed it as challenging the legitimacy of the TRIPS Agreement.[5] Furthermore, in August 2000, the CHR's Sub-Commission on Human Rights adopted a resolution that explicitly referred to '*apparent conflicts between the intellectual property rights embodied in the TRIPS Agreement, on the one hand, and international human rights law, on the other*'.[6]

Moreover, DCs presented a draft resolution to the CHR, which was adopted on 20 April 2001, under the agenda item on 'access to medication in the context of pandemics such as HIV/AIDS.'[7] The resolution, inter alia, encourages states '*to adopt legislation or other measures, in accordance with applicable international law, including international agreements acceded to, to safeguard access to such preventive, curative or palliative pharmaceuticals or medical technologies from any limitations by third parties*'.[8]

The resolution was in part directed at ICs, and particularly US policy, which a few weeks earlier had requested the establishment of a panel in its WTO case against Brazil. Clearly the reference to 'legislation or other measures', was meant to encompass Brazil's presidential decree, Article 68 of its industrial property law, and South Africa's Medicines Amendment Act. Moreover, these would ultimately entail compulsory licensing and

[3] The Commission on Human Rights is an organ of the United Nations' Economic and Social Council.

[4] World Health Assembly Res No WHA52.19 (24 May 1999). Emphasis added.

[5] See Daniel Pruzin *WHO Members Ratify Drug Strategy Opposed by US Pharmaceutical Companies* 16 Int'l Trade Rep (BNA) 881 (26 May 1999).

[6] United Nations Commission on Human Rights, Sub-commission on the Promotion and Protection of Human Rights 'Intellectual Property Rights and Human Rights' Res No 2000/7 E/CN.4/SUB.2/RES/2000/7 (17 Aug 2000) para 2.

[7] United Nations Commission on Human Rights Res No 2001/33 E/CN.4/RES/2001/33 (20 Apr 2001).

[8] ibid para 3(b).

parallel imports. The resolution was adopted unanimously, with the single abstaining vote being that of the United States. The United States representative at the Commission explained the decision to abstain by arguing that the resolution 'appears to question the validity of internationally agreed protections of intellectual property rights. . . .'[9]

With such multilateral action, the way was sufficiently paved for DCs to seek action at the WTO in respect of the TRIPS Agreement and its interpretation. Zimbabwe, on behalf of the African Group, initiated the drive. During the TRIPS Council's meeting in April 2001, Zimbabwe requested that the Council devote a one-day discussion of the topic in its upcoming formal meeting scheduled for June 2001.[10] The request presented emphasized 'the need to clarify the role of intellectual property rights protection in dealing with pandemics such as HIV/AIDS and other life-threatening diseases'.[11] Developing countries were linking this need not only to the lack of such clarity in the interpretation and/or application of relevant TRIPS provisions, but also to pressures by ICs on DCs to apply TRIPS-plus measures.[12] The proposal was almost universally supported by WTO members, most notably by the US and EC. However, the latter two stressed the multidimensional nature of efforts needed to deal with the AIDS crisis, that TRIPS issues were but among many other factors.[13]

The preceding multilateral action in international organizations, in addition to the dominance of the issue at the international arena, almost guaranteed DCs their quest to hold formal WTO discussions on the topic. The legitimacy of the WTO would have been put into question if it had chosen not to engage in a formal debate on the issue, while other organizations were discussing issues directly related to its TRIPS Agreement. As the Tanzanian delegation stated on behalf of the least developed countries,

> it was such a great anomaly that while NGOs and other groups were loudly expressing their concern at the negative impact of the TRIPS Agreement on the greatest human tragedy of our times . . . the WTO and especially this Council [TRIPS Council] should remain silent.[14]

[9] Reported in US *Attacks Brazilian Resolution in UN Commission on Access to Medicine* 18 Int'l Trade Rep (BNA) 671 (26 Apr 2001).

[10] WTO *Council for Trade-Related Aspects of Intellectual Property Rights, Minutes of Meeting, 2-5 April, 2001* IP/C/M/30 (1 June 2001) paras 229 and 231, [hereinafter April Minutes of Meeting].

[11] ibid para 229.

[12] ibid para 230.

[13] ibid paras 235 and 243.

[14] WTO *Council for Trade-Related Aspects of Intellectual Property Rights, Minutes of Meeting, Special Discussion on Intellectual Property and Access to Medicines, during the meeting of the Council from 18 to 22 June 2001* IP/C/M/31 (10 July 2001) 28, [hereinafter June Minutes of Meeting].

The June 2001 meeting was therefore tasked to undertake a special discussion on intellectual property and access to medicines. Specifically, members planned to focus on the interpretation and application of the relevant provisions of the TRIPS Agreement with a view to clarifying the flexibility to which Members were entitled under the Agreement and the relationship between the TRIPS Agreement and affordable access to medicines.[15]

(II) STAKEHOLDERS' POSITIONS

(A) Developing Countries' Position

Having succeeded in scheduling a formal meeting on TRIPS and access to medicines in the TRIPS Council, DCs proceeded to formulate their position for presentation to the meeting in June.[16] This exercise resulted in a document entitled 'TRIPS and Public Health,' presented by Brazil on behalf of a group of DCs including the African Group, to the TRIPS Council.[17] The fundamental premise of developing countries' action in the WTO was to reach an authoritative declaration that '*nothing in the TRIPS Agreement should prevent Members from taking measures to protect public health*'.[18] From this premise, they undertook to: (1) identify what they deemed to be the proper scope of discussions; (2) elaborate upon what they considered to be the proper interpretation of specific TRIPS provisions ensuring flexibility in dealing with public health crises; and (3) propose steps the WTO should undertake to address this matter. These three elements are discussed below.

With regard to the scope of discussions, DCs argued that the June meeting should not be a one-off event, but rather part of a process that would ultimately guarantee them freedom of action to pursue their legitimate public health policies, unhindered by the TRIPS regime.[19] Furthermore, they emphasized that discussions should focus on issues pertaining to TRIPS, and not wander into areas such as differential pricing, financing, or health-related infrastructure needs.[20] Developing countries feared that ICs

[15] April Minutes of Meeting (n 10) para 251.

[16] The Special Discussion was held on 20 June 2001, as part of the TRIPS Council's meeting of 18–22 June 2001. See June Minutes of Meeting (n 14).

[17] WTO *TRIPS Council, Submission by the African Group, Barbados, Bolivia, Brazil, Cuba, Dominican Republic, Ecuador, Honduras, India, Indonesia, Jamaica, Pakistan, Paraguay, Philippines, Peru, Sri Lanka, Thailand and Venezuela* IP/C/W/296 (29 June 2001), [hereinafter DCs June Paper].

[18] Statement of Zimbabwe (on behalf of the African Group), in June Minutes of Meeting (n 14) 3.

[19] DCs June Paper (n 17) para 3.

[20] Specifically, DCs stressed that the WTO has no mandate to establish public health policies. See ibid para 2.

would attempt to divert the focus from TRIPS provisions into those other areas addressing the issue of access to medicine. Developing countries' fears were well founded where shortly before the June discussion, the WTO Secretariat in collaboration with the WHO Secretariat held a workshop entitled 'Differential Pricing and Financing of Essential Drugs'.[21] While such areas were undoubtedly relevant, yet DCs were correct in arguing that they were more appropriately dealt with in other forums such as the WHO.[22]

Secondly, DCs undertook to clarify what they considered a proper interpretation of flexibilities inherent in TRIPS that can be used to address the public health crisis. Developing countries acknowledged that some TRIPS provisions may elicit different interpretations, due mainly to drafting during the Uruguay Round aiming to accommodate different countries' perspectives.[23] Table 13.1 below offers a summary of DC interpretations of the flexibilities in specific TRIPS provisions.

Of paramount importance to DCs interpretations of TRIPS flexibility were its objectives and principles codified in Articles 7 and 8. They noted that each provision of TRIPS should be read in their light. Taken individually, they stressed that the Agreement's objectives do not simply focus on the protection of IPRs, but that promoting technological innovation and the transfer and dissemination of technology are key to its fulfilment. With regard to the principles of the Agreement, DCs emphasized the reading that nothing in the Agreement prevents Members from adopting measures to protect public health.

The second and third classes of provisions referred to by DCs concerned those relating to flexibilities in Members' pursuit of policies on parallel imports and compulsory licences. They emphasized that TRIPS grants countries freedom to apply an international exhaustion regime, and consequently full freedom to resort to parallel imports to enable access to medicines.[24] They also warned that ICs' emphasis on differential pricing should in no way restrict the permissibility of parallel imports under TRIPS.[25] Developing countries also sought broad flexibility in the interpretation of TRIPS compulsory licences provisions.[26] According to Article 31, there was freedom to determine the grounds upon which compulsory licences could

[21] See WTO *WTO, WHO Secretariats Workshop on Affordable Drugs* <http://www.wto.org/english/tratop_e/trips_e/tn_hosbjor_e.htm> (last visited 22 Mar 2006).

[22] DCs June Paper (n 17) para 35. See also Statement by India, in June Minutes of Meeting (n 14) 21.

[23] DCs June Paper (n 17) para 5.

[24] DCs June Paper (n 17) paras 24–27. See also Statement by India in June Minutes of Meeting (n 14) 25.

[25] DCs June Paper (n 17) para 37.

[26] ibid paras 28–34.

Table 13.1: Developing Countries' Interpretations of the Flexibilities Inherent in TRIPS Provisions Relating to Public Health[27]

Objectives and Principles of the Agreement	
Article 7	Establishes that the protection and enforcement of intellectual property rights do not exist in a vacuum. The mere existence and the exercise of IPRs, such as patents, do not necessarily result in the fulfilment of the objectives of the Agreement. The objective of promoting technological innovation and the transfer and dissemination of technology encourages the development of domestic production of pharmaceutical products and Members may take measures to do so.
Article 8	Nothing in TRIPS will prevent Members from adopting measures to protect public health, as well as from pursuing the overarching policies defined in this article.
Parallel Imports:	
Article 6	Members should confirm their right of applying regimes of exhaustion of rights in their jurisdiction.
Compulsory Licences	
Article 31	Members are free to determine the grounds upon which to issue compulsory licences.
Article 5A Paris Convention	Based on this article and TRIPS article 31, governments may issue compulsory licences as a way of ensuring that medicines will be available at more affordable prices.
Articles 27.1 and 28	In no way do these two articles limit the right of members to issue compulsory licences.
Article 31(f)	Nothing in TRIPS will prevent Members from granting compulsory licences to supply foreign markets.
Other Issues	
Article 1.1	Freedom to implement TRIPS in ways that best accommodates the protection of health policies in national legislation.

[27] Information in this table is based on DC positions in the DCs June Paper (n 17); and the DC statements in the meeting of 20 June 2001.

Objectives and Principles of the Agreement	
Article 39.3	Permits a national competent authority to rely on data in its possession to assess further applications relating to the same drug, since this would not imply any 'unfair commercial use'.
Articles 65.4 and 66.1	TRIPS Council could consider extending the transitional periods.
Article 64.3	It seems inconceivable that a non-violation complaint could be applied to measures to protect public health, in particular measures for providing access to essential medicines.

be issued.[28] Similarly, they considered that Articles 27.1 and 28 should in no way restrict Members' rights to issue compulsory licences. Furthermore, DCs argued that Article 5A of the Paris Convention taken together with TRIPS Article 31 would allow the issuance of a compulsory licence to ensure medicines would be available at more affordable prices. This was best exemplified in Brazil's policy towards the pharmaceutical MNEs, as discussed earlier. Finally, the issue of Article 31(f) stipulating that the issuance of a compulsory licence be predominantly for the supply of the domestic market was raised by DCs, arguing that it should not prevent members from issuing licenses for the supply of a foreign market. Specifically, DCs noted that there was nothing to prevent Members from issuing a compulsory licence for a foreign manufacturer to supply the domestic market of the issuing Member.[29]

Table 13.1 refers to interpretations of other TRIPS provisions. An important provision therein was Article 39.3 concerning the protection of undisclosed test or other data submitted for marketing approval of pharmaceutical or agricultural chemical products, which utilize new chemical entities. DCs were particularly concerned about this provision as significant pressure was being exerted by ICs and MNEs for it to be implemented in a TRIPS-plus manner that effectively hindered generic competition.[30] Developing countries therefore provided a strict interpretation of this article

[28] The African Group noted three particular grounds for such issuance: where there is non-working or insufficient working of a patent; for the importation of a product under patent protection; and for the export of a product under patent protection. See Zimbabwe Statement in June Minutes of Meeting, (n 14) 5.

[29] DCs June Paper note 17, para 34.

[30] See Carlos Correa *Public Health and Patent Legislation in Developing Countries* 3 Tul J Tech and IP 1 (2001) 49–50.

arguing that there was nothing to prevent a competent national authority from relying on such data in its possession for marketing approval of further applications of the same product, and that this did not constitute 'unfair commercial use'.[31]

Finally, the third element of the DC strategy was to propose concrete steps for the WTO to undertake. Primarily, they sought a special declaration at the forthcoming Ministerial Meeting scheduled for November in Doha, that '*nothing in the TRIPS Agreement should prevent Members from taking measures to protect public health*'. Secondly, DCs called for an extension of the transitional periods under Article 65.4 specifically for pharmaceutical products and processes, and an extension of the transitional period for least-developed country Members under Article 65.1.[32] Finally, DCs proposed a moratorium in the dispute settlement mechanism to allow members to take measures to protect public health, and for the immediate cessation of ongoing disputes against DCs that hinders their ability to promote access to medicines and protect public health.[33] This last proposal clearly implied the ongoing DSU action by the US against Brazil.

In presenting their position at the WTO, DCs exhibited an almost unprecedented degree of organization and solidarity in the history of DC GATT/WTO action.[34] This degree of cohesion was similarly supported by the highly effective politics of civil society groups and global public opinion in favour of their position. However, DCs were also aware of the agenda of ICs, and perceived how it might be brought to work in their favour. Industrialized countries were pushing for the initiation of a new round of multilateral trade negotiations under the ambit of the WTO, partly as a need to revitalize their economies, but also to carry on a backlog of issues from the Uruguay Round and previous ministerial conferences. Developing countries were aware of the fact that ICs needed their support, and were hence willing to oblige them towards that goal. This realization was hinted at by Brazil, arguing that a positive outcome for DCs on the TRIPS and public health issue:

> should go a long way to build the required confidence between developed and developing countries for any future negotiations we may embark on, not only on this subject. It would also send a powerful

[31] DCs June Paper (n 17) paras 39–40.

[32] ibid para 41. DCs had long argued for an extension of transitional periods under TRIPS. See WTO *Proposal Regarding Extension of Transition Period: Communication from Cuba, Dominican Republic, Egypt and Honduras* WT/GC/W/209 (17 June 1999). See also Press Release, World Trade Organization WTO General Council Informal Meeting (28 Mar 2000) Press/173.

[33] Statement of Zimbabwe in June Minutes of Meeting (n 14) 6.

[34] Professor Abbott presents three particular reasons for this cohesion amongst the ranks of DCs, namely: shared common interests; assistance for the systematic development of coordinated WTO policy among DCs; and realizing the importance of concerted efforts in WTO matters. See Abbott (2002) (n 1) 479–80.

message to all those growing sectors of civil society, both in the North and in the South, that see the WTO as a soulless organization at the service of the rich and the powerful.[35]

(B) Industrialized Countries' Positions

Contrary to the unified front that ICs had exhibited in the Uruguay Round negotiations on TRIPS particularly following its initial phase, there emerged a significant schism in their positions during the TRIPS Council discussions on public health.[36] This was particularly the case between the positions of the United States and the EC. As early as July 2000, during the UN General Assembly's Special Session on Social Development, the EC had alluded to the 'inherent flexibilities' in the TRIPS Agreement concerning DCs' aims of improving access to medicines.[37] Furthermore, the EC had also contributed a detailed paper ahead of the TRIPS Council's discussion in June.[38] On the other hand, the United States joined by Switzerland had maintained a less accommodating policy concomitant to the interests of pharmaceutical MNEs, and appeared as one commentator described it, to be discounting that the problem existed, 'drawing battle lines rather than establishing bases for further discussion'.[39] This divergence in positions was clear in their varying readings of the flexibilities inherent in TRIPS provisions as will be discussed below.

However, prior to this discussion, and despite this divergence in positions, three key precepts were maintained in the majority of IC positions, albeit in varying degrees of emphasis. First, ICs maintained the paramount importance of intellectual property rights in fostering innovation, and the importance of its protection as a means of making future treatments of diseases possible.[40] Secondly, they stressed the existence of an inherent balance in TRIPS between the interests of right holders on the one hand, and those of consumers on the other.[41] This was put most clearly by Canada, where it argued that

[35] Statement of Brazil in June Minutes of Meeting (n 14) 9–10.

[36] See Abbott (2002) (n 1) 481–88.

[37] International Intellectual Property Institute (IIPI) *Patent Protection and Access to HIV/AIDS Pharmaceuticals in Sub-Saharan Africa* Report Prepared for the World Intellectual Property Organization (2000) 18 <http://www.wipo.int/about-ip/en/studies/pdf/ iipi_hiv.pdf> (last visited 22 Mar 2006).

[38] WTO *TRIPS Council, Communication from the European Communities and their Member States, The Relationship Between the Provisions of the TRIPS Agreement and Access to Medicines* IP/C/W/280 (12 June 2001), [hereinafter EC June Paper].

[39] Abbott (2002) (n 1) 482–3.

[40] EC June paper (n 38) para 7; US Statement in June Minutes of Meeting (n 14) 33 and 35–6; Swiss Statement in June Minutes of Meeting (n 14) 44; and Japan Statement in June Minutes of Meeting (n 14) 47–8.

[41] Swiss Statement in June Minutes of Meeting (n 14) 44–5; EC June Paper (n 38) para 17; Japan Statement in June Minutes of Meeting (n 14) 48; and US Statement in June Minutes of Meeting (n 14) 33.

> [t]he TRIPS Agreement attempts to provide the necessary balance between encouraging innovation and development of new products, and the needs of those requiring access to such products. That balance, and the flexibility in the TRIPS Agreement, plays an important part in finding a solution to the HIV/AIDS health crisis.[42]

Thirdly, ICs underscored that the access to medicines debate engulfs more than merely the question of patents or the TRIPS Agreement. In this light, they argued that particular attention was required to attend to other important issues such as infrastructure needs, financing, and most notably, differential pricing.[43] However, at one extreme, the United States seemed to discount the relevance of patents in this discussion, referring to a controversial study that casts doubt on the link between patents and access to ARV treatment in African countries.[44]

In their positions regarding TRIPS flexibilities, ICs focused mainly on parallel imports (Article 6), the objectives and principles of the Agreement (Articles 7 and 8), and compulsory licensing (Articles 30 and 31). With regard to the interpretation of Article 6, ICs were divided on the TRIPS legality of parallel imports under this provision.[45] The United States cautioned that it does not authorize parallel imports, as it does not alter the substantive provisions of Part II of the Agreement.[46] On the other hand, the EC, Japan, Canada, and Norway all acquiesced in members' right under TRIPS to establish their own exhaustion regime.[47] However, ICs were predominantly lukewarm to the desirability of a policy of parallel imports to handle the access to medicine dilemma. Such a policy they warned could create problems for achieving a differential pricing mechanism, where producers could shy away from undertaking such a scheme if they believed that discounted products could find their way back to the rich markets of the ICs.[48]

[42] Canada Statement in June Minutes of Meeting (n 14) 58.

[43] US Statement in June Minutes of Meeting (n 14) 34; EC June Paper (n 38) para 19; Swiss Statement in June Minutes of Meeting (n 14) 45; and Canada Statement in June Minutes of Meeting (n 14) 57.

[44] See US Statement in June Minutes of Meeting (n 14) 34–5.

[45] ICs concurred however on the definition of parallel imports, as those extending to goods produced by the patent holder or through his consent. As such, this excluded goods produced through a compulsory licence. This definition was criticized by India arguing that in the event of a compulsory licence, the right holder was entitled to adequate remuneration, therefore his consent was not imperative. See WTO *TRIPS Council, Minutes of Meeting on 19 and 20 September 2001* IP/C/M/33 (2 Nov 2001) para 241, [hereinafter September Minutes of Meeting].

[46] US Statement in June Minutes of Meeting (n 14) 40.

[47] EC Statement in June Minutes of Meeting (n 14) 8; Japan Statement in June Minutes of Meeting (note 14) 48; Canada Statement in September Minutes of Meeting (n 45) para 170; and Norway Statement in September Minutes of Meeting (n 45) para 174.

[48] See Japan Statement in June Minutes of Meeting (n 14) 49; US Statement in June Minutes of Meeting (n 14) 40; and EC Statement in June Minutes of Meeting (n 14) 8.

Articles 7 and 8, enumerating the Agreement's objectives and principles, have been at the forefront of the EC's emphasis on the flexibilities inherent in TRIPS. The EC noted that while these two articles were not drafted as general exception clauses, they were important for interpreting other provisions in the Agreement, particularly those provisions allowing members to fine-tune the balance between the rights of the right holders and those of the public.[49] The EC explained that Article 7 '*made clear that implementation was not just a matter of protecting private rights but should be done in a manner which achieved the objectives set out in that provision. . . .*'[50] Canada noted that Article 7 called for a balance between IPRs and other important socio-economic goals, including public health.[51] In the closest interpretive construction to that of the DCs, Norway also noted this balance of interests adding that the overriding goal was to achieve technological progress and social and economic welfare, and that Article 8 referred to Members' rights to take measures to protect public health and to prevent abuse of IPRs by right-holders.[52] The United States however took the extreme position that Article 7, rather than guiding TRIPS implementation, it '*set out the objectives that full implementation of the TRIPS Agreement was intended to achieve*'.[53] Hence, the US argument was that only through full implementation of TRIPS provisions, including patent protection, were countries then in a position to reap the rewards of technological innovation and the transfer and dissemination of technology. A similar position was also expressed by Switzerland.[54] With regard to Article 8, the US maintained that it should not be seen as a tool for interpreting the TRIPS Agreement, but rather as another of the flexibilities built into the Agreement that ensured that the objectives listed in Article 7 were achieved.[55]

As to compulsory licensing, ICs agreed that public health was a legitimate ground for such an issuance, particularly in national emergencies or other circumstances of extreme urgency. Industrialized countries also conceded that certain levels of HIV/AIDS comprised a national emergency or a situation of extreme urgency.[56] However, the United States and

49 EC June Paper (n 38) para 12; and EC Statement in September Minutes of Meeting (n 45) para 155.

50 EC Statement in September Minutes of Meeting (n 45) para 155.

51 Canada Statement in September Minutes of Meeting (n 45) para 169.

52 Norway Statement in September Minutes of Meeting (n 45) para 172.

53 US Statement in September Minutes of Meeting (n 45) para 161.

54 Swiss Statement in September Minutes of Meeting (n 45) para 181.

55 US Statement in September Minutes of Meeting (n 45) para 162.

56 EC June Paper (n 38) paras 11 and 12; US Statement in June Minutes of Meeting (n 14) 38; Japan Statement in June Minutes of Meeting (n 14) 49; Canada Statement in September Minutes of Meeting (n 45) para 171; and Swiss Statement in September Minutes of Meeting (n 45) para 182.

Switzerland both contended that Article 31 must be read in light of Articles 27.1 and 28, prohibiting discrimination as to whether products are imported or domestically produced, a reference to the situation in Brazil, as previously discussed.[57] Moreover, contrary to the position of other ICs, the US and Switzerland cautioned against the use of compulsory licensing, as it was not intended to be a mechanism for directing industrial development nor a normal course of doing business.[58] Switzerland, during the September 2001 meeting of the TRIPS Council, stated that it perceived a consensus was emerging that voluntary licences were preferable to compulsory licences,[59] a proposition immediately challenged by India.[60]

The EC was also more accommodating on the issue of Article 31(f) concerning countries that lack manufacturing capacity. Along lines similar to DCs' interpretation, the EC presented that a member could issue a compulsory licence to a manufacturer in another country provided that this other country recognized the licence, and that all goods manufactured under the licence were exported to the country granting the licence.[61] The EC however cautioned that this latter option might not stand scrutiny by a panel or the Appellate Body. The United States emphasized that what was relevant in that situation was whether the licensee would be infringing a patent in his own country, when he acts under a compulsory licence issued in another country.[62]

In their various interpretations, ICs also referred to other provisions in TRIPS, including the issue of exceptions under Article 30,[63] and the protection of undisclosed data in Article 39.3. The majority of ICs adopted a strict interpretation that such data could not be relied upon for marketing approval of equivalent products for a specified period of time.[64] However, the EC, Japan and Switzerland added that this article did not oblige members either to have marketing approval procedures nor does it prescribe what those should be.[65] This was to indicate that DCs were free to adopt regulatory approval measures that circumvented the constraints that might face the introduction of generic medicines under that article.

The preceding examination reveals that DCs had succeeded in presenting a detailed and united stance concerning what they deemed a proper clarifi-

[57] US Statement in June Minutes of Meeting (n 14) 37–8; and Swiss Statement in September Minutes of Meeting (n 45) para 182.

[58] US Statement in June Minutes of Meeting (n 14) 38–9.

[59] Swiss Statement in September Minutes of Meeting (n 45) paras 182 and 239.

[60] India Statement in September Minutes of Meeting (n 45) paras 217 and 241.

[61] EC June Paper (n 38) para 13.

[62] US Statement in June Minutes of Meeting (n 14) 38–9.

[63] EC June Paper (n 38) para 14; and US Statement in June Minutes of Meeting (n 14) 37.

[64] EC June Paper (n 38) para 15; and US Statement in June Minutes of Meeting (n 14) 40.

[65] EC June Paper (n 38) para 16; Japan Statement in June Minutes of Meeting (n 14) 50; and Swiss Statement in June Minutes of Meeting (n 14) 45.

cation of TRIPS flexibilities, and a course of action to be undertaken by the WTO in support thereof. On the other hand, ICs, but mainly the United States and Switzerland, prodded by pharmaceutical MNEs' interests, opposed this DC drive, fearing that it might undermine the effectiveness of TRIPS as an instrument supportive of a highly protectionist patent regime.

(III) CONTESTATIONS AND DEVELOPMENTS

By late September 2001, following two formal and two informal meetings of the TRIPS Council,[66] a consensus had emerged that a political declaration by the Ministerial Conference on the issue of public health/access to medicines was necessary.[67] In this regard two drafts were presented. The first was a draft declaration presented by DCs,[68] and the second was a document containing preambular language presented by the United States, Switzerland, Japan, Canada, and Australia.[69] The operative language of the US-sponsored draft was presented informally two days later.[70] The EC also presented a draft declaration that it subsequently withdrew.[71] During the period leading up to the Doha Ministerial and the eventual adoption of the Doha Declaration, DCs and ICs were engaged in an acute contest over three main issues: (1) the scope of the declaration; (2) key declaratory language; and (3) TRIPS provisions to be referred to in the declaration. Each of these is examined below, in addition to a discussion of the eventual drafting of a compromise text presented by the Chairperson of the General Council to the Doha Ministerial meeting.

66 The formal meetings were held on 20 June 2001 and 19 September 2001. The two informal meetings were held on 25 July 2001 and 21 Sept 2001.

67 Statement by the Chairperson of the TRIPS Council in September Minutes of Meeting (n 45) para 149.

68 WTO *TRIPS Council, Proposal by the African Group, Bangladesh, Barbados, Bolivia, Brazil, Cuba, Dominican Republic, Ecuador, Haiti, Honduras, India, Indonesia, Jamaica, Pakistan, Paraguay, Philippines, Peru, Sri Lanka, Thailand and Venezuela, Ministerial Declaration on the TRIPS Agreement and Public Health* IP/C/W/312; WT/GC/W/450 (4 Oct 2001), [hereinafter DC Draft Declaration].

69 WTO *TRIPS Council, Preambular Language for Ministerial Declaration, Contribution from Australia, Canada, Japan, Switzerland and the United States, Access to Medicines for HIV/AIDS and other Pandemics* IP/C/W/313 (4 Oct 2001), [hereinafter US-Sponsored Draft].

70 This particular US 'non-paper' is not available at the WTO website. The author relies on a copy made available in an email communication from Cecilia Oh of the Third World Network, available at the IP-Health Database, <http://lists.essential.org/pipermail/ip-health/2001-September/ 001891.html> (last visited 16 Dec 2003) [hereinafter US 'Non-Paper'].

71 The EC 'non-paper', with comments thereon by Act UP-Paris, is available in posting of Gaelle Kirkorian, galk@compuserve.com, to IP-Health@lists.essential.org (10 Oct 2001) <http://lists.essential.org/pipermail/ip-health/2001-October/002046.html> (last visited 16 Dec 2003).

(A) Scope of the Declaration

With regard to the issue of scope, DCs as was evident from the title of their declaration: 'Ministerial Declaration on the TRIPS Agreement and Public Health', sought to capture the broad issue of public health. Brazil, India, and Zimbabwe argued that it was necessary for the eventual statement to go beyond the narrow albeit important issue of the HIV/AIDS crisis.[72] For Brazil, as important as the HIV/AIDS crisis was, yet it argued that there were other diseases that affected its population, and it could not accept that other sectors of its constituency would be denied the privilege of having a declaration citing flexibilities within TRIPS encompass their concerns.[73] Moreover, Zimbabwe and India noted that the TRIPS Agreement itself, in its Article 8.1, specifically referred to 'public health and nutrition',[74] and argued that Members should therefore be aiming to pronounce on the flexibilities at least regarding public health.[75] In this light, the DCs' draft declaration, apart from its indicative title, contained references to public health in four of its 17 preambular recitals, and in five of its fourteen operative paragraphs.

On the other hand, entitling their draft 'Access to Medicines for HIV/AIDS and other Pandemics,' the US, Switzerland, and the other ICs to varying degrees, strove to limit the scope to the narrower topic of access to medicines, and specifically to HIV/AIDS and similar pandemics. Both Switzerland and the EC noted that the original mandate for this discussion, as delineated in the April 2001 TRIPS Council meeting, referred explicitly to the '*relationship between the TRIPS Agreement and affordable access to medicines*'.[76] Switzerland added that broadening the mandate risked that discussions would not be result-oriented and would fail to reach concrete results.[77] As such, the US-sponsored draft referred only to 'HIV/AIDS and other pandemics', and established the roots of the problem in different issues such as infrastructure and education.[78]

(B) Declaratory Language

Apart from the issue of scope, DCs sought to include their key declaratory language that '*nothing in the TRIPS Agreement shall prevent Members*

[72] See India Statement in September Minutes of Meeting (n 45) para 150.
[73] Brazil Statement in September Minutes of Meeting (n 45) para 157.
[74] India Statement in September Minutes of Meeting (n 45) para 151.
[75] Zimbabwe Statement in September Minutes of Meeting (n 45) para 240.
[76] Swiss Statement in September Minutes of Meeting (n 45) para 179; and EC Statement in September Minutes of Meeting (n 45) para 154.
[77] ibid.
[78] US-Sponsored Draft (n 69) at first and fourth recitals.

from taking measures to protect public health'.[79] The United States and Switzerland were uneasy with such language, even though as a leading commentator put it, this was in fact stating the obvious.[80] Even the EC, acting the role of the mediator, endeavoured to soften the impact of the DC statement, proposing that it could be transformed into a more positive statement that 'implementation of the TRIPS Agreement should contribute to enabling Members to have access to affordable medicines'.[81] Developing countries were however adamant. Brazil argued that the inclusion of this language was crucial to clarify TRIPS provisions vis-à-vis public health policies, a sovereign prerogative of States.[82] It added that it would be surprised if such language was to prove controversial, and if it was shown to be, then a broader question would have to be addressed concerning the actual scope of the TRIPS Agreement, an implicit threat that DCs could possibly call for expanding the scope of review of the TRIPS Agreement.[83]

In contrast to this DC language, the US-sponsored draft reaffirmed in its preamble the contribution of the TRIPS Agreement to the availability of medicines, and in allowing sufficient flexibility whereby members could ensure that medicines for HIV/AIDS and other pandemics are available to their citizens.[84] This contention was refused by DCs, where Brazil argued that it would not agree to such language as there was no conclusive evidence that TRIPS provided access to pharmaceuticals.[85] Similarly, DCs were critical of the fact that the preamble, while referring to factors affecting access to medicines, omitted any mention of patents.[86] Moreover, India was also uncertain of the absolute validity of the fifth recital in the preamble, which recognizes that intellectual property contributes to public health objectives globally.[87]

(C) TRIPS Provisions Covered

The DC draft declaration contained references to those provisions of TRIPS that they had pronounced on when stating their position earlier in the process. Most importantly, on parallel imports, they postulated that each Member has the right to establish its own policy and rules regarding the

[79] DC Draft Declaration (n 68) para 1.
[80] Abbott (2002) (n 1) 483.
[81] EC Statement in September Minutes of Meeting (n 45) para 220.
[82] Brazil Statement in September Minutes of Meeting (n 45) para 201.
[83] ibid.
[84] US-Sponsored Draft (n 69) at sixth and seventh recitals.
[85] Brazil Statement in September Minutes of Meeting (n 45) para 204.
[86] India Statement in September Minutes of Meeting (n 45) para 218
[87] ibid.

exhaustion of IPRs.[88] On compulsory licences, DCs sought the freedom of members to issue such licences without the authorization of right holders, to determine the grounds for such use, and in the case of a national emergency or other situation of extreme urgency, to do so without prior efforts on the part of the user to obtain a voluntary licence.[89] Moreover, in the case of Members with no production capacity, and to solve the Article 31(f) restriction, DCs proposed that a compulsory licence issued by a Member may be given effect by another Member, and that production and export in the licensee's country do not infringe the rights of the patent holder, in so doing relying on an Article 30 exception.[90]

Industrialized countries' however expressed concerns with the DC draft declaration in what they considered a broadening by DCs of the provisions under discussion. Industrialized countries emphasized that the Chairperson had identified three particular focus areas of TRIPS provisions for discussions, namely: objectives and principles of the Agreement in Articles 7 and 8; provisions relating to compulsory licences; and provisions relating to parallel imports.[91] However, in their draft declaration, DCs went beyond those specific areas. Developing countries called for restraint in dispute settlement proceeding relating to DC and LDC measures to protect and promote public health (paragraph 11), and that non-violation complaints should not apply to measures adopted, particularly by DCs and LDCs, to protect and promote public health (paragraph 12). They also called for an extension of transition periods under Articles 65.4 and 66.1 for an additional period of five years (paragraph 13). Moreover, the DC draft declaration also referred to TRIPS Article 39.3, where it called for flexibility with regard to marketing approval procedures for generic medicines specifically relating to information used in the grant of prior approvals for equivalent products (paragraphs 7 and 8). Finally, DCs also called for a cessation by Members of the exertion of pressure including imposing or threatening to impose sanctions which would curtail the ability of DCs and LDCs to avail themselves of every option to protect and promote public health (paragraph 10).

In contrast to this exhaustive coverage of TRIPS provisions in the DC draft, the operative paragraphs of the US-sponsored 'non-paper' covered only three issues. Primarily, it noted that each provision of TRIPS must be interpreted in accordance with the customary rules as reflected in the Vienna Convention on the Law of Treaties. Significantly, however, no reference was made to the objectives and principles of TRIPS in Articles 7 and

88 DC Draft Declaration (n 68) para 2.
89 ibid paras 3 and 4.
90 ibid paras 5 and 9.
91 See Canada Statement in September Minutes of Meeting (n 45) para 206. This referred to the summary of the Chair's statement, para 149.

8.[92] Secondly, on the issue of compulsory licensing, the 'non-paper' while acknowledging freedom to determine grounds for the grant of compulsory licences, sought to limit the recourse to Article 31(b) national emergency or other situations of extreme urgency to '*pandemics of life-threatening communicable diseases such as HIV/AIDS, malaria and tuberculosis*'.[93] Finally, with regard to the issue of parallel imports, it conceded members' right to adopt the exhaustion regime they preferred, but limited it to goods placed on the market by the consent of the right holder, and made allowance for measures on differential pricing.[94]

(D) Developments and the Chairman's Draft

While the contestations discussed above were verging on a stalemate between DCs on the one hand and the ICs, particularly the US, on the other, preparations for the Doha Ministerial Meeting were proceeding at the WTO's General Council. Already, that higher body of the WTO had issued a draft of the main Ministerial Declaration, and it was there that the TRIPS Council decided to submit its work thus far on the issue of TRIPS and public health/access to medicines. Taking the initiative, the Chairman of the General Council requested the Secretariat of the WTO to prepare a draft declaration proposal that would reflect the positions of the members thus far. This exercise resulted in a document with bracketed language that contained two options.[95] The two options in the draft related to its title, and the key operative paragraph 4. The options in the title reflected the differences over the scope for which the declaration would refer to, either 'access to medicines', or 'public health'. As regards the options for paragraph 4, Option 1 contained the language preferred by DCs that '*nothing in the TRIPS Agreement shall prevent Members from taking measures to protect public health. . . .*' Option 2 on the other hand, supported by the US, stipulated that '*we affirm a Member's ability to use, to the full, the provisions in the TRIPS Agreement which provide flexibility to address public health crises such as HIV/AIDS and other pandemics. . . .*'

A development in the Chairman's Draft however, was the inclusion of two paragraphs that were originally proposed by the United States. First, paragraph 10 grants least-developed country members an extension of their transitional period with respect to pharmaceutical products until 1 January 2016. Secondly, paragraph 11 agrees a moratorium on WTO DSU action

92 US 'non-paper' (n 70) para 1.

93 ibid paras 2 and 3.

94 ibid paras 4–6.

95 WTO *Draft Declaration on Intellectual Property and [Access to Medicines] [Public Health]* JOB(01)/155 (27 Oct 2001) <http://www.ictsd.org/ministerial/doha/docs/IP27oct.pdf> (last visited 22 Mar 2006) [hereinafter Chairman's Draft].

with respect to '*any non-discriminatory intellectual property law, regulation or other measure*', of a sub-Saharan African country member that improves access to medicines used in treating HIV/AIDS and other pandemics. These paragraphs were based on a US proposal that was made on 13 October 2001, at the so-called Singapore 'mini-ministerial'.[96] This proposal however, was widely regarded as being designed to instil a fissure in the cohesion of the DC group.[97] As such, the proposal for a moratorium, given its exclusion of regions other than sub-Saharan Africa, was rejected by DCs, a laudable act to cement DC cohesion.

A significant incident, outside of the context of WTO action by DCs, yet germane to the core of their argument related to developments concerning the anthrax scare in North America following the 11 September terrorist attacks on the United States. As a precautionary measure against this risk, on 18 October 2001, the Canadian Government announced it would issue a compulsory licence for the drug Ciprofloxacin, used in the treatment of anthrax and patented by the German pharmaceutical MNE Bayer, to a generic manufacturer to obtain a low-cost version of the drug.[98] Similarly, a few days later, the US Health and Human Services (HHS) Secretary, threatened Bayer with similar action if it did not reduce the price in the United States of the same drug, and succeeded in persuading Bayer to cut the price by 50 per cent.[99]

The implications of the Cipro case, coming at a crucial moment in the negotiations in the WTO on TRIPS and public health were considerable and added a further emphasis and legitimacy to the DC position and claims. Developing countries had just to point out that the United States itself, as well as Canada, when facing a threat to the public health of their citizens, cast aside their IPR rhetoric and threatened to break patents on key pharmaceutical products necessary to maintain public health. Indeed, the USTR was on the defensive in reply to such charges, arguing that the action by the HHS Secretary were 'fully consistent with the international agreements to which the United States is party'.[100] Developing countries, when facing a

[96] See USTR *Background Paper, TRIPs and Health Emergencies*, 5 (10 Nov 2001) <http://www.wtowatch.org/library/admin/uploadedfiles/TRIPs_and_Health_Emergencies.htm> (last visited 23 June 2003) [hereinafter USTR Background Paper].

[97] See Cecilia Oh 'An Update on the Progress of Consultations on the Proposed Ministerial Declaration on TRIPS and Public Health' TWN Info Service on WTO Issues (26 Oct 2001) <http://lists.essential.org/pipermail/ip-health/2001-October/002266.html> (last visited 19 Jan 2004). See also Gary G Yerkey US *Says Support Growing for Proposal on Drug Patents in Run-Up to WTO Meeting* 18 Int'l Trade Rep (BNA) 1779 (8 Nov 2001).

[98] See Amy Harmon and Robert Pear *Canada Overrides Patent for Cipro to Treat Anthrax* NY TIMES (19 Oct 2001). Canada however did not issue the compulsory license as it had reached an understanding with Bayer.

[99] See *Industry Observers Debate Implications of HHS Secretary's Remarks on Cipro Patent* 18 Int'l Trade Rep (BNA) 1783 (8 Nov 2001); and Abbott (2002) 487.

[100] USTR Background Paper (n 96) 3–4.

greater threat to the public health of their citizens, as the HIV/AIDS pandemic undoubtedly was, should not be expected to demand any less freedom of action in addressing this threat. This was the action Brazil pursued, it was the action South Africa sought, and it was the action that they demanded a pronouncement on from the Doha ministerial meeting.

(IV) DOHA DECLARATION ON TRIPS AND PUBLIC HEALTH AND ITS AFTERMATH

(A) Understanding the Declaration

The WTO Doha Ministerial Conference adopted the Declaration on the TRIPS Agreement and Public Health on 14 November 2001.[101] The Declaration came to resemble more closely the positions advocated by DCs rather than those of ICs, particularly that of the United States and Switzerland. Primarily, its title came to refer to 'public health', and not the narrower reference to HIV/AIDS and other pandemics, as desired by ICs. Similarly, its pronouncements followed more closely the DCs' position. The first three paragraphs of the Declaration acted in framing the background to the Declaration.[102] They recognized the gravity of public health problems affecting DCs and LDCs, and stressed the need for TRIPS to be part of the action to address these problems (paragraphs 1 and 2). Moreover, in a balanced tone, the Declaration also recognized that intellectual property protection is important for the development of new medicines, yet also acknowledged the concerns about its effects on prices (paragraph 3).

The most important item in the Declaration however was paragraph 4. This paragraph states in its first part:

> We agree that the TRIPS Agreement does not and should not prevent Members from taking measures to protect public health. Accordingly, while reiterating our commitment to the TRIPS Agreement, we affirm that the Agreement can and should be interpreted and implemented in a manner supportive of WTO Members' right to protect public health and, in particular, to promote access to medicines for all.

This language was based on Option 1 of the Chairman's draft text, which was championed by DC negotiators. In fact, the limited change that was introduced, replacing '*Nothing in the TRIPS Agreement shall prevent*' with

[101] WTO *Ministerial Conference, Fourth Session, Doha, 9-14 November, 2001, Declaration on the TRIPS Agreement and Public Health* WT/MIN(01)/DEC/2 (20 Nov 2001) para 5(d), [hereinafter Doha Declaration].

[102] See Divya Murthy *The Future of Compulsory Licensing: Deciphering the Doha Declaration on the TRIPS Agreement and Public Health* 17 Am U Int'l L Rev 1299 (2002) 1321–2.

'*the TRIPS Agreement does not and should not prevent*', was presented as being slightly more of an improvement for the DCs' position.[103] Paragraph 4 proceeds to reaffirm the right of Members to use, to the full, TRIPS provisions that provide flexibility for measures to protect public health. In a sense, what imbues paragraph 4 with such importance is that it is the key paragraph in the Declaration, performing the function of a *chapeau* under whose interpretations the flexibilities in TRIPS are listed in paragraph 5.

Indeed, paragraph 5 proceeds to list these flexibilities '*in the light of paragraph 4*'. Four flexibilities are enumerated in paragraph 5. Primarily, it acknowledges that in interpreting the Agreement, each of its provisions must be read in light of its objectives and principles, a key DC demand. With regard to interpreting flexibilities for compulsory licensing, it recognizes each Member's right to grant such licences, and the freedom to determine the grounds upon which they are granted. Equally, it acknowledges each Member's right to determine what constitutes a national emergency or other circumstances of extreme urgency, while specifically referring to HIV/AIDS, tuberculosis, malaria, and other epidemics as fitting under these conditions. Finally, it unquestionably asserts each Member's right to freely establish its own regime of exhaustion without challenge. This last interpretation importantly makes no mention of any reference to differential pricing arrangements as was being advocated by ICs, and that could have acted as a limitation on such a right.

Among the Declaration's other significant achievements for LDCs was paragraph 7. Under its terms, LDCs will not be obliged, with respect to pharmaceutical products, to implement or apply TRIPS provisions on patents and the protection of undisclosed information (sections 5 and 7 of part II of the Agreement), until 1 January 2016. It also acknowledged their right to apply for further extensions as stipulated in TRIPS. This same paragraph also calls on ICs to provide incentives to promote and encourage technology transfer to LDCs.

Finally, the Declaration contained in its paragraph 6, a reference to the issue of the difficulties facing countries with insufficient or no manufacturing capacity in the pharmaceutical sector in making use of compulsory licences. Clearly a contentious issue, given the restrictions imposed by Article 31(f), it was not possible to reach a solution to this problem by the time of the Ministerial Conference. This was perhaps one of the issues that DCs were unable to prevail on, given their earlier calls that nothing in TRIPS prevents Members to grant compulsory licences to foreign suppliers to provide medicine in the domestic market.[104] Nonetheless, paragraph 6 of

[103] Abbott (2002) (n 1) 488–89.

[104] See Alan O Sykes *TRIPS, Pharmaceuticals, Developing Countries, and the Doha 'Solution'* 3 Chi. J Int'l L 47 (2002) 54–5.

the Declaration acknowledged this problem, and instructed the TRIPS Council to find an expeditious solution and report to the General Council before the end of 2002. This important yet narrow issue was to engage once more DCs and ICs in further negotiations, and was settled briefly before the Fifth Ministerial Conference of the WTO in August 2003, that is many months beyond the original deadline.[105]

(B) Significance of the Declaration

The Declaration on the TRIPS Agreement and Public Health proved a milestone in the history of the TRIPS Agreement, and indeed, of DC action in the WTO. Due to this fact, there has been considerable commentary on its significance. Scholars have pondered on its legal significance. A number of such analyses have concluded that the Declaration is not legally significant, or at the most legally dubious.[106] This lack of legal significance was argued to derive from the nature of the Declaration itself, being a recount of the flexibilities that are already part of the TRIPS Agreement itself.[107] Other opinions address the question of whether WTO ministerial 'declarations' are capable of legal effect, specifically as they are differentiated from ministerial 'decisions' that are explicitly referred to under the WTO Agreement,[108] ultimately arguing that there is no clear answer.[109]

On the other hand, other scholars have referred to the legal value of the Declaration, particularly in relation to interpretations of TRIPS provisions as might be used by panels and the Appellate Body.[110] While noting that ministerial declarations are not legally binding, yet Professor Sykes argues that this Declaration is interpretive of imprecise obligations in TRIPS, and does not appear to contradict the Agreement, he therefore presents that 'it

[105] WTO *Implementation of Paragraph 6 of the Doha Declaration on the TRIPS Agreement and Public Health* IP/C/W/405 (30 Aug 2003). The deal reached was based on a temporary waiver of obligations under Art 31(f), and the establishment of a notification procedure for importing and exporting countries. For a good analysis of the negotiations over para 6 of the Doha Declaration, see Duncan Matthews *WTO Decision on the Implementation of Paragraph of the Doha Declaration on the TRIPS Agreement and Public Health: A Solution to the Access to Essential Medicines Problem?* 7 J INT'L ECON L 73 (2004).

[106] See Jeffrey J Schott *Comment on the Doha Ministerial* 5 J Int'l Econ L 191 (2002) 194–5; Gary N Horlick *Over the Bump in Doha?* 5 J Int'l Econ L 195 (2002) 199–200; Steve Charnovitz *The Legal Status of the Doha Declarations* 5 J Int'l Econ L 207 (2002) 207–11; and Carmen Otero Garcia-Castrillon *An Approach to the WTO Ministerial Declaration on the TRIPS Agreement and Public Health* 5 J Int'l Econ L 212 (2002) 218–19.

[107] Schott (2002) (n 106) 195; and Horlick (2002) (n 106)199–200.

[108] Marrakesh Agreement Establishing the World Trade Organization arts III:2, IV:1, and IX:1 (15 Apr 1994) 33 ILM 1144 (1994).

[109] Charnovitz (2002) (n 106) 208–11.

[110] See James Thuo Ghatii *The Legal Status of the Doha Declaration on TRIPS and Public Health Under the Vienna Convention on the Law of Treaties* 15 Harv J L and Tech 291 (2002) 292–3, and 299–313.

is likely to be persuasive authority in the interpretation of TRIPs in the event of a dispute.'[111] Moreover, Professor Abbott contends that specifically regarding paragraph 4 of the Declaration, the use of the initial 'we agree' imbues this paragraph with the characteristic of a 'decision', and hence appeared to

> constitute an agreement on the method of application of the agreement within the meaning of Article 31(3)(a) of the Vienna Convention . . . the substantive equivalent of an interpretation of the TRIPS Agreement.[112]

More encouragingly, even those accounts that cast doubt on the legal validity of the Declaration, acknowledge that its political importance is significant, particularly in making it politically unfeasible for actions under the DSU relating to public health measures.[113]

Apart from its legal and political value, another important indication of the significance of the Declaration was its perception by two key stakeholders in the debate: pharmaceutical MNEs, and NGOs. Initial reactions by pharmaceutical MNEs as expressed by their industry associations, was negative and outright hostile to the content of the Declaration.[114] On the eve of the Doha Ministerial, Harvey Bale, Director-General of the International Federation of Pharmaceutical Manufacturers Associations (IFPMA), described Option 1 in the Chair's draft, backed by DCs, and which the Declaration was eventually based on, as a 'lawless option', that would destroy the rule of law system.[115] Moreover, of the final Declaration, Bale added that it was ambiguous and that it would be difficult for him to convince his members of its value. However, after this initial rejection, MNEs changed their tone, undoubtedly they sought to cast an image on the Declaration that was favourable to their interests. Emphasis was placed that the Declaration was a political statement, and hence 'not a legal change to the WTO rules'.[116] However, individual MNEs such as the Swiss Novartis, still expressed concern about the effect

[111] Sykes (2002) (n 104) 54.

[112] Abbott (2002) (n 1) 491. The same contention with regard to the effect of the Declaration is presented in Murthy (2002) (n 102) 1328.

[113] See Schott (2002) (n 106) 195; and Garcia-Castrillon (2002) (n 106) 219.

[114] For commentary on pharmaceutical MNEs' response to the Declaration, see Ellen 't Hoen *TRIPS, Pharmaceutical Patents, and Access to Essential Medicines: A Long Way From Seattle to Doha* 3 Chi J Int'l L 27 (2002) 43–4.

[115] *Global Drug Industry Association Blasts 'Nutty' WTO Text on TRIPs, Public Health* 18 Int'l Trade Rep (BNA) 1782 (8 Nov 2001).

[116] Statement by Brian Ager, Director-General, European Federation of Pharmaceutical Industries and Associations (EFPIA), quoted in Geoff Winestock and Helene Cooper *Deal Will Allow Poor Nations to Ignore Patents to Meet Public-Health Needs* WALL STREET JOURNAL (14 Nov 2001).

of the Declaration.[117] The most important statement on the issue however came from PhRMA, where it stressed the Declaration was a 'political statement', that 'explicitly maintains TRIPS Agreement rights and obligations reaffirming that intellectual property protection promotes public health by encouraging the discovery and development of vaccines and medicines. . . .'[118] Finally, the International Intellectual Property Institute (IIPI), commenting on how the Declaration was perceived as a victory by NGO activists, argued:

> It is the view of the Institute that this is naïve and short sighted. Whenever property rights are challenged . . . and the country which has taken steps to abrogate those rights is perceived to have used its discretion unwisely, the property right holder will challenge the decision made. This will happen with or without a declaration of the nature as that contained in the Draft [sic] Declaration on the TRIPS Agreement and Public Health. . . .[119]

On the other hand, NGOs considered the Declaration a major step forward in their efforts to ensure access to medicines, and in the pursuit of DCs of their interest vis-à-vis IC and MNE pressure.[120] Oxfam in particular alluded to the continuation of pressure building up from the 'victories' in the South Africa and Brazil cases, and that it will be much harder for the US and the MNEs to 'bully' poor countries over their patent policies.[121] However, there was still some concern that a stronger statement might still be needed. In particular, James Love of the Consumer Project on Technology, expressed disappointment that the paragraph 6 issues remained unresolved, alluding that it will be the next battleground.[122] The Declaration, just as it proved an important achievement for DC interests, representing the first time that they can be said to have prevailed on TRIPS issues in the WTO, it was equally significant for NGOs. It must be acknowledged that without the support of NGOs and their incessant campaigning, DCs would have found it difficult to prevail in their WTO action.

[117] Daniel Vasella, Chairman and CEO, Novartis AG, quoted in ibid.

[118] Press Release, PhRMA WTO Doha Declaration Reaffirms Value of Intellectual Property Protection (14 Nov 2001) (on file with author).

[119] Lee Gillespie-White 'What did Doha Accomplish?' (19 Nov 2001) <http://lists. essential.org/pipermail/ip-health/2002-February/002724.html> (last visited 19 Jan 2004).

[120] See statement on the Declaration by Oxfam, Third World Network, HAI, CPT, and MSF among others, compiled in posting by James Love, love@cptech.org, to IP-Health@lists.essential.org (13 Nov 2001) <http://lists.essential.org/pipermail/ip-health/2001-November/002401.html> (last visited 16 Dec 2003).

[121] ibid.

[122] ibid.

PART FIVE

TOWARDS A BETTER 'PLAYING-FIELD'

This book has explored the issue of fairness in international economic rule-making, between the interests of developing countries and those of multinational enterprises and industrialized countries. This exploration was carried out within the context of the pharmaceutical-related provisions of the TRIPS Agreement. Analysis covered three phases in the Agreement's trajectory; its negotiation, its implementation, and finally, disputes and conflicts concerning its implementation and interpretation. The argument was maintained throughout, that due to a rule-making process disadvantageous to DC interests characterized as an instance of 'top-down' rule-making, DCs resisted the implementation of TRIPS standards into their domestic legislation, and ultimately engaged in action commensurate to 'bottom-up' retorting against the TRIPS pharmaceutical-related standards. In Chapter 14, this characterization of the twin dynamic involved in the history of the TRIPS Agreement is revisited, and its main characterizations and implications briefly examined. Finally, as a proposed antidote to future rule-making endeavours suffering from a similar malady, a set of selective suggestions are presented. These suggestions, presented in Chapter Fifteen, are designed to tackle inconsistencies in the rule-making exercise itself, and are therefore of generic value to various areas of international economic regulation, involving DCs, ICs, and MNEs interests.

Chapter 14

The Twin Dynamic of 'Top-Down' Rule-Making and 'Bottom-up' Retorting Action

The problem as examined in this book was captured as entailing two principal dynamics. Primarily, there is the rule-making process, that of the negotiation of the TRIPS Agreement itself. This dynamic was flawed, as it largely accounted for the interests of one set of actors, the pharmaceutical MNEs, at the expense of those of DCs and their domestic stakeholders. Indeed, the period during the rule-making of the TRIPS Agreement can be described as the golden era of MNEs' influence.[1] On the other hand, DCs were incapable of resisting this exercise of 'top-down' rule-making. In retrospect, a number of factors contributed significantly to this dynamic of the rule-making of the TRIPS Agreement: the success of the MNE strategy; the role of ICs, essentially that of the United States; deficiencies in DC strategy; and the GATT/WTO negotiating set-up. Due to this limited capacity to impact the Uruguay Round negotiations on TRIPS, DCs lacked a 'sense of ownership' of its results.[2]

As such, the second dynamic, set in motion and diametrically opposed to the first, comprised the retorting action engaged in by DCs, their stakeholders, and global civil society groups. At the centre of this dynamic was the attempt to restore a minimum of DC interests in the TRIPS pharmaceutical-related regime. In reading it as such, it must be pointed out that a degree of damage was done to the legitimacy of the WTO during this second dynamic, and a sense of unpredictability emerged over the rules of the trading system as they related to IP. On the other hand, and more importantly, there are positive elements that should be highlighted and built upon towards the goal of asserting a viable level of representational fairness for DCs in the rule-making process.

1 It has been noted that the MNE solidarity over TRIPS, characteristic of the Uruguay Round era no longer holds true, as signs of business fragmentation arise that risk sacrificing the effectiveness of MNE influence. See DUNCAN MATTHEWS, GLOBALISING INTELLECTUAL PROPERTY RIGHTS: THE TRIPS AGREEMENT 105–106, 124–28 (2002).

2 This point was raised in J Michael Finger and Philip Schuler *Implementation of Uruguay Round Commitments: The Development Challenge* WORLD BANK WORLD POLICY RESEARCH WORKING PAPER NO 2215, 3–5 (1999) <http://www-wds.worldbank.org/servlet/WDSContentServer/WDSP/IB/2001/02/10/000094946_01013005324822/Rendered/PDF/multi_page.pdf> (last visited 22 Mar 2006).

(I) TRIPS PATENT NEGOTIATIONS: TOP-DOWN RULE-MAKING

The evidence presented in Part Two above reveals that the TRIPS negotiations, specifically as they pertained to patent standards, were the product of a process that was disproportionately influenced by the interests of pharmaceutical MNEs at the expense of DC interests, resulting in a 'top-down' model of rule-making. This section will first deal with the factors that led to this format in the TRIPS rule-making process. It will then briefly discuss the implications of the TRIPS negotiation phase on the issue of fairness in GATT/WTO rule-making.

(A) Pharmaceutical MNEs and the TRIPS Patent Negotiations Outcome

The role of the pharmaceutical MNEs, particularly as represented by the US Pharmaceutical Manufacturers Association (later known as Pharmaceutical Research and Manufacturers of America), and more generally by the Intellectual Property Committee, has undoubtedly been a major catalyst, if not the raison-d'être, for the drive towards the relevant standards on patent protection in the TRIPS Agreement. Indeed, in our attempt to understand the flaws in this process, it is not so much what went wrong as it is what did the MNEs do right. The reason for this success by the pharmaceutical MNEs was due to a number of factors.

The first two factors relate respectively to the cohesion and organizational prowess of the pharmaceutical MNE lobby. Arguably, the nature of the 'piracy' problem faced by the pharmaceutical giants was peculiar in eliciting a high level of cohesion within their ranks, as it posed a common problem faced by most of them especially in the larger DC markets. This facilitated the emergence of a strong cohesive stance revealed in the formation of the IPC, which involved a number of pharmaceutical MNE members, as well as a clear stance by the PMA on the issue. It was further reinforced by international solidarity primarily through the IPC-UNICE-Keidanren unified position,[3] and secondly, through the efforts of the international federation, IFPMA. Related to the factor of cohesion in the success of the pharmaceutical MNE effort is that of their organizational prowess. Not only were these MNEs financially well resourced but they were equally successful in having exceptional human resources to bring to bear on the issue. The experience and networks of such key figures as

[3] This led to the publication of the Trilateral Report. See KEIZAI DANTAI RENGOKAI, UNICE, INTELLECTUAL PROPERTY COMMITTEE, BASIC FRAMEWORK OF GATT PROVISIONS ON INTELLECTUAL PROPERTY: STATEMENT OF VIEWS OF THE EUROPEAN, JAPANESE AND UNITED STATES BUSINESS COMMUNITIES (1988) [hereinafter Trilateral Report].

Edmund Pratt,[4] Gerald Mossinghoff,[5] and Richard Arnold,[6] among others, were major contributing factors in this regard.[7] Furthermore, the coordination of work by the pharmaceutical lobby in 'working' Capitol Hill and the Administration, and in information gathering and direct lobbying of delegates in Geneva, as largely conducted by IFPMA, was also an organizational ability unmatched by the majority of DC delegations.

Also related to the MNEs organizational abilities, the third factor was their success in defining the problem, in devising a solution, and ultimately in supplying it in a legal format. Earlier, the 'genius' of framing the IP problem in a trade context was discussed. Furthermore, the utility of providing a proposed draft document very close to treaty language in the form of the Trilateral Report at the early stages of the negotiations proved an effective tool in gaining momentum. Finally, the fourth factor relates to the ability of the MNEs to effectively lobby the dominant state actor(s) during the Uruguay Round negotiations and particularly on the TRIPS patent standards provisions.

Supported by other IC delegations (particularly the EC) during the Uruguay Round negotiations, the role performed by the United States also contributed to this 'top-down' rule-making process. Apart from the bilateral diplomatic pressures and unilateral sanctions applied mainly by the United States,[8] IC delegations were engaged in manipulative negotiating tactics with DC delegations partly through their ability to offer concessions to DCs in other areas of the Uruguay Round negotiations such as in textiles and agriculture. However, they were also able to exclude DC delegations from key decision-making, notoriously in the 'green room' process of negotiations among the like-minded ICs with the results offered on a take it or leave it basis for DCs.

Two further factors contributed to this characterization of a 'top-down' rule-making process. Primarily, the forum of the GATT was amenable to advantage the interests of ICs. The GATT/WTO system and particularly its rule-making process in the form of rounds of negotiations to be carried forward as a single undertaking with the end product in the form of a package, lends itself to those negotiating delegations with the most bargain-

[4] Edmund Pratt is former CEO of Pfizer and convenor/founder of the IPC.

[5] Gerald Mossinghoff was President of PMA during the Uruguay Round and former US Undersecretary of Commerce and Commissioner of Patents.

[6] Richard Arnold was Executive Vice-President of IFPMA during the Uruguay Round.

[7] Braithwaite and Drahos enumerate 'individuals' as important actors involved in international economic regulation. For their analysis, see JOHN BRAITHWAITE AND PETER DRAHOS, GLOBAL BUSINESS REGULATION 494–7 (2000).

[8] For an attack by certain delegations during the negotiations on the 'Special 301' process being a violation of the commitments under the Punta del Este Declaration, specifically with regard to standstill and rollback, see GATT *Meeting of Negotiating Group of 27 and 28 June 1991—Note by the Secretariat* MTN.GNG/TRIPS/1 (25 July 1991) paras 4–5.

ing power. Particularly, the ability of the US and EC to offer DCs concessions in important areas was paralleled by their ability to force a capitulation on the part of DCs on the issue of TRIPS. Finally, the lack of cohesion among DC delegations on the issue of TRIPS, as in other issues during the Uruguay Round, facilitated this process and made them an easier target of IC pressure.[9]

(B) Implications of the TRIPS Negotiations on Patents

As becomes evident, DCs and the pharmaceutical MNEs approached the issue of patent protection from different perspectives. As their interests were at odds, the discourse employed by each party in the debate to justify their positions was different. While we warned earlier of the dangers of falling into the trap of an ideologically grounded debate on the relevant merits of either party's position and their approach to the issue, it is important to note the opposed nature of some of their justifications. MNEs argued that existing international IP regimes, most notably the Paris Convention, were never intended to address trade-related distortions, and hence the existence of a problem in international economic regulation that required to be addressed in a new fashion.[10] On the other hand and diametrically opposed to this contention, was the argument by DCs, as expressed by India's submission to the negotiating group on TRIPS. Their argument was that the philosophy behind regimes for the protection of IP was to encourage and promote public policy priorities, and that the trade-related problems associated with it were the quest of IP owners to distort such a goal to fulfil their narrower interests.[11]

The *fait accompli* resulting in the adoption of the TRIPS Agreement at the end of the Uruguay Round was by no means the end of the line with regard to the TRIPS pharmaceutical patent dilemma. Its implementation proved beyond doubt that the debate on its relative 'fairness' has not been settled. This complicated the implementation process and led to legal and political disputes that have proven problematic not only to the TRIPS and WTO regime, but also to the interests of all parties involved including DCs and MNEs.[12]

[9] On the breaking up of 'third world unity' during the Uruguay Round see CHAKRAVARTHI RAGHAVAN, RECOLONIZATION: GATT, THE URUGUAY ROUND AND THE THIRD WORLD 75–7 (1990).

[10] See Trilateral Report (n 3) 15.

[11] See GATT *Standards and Principles Concerning the Availability, Scope and Use of Trade-Related Intellectual Property Rights—Communication from India* MTN.GNG/NG11/W/37 (10 July 1989), and commentary thereon in GATT *Meeting of Negotiating Group of 12–14 July 1989* MTN.GNG/NG11/14 (12 Sept 1989).

[12] Ryan notes that US IP diplomacy was mainly a 'rule-writing' effort, and that it did not

(II) TRIPS IMPLEMENTATION AND DISPUTES: BOTTOM-UP RETORTING

A genuine perception exists in DCs that TRIPS ultimately represents an unbalanced regime that favours the interests of IC corporate actors, and most notably pharmaceutical MNEs. As captured by two analysts of the TRIPS regime, ICs were essentially telling DCs 'do it my way.'[13] Apart from disillusionment with the rule-making process, DCs were acutely aware of the negative impact TRIPS would have on their public health policy and pharmaceutical industry. This was apparent in the debates over implementation in Egypt. The Ministry of Health, supported by domestic pharmaceutical industry magnates, engaged in exhaustive efforts to attempt to lessen the impact of TRIPS provisions as they were incorporated into the new IP legislation. DC media was also shown to be unwaveringly critical of TRIPS implementation.

Given this recalcitrance, pharmaceutical MNEs and ICs, chiefly the United States, engaged in pressure that was designed to speed this implementation process, and furthermore to move beyond what was achieved in TRIPS. While DCs had anticipated a cessation of bilateral pressure as a result of TRIPS, a promise ICs had made during the Uruguay Round negotiations, they found themselves prodded for further revisions beyond TRIPS standards in a number of instances, and subject to the same bilateral 'bullying' tactics including continued use of the US 301 process. In the words of Professor Correa,

> [t]he expectations created by the Agreement as an instrument to eliminate tensions and institutionalise conflicts have been undermined by actions against some developing countries to amend IPRs laws before the expiration of the transitional periods, and to provide protection beyond the requirements of the TRIPs Agreement.[143]

This fact added further to DC resentment against the imposition of the TRIPS regime. Furthermore, and as alluded to by Dr El Sayed, Head of the Egyptian Medical Union, and Chairman of the lower house of Parliament's Health Committee, the direct effects of TRIPS standards on pharmaceuticals in DCs has not yet taken its full toll.[15]

stop at the signing of the TRIPS Agreement, but continues well into its implementation phase into DC legislation. See MICHAEL P RYAN, KNOWLEDGE DIPLOMACY: GLOBAL COMPETITION AND THE POLITICS OF INTELLECTUAL PROPERTY 86–87 (1998).

[13] J Michael Finger and Philip Schuler (n 2).

[14] Carlos Correa *Implementation of the TRIPS Agreement in Latin America and the Caribbean* 19 EUR INTELL PROP REV 435, 438 (1997).

[15] Interview with Dr Hamdy El Sayed, Head of the Egyptian Medical Union and Chairman, Health Committee, People's Assembly, Cairo (6 Apr 2004).

Nonetheless, and as discussed in Part Three above, DCs enacted legislation largely in compliance with TRIPS provisions. However, legislative compliance has not spared the TRIPS regime, nor that of the WTO, the pressure generated and retorting action undertaken by DC governments, their domestic stakeholders, global civil society groups, and indeed certain international governmental organizations, against the impediments that TRIPS standards and certain interpretations of them levy on DC public policy. It has been noted that '[c]oercion is...a delicate, risky, and possibly counterproductive strategy, one that could easily backfire on those governments that succumb to this temptation.'[16] The TRIPS regime therefore entered a third stage in its trajectory following those of its negotiation and implementation; that of the disputes and challenges emerging over certain of its provisions, and of IC and MNE favoured interpretations of its text. That stage was initiated through a series of WTO dispute settlement actions against violations of certain TRIPS provisions in a number of DC legislations, but quickly transfixed on the broader issue of access to medicine.

Part Four focused its examination on retorting action against the implementation and inflexible interpretation of the pharmaceutical-related provisions of the TRIPS Agreement. Through an analysis of that action at three framework levels, it has shown that the discourse on TRIPS has undergone a significant change from that existing during its negotiation in the Uruguay Round. Undoubtedly, the TRIPS Agreement as an international legal instrument linked to the multilateral trading system cannot be 'undone'.[17] But it is equally undeniable that TRIPS, as revealed by the examination above, has been a regime in crisis. Jacques Gorlin, an architect of the pharmaceutical industry's construction of TRIPS during the Uruguay Round lamented this crisis, arguing that

> we had assumed that most countries would accept the TRIPS obligations, and dispute settlement would fix a few of the problems. What has happened however, is that we are starting to see dispute settlement cases that cover the wholesale failure to implement TRIPS.[18]

In appreciating this evolution of events, and in concluding this discussion on retorting action, three particular perspectives on those events should be considered.

[16] JH Reichman and David Lange *Bargaining Around the TRIPS Agreement: the Case for Ongoing Public-Private Initiatives to Facilitate Worldwide Intellectual Property Transactions* 9 DUKE J COMP AND INT'L L 11, 48 (1998).

[17] See Susan K Sell *Industry Strategies for Intellectual Property and Trade: The Quest for TRIPS, and Post-TRIPS Strategies* 10 Cardozo J Int'l and Comp L 79, 99 (2002).

[18] Jacques J Gorlin US *Industries, Trade Associations, and Intellectual Property Lawmaking* 10 Cardozo J Int'l and Comp L 5, 10 (2002).

Primarily, one way of perceiving this evolution of events relating to the TRIPS regime, is the attempt by DCs to extricate their public policy flexibility from the constraints of TRIPS implementation and certain of its interpretations. As the first framework of retorting action revealed, DC governments and domestic stakeholders were resisting TRIPS implementation, most clearly in the cases of India and Argentina. This resistance extended in the case of Brazil to a conflict between interpretations of TRIPS provisions and DCs' ability to undertake an effective public policy to address an important health issue. In the case of South Africa, this conflict erupted into a serious impediment to the South African government's ability to respond to a major health crisis. Action was hence imperative to address these constraints.

A second perspective on those events is the gradual evolution of retorting action carried out by DCs. This can best be described as a gradual maturing in the discourse adopted by DCs, from the crude negativity of a tactic of delay in the India WTO DSU cases, to the positive acumen of a strategy that led to the adoption of the Doha Declaration. In a post-TRIPS world, individual DCs were initially delaying and attempting to circumvent full TRIPS implementation. This was however countered by stringent US monitoring of its implementation and enforcement through DSU action. A qualitative shift in retorting action ensued with the rise of the access to medicines debate, as examined in the second framework. Developing countries and NGOs were now methodically engaging in criticism of certain TRIPS provisions and their interpretation by IC and MNE interests. The passivity exhibited by DCs in accepting a 'top-down' imposition of rules concerning intellectual property had reached its apex with the signing of TRIPS and the earlier stages of DSU action. At hand in the latter 1990s however, was a situation where ICs and MNEs were finding it increasingly more difficult to impose their will, and were on the defensive towards DC and NGO charges of 'valuing profits over life'. Eventually, as examined in the third framework, DC action succeeded in re engaging debate on an interpretation of TRIPS provisions. Back at the WTO, it was DCs who were now taking the initiative and setting the agenda for ICs to respond to.

Finally, a third perspective on those events concerns the rise of new issues relating to the TRIPS Agreement, and the rise of new actors in the debate surrounding it. The trade-related nature of the debate surrounding the TRIPS negotiations during the Uruguay Round has gradually transformed into a debate surrounding the implications of TRIPS on public health issues. This evolution has led to what has been described as a conflict between the commercial and social agendas in the context of TRIPS.[19] Furthermore,

[19] See Susan K Sell *Post-TRIPS Developments: The Tension Between Commercial and Social Agendas in the Context of Intellectual Property* 14 Florida J Int'l L 193, 201 (2002).

while industry concerns, and especially the pharmaceutical MNEs and their business organizations, had a near monopoly on non-state actor involvement during the Uruguay Round negotiations on TRIPS, this was no longer the case. Throughout the discussion in Part Four, NGOs were shown to effectuate a role that was central in the dynamic of the debate surrounding the post-Uruguay Round TRIPS regime. As captured in a news report during the Doha ministerial:

> Lobbyists from US, Swiss and European drug companies all descended on the meeting to protect their patents. But unlike in 1993, when intellectual-property protections were first negotiated as part of the initial WTO pact, this time the lobbyists were matched by AIDS activists who proved to be a well-coordinated group of opponents.[20]

This dual phenomenon of the rise of new issues and the involvement of new actors is an important unfolding aspect of international rule-making, specifically as it affects WTO rule-making and the question of representational fairness therein.

[20] Geoff Winestock and Helene Cooper *Deal Will Allow Poor Nations to Ignore Patents to Meet Public-Health Needs* WALL STREET JOURNAL (14 Nov 2001).

Chapter 15

Suggestions Towards a Viable Level of Representational Fairness

In this final chapter, a set of selective suggestions are presented, distilling the lessons that can be derived from the analysis in this book, as to how the rule-making process, as it concerns the WTO, could avoid imbalances and ensuing conflicts in its future rule-making undertakings. Clearly, there is no set formula whereby all stakeholders in any given set of negotiations would have no misgivings over its outcome. It is a *sine qua non* of the multilateral trading system that negotiations occur simultaneously over a wide panoply of issues, the so-called 'single undertaking' format. An example of this fact is what was alluded to above that while the interests of the MNEs had largely eclipsed those of DCs during the TRIPS negotiation process, MNEs still found faults in the Agreement, being critical of the inclusion of transitional periods and the lack of provisions on pipeline protection. However, in light of the discussion in this book, there clearly is a need for some viable level of representational fairness in the rule-making process that would serve to uphold a minimum of DC interests. In this regard, the set of selective suggestions presented derive from the context of the experience of the TRIPS pharmaceutical-related provisions.

It is the purpose of this prescriptive approach to the suggestions for attaining a minimum level of representational fairness for DCs in the rule-making process that it should be informed by the elements discussed in the preceding chapter. The extent to which a level of fairness may be achieved is naturally contingent on a broad set of factors, and relates directly to the negotiating 'power' of the parties involved. While comprising the vast majority of the membership of the WTO, developing countries still lag behind in terms of their 'market power' and are therefore a 'weaker' party as a block compared to the ICs as a block. It is often presented as a truism of the GATT/WTO system that when the US and the EC are in unison over an issue, they usually prevail. This is undoubtedly more so the case when the 'quad' (US, EC, Japan, and Canada), are in agreement over an issue. Nonetheless, this should not, and luckily has not, been perceived as impeding DC action. It is in this particular situation that the craft of diplomacy is most valuable, if properly deployed, to orchestrate a set of 'safety valves' in the rule-making process to guarantee

DCs a viable level of representational fairness. Below, four suggestions are presented towards that end.

(I) DEVELOPING COUNTRIES' ACTION

As discussed in Part Two above, during the Uruguay Round DCs failed to engage effectively in the negotiations. However, this DC condition changed during the lead up to, and at the Doha Ministerial. Arguably, the increase in DC involvement in the post-Uruguay Round multilateral trading system has led DCs into a learning curve that started to reap benefits.[1] It is important to note that in seeking a viable level of representational fairness in WTO rule-making, notwithstanding the other important suggestions referred to below, concerted DC action remains the most important basis for achieving this goal. DCs are formal parties to the rule-making process, and hence have a direct avenue for influencing its outcome. In this regard, DCs have a number of tasks to perform to act as effective parties in a rule-making process, most importantly: a thorough research of the issues involved; the engagement of experts with specialized knowledge of the issues involved; and concerted action to present as much as possible a unified position on the subject matter of the rule-making undertaking.

Of great importance is their need to carry out proper research into the particular issues at hand, and that necessitates a broad research undertaking that captures the effects of all the issues being negotiated in parallel. This is of course necessary within the WTO negotiating set-up where various issues are under discussion within the ambit of the 'single undertaking'. This research task, in order to be effective, must also reach into an understanding of IC positions in the negotiations, and indeed of developments in other regulatory bodies outside of the WTO system. Background papers, and other 'ideas' related to the issue at hand are often floated from a multitude of sources. These include those from negotiating parties, from the WTO Secretariat, produced by other international development agencies (eg UNCTAD, WIPO, World Bank, etc), from NGOs (including those produced by business associations representing MNE interests), and academic publications, among others. However, while these sources are undoubtedly of great use, yet they do not release DCs from the task of doing their own 'homework' themselves. By conducting their own research on the issues, DCs will not only be better able to appreciate the complexity of the

[1] See Diana Tussie and Miguel F Lengyel *Developing Countries: Turning Participation into Influence* in DEVELOPMENT, TRADE, AND THE WTO: A HANDBOOK 485–88 (Bernard Hoekman, Aaditya Mattoo and Philip English eds 2002).

issues at stake, but more importantly, will include in this analysis conditions germane to their domestic situations. It is important that this research is carried out at an early stage prior to the initiation of negotiations. In so doing, they will be able to make full use of this research in terms of identifying where their interests lie and what their negotiating position should be. Equally important is that this research needs to be conducted by 'experts' in the particular field, or at least in close collaboration with them. With the benefit of hindsight, it is greatly regrettable that not sufficient in-depth research was carried out in the earlier stages of the Uruguay Round concerning the impact of TRIPS on DCs. Perhaps this might have shed light on a feasible incongruity of TRIPS standards with certain public health policies, and as such might have gone some way towards realizing a more balanced text. DCs have learned that once the 'ink has dried' on a given instrument, particularly so in the GATT/WTO context, it is much harder to amend than when it is still being written.

This last point raised concerning the need to involve 'experts' in the fields leads to another important aspect of DC action, that of their staff capacity. For the vast majority of DC delegations involved in WTO processes, they tend to be overstretched engaging in multiple issues simultaneously, and in most cases covering other international organizations headquartered in Geneva. This capacity problem has been paid particular attention at the WTO with funds being made available from IC members to support DCs in this regard. It must dawn on DCs that the era of the diplomatic emissary based in a foreign office and in charge of a plethora of issues is incompatible with 'regulatory globalization'. Undoubtedly this function is important to provide general direction to a country's negotiations, yet the need for specialized negotiators for specific issues cannot be stressed sufficiently. It is appreciated that many DCs and the vast majority of LDCs cannot afford such specialization, and it is exactly at this stage that a concerted DC negotiating strategy is important.

The ability of DCs to act in concert in terms of adopting, to the extent possible, a unified negotiating position is a necessary but not a sufficient condition ensuring a viable level of representational fairness in WTO rule-making efforts. It is acknowledged that reaching a common position on the various issues that could come under WTO disciplines is a complicated task. Primarily, the DC block encompasses countries with different market structures and size, and more importantly varying levels of economic development. This fact, in addition to ICs policies of offering different concessions to different groups of DCs over the various issues under consideration, result in severe strains on attempts to forge a unified DC position. The lesson learnt from DC action during the WTO deliberations on TRIPS leading to the Doha Declaration is that concerted action is possible and most effective when DCs identify common interest that are sufficiently critical and can be translated into a concrete regulatory proposal.[2]

(II) BALANCING NON-STATE ACTORS' INVOLVEMENT

A major challenge to representational fairness during the rule-making of the TRIPS Agreement has been the ability of MNEs, through their business associations and alliances to monopolize non-state actor involvement in this process. While DCs and ICs engaged in preparatory work and debates prior to, and during the negotiations, MNEs were the only non-state actors involved with an effective influence. Therefore, DCs had been more easily outmanoeuvred in facing this combination of IC and MNE involvement. The limited involvement of intergovernmental organizations such as the GATT secretariat and that of WIPO did not have much of an impact in supporting DCs positions. On the other hand, this situation was reversed during the lead up to the Doha Ministerial, where the involvement of NGOs[3] based in both ICs and DCs had a highly effective role in promoting a greater degree of representational fairness between the interests of DCs and those of MNEs/ICs. This fact drives an important lesson for DCs that they should capitalize on.

Developing countries had traditionally assumed a posture averse to the involvement of non-state actors, including NGOs, in international economic regulation, and particularly in WTO matters. This was most pointedly revealed in the alarm and refusal expressed by DCs on the question of the admission of *amicus curiae* briefs from NGOs in WTO dispute settlement proceedings.[4] Such disenchantment with NGO involvement can be attributed to a traditional, and partly correct nonetheless, DC view of NGOs as primarily IC-based groups with an aggressive regulatory agenda incompatible with DC interests, and the association of such groups to increasing calls for the trade linkage of issues such as environment and labour standards within the WTO ambit and purview. Nonetheless, DCs would be foolhardy to deny that their degree of success at Doha was to no

[2] See also Frederick M Abbott *The Doha Declaration on the TRIPS Agreement and Public Health: Lighting A Dark Corner at the WTO* 5 J Int'l Econ L 469, 479–80 (2002).

[3] Reference to NGOs in this context, as it has been throughout this volume, is made to non-business civil society based groups, often revolving around a particular regulatory issue. In the course of this discussions on TRIPS, the most commonly cited IC-based groups include Oxfam, MSF, and Ralph Nader's and James Love's Consumer Project on Technology (CPT). Among the DC-based groups have been Third World Network (TWN) and Zackie Achmat's Treatment Action Campaign (TAC).

[4] See WTO *Minutes of Meeting of the General Council of 22 November 2000*, paras 9–10, 16, and 22–42 WT/GC/M/60 (23 Jan 2001).

small measure due to aggressive NGO campaigning action. The lesson is therefore also one of a coincidence of interests.

On the other hand, regardless of the views of DCs towards the role of NGOs in international economic regulation, theirs is increasingly an established role and a healthy development towards the aim of representational fairness, particularly with regard to WTO rule-making.[5] Nongovernmental organizations are capable of performing a role that strikes a degree of balance to the impact of MNEs on international rule-making, and hence of restoring a level of representational fairness in the process. The effectiveness of the NGO role was demonstrated in the 'Access to Medicine' campaign as discussed in Part Four of this book. An insightful example of the ability of NGOs to counter the influence of MNEs in an international rule-making effort was that of the OECD negotiations over the draft Multilateral Agreement on Investment (MAI) during the mid 1990s.[6]

The effectiveness of NGOs in instilling a viable level of representational fairness in international rule-making efforts lies in their ability to perform a number of important functions. Three such functions are particularly relevant in this context. Primarily, NGOs perform an information and publicity function. Being specialized groups, NGOs have the ability to develop particular expertise on a given issue of regulation, and in many cases, of having access to facts on the ground that are sometimes beyond the ability of governments or intergovernmental organizations to gather. The specialization of a group like MSF in tackling the global AIDS crisis and its access to data from its fields of operation has been an important factor in its ability to draw attention to the extent of the crisis. The South African TAC has through its efforts publicized the extent of the disease in South Africa, and questioned the government's seeming tendency to bend to intense MNE and IC pressure. Similarly, the legal expertise of groups such as CPT, in part available due to their ability to draw from leading academic scholars, has highlighted aspects of TRIPS that are disadvantageous to DCs, as well as warning of impedimentary interpretations of TRIPS provisions. Another aspect of this information function of NGOs is their ability to respond to MNE positions and claims. In this book, reference was made to Oxfam's 'Cut the Cost' campaign, which was effective in countering the claims of the major pharmaceutical MNEs with regard to their drug pricing policies. Furthermore, the response of the global coalition of NGOs to the lawsuit

[5] In their review of the involvement of civil society groups and broader epistemic communities in 'global business regulation', Braithwaite and Drahos commend such a role as tantamount to the empowerment of the individual among the clashing titans of international regulation. See JOHN BRAITHWAITE AND PETER DRAHOS, GLOBAL BUSINESS REGULATION 34–6 (2000).

[6] See Mohamed Omar Gad, Non-State Actors and the Negotiation of Multilateral Economic Instruments: A Case Study of the Multilateral Agreement on Investment (1998) (unpublished LLM dissertation, University of Warwick) (on file with author).

filed by the pharmaceutical MNEs in South Africa has led not only to the withdrawal of the court action, but produced a major public relations defeat for these MNEs.

A second function performed by NGOs is their potential to instil a degree of 'moral legitimacy' on the positions they advocate. This 'legitimizing' function is due to two attributes of NGOs: their independence from government and corporate influence, and their representation of grassroots interests. Naturally, not all NGOs enjoy such attributes equally nor all score highly on these attributes, but those that do, such as the NGOs discussed in the context of this book (TAC, MSF, ACT UP, etc), have prevailed largely due to the 'moral authority' with which their arguments have been received by global public opinion and the various parties to the regulatory agenda. In turn, the persuasiveness of their arguments, when they coincide with DC interests, as they did during the Doha process, strengthens DCs negotiating position and thus serves the interests of representational fairness.

Finally a third important function performed by NGOs is their capacity to influence the policy positions of key ICs. As discussed above, during the Uruguay Round negotiations on TRIPS, MNEs had a monopoly position in terms of their ability to influence IC negotiating positions, particularly that of the United States. However, NGOs have shown that by defining key positions and policies, and by exploiting the political position and campaigning action of IC political candidates, they bring a powerful force to bear on the outcome of IC policies. This was clearly revealed during the presidential campaign of Albert Gore where US-based NGOs, mainly ACT UP and CPT, exerted considerable pressure. This pressure, in the form of direct communications to the White House and the USTR and disruption of the presidential campaign of Al Gore over US policies on access to medicines under the TRIPS regime, specifically towards South Africa, was successful in changing the course of US policy, as discussed above.

(III) DC-MNE DIALOGUE

A third suggestion presented for achieving a level of representational fairness in international rule-making between the interests of DCs and those of MNEs is fostering a DC-MNE dialogue. While in the case of the TRIPS Agreement, the regulatory preferences of both sides were at odds, and so are they expected to be on a number of issues relating to international economic regulation, yet this should not obviate the need for this dialogue. On the contrary, it is in the interest of both parties to engage in a discussion of problematic issues, even when they are both initially aware that the gap between their respective interests and positions is wide. During the rule-making process of the TRIPS Agreement, no such dialogue existed. MNEs focused their strategy on ICs and their negotiators. Indeed, a leading lobbyist for the US business community during the Uruguay Round confirmed that the idea of a dialogue with DCs was not considered, even when business representatives contacted delegates in Geneva, they limited such contacts to IC delegations and the GATT secretariat.[7]

Once again, with hindsight, had a communication channel been established between the MNEs and DCs during the negotiations over TRIPS, and had MNEs themselves acknowledged the need for such a link rather than relying as they did, and continued to do during TRIPS implementation, on lobbying ICs for a coercive approach, problems with the TRIPS Agreement might have been less acute. Indeed, the confrontation that ensued over the implementation and interpretation of certain TRIPS provisions between DC governments and the pharmaceutical MNEs can be attributed to this lack of a channel of dialogue. In the case of South Africa and that of Brazil, this confrontational discourse as it transpired led to negative developments, a lawsuit in the former case, and threats of compulsory licensing in the latter, as was discussed in Chapter 11.

In presenting this suggestion however, the gap in positions between DCs and MNEs is appreciated, and it is not to be expected that merely through a dialogue, a resolution of differences might occur. The notion for such an undertaking was advocated in a project initiated at the Duke Law School that sought the promotion of dialogue over the TRIPS Agreement among DCs, their stakeholders and IP rights holders:

> we believe that the relevant interest groups in both developed and developing countries should consider treating the TRIPS Agreement as a set of default rules to be bargained around within a cooperative framework that removes impediments to the 'rule of law' on a transactional basis and that seeks to maximize gains for participating rights holders on a case-by-case approach. In other words, we see the need to establish an operational framework outside of the TRIPS Agreement's own institutional machinery that would be conducive to 'unofficial' cooperative strategies likely to produce win-win results for both public and private actors, regardless of the tensions that the TRIPS implementation process otherwise may generate among WTO member states.[8]

While clearly a worthwhile initiative, however, such a dialogue proposes a 'bargain' around the parameters already established by TRIPS, and as such

[7] Interview with Gerald J Mossinghoff, former President, Pharmaceutical Manufacturers Association, in Washington DC (29 Aug 2002).

[8] JH Reichman and D Lange *Bargaining Around the TRIPS Agreement: The Case for Ongoing Public–Private Initiatives to Facilitate Worldwide Intellectual Property Transactions* 9 DUKE J COMP AND INT'L L 11, 15–16 (1998).

is less favourable to DCs given the ontological basis of these parameters arrived at in a flawed rule-making process. What is therefore suggested here is to take such a set-up a step back, and to establish a mechanism of dialogue between DCs and MNEs to function prior to and during the rule-making process.

(IV) ISSUE LINKAGE AND CONSIDERATIONS OF HUMAN RIGHTS

An important lesson that is drawn from the analysis in this book on TRIPS has been that the nature of the conflicts that were eventually generated over its provisions and their interpretations, concerned a set of issues that did not figure during its negotiation phase. The core conflict emerging over 'access to medicine' in the context of global pandemics such as HIV/AIDS has increasingly led to calls linking TRIPS to issues of human rights, the public policy prerogatives of 'sovereign' States, and the obligations of governments towards their people.[9] Such issues, while they might have been alluded to in a general form by DCs during the TRIPS negotiations, have been side stepped in favour of focusing the debate on the technicalities of IPR protection in the context of international trade, its 'trade-related' aspects. It is becoming increasingly apparent that there cannot be a predominance of one interpretation nor of a singularly informed discourse in matters relating to international economic regulation. International regulatory norms are in a constellation, where each and every cluster should relate to the others. A disregard for such a notion, as it led to disputes and conflicts in the context of the pharmaceutical-related TRIPS provision, was best characterized by Sell as a conflict between the commercial and social agendas.[10] The rule-making effort should therefore acknowledge the diversity of issues involved in a given area of regulation in order to avoid the dismissal of the treatment of a particular issue that could lead to future complication in the resulting instrument.

This lesson therefore establishes the need for issue linkage in WTO rule-making efforts.[11] It should be noted that in the post-Uruguay Round international trading system, ICs have led the way in the call for the integration of certain issues including the environment and labour standards into the

[9] In this context, Ostergard argues the thesis that the responsibility of a state to provide for the physical welfare of its people takes precedence over a right holder's right to profit from his invention. See Robert Ostergard Jr *Intellectual Property: A Universal Human Right?* 21 HUM RTS Q 156, 157 (1999).

[10] Susan K Sell *Post-TRIPS Developments: The Tension Between Commercial and Social Agendas in the Context of Intellectual Property*, 14 Florida J Int'l L 193, 201 (2002).

[11] A recent symposium held by the American Journal of International Law focused on issue linkage in the work of the WTO, see Jose E Alvarez (ed) *Symposium: The Boundaries of the WTO* 96 Am J Int'l L 1 (2002).

system's trade discourse.[12] This tendency has in part been a resonance of calls by affected interest groups and NGO campaigners. On the other hand, these calls have been met with apprehension by DCs suspicious of an IC agenda of disguised protectionism, particularly as these links will affect trade in goods where DCs are increasingly enjoying a comparative advantage in.[13] However, DCs must recognize that while the linking of certain issues might potentially harm their interests, others will enhance them.

This potential for issue linkage to enhance DC interests, as they positively contribute to representational fairness in rule-making efforts, is most notably the case with regard to the admission of human rights considerations, and ensuring the conformity of future WTO instruments with the precepts of international human rights law. This was clearly seen in the discourse that emerged over the human rights implications of certain TRIPS provisions where, as discussed in Part Four, pronouncements issued by the United Nation's Sub-Commission on Human Rights, and the WHO's World Health Assembly, in addition to other UN reports, indicated a possible inconsistency between TRIPS provisions and certain international human rights instruments.[14] It is therefore important that future WTO negotiations, specifically as they admit new subject matter in its rule-making undertakings, should be viewed with the lens of consistency with international human rights law. A further issue area that might be considered as a safety gauge for DC interests is a consideration of competition policy.

The four suggestions discussed above entailed proposals concerning the involvement of actors and issues in a given rule-making process, that might serve to instil a viable level of representational fairness in the undertaking. Finally, in conclusion, it is important to point out that these proposals ultimately wind up into the mechanisms of the WTO rule-making process itself. This includes the format of negotiations as a 'single undertaking' and the need for 'qualifying' it, and the limited key decision-making format of the 'green room' process. Ultimately it covers issues of transparency and democratic governance in the WTO, an area at the vanguard of what the organization will have to grapple with in the years ahead.

[12] See Chantal Thomas *Trade-Related Labor and Environment Agreements?* 5 J INT'L ECON L 791 (2002).

[13] ibid 817–19. See also Jose E Alvarez *Symposium: The Boundaries of the WTO: Foreword* 96 AM J INT'L L 1 (2002).

[14] Two excellent accounts noted the need for international human rights law considerations to be adopted in the discourse over TRIPS. See Peter Drahos *Intellectual Property and Human Rights* 3 INTELL PROP Q 349 (1999); and Richard Elliott *TRIPS and Rights: International Human Rights Law, Access to Medicines, and the Interpretation of the WTO Agreement on Trade-Related Aspects of Intellectual Property Rights* CANADIAN HIV/AIDS LEGAL NETWORK (Nov 2001) <http://www.aidslaw.ca/ Maincontent/issues/cts/briefs/TRIPS-human-rights-briefPDF.pdf> (last visited 22 Mar 2006).

Bibliography

INTERNATIONAL TREATIES AND AGREEMENTS

Agreement on Trade-Related Aspects of Intellectual Property Rights, Annex 1C to the Marrakesh Agreement Establishing the World Trade Organization (15 April 1994) 33 ILM 1197.

Marrakesh Agreement Establishing the World Trade Organization (15 April 1994) 33 ILM 1144.

General Agreement on Tariffs and Trade 1994, Annex 1A to the Marrakesh Agreement Establishing the World Trade Organization (15 April 1994) 33 ILM 1153.

General Agreement on Trade in Services, Annex 1B to the Marrakesh Agreement Establishing the World Trade Organization (15 April 1994) 33 ILM 1167.

Understanding on Rules and Procedures Governing the Settlement of Disputes, Annex 2 to the Marrakesh Agreement Establishing the World Trade Organization (15 April 1994) 33 ILM 1226.

Paris Convention for the Protection of Industrial Property (20 March 1883) 21 UNTS 305 (as revised at Stockholm on 14 July 1967, and as amended on 28 September 1979).

Berne Convention for the Protection of Literary and Artistic Works (24 July 1971) 828 UNTS 221 (as revised in Paris on 24 July 1971, and amended on 28 September 1979).

Vienna Convention on the Law of Treaties (23 May 1969) 8 ILM 679.

Vienna Convention on the Law of Treaties Between States and International Organizations or Between International Organizations, (1986) 25 ILM 543

Convention Establishing the World Intellectual Property Organization (14 July 1967) 828 UNTS 3 (as amended on 28 September 1979).

LEGISLATION BY COUNTRY

Argentina

Law No 111 on Patents of Invention of 11 October 1864.

Law No 6,673 on Industrial Models and Designs of 9 August 1963.

Law No 24,481 on Patents and Utility Models of 30 March 1995 (as amended by Law No 24.572 of 20 March 1996).

Brazil

Law No 9.279 on Industrial Property of 14 May 1996.
Normative Act No 127/97 on Industrial Property of 5 March 1997.
Decree No 3.201 on Patents (Compulsory Licenses) of 6 October 1999.
Normative Act No 127 on Patents of 1997.
Decree No 2.553 on Patents of 16 April 1998.
Ministerial Ordinance No 322 on Patents of 16 April 1998.
Ministerial Ordinance No 88 on Patents of 16 April 1998.
Law No 8.884 on Prevention of Abuse of 11 June 1994.

Egypt

Law No 132 on Patents for Inventions, Designs and Industrial Models of 1949.
Ministerial Decree No 547 Organising the Implementation of Article 70(9) of the TRIPS Agreement of 8 March 2000.
Ministerial Decree No 2211 Concerning Data Exclusivity of Chemical and Pharmaceutical Products of 25 November 2000.
Law No 182 on the Protection of Intellectual Property Rights of 2 June 2002.

India

Patents Act No 39 of 19 September 1970.
Patents Ordinance (Amendment) No 13 of 1994.
Patents (Amendment) Act No 17 of 6 March 1999.
Patents (Amendment) Act No 38 of 25 June 2002.

South Africa

Patents Act (Consolidation) No 57 (No 76) of 26 April 1978 (1988).
Patents Act (Consolidation) No 57 (No 49) of 26 April 1978 (1996).
Patents Regulations No R6247 of 15 December 1978.
Anti-competitive Practices (Art. 2) Act (Consolidation) No 96 (No51) of 21 June 1979 (1991).
Medicines and Related Substances Control Amendment Act No 90 of 1997.

United States

Uruguay Round Agreements Act Pub L No 103–465 (1994).
Omnibus Trade and Competitiveness Act of 1988 Pub L No 100–418 (1988).

Trade Act of 1974 Pub L No 93–618 (1975).

Omnibus Consolidated and Emergency Supplemental Appropriations Act Pub L No 105–277 (1999).

WTO CASES

Panel Reports

India—Patent Protection for Pharmaceutical and Agricultural Chemical Products—Complaint by the United States. 5 September 1997. WT/DS50/R.

India—Patent Protection for Pharmaceutical and Agricultural Chemical Products—Complaint by the European Communities and their Member States. Report of the Panel. 24 August 1998. WT/DS79/R.

Canada—Patent Protection of Pharmaceutical Products—Complaint by the European Communities and their Member States. 17 March 2000. WT/DS114/R.

Canada—Term of Patent Protection—Complaint by the United States. 5 May 2000. WT/DS170/R.

Appellate Body Reports

India—Patent Protection for Pharmaceutical and Agricultural Chemical Products. 19 December 1997. WT/DS50/AB/R.

Canada—Term of Patent Protection. 18 September 2000. WT/DS170/AB/R.

Japan—Taxes on Alcoholic Beverages. 4 October 1996. WT/DS8/AB/R; WT/DS10/AB/R; WT/DS11/AB/R.

WTO Documents (arranged by date)

Document Symbol	Document Title	Document Date
IP/C/2	Procedures for Notification of, and Possible Establishment of a Common Register of, National Laws and Regulations Under Article 63.2: Decision of the Council for TRIPS of 21 November 1995.	30 November 1995

Document Symbol	Document Title	Document Date
WT/GC/W/209	Communication from Cuba, Dominican Republic, Egypt and Honduras	17 June 1999
JOB(99)/6928	Procedures for the Notification and Review of Legislation: Note by the Secretariat.	18 November 1999
Press/173		28 March 2000
WT/DS199/1	Brazil—Measures Affecting Patent Protection—Request for Consultation by the United States.	8 June 2000
IP/C/W/207	Review of Legislation: Questions Posed by Switzerland to Chile, Colombia, Egypt, Estonia, Kuwait, Paraguay, Peru, Turkey, and the United Arab Emirates.	20 September 2000
IP/C/W/208	Review of Legislation: Questions Posed by Japan to Chile, Colombia, Egypt, Estonia, Guatemala, Kuwait, Paraguay, Peru, Qatar, Saint Lucia and Turkey.	20 September 2000
IP/C/W/215	Review of Legislation: Questions Posed by the United States (includes to Egypt).	3 October 2000
IP/C/22	Annual Report (2000) of the Council for TRIPS.	6 December 2000
WT/GC/M/60	Minutes of Meeting of the General Council of 22 November 2000.	23 January 2001
JOB(01)/4	Members Whose Legislation is Scheduled to be Reviewed in 2001: Note by the Chairman.	30 January 2001
IP/C/W/261	Review of Legislation: Questions posed by Canada (including to Argentina and Egypt)—attached to an Egypt Geneva Mission fax.	9 May 2001
IP/C/W/263	Review of Legislation: Questions posed by Switzerland (includes to Argentina and Egypt).	14 May 2001

Document Symbol	Document Title	Document Date
IP/C/W/268	Review of Legislation: Questions posed by the United States (includes to Argentina and Egypt).	31 May 2001
IP/C/W/274	Review of Legislation: Questions posed by the European Communities and their member States (includes to Argentina and Egypt).	12 June 2001
IP/C/W/278	Review of Legislation: Responses from Egypt to the questions posed by Japan, Switzerland and the United States.	12 June 2001
IP/C/W/280	Communication from the European Communities and their Member States.	12 June 2001
IP/C/W/261/Add1	Review of Legislation: Questions posed by Canada: Addendum (including to Egypt)—attached to an Egypt Geneva Mission fax.	13 June 2001
IP/C/W/268/Add.2	Review of Legislation: Follow-up questions posed by the United States: Addendum (includes to Argentina and Egypt).	22 June 2001
Press/233	TRIPS Council Meeting on Access to Medicines: WTO Members to Press On, Following 'Rich Debate' on Medicines.	22 June 2001
IP/C/W/296	Submission by the African Group, Barbados, Bolivia, . . .	29 June 2001
IP/C/M/31	Special Discussion on Intellectual Property and Access to Medicines.	10 July 2001
WT/DS199/4	Brazil—Measures Affecting Patent Protection—Notification of Mutually Agreed Solution.	19 July 2001
IP/C/W/312 WT/GC/W/450	Proposal by the African Group, Bangladesh, Barbados, Bolivia, Brazil, Cuba, Dominican Republic, Ecuador, Haiti, Honduras [...] Lanka, Thailand, and Venezuela.	4 October 2001

Document Symbol	Document Title	Document Date
IP/C/W/313	Preambular Language for Ministerial Declaration—Contribution from Australia, Canada, Japan, Switzerland and the United States.	4 October 2001
IP/C/23	Annual Report (2001) of the Council for TRIPS.	5 October 2001
WT/MIN(01)/DEC/2	Declaration on the TRIPS Agreement and Public Health—Adopted on 14 November 2001.	20 November 2001
IP/N/1/ARG/2	Notification of Laws and Regulations Under Article 63.2 of the Agreement: Argentina.	22 October 2002
IP/C/W/326/Add.3	Review of Legislation: Responses from India to the questions posed by Australia, the European Communities and their member States, Japan and the United States and to follow-up questions posed by the European Communities and their member States and Switzerland: Addendum.	12 November 2002
IP/C/W/405	Implementation of Paragraph 6 of the Doha Declaration on the TRIPS Agreement and Public Health.	30 August 2003

TRIPS Negotiations Documents (arranged by date, from 9 February to 29 November 1993:

Document Symbol	Document Title	Document Date
MTN.GNG/5	Fifth Meeting of the Group of Negotiations on Goods—Record of Decisions Taken.	9 February 1987
MTN.GNG/W/9	Chairmen of Negotiating Groups.	12 February 1987
MTN.GNG/NG11/W/1	Communication From the Director General of the World Intellectual Property Organization.	25 February 1987

Document Symbol	Document Title	Document Date
MTN.GNG/ NG11/W/2	Statement by United States at Meeting of 25 March 1987.	3 April 1987
MTN.GNG/ NG11/W/3	EC Council Regulation Laying Down Measures to Prohibit the Release for Free Circulation of Counterfeit Goods—Communication from European Communities.	3 April 1987
MTN.GNG/ NG11/1	Meeting of the Negotiating Group of 25 March 1987—Note by the Secretariat.	10 April 1987
MTN.GNG/ NG11/W/4	Work Undertaken in GATT Concerning Trade-Related Aspects of Intellectual Property Rights, including Trade in Counterfeit Goods—Note by the Secretariat.	6 May 1987
MTN.GNG/ NG11/W/5	Information From Other International Organizations—Communication from WIPO.	19 May 1987
MTN.GNG/ NG11/W/6	GATT Provisions Bearing on Trade-Related Aspects of Intellectual Property Rights—Note by the Secretariat.	22 May 1987
MTN.GNG/ NG11/W/5/Add.1	Information From Other International Organizations—Communication from the Customs Co-operation Council.	29 May 1987
MTN.GNG/ NG11/W/7	Submissions from Participants on Trade Problems Encountered in Connection with Intellectual Property Rights.	29 May 1987
MTN.GNG/ NG11/W/8	Notifications in the Inventory of Non-Tariff Measures (Industrial Products) Relating to Intellectual Property Rights—Note by the Secretariat.	29 May 1987
MTN.GNG/ NG11/W/5/Add.2	Information From Other International Organizations—Communication from UNESCO.	4 June 1987

Document Symbol	Document Title	Document Date
MTN.GNG/ NG11/W/7/Add.1	Submissions from Participants on Trade Problems Encountered in Connection with Intellectual Property Rights—Addendum.	9 June 1987
MTN.GNG/ NG11/2	Meeting of the Negotiating Group of 10 June 1987—Note by the Secretariat.	23 June 1987
MTN.GNG/ NG11/W/9	Draft Agreement to Discourage the Importation of Counterfeit Goods.	25 June 1987
MTN.GNG/ NG11/W/10	Decree Prohibiting the Importing of Goods Illegally Bearing Marks Registered in Mexico—Communication from Mexico.	30 June 1987
MTN.GNG/ NG11/W/11	The Madrid Agreement for the Repression of False or Deceptive Indications of Source on Goods—Suggestion by Brazil.	9 July 1987
MTN.GNG/ NG11/W/5/Add.3	Information From Other International Organizations—Communication from WIPO, Addendum.	21 July 1987
MTN.GNG/ NG11/W/7/Add. 2	Submissions from Participants on Trade Problems Encountered in Connection with Intellectual Property Rights—Switzerland.	5 August 1987
MTN.GNG/ NG11/W/12	Compilation of Written Submissions and Oral Statements—Prepared by the Secretariat.	11 August 1987
MTN.GNG/ NG11/W/13	International Conventions Regarding Intellectual Property and their Membership—Note by the Secretariat.	2 September 1987
MTN.GNG/ NG11/W/5/Add.4	Information From Other International Organizations—Communication from WIPO, Addendum.	17 September 1987
MTN.GNG/ NG11/INF/1	List of Representatives.	23 September 1987

Document Symbol	Document Title	Document Date
MTN.GNG/ NG11/3	Meeting of the Negotiating Group of 23 September 1987—Note by the Secretariat.	8 October 1987
MTN.GNG/ NG11/W/14	Suggestion by the United States for Achieving the Negotiating Objective.	20 October 1987
MTN.GNG/ NG11/W/12/ Add.1	Compilation of Written Submissions and Oral Statements—Prepared by the Secretariat.	21 October 1987
MTN.GNG/ NG11/W/15	Suggestion by Switzerland for Achieving the Negotiating Objective.	26 October 1987
MTN.GNG/ NG11/4	Meeting of the Negotiating Group of 28 October 1987—Note by the Secretariat.	17 November 1987
MTN.GNG/ NG11/W/16	Guidelines Proposed by the European Community for the Negotiations on Trade-Related Aspects of Intellectual Property Rights.	20 November 1987
MTN.GNG/ NG11/W/17	Suggestion by Japan for Achieving the Negotiating Objective.	23 November 1987
MTN.GNG/ NG11/5	Meeting of the Negotiating Group of 23–24 November 1987—Note by the Secretariat.	14 December 1987
MTN.GNG/ NG11/W/5/Add.5	Information From Other International Organizations—Communication from the Customs Co-operation Council, Addendum.	25 January 1988
MTN.GNG/ NG11/W/19	Provisions of Existing International Conventions Providing Protection for Intellectual Property—Communication from the UNESCO Secretariat.	4 February 1988
MTN.GNG/ NG11/W/12/ Rev.1	Compilation of Written Submissions and Oral Statements—Prepared by the Secretariat—Revision.	5 February 1988

Document Symbol	Document Title	Document Date
MTN.GNG/ NG11/W/20	Activities in Other International Organizations of Possible Interest in Relation to Matters Raised in the Group—Note by the Secretariat.	8 February 1988
MTN.GNG/ NG11/W18	Provisions on Enforcement in International Agreements on Intellectual Property Rights—Note by the Secretariat.	10 February 1988
MTN.GNG/ NG11/W/21	Provisions of Existing International Conventions Providing Protection for Intellectual Property—Communication from the WIPO Secretariat.	12 February 1988
MTN.GNG/ NG11/W/22	Suggestion by the Nordic Countries for Achieving the Negotiating Objective.	12 February 1988
MTN.GNG/ NG11/6	Meeting of the Negotiating Group of 29 February–3 March 1988—Note by the Secretariat.	8 April 1988
MTN.GNG/ NG11/W/23	Trade in Counterfeit Goods: Compilation of Written Submissions and Oral Statements—Prepared by the Secretariat.	26 April 1988
MTN.GNG/ NG11/W/24	Existence, Scope and Form of Generally Internationally Accepted and Applied Standards/ Norms for the Protection of Intellectual Property—Note prepared by the International Bureau of WIPO.	5 May 1988
MTN.GNG/ NG11/W/24/ Add.1	Existence, Scope and Form of Generally Internationally Accepted and Applied Standards/Norms for the Protection of Intellectual Property—Note prepared by the International Bureau of WIPO—Addendum.	15 June 1988

Document Symbol	Document Title	Document Date
MTN.GNG/ NG11/W/5/Add.6	Other International Information From Organizations—Communication from WIPO, Addendum.	20 June 1988
MTN.GNG/ NG11/7	Meeting of the Negotiating Group of 16–19 May 1988—Note by the Secretariat.	21 June 1988
MTN.GNG/ NG11/W/24/ Add.2	Existence, Scope and Form of Generally Internationally Accepted and Applied Standards/ Norms for the Protection of Intellectual Property—Note prepared by the International Bureau of WIPO—Addendum.	27 June 1988
MTN.GNG/ NG11/W/26	Guidelines and Objectives Proposed by the European Community for the Negotiations on Trade Related Aspects of Substantive Standards of Intellectual Property Rights.	7 July 1988
MTN.GNG/ NG11/8	Meeting of the Negotiating Group of 5–8 July 1988—Note by the Secretariat.	29 August 1988
MTN.GNG/ NG11/W/24/ Rev.1	Existence, Scope and Form of Generally Internationally Accepted and Applied Standards/ Norms for the Protection of Intellectual Property—Note prepared by the International Bureau of WIPO—Revision.	15 September 1988
MTN.GNG/ NG11/W/27	Statement by Thailand at the Meeting of 12–14 September 1988.	21 September 1988
MTN.GNG/ NG11/W/17/Add.1	Submission by Japan—Addendum.	23 September 1988
MTN.GNG/ NG11/9	Meeting of the Negotiating Group of 12–14 September 1988—Note by the Secretariat.	13 October 1988
MTN.GNG/ NG11/W/14/ Rev.1	Suggestion by the United States for Achieving the Negotiating Objective—Revision.	17 October 1988

Document Symbol	Document Title	Document Date
MTN.GNG/ NG11/W/28	Statement by the Delegation of Mexico at the Meeting of 17, 18 and 21 October 1988.	19 October 1988
MTN.GNG/ NG11/W/29	Communication from the Nordic Countries.	20 October 1988
MTN.GNG/ NG11/W/30	Submission from Brazil.	31 October 1988
MTN.GNG/ NG11/10	Meeting of the Negotiating Group of 17–21 October 1988—Note by the Secretariat.	30 November 1988
MTN.GNG/ NG11/11	Meeting of the Negotiating Group of 14–15 November 1988—Note by the Secretariat.	1 December 1988
MTN.TNC/ 7(MIN)	Trade Negotiating Committee Meeting at Ministerial Level—Montreal, December 1988.	9 December 1988
MTN.TNC/9	Trade Negotiating Committee Meeting at Level of High Officials—Geneva, 5–8 April 1989.	11 April 1989
MTN.TNC/11	Mid-Term Meeting.	21 April 1989
MTN.GNG/ NG11/W/31	Proposal by the European Community for the Negotiations on the Enforcement of Trade-Related Intellectual Property Rights.	30 May 1989
MTN.GNG/ NG11/W/32	Synoptic Tables Setting Out Existing International Standards and Proposed Standards and Principles—Prepared by the Secretariat.	2 June 1989
MTN.GNG/ NG11/12	Meeting of the Negotiating Group of 11–12 May 1989—Note by the Secretariat.	13 June 1989
MTN.GNG/ NG11/W/34	Basic Principles of the Main Multilateral Treaties in the Field of Intellectual Property—Paper Prepared by the International Bureau of the World Intellectual Property Organization.	16 June 1989

Document Symbol	Document Title	Document Date
MTN.GNG/ NG11/W/13/ Rev.1	International Conventions Regarding Intellectual Property and their Membership—Note by the Secretariat—Revision.	19 June 1989
MTN.GNG/ NG11/W/5/Add.7	Information From Other International Organizations—Communication from WIPO, Addendum.	20 June 1989
MTN.GNG/ NG11/W/35	Standards and Norms for Negotiations on Trade-Related Aspects of Intellectual Property Rights—Communication from Australia.	10 July 1989
MTN.GNG/ NG11/W/36	Proposal by the Nordic Countries for the Negotiations on Standards and Principles for Trade-Related Aspects of Intellectual Property Rights.	10 July 1989
MTN.GNG/ NG11/W/37	Standards and Principles Concerning the Availability, Scope and Use of Trade-Related Intellectual Property Rights—Communication from India.	10 July 1989
MTN.GNG/ NG11/W/38	Standards and Principles Concerning the Availability, Scope and Use of Trade-Related Intellectual Property Rights—Communication from Switzerland.	11 July 1989
MTN.GNG/ NG11/W/35/ Corr.1	Standards and Norms for Negotiations on Trade-Related Aspects of Intellectual Property Rights—Communication from Australia—Corrigendum.	12 July 1989
MTN.GNG/ NG11/13	Meeting of the Negotiating Group of 3–4 July 1989—Note by the Secretariat.	16 August 1989
MTN.GNG/ NG11/W/39	Applicability of the Basic Principles of the GATT and of Relevant International Intellectual Property Agreements or Conventions—Communication from India.	5 September 1989

Document Symbol	Document Title	Document Date
MTN.GNG/ NG11/W/40	Enforcement of Trade-Related Intellectual Property Rights—Communication from India.	5 September 1989
MTN.GNG/ NG11/W/41	Multilateral Framework for International Trade in Counterfeit Goods—Communication from India.	5 September 1989
MTN.GNG/ NG11/W/42	Enforcement of Trade-Related Intellectual Property Rights—Submission from Canada.	5 September 1989
MTN.GNG/ NG11/14	Meeting of the Negotiating Group of 12–14 July 1989—Note by the Secretariat.	12 September 1989
MTN.GNG/ NG11/W/43	Enforcement of Trade-Related Intellectual Property Rights—Proposal by Japan.	12 September 1989
MTN.GNG/ NG11/W/32/ Rev.1	Synoptic Tables Setting Out Existing International Standards and Proposed Standards and Principles—Prepared by the Secretariat—Revision.	29 September 1989
MTN.GNG/ NG11/W/46	Standards and Principles for Negotiations on Trade-Related Aspects of Intellectual Property Rights—Communication from New Zealand.	24 October 1989
MTN.GNG/ NG11/W/44	Enforcement of Trade-Related Intellectual Property Rights—Statement by Switzerland.	25 October 1989
MTN.GNG/ NG11/W/47	Standards for Trade-Related Intellectual Property Rights—Submission from Canada.	25 October 1989
MTN.GNG/ NG11/W/48	Standards and Enforcement of Intellectual Property Rights—Communication from the Republic of Korea.	26 October 1989
MTN.GNG/ NG11/15	Meeting of the Negotiating Group of 11–13 September 1989—Note by the Secretariat.	26 October 1989

Document Symbol	Document Title	Document Date
MTN.GNG/ NG11/W/45	Guidelines for Negotiations that Strike A Balance Between Intellectual Property Rights and Development Objectives—Communication from Peru.	27 October 1989
MTN.GNG/ NG11/W/17/Add.2	Submission by Japan—Addendum.	30 October 1989
MTN.GNG/ NG11/W/43/ Add.1	Enforcement of Trade-Related Intellectual Property Rights—Proposal by Japan—Addendum.	30 October 1989 14 November 1989
MTN.GNG/ NG11/W/49	Trade-Related Aspects of Intellectual Property Rights—Submission from the European Communities.	
MTN.GNG/ NG11/W/50	Proposals on Behalf of the Least-Developed Countries—Communication from Bangladesh.	17 November 1989
MTN.GNG/ NG11/W/51	Standards for Trade-Related Intellectual Property Rights—Submission from Hong Kong.	29 November 1989
MTN.GNG/ NG11/16	Meeting of the Negotiating Group of 30 October–2 November 1989—Note by the Secretariat.	4 December 1989
MTN.GNG/ NG11/W/52	Data on Maintenance of Patents Through Payment of Maintenance Fees—Note by the Secretariat.	4 December 1989
MTN.GNG/ NG11/W/53	Enforcement of Trade-Related Intellectual Property Rights—Submission by Australia.	6 December 1989
MTN.GNG/N G11/W/54	Enforcement of Intellectual Property Rights—Submission from Hong Kong.	7 December 1989
MTN.GNG/ NG11/W/17/ Add.3	Submission by Japan—Addendum—Patents: Non-Voluntary Licences.	8 December 1989
MTN.GNG/ NG11/W/55	Trade-Related Intellectual Property Rights—Submission by Austria.	8 December 1989

Document Symbol	Document Title	Document Date
MTN.GNG/ NG11/W/56	Transitional Dispositions Relating to a GATT 'Minimum Standard Agreement— Communication by Hungary.	8 December 1989
MTN.GNG/ NG11/W/38/ Add.1	Standards and Principles Concerning the Availability, Scope and Use of Trade-Related Intellectual Property Rights— Communication from Switzerland—Addendum on Proprietary Information.	11 December 1989
MTN.GNG/ NG11/W/57	Communication from Brazil.	11 December 1989
MTN.GNG/ NG11/W/58	Enforcement of Trade-Related Intellectual Property Rights— Submission from the Nordic Countries.	12 December 1989
MTN.GNG/ NG11/W/59	Dispute Settlement— Communication from the Nordic Countries.	14 December 1989
MTN.GNG/ NG11/W/60	Communication from Mexico.	22 January 1990
MTN.GNG/ NG11/W/61	Communication from Chile.	22 January 1990
MTN.GNG/ NG11/17	Meeting of the Negotiating Group of 11, 12 and 14 December 1989—Note by the Secretariat.	23 January 1990
MTN.GNG/ NG11/W/62	Enforcement of Intellectual Property Rights—Submission by Austria.	29 January 1990
MTN.GNG/ NG11/W/63	Technical Assistance Provided by International Organizations— Communication from WIPO.	30 January 1990
MTN.GNG/ NG11/W/63/ Add.1	Technical Assistance Provided by International Organizations— Communication from CCC.	1 February 1990
MTN.GNG/ NG11/W/63/ Add.2	Technical Assistance Provided by International Organizations— Communication from UNESCO.	1 February 1990

Document Symbol	Document Title	Document Date
MTN.GNG/ NG11/W/64	National Legislation and Practices Deemed Restrictive in Connection with Intellectual Property Rights—Note by the Secretariat.	1 February 1990
MTN.GNG/ NG11/W/32/Rev.2	Synoptic Tables Setting Out Existing International Standards and Proposed Standards and Principles—Prepared by the Secretariat—Revision.	2 February 1990
MTN.GNG/ NG11/W/63/ Add.3	Technical Assistance Provided by International Organizations—Communication from UNCTAD.	2 February 1990
MTN.GNG/ NG11/18	Meeting of the Negotiating Group of 5–6 February 1990—Note by the Secretariat.	27 February 1990
MTN.GNG/ NG11/18/Corr.1	Meeting of the Negotiating Group of 5–6 February 1990—Note by the Secretariat—Corrigendum.	28 February 1990
MTN.GNG/ NG11/W/66	Beneficiaries of and Exceptions to National Treatment Under Treaties Administered by WIPO—Communication from WIPO.	28 February 1990
MTN.GNG/ NG11/W/67	List of Documents—Note by the Secretariat.	2 March 1990
MTN.GNG/ NG11/W/66/ Corr.1	Beneficiaries of and Exceptions to National Treatment Under Treaties Administered by WIPO—Communication from WIPO—Corrigendum.	6 March 1990
MTN.GNG/ NG13/W/37/ Add.2	Negotiating Group on Dispute Settlement — Discussion and Proposals in Other Negotiating Groups and in the Code Committees Relating to Dispute Settlement.	26 March 1990
MTN.GNG/ NG11/19	Meeting of the Negotiating Group of 6 and 9 March 1990—Note by the Secretariat.	28 March 1990

Document Symbol	Document Title	Document Date
MTN.GNG/ NG11/W/68	Draft Agreement on Trade-Related Aspects of Intellectual Property Rights.	29 March 1990
MTN.GNG/ NG11/W/65	Synoptic Table Setting Out Proposals on Procedures for the Acquisition and Maintenance of IPRs—Prepared by the Secretariat.	30 March 1990
MTN.GNG/ NG11/W/67/ Rev.1	List of Documents—Note by the Secretariat—Revision.	30 March 1990
MTN.GNG/ NG11/W/69	Transitional Arrangements in a TRIPS Agreement—Communication from a Number of Participants.	30 March 1990
MTN.TNC/W/19	Trade Negotiations Committee—Statement by the Informal Group of Developing Countries at the Trade Negotiations Committee of the GATT Uruguay Round, Geneva, 9–10 April 1990.	9 April 1990
MTN.GNG/ NG11/20	Meeting of the Negotiating Group of 2, 4 and 5 April 1990—Note by the Secretariat.	24 April 1990
MTN.GNG/ NG11/W/70	Draft Agreement on the Trade-Related Aspects of Intellectual Property Rights—Communication from the United States.	11 May 1990
MTN.GNG/ NG11/W/71	Communication from Argentina, Brazil, Chile, China, Colombia, Cuba, Egypt, India, Nigeria, Peru, Tanzania and Uruguay.	14 May 1990.
MTN.GNG/ NG11/W/72	Communication from Chile.	14 May 1990
MTN.GNG/ NG11/W/73	Draft Amendment to the General Agreement on Tariffs and Trade on the Protection of Trade-Related Intellectual Property Rights—Communication from Switzerland.	14 May 1990

Document Symbol	Document Title	Document Date
MTN.GNG/ NG11/W/74	Main Elements of a Legal Text for TRIPS —Communication from Japan.	15 May 1990
MTN.GNG/ NG11/W/75	Draft Text on Geographical Indications—Communication from Australia.	13 June 1990
MTN.GNG/ NG11/W/73/ Corr.1	Draft Amendment to the General Agreement on Tariffs and Trade on the Protection of Trade-Related Intellectual Property Rights—Communication from Switzerland.	14 June 1990
MTN.GNG/ NG11/21	Meeting of the Negotiating Group of 14–16 May 1990—Note by the Secretariat.	22 June 1990
MTN.GNG/ NG13/W/37/ Add.4	Negotiating Group on Dispute Settlement —Discussion and Proposals in Other Negotiating Groups and in the Code Committees Relating to Dispute Settlement—Update to Note by Secretariat.	6 July 1990
MTN.GNG/ NG11/W/76	Status of Work in the Negotiating Group—Chairman's Report to the GNG.	23 July 1990
MTN.TNC/15	Trade Negotiations Committee—Chairman's Summing-Up at Meeting of 26 July 1990.	30 July 1990
MTN.TNC/W/24	Trade Negotiations Committee—Statement by Bangladesh on Behalf of the Least Developed Countries.	30 July 1990
MTN.TNC/W/26	Trade Negotiations Committee—Statement by Mexico at the Meetings of the GNG and the TNC in July 1990.	3 August 1990
MTN.GNG/ NG11/22	Meeting of the Negotiating Group of 25 and 29 June 1990—Note by the Secretariat.	22 August 1990
MTN.GNG/ NG11/23	Meeting of the Negotiating Group of 13 July 1990—Note by the Secretariat.	22 August 1990

Document Symbol	Document Title	Document Date
MTN.GNG/4 NG11/2	Meeting of the Negotiating Group of 20 July 1990—Note by the Secretariat.	22 August 1990
MTN.GNG/ NG11/25	Meeting of the Negotiating Group of 10–21 September 1990—Note by the Secretariat.	8 October 1990
MTN.GNG/ NG11/26	Meeting of the Negotiating Group of 8 and 18 October 1990—Note by the Secretariat.	31 October 1990
MTN.GNG/ NG11/27	Meeting of the Negotiating Group of 1 November 1990—Note by the Secretariat.	14 November 1990
MTN.TNC/W/33 MTN.GNG/W/25	Trade Negotiations Committee—Group of Negotiations on Goods—Communication from Various Delegations.	21 November 1990
MTN.GNG/ NG11/28	Meeting of the Negotiating Group of 22 November 1990—Note by the Secretariat.	29 November 1990
MTN.TNC/W/41 MTN.GNG/W/27	Trade Negotiations Committee—Group of Negotiations on Goods—Evaluation on the Situation of the Uruguay Round—Communication from the Permanent Representative of Uruguay on Behalf of SELA.	29 November 1990
MTN.TNC/W/42	Trade Negotiations Committee—Statement by the Representative of the Philippines.	29 November 1990
MTN.TNC/W/45	Trade Negotiations Committee—Statement by the Representative of Bangladesh.	29 November 1990
MTN.TNC/W/56	Trade Negotiations Committee—Communication from the ACP Countries —Conclusions of the Special ACP Ministerial Meeting on the Uruguay Round.	5 December 1990
MTN.TNC/W/69	Trade Negotiations Committee—Programme of Work—Proposal by the Chairman at Official Level.	26 February 1991

Document Symbol	Document Title	Document Date
MTN.GNG/ TRIPS/W/1	Proposal for the Establishment of Dispute Prevention System in Respect of Transfer of Technologies—Communication from the Republic of Korea.	2 July 1991
MTN.GNG/ TRIPS/1	Meeting of Negotiating Group of 27 and 28 June 1991—Note by the Secretariat.	25 July 1991
MTN.GNG/W/28	Group of Negotiations on Goods—Communication from the Chairman of the Group of Negotiations on Goods to the Trade Negotiations Committee.	29 July 1991
MTN.GNG/ TRIPS/2	Meeting of Negotiating Group of 16 and 20 September 1991—Note by the Secretariat.	7 October 1991
MTN.GNG/ TRIPS/W/2	Communication from Colombia.	16 October 1991
MTN.TNC/W/89	Trade Negotiations Committee—Stocktaking of the Uruguay Round Negotiations by the Chairman of the Trade Negotiations Committee at Official Level.	7 November 1991
MTN.TNC/ W/89/Add.1	Trade Negotiations Committee—Progress of Work in Negotiating Groups: Stocktaking.	7 November 1991
MTN.TNC/23	Trade Negotiations Committee—Nineteenth Meeting: 7 November 1991.	13 November 1991
MTN.GNG/ TRIPS/3	Meeting of Negotiating Group of 16 and 22 October 1991—Note by the Secretariat.	18 November 1991
MTN.TNC/W/90	Communication from the Republic of Korea.	25 November 1991
MTN.GNG/ TRIPS/4	Meeting of Negotiating Group of 25 and 29 November 1991—Note by the Secretariat.	9 December 1991
MTN.GNG/ TRIPS/5	Meeting of Negotiating Group of 9 December 1991—Note by the Secretariat.	31 January 1992

Document Symbol	Document Title	Document Date
MTN.GNG/TRIPS/6	Meeting of Negotiating Group of 16 December 1991—Note by the Secretariat.	31 January 1992
MTN.TNC/W/107	Trade Negotiations Committee—Communication from Bangladesh.	21 January 1993
MTN.SB/SN/26	Surveillance Body—Standstill—Notification.	15 June 1993
MTN.TNC/W/122 MTN.GNG/W/30	Trade Negotiations Committee—Group of Negotiations on Goods—An Analysis of the Proposed Uruguay Round Agreement, with Particular Emphasis on Aspects of Interest to Developing —GATT Secretariat.	29 November 1993

GOVERNMENT DOCUMENTS

European Communities Documents

European Communities, Council of Ministers (1986) 'Overall Approach: New Round of Trade Negotiations in Defence of Open Multilateral Trade' EEC Doc No 7748/86, PV/CONS.33 Ext. 1 GATT 107 (June 1986).

EC Communication 'Accelerated Action Targeted at Major Communicable Diseases Within the Context of Poverty Reduction' COM (2000) 585 (20 Sept 2000).

European Parliament, Resolution B5-0182/2001 'Access to Medicines for AIDS Patients in the Third World' (15 Mar 2001).

United States Government Documents

Congressional Committee Prints and Reports

US Congress, Congressional Budget Office (1987) 'The GATT Negotiations and US Trade Policy.' (June 1987).

US House of Representatives (1988) 'Omnibus Trade and Competitiveness Act of 1988: Conference Report to Accompany H.R. 3.' 100th Congress, 2nd Session (20 April 1988).

US House or Representatives, Committee on the Judiciary, Subcommittee on Courts, Civil Liberties, and the Administration of Justice (1982) 'Revision of the Paris Convention on Industrial Property' 97th Congress, 2nd Session (December 1982).

US Senate, Committee on Finance (1987) 'Omnibus Trade Act of 1987: Report of the Committee on Finance' 100th Congress, 1st Session (12 June 1987).

US Senate, Special Committee on Aging (1991) 'The Drug Manufacturing Industry: A Prescription for Profits: Staff Report of the Special Committee on Aging' 102nd Congress, 1st Session, (September 1991).

Congressional Hearings

US Congress, House Committee on the Judiciary and Senate Committee on the Judiciary (1994) 'General Agreement on Tariffs and Trade (GATT): Intellectual Property Provisions: Joint Hearing Before the Subcommittee on Intellectual Property and Judicial Administration of the House Committee on the Judiciary and the Subcommittee on Patents, Copyrights and Trademarks of the Senate Committee on the Judiciary' 103rd Congress, 2nd Session (12 August 1994).

US House of Representatives, Committee on Energy and Commerce (1985) 'Unfair Foreign Trade Practices (Part 2): Hearings Before the Subcommittee on Oversight and Investigations and the Committee on Energy and Commerce.' 99th Congress, 1st Session (25, 26, 30 July and 17 October 1985).

US House of Representatives, Committee on Energy and Commerce, Subcommittee on Oversight and Investigations (1989) 'Unfair Foreign Trade Practices: Hearings Before the Subcommittee on Oversight and Investigations of the Committee on Energy and Commerce' 101st Congress, 1st Session (1 and 2 March 1989).

US House of Representatives, Committee on Foreign Affairs, Subcommittee on International Economic Policy and Trade (1986) 'Status of Intellectual Property Protection: Hearing Before the Subcommittee on International Economic Policy and Trade of the Committee on Foreign Affairs' 99th Congress, 2nd Session (31July 1986).

US House of Representatives, Committee on Foreign Affairs, Subcommittee on Economic Policy, Trade and Environment (1994) 'GATT: The Impact on American Industries: Hearing and Markup on H. Res. 362 France's Embargo of US Exports of Seafood Before the Subcommittee on Economic Policy, Trade and Environment of the Committee on Foreign Affairs' 103rd Congress, 2nd Session (8 March 1994).

US House of Representatives, Committee on Foreign Affairs, Subcommittee on Economic Policy, Trade and Environment (1994) 'Jobs Through Anti-

Piracy: Hearing Before the Subcommittee on Economic Policy, Trade and Environment of the Committee on Foreign Affairs' 103rd Congress, 2nd Session (3 May 1994).

US House of Representatives, Committee on International Relations (1999) 'Violations of Intellectual Property Right: How Do We Protect American Ingenuity?: Hearing Before the Committee on International Relations' 106th Congress, 1st Session (13 October 1999).

US House of Representatives, Committee on Science, Space, and Technology, Subcommittee on Technology and Competitiveness (1991) 'Trade and Technology: Implications of the GATT Negotiations: Hearing Before the Subcommittee on Technology and Competitiveness of the Committee on Science, Space, and Technology' 102nd Congress, 1st Session (30 July 1991).

US House of Representatives, Committee on the Judiciary, Subcommittee on Courts, Intellectual Property, and the Administration of Justice (1989) 'Intellectual Property, Domestic Productivity and Trade: Hearing Before the Subcommittee on Courts, Intellectual Property and the Administration of Justice of the Committee on the Judiciary' 101st Congress, 1st Session (25 July 1989).

US House of Representatives, Committee on the Judiciary, Subcommittee on Courts, Intellectual Property, and the Administration of Justice (1987) 'Intellectual Property and Trade—1987: Oversight Hearings Before the Subcommittee on Courts, Civil Liberties, and the Administration of Justice of the Committee on the Judiciary' 100th Congress, 1st Session (18 and 26 March 1987).

US House of Representatives, Committee on the Judiciary, Subcommittee on Courts, Civil Liberties and the Administration of Justice (1986) 'Intellectual Property and Trade: Hearings Before the Subcommittee on Courts, Civil Liberties, and the Administration of Justice of the Committee on the Judiciary' 99th Congress 2nd Session (19 Feb, 23 Apr, and 21 May 1986).

US House of Representatives, Committee on the Judiciary, Subcommittee on Intellectual Property and Judicial Administration (1991). 'Intellectual Property and International Issues: Hearings Before the Subcommittee on Intellectual Property and Judicial Administration of the Committee on the Judiciary' 102nd Congress, 1st Session (15 and 16 May 1991).

US House of Representatives, Committee on Ways and Means (1987) 'Comprehensive Trade Legislation: Hearings Before the Committee on Ways and Means and its Subcommittee on Trade' 100th Congress, 1st Session (5, 10, 18, 20, 26, and 27 February 1987).

US House of Representatives, Committee on Ways and Means (1994) 'Trade Agreements Resulting From the Uruguay Round of Multilateral Trade Negotiations: Hearings Before the Committee on Ways and Means and its Subcommittee on Trade' 103rd Congress, 2nd Session (26 January, 1, 2, 8, and 22 Februaury 1994).

US House of Representatives, Committee on Ways and Means, Subcommittee on Trade (1989) 'USTR Identification of Priority Practices and Countries Under Super 301 and Special 301 Provisions of the Omnibus Trade and Competitiveness Act of 1988: Hearing Before the Subcommittee on Trade of the Committee on Ways and Means' 101st Congress, 1st Session (8 June 1989).

US House of Representatives, Committee on Ways and Means, Subcommittee on Trade (1992) 'US International Trade Performance and Outlook: Competitive Position in the Automotive, Aerospace, and Chemical and Pharmaceutical Sectors: Hearings Before the Subcommittee on Trade of the Committee on Ways and Means' 102nd Congress, 2nd Session (11, 23, 30, 31 March; and 7 April 1992).

US House of Representatives, Committee on Ways and Means, Subcommittee on Trade (1993) 'Uruguay Round of Multilateral Trade Negotiations: Hearings Before the Subcommittee on Trade of the Committee on Ways and Means' 103rd Congress, 1st Session (4 and 5 November 1993).

US House of Representatives, Committee on Ways and Means, Subcommittee on Trade (1996) 'World Trade Organization Singapore Ministerial Meeting: Hearing Before the Subcommittee on Trade of the Committee on Ways and Means' 104th Congress, 2nd Session (11 September 1996).

US House of Representatives, Committee on Ways and Means, Subcommittee on Trade (1996) 'Implementation of Uruguay Round Agreements and the World Trade Organization: Hearing Before the Subcommittee on Trade of the Committee on Ways and Means' 104th Congress, 2nd Session (13 March 1996).

US Senate, Committee on Finance (1986) 'Possible New Round of Trade Negotiations: Hearing Before the Committee on Finance' 99th Congress, 2nd Session (23 July 1986).

US Senate, Committee on Finance (1989) 'Oversight of the Trade Act of 1988: Hearing Before the Committee on Finance: Part 2 of 3' 101st Congress, 1st Session (20 April 1989).

US Senate, Committee on Finance (1993) 'Uruguay Round of Multilateral Trade Negotiations: Hearing Before the Committee on Finance' 103rd Congress, 1st Session (10 November 1993).

US Senate, Committee on Finance, Subcommittee on International Trade (1986) 'Intellectual Property Rights: Hearing Before the Subcommittee on International Trade of the Committee on Finance' 99th Congress, 2nd Session (14 May 1986).

US Senate, Committee on Finance, Subcommittee on International Trade

(1992). 'Intellectual Property Rights Protection Under Special 301: Hearing Before the Subcommittee on International Trade of the Committee on Finance.' 102nd Congress, 2nd Session, (March 6, 1992).

US Senate, Committee on Finance, Subcommittee on International Trade (1993) 'Special 301 and the Fight Against Trade Piracy: Hearing Before the Subcommittee on International Trade of the Committee on Finance' 103rd Congress, 1st Session (19 April 1993).

US Senate, Committee on Finance, Subcommittee on International Trade (1994) 'Special 301 Trade Remedy: Hearing Before the Subcommittee on International Trade of the Committee on Finance' 103rd Congress, 2nd Session (24 June 1994).

US Senate, Committee on the Judiciary (1996) 'Pharmaceutical Patent Issues: Interpreting GATT: Hearings Before the Committee on the Judiciary' 104th Congress, 2nd Session (27 February and 5 March 1996).

US Senate, Committee on the Judiciary, Subcommittee on Antitrust, Monopolies and Business Rights (1987) 'Competitive Problems in the Pharmaceutical Drug Industry: Hearing Before the Subcommittee on Antitrust, Monopolies and Business Rights of the Committee on the Judiciary' 100th Congress, 1st Session (21 October 1987).

US Senate, Committee on the Judiciary, Subcommittee on Patents, Copyrights and Trademarks (1991) 'Hearings on Fast Track: Intellectual Property: Hearings Before the Subcommittee on Patents, Copyrights and Trademarks of the Committee on the Judiciary' 102nd Congress, 1st Session (14 and 16 May 1991).

US Senate, Committee on the Judiciary, Subcommittee on Patents, Copyrights and Trademarks (1992) 'International Piracy of Intellectual Property: Hearing Before the Subcommittee on Patents, Copyrights and Trademarks of the Committee on the Judiciary' 102nd Congress, 2nd Session, (29 September 1992).

United States Trade Representative Documents

Office of the US Trade Representative (1985) Annual Report on National Trade Estimates 1985.

Office of the US Trade Representative (1986) National Trade Estimate: 1986 Report on Foreign Trade Barriers.

Office of the US Trade Representative, Department of Agriculture, and Department of Commerce (1987) 1987 National Trade Estimate Report on Foreign Trade Barriers.

Office of the US Trade Representative (1989) 1989 National Trade Estimate Report on Foreign Trade Barriers.

Office of the US Trade Representative (1990) 1990 National Trade Estimate Report on Foreign Trade Barriers.

Office of the US Trade Representative (1991) 1991 National Trade Estimate Report on Foreign Trade Barriers.
Office of the US Trade Representative (1992) 1992 National Trade Estimate Report on Foreign Trade Barriers.
Office of the US Trade Representative (1993) 1993 National Trade Estimate Report on Foreign Trade Barriers.
Office of the US Trade Representative (1994) 1994 National Trade Estimate Report on Foreign Trade Barriers.
Office of the US Trade Representative (1995) 1995 National Trade Estimate Report on Foreign Trade Barriers.
Office of the US Trade Representative (1996) 1996 National Trade Estimate Report on Foreign Trade Barriers.
Office of the US Trade Representative (1997) 1997 National Trade Estimate Report on Foreign Trade Barriers.
Office of the US Trade Representative (1998) 1998 National Trade Estimate Report on Foreign Trade Barriers.
Office of the US Trade Representative (1999) 1999 National Trade Estimate Report on Foreign Trade Barriers.
Office of the US Trade Representative (2000) 2000 National Trade Estimate Report on Foreign Trade Barriers.
Office of the US Trade Representative (2001) 2001 National Trade Estimate Report on Foreign Trade Barriers.
Office of the US Trade Representative (2002) 2002 National Trade Estimate Report on Foreign Trade Barriers.
Office of the US Trade Representative (2003) 2003 National Trade Estimate Report on Foreign Trade Barriers.

Section 301 Cases

Office of the US Trade Representative. Public Docket No 301–52, 'Korea: Intellectual Property Rights.' Self-Initiated on 4 November 1985.
Office of the US Trade Representative. Public Docket No 301–61 'Brazil—Pharmaceuticals' Initiated 23 July 1987.
Office of the US Trade Representative Public Docket No 301–68 'Argentina—Pharmaceuticals—Denial of Intellectual Property Rights' Initiated 23 September 1988.
Office of the US Trade Representative Public Docket No 301–84 'Thailand—Patent Protection' Initiated 15 March 1991.
Office of the US Trade Representative Public Docket No 301–85 'India—Intellectual Property Protection' Self-Initiated on 26 May 1991.
Office of the US Trade Representative Public Docket No 301–91 'Brazil—Intellectual Property Rights' Self-Initiated 28 May 1993.

Other USTR Publications and Documents

Office of the US Trade Representative (1985) Task Force on Intellectual Property, Summary of Phase I: Recommendations of the Task Force on Intellectual Property to the Advisory Committee for Trade Negotiations (October 1985) Washington DC: USTR.

Office of the US Trade Representative (1986) Advisory Committee for Trade Negotiations Task Force on Intellectual Property Rights, Summary of Phase II: Recommendations of the Task Force, (April 1986). Washington DC: USTR.

Office of the US Trade Representative (1989–2002) Various Submissions for Designation of Countries Under Section 182 'Super 301' of the Omnibus Trade and Competitiveness Act of 1988. Washington DC: USTR.

Office of the US Trade Representative (1990) Submission from the Pharmaceutical Manufacturers Association (PMA) on the 'November 20, 1990 Chairman's Text on the GATT TRIP Negotiation' Washington DC: USTR.

Office of the US Trade Representative (1992) Report to Congress on Section 301 Developments Required by Section 309(a)(3) of the Trade Act of 1974 (July–December 1992) Washington DC: USTR.

Office of the US Trade Representative (1993) Report to Congress on Section 301 Developments Required by Section 309(a)(3) of the Trade Act of 1974 (July–December 1993) Washington DC: USTR.

Office of the US Trade Representative (1994) Report to Congress on Section 301 Developments Required by Section 309(a)(3) of the Trade Act of 1974 (July–December 1994) Washington DC: USTR.

Office of the US Trade Representative (1994) Uruguay Round: Jobs for the United States, Growth for the World. Uruguay Round White Paper. Washington DC: USTR.

Office of the US Trade Representative (1998–2000) Submissions from the Pharmaceutical Research and Manufacturers of America (PhRMA) With Respect to the Annual Trade Estimate Report on Foreign Trade Barriers. Washington DC: USTR.

Other US Government Documents

Advisory Committee on Trade Policy and Negotiations (1994) 'The Uruguay Round of Multilateral Trade Negotiations: Report of the Advisory Committee on Trade Policy and Negotiations' (January 1994).

Industry Policy Advisory Committee (1994) 'The Uruguay Round of Multilateral Trade Negotiations: Report of the Industry Policy Advisory Committee' (January 1994).

Industry Sector and Functional Advisory Committees (1994) 'The Uruguay Round of Multilateral Trade Negotiations: Report of the Industry Sector and Functional Advisory Committees' (January 1994).

United States, General Accounting Office (1993) 'Intellectual Property Rights: US Companies' Patent Experiences in Japan: Report to the Honorable John D Rockefeller IV and the Honorable Dennis DeConcini, US Senate.' United States General Accounting Office Washington DC.

United States, International Trade Commission (1988) 'Foreign Protection of Intellectual Property Rights and the Effect on US Industry and Trade: Report to the United States Trade Representative, Investigation No 332–245, Under Section 332(g) of the Tariff Act of 1930' Washington DC: US International Trade Commission.

United States, International Trade Commission (1991) 'Global Competitiveness of US Advanced-Technology Manufacturing Industries: Pharmaceuticals: Report to the Committee on Finance, US Senate, on Investigation No 332–302 Under Section 332(g) of the Tariff Act of 1930' Washington DC: US International Trade Commission.

INTERVIEWS

Mr Steve Bondy, First Secretary US Embassy Egypt (Cairo Monday 13 January 2003).

Dr Mohamed Bahaa El-Din Fayez, National Research Centre Egypt (Cairo Monday 5 May 2003).

Dr Mustafa El Hadary, Former Head of Drug Policies, Ministry of Health, Egypt (Cairo Sunday 11 May 2003).

Dr Ahmed El Hakim, Manager, Pfizer Egypt SAE; Secretary, PHRMA Egypt (Cairo January 2003).

Dr Raouf Hamed, National Organization for Drug Control and Research (NODCAR), Egypt (Cairo Saturday 3 May 2003).

Dr Hossam Loutfi, Legal Advisor to IP Law Drafting Committee, Ministry of Justice, Egypt (Cairo Tuesday 6 May 2003).

Ms Jaleen Moroney, Chief of Party, TIPRE Project, USAID, Egypt (Cairo Wednesday 23 April 2003).

Hon Gerald J Mossinghoff, Former US Commissioner of Patents; Former President, Pharmaceutical Manufacturers Associations (Washington DC Thursday 29 August 2002).

Dr Fawzy Al Rifoey, President of the Academy of Scientific Research and Technology of Egypt (Cairo Sunday 4 May 2003).

Dr Hamdy El Sayed, Head of the Egyptian Medical Union, and Chairman, Health Committee, People's Assembly of Egypt (Cairo Tuesday 6 April 2004).

Mr Serge Scotto, Managing Director, Novartis Egypt; Chairman, American

Chamber of Commerce Health and Pharmaceutical Committee, Egypt (Cairo Monday 5 May 2003).

HE Dr Moufid Shehab, Minister of Higher Education and of State for Scientific Research, Egypt (Cairo Sunday 4 May 2003).

HE Ambassador Mounir Zahran, Former Permanent Representative of Egypt to the World Trade Organization (1991–1998) (Cairo Sunday 27 April 2003).

SECONDARY SOURCES

Abbott, Frederick M 'Protecting First World Assets in the Third World: Intellectual Property Negotiations in the GATT Multilateral Framework' (1989) Vanderbilt Journal of Transnational Law 22: 689–745.

Abbott, Frederick M 'Commentary: The International Intellectual Property Order Enters the 21st Century' (1996a) Vanderbilt Journal of Transnational Law 29: 471–479.

Abbott, Frederick M 'The WTO TRIPS Agreement and Global Economic Development' (1996b) Chicago-Kent Law Review 72: 385–405.

Abbott, Frederick M 'First Report (final) to the Committee on International Trade Law of the International Law Association on the Subject of Parallel Importation' (1998) Journal of International Economic Law 1: 607–636.

Abbott, Frederick M 'The Enduring Enigma of TRIPs: A Challenge for the World Economic System' (1998) Journal of International Economic Law 1: 497–521.

Abbott, Frederick M 'TRIPS in Seattle: the Not-So-Surprising Failure and the Future of the TRIPS Agenda' (2000) Berkeley Journal of International Law 18: 165–179.

Abbott, Frederick M 'The TRIPS Agreement, Access to Medicines and the WTO Doha Ministerial Conference' (2001a) Quaker United Nations Office—Geneva, Occasional Paper No 7 (September 2001) <http://hostings.diplomacy.edu/quaker/new/doc/ OP7%20Abbott1.pdf> (last visited 11 January 2002).

Abbott, Frederick M 'The TRIPS-Legality of Measures Taken to Address Public Health Crises: A Synopsis' (2001b) Widener Law Symposium Journal 7: 71–85.

Abbott, Frederick M 'The Doha Declaration on the TRIPS Agreement and Public Health: Lighting A Dark Corner at the WTO' (2002a) Journal of International Economic Law 5: 469–505.

Abbott, Frederick M 'WTO TRIPS Agreement and Its Implications for Access to Medicines in Developing Countries' (2002b) Commission on Intellectual Property Rights Study Paper 2a <http://www.iprcommission. org/documents%5CAbbott% 20study.doc> (last visited 18 February 2002).

Abbott, Kenneth W 'Modern International Relations Theory: A Prospectus for International Lawyers' (1989) Yale Journal of International Law 14: 335 ff.

Abouelenein, A 'Trade-Related Aspects of Intellectual Property Rights (TRIPS) and the Pharmaceutical Industry in Egypt' (Cairo Federation of Egyptian Industries 1996).

Adelman, MJ and Sonia Baldia 'Prospects and Limits of the Patent Provision in the TRIPS Agreement: The Case of India' (1996) Vanderbilt Journal of Transnational Law 29: 507–533.

Ahuja, Sudhir D 'GATT and TRIPS—the Impact on the Indian Pharmaceutical Industry.' (1994) Patent World 65: 28 ff.

Al-Ali, Nermien 'The Egyptian Pharmaceutical Industry After TRIPS: A Practitioner's View' (2003) Fordham International Law Journal 26: 274–314.

Alford, W 'Making The World Safe For What? Intellectual Property Rights, Human Rights and Foreign Economic Policy in the Post-European Cold War World' (1996) New York University Journal of International Law and Politics 29: 135–152.

Alford, William P 'Intellectual Property, Trade and Taiwan: A GATT-Fly's View' (1992) Columbia Business Law Review 1992: 97–107.

Allam, Abeer 'Seeking Investment, Egypt Tries Patent Laws' New York Times (4 October 200???)

Allison, Graham 'Essence of Decision: Explaining the Cuban Missile Crisis' (Little Brown and Co Boston 1971).

Almeida, P R de 'The Political Economy of Intellectual Property Protection: Technological Protectionism and Transfer of Revenue among Nations' (1995) International Journal of Technology Management 10: 214–29.

American Chamber of Commerce in Egypt 'The Egyptian Pharmaceutical Industry' (American Chamber of Commerce Cairo 2001).

Anderman, SD 'Intellectual Property Rights, EEC Policy' Les Nouvelles (March 1990) 33–38.

Archer, Clive *International Organizations* (2nd edn Routledge London 1992).

Arup, Christopher The New World Trade Organization Agreements: Globalizing Law Through Services and Intellectual Property (Cambridge University Press Cambridge; New York 2000).

Attaran, Amir (2002). 'The Doha Declaration on the TRIPS Agreement and Public Health, Access to Pharmaceuticals, and Options Under WTO Law.' Fordham Intellectual Property, Media and Entertainment Law Journal 12: 859–885.

Attaran, Amir 'Assessing and Answering Paragraph 6 of the Doha Declaration on the TRIPS Agreement and Public Health: The Case for Greater Flexibility and a Non-Justiciable Solution' (2003) Emory International Law Review 17: 743–80.

Aust, Anthony I *Modern Treaty Law and Practice* (CUP Cambridge 2000).

Aziz, Sahar 'Linking Intellectual Property Rights in Developing Countries with Research and Development, Technology Transfer, and Foreign Direct Investment Policy: A Case Study of Egypt's Pharmaceutical Industry' (2003) ILSA Journal of International and Comparative Law 10: 1–34.

Bainbridge, David I *Intellectual Property* (4th edn Pitman London 1999).

Baldwin, Robert and Martin Cave *Understanding Regulation: Theory, Strategy, and Practice* (OUP Oxford 1999).

Baldwin, Robert, Colin Scott and Christopher Hood *A Reader on Regulation* (OUP Oxford 1998).

Bale H 'AIDS in Africa' (24 Feb 2000) <http://www.ifpma.org/pdfifpma/testimony-Feb24.pdf> (last visited 19 Jan 2004).

Bale, H 'The Conflicts Between Parallel Trade and Product Access and Innovation: the Case of Pharmaceuticals' (1998) Journal of International Economic Law 1, 637–653.

Baljer, Nico 'Between Rent-Seekers and Free-Marketeers: the Economic Policy Preferences and Political Influence of German and Swiss Pharmaceutical Multinationals and Banks' (PhD Thesis London School of Economics University of London 2001).

Ballance, Robert H, Janos Pogany and Helmut Forstner *The World's Pharmaceutical Industries: an International Perspective on Innovation, Competition and Policy*. Prepared for the United Nations Industrial Development Organization (Edward Elgar Aldershot 1992).

Barber, Simon 'Discounted AIDS Drugs Can Be Profitable' Business Day (Johannesburg 1 December 2000).

Barfield, Claude E 'Services, Intellectual Property and the Major Issues of the Uruguay Round' (1989) Georgia Journal of International and Comparative Law 19, 307–13.

Barnet, Richard J, and Ronald E Muller *Global Reach: The Power of the Multinational Corporation* (Simon and Schuster New York 1974).

Bass, Naomi A 'Implications of the TRIPS Agreement for Developing Countries: Pharmaceutical Patent Laws in Brazil and South Africa in the 21st Century' (2002) George Washington International Law Review 34, 191–222.

Bauer, Raymond A, Ithiel de Sola Pool, and Lewis A Dexter *American Business and Public Policy* (Aldine Chicago 1963).

Bawa, Rafik 'The North–South Debate Over the Protection of Intellectual Property' (1997) Dalhousie Journal of Legal Studies 6, 77–119.

Baxter, JW (2001). World Patent Law and Practice. Vols. 2 and 2A. Newark, NJ: Lexis Nexis.

Behrman, JN and Robert E Grosse *International Business and Governments: Issues and Institutions* (University of South Carolina Press Columbia SC 1990).

Beier, Friedrich-Karl and Gerhard Schricker (eds) *GATT or WIPO? New Ways in the International Protection of Intellectual Property* (IIC Studies VCH Munich 1989).

Beier, Friedrich-Karl and Gerhard Schricker (eds) *From GATT to TRIPs: the Agreement on Trade-Related Aspects of Intellectual Property Rights* (VCH New York 1996).

Bello, Judith H 'Some Practical Observations About WTO Settlement of Intellectual Property Disputes' (1997) Virginia Journal of International Law 37, 357–67.

Bello, Judith Hippler and Alan F Holmer 'Significant Recent Developments in Section 301 Unfair Trade Cases' (1987) International Lawyer 21, 211–32.

Benko, Robert P *Protecting Intellectual Property Rights: Issues and Controversies* (American Enterprise Institute for Public Policy Research Washington DC 1987).

Bennett, Philippe 'TRIPs—a Victory for US Industry' (1994) Patent World 66 (May 1994) 31–5.

Bently, Lionel and Brad Sherman *Intellectual Property Law* (Oxford University Press New York 2001).

Berliner, Brian Mark 'Making Intellectual Property Pirates Walk the Plank: Using 'Special 301' to Protect the United States' Rights' (1990) Loyola of Los Angeles International and Comparative Law Journal 12, 725–752.

Bertin, Gilles Y and Sally Wyatt *Multinationals and Industrial Property: The Control of the World's Technology* (Harvester Wheatsheaf Hertfordshire 1988).

Bhagwati, Jagdish and HT Patrick (eds) *Aggressive Unilateralism: America's 301 Trade Policy and the World Trading System* (University of Michigan Press Ann Arbor 1990).

Bhagwati, Jagdish and Mathias Hirsch (eds) *The Uruguay Round and Beyond: Essays in Honor of Arthur Dunkel* (University of Michigan Press Ann Arbor 1998).

Bhorali, D *GATT Agreement Or Dunkel Draft Treaty: Its Impact on Agriculture Industry, TRIPs and TRIMs and Drug Industry* (Mittal Publications New Delhi 1994).

Bickham, Timothy C 'Protecting US Intellectual Property Rights Abroad with Special 301' (1995) AIPLA Quarterly Journal 23, 195–220.

Bikoff, James L and David I Wilson 'Intellectual Property Protection Under NAFTA and TRIPS and the Future of Bilateral Intellectual Property Initiatives—Part I' (1994) Patent World 66 (October 1994) 21–7.

Bikoff, James L and David I Wilson 'Intellectual Property Protection Under NAFTA and TRIPS and the Future of Bilateral Intellectual Property Initiatives—Part II' (1994) Patent World 66 (November1994) 31–6.

Bilzi, Carol J 'Towards an Intellectual Property Agreement in the GATT:

View of the Private Sector' (1989) Georgia Journal of International and Comparative Law 19, 343–51.

Blackhurst, Richard 'Reforming WTO Decision Making: Lessons from Singapore and Seattle' in Klaus Gunter Deutsch and Bernhard Speyer (eds) *The World Trade Organization Millennium Round: Free Trade in the Twenty-First Century* (Routledge London 2001).

Blakeney, Michael *Trade Related Aspects of Intellectual Property Rights: A Concise Guide to the TRIPS Agreement* (Sweet & Maxwell London 1996).

Blakeney, Michael 'Intellectual Property in the Millennium Round—the TRIPS Agreement After Seattle' in Ian Fletcher *et al* (eds) *Foundations and Perspectives of International Trade Law* (Sweet & Maxwell London 2001).

Bloch, Marla R 'The Expansion of the Berne Convention and the Universal Copyright Convention to Protect Computer Software and Future Intellectual Property' (1985) Brooklyn Journal of International Law 11, 283–323.

Bloche, M Gregg 'Introduction: Health and the WTO' (2002) Journal of International Economic Law 5, 821–3.

Bloche, M Gregg 'WTO Defence to National Health Policy: Toward an Interpretive Principle' (2002) Journal of International Economic Law 5, 825–48.

Boddewyn, Jean J 'International Public Affairs' in Ingo Walter and Tracy Murray (eds) *Handbook of International Business* (Wiley New York 1988).

Boddewyn, Jean J 'Political Aspects of MNE Theory' (1988) Journal of International Business Studies 19, 341–63.

Bodenhausen, GCH *Guide to the Application of the Paris Convention for the Protection of Industrial Property: As Revised at Stockholm in 1967* (United International Bureaux for the Protection of Intellectual Property Geneva 1968).

Bodenhausen, GHC *Guide to the Application of the Paris Convention for the Protection of Industrial Property, as Revised at Stockholm in 1967* (United International Bureaux for the Protection of Intellectual Property Geneva 1968).

Bogsch, Arpad *Brief history of the first 25 years of the World Intellectual Property Organization* (WIPO Geneva 1992).

Booth Ken and Steve Smith (eds) *International Relations Theory Today* (Polity Press Cambridge 1995).

Bradley, A Jane 'Intellectual Property Rights, Investment, and Trade in Services in the Uruguay Round: Laying the Foundations' (1987) Stanford Journal of International Law 23, 57–98.

Braithwaite, John and Peter Drahos *Global Business Regulation* (CUP Cambridge 2000).

Brenner-Beck, Dru 'Do As I Say, Not As I Did' (1992) UCLA Pacific Basin Law Journal 11, 84–117.

Brewer, Thomas L 'An Issue-Area Approach to the Analysis of MNE-Government Relations' (1992) Journal of International Business Studies 23, 295–309.

Brittan, L 'Uruguay Round.' (1994) Common Market Law Review 31, 229–34.

Bronckers, Marco 'The Impact of TRIPS: Intellectual Property Protection In Developing Countries' (1994) Common Market Law Review 31, 1245–1282.

Bronckers, Marco 'The Exhaustion of Patent Rights Under World Trade Organization Law' (1998) Journal of World Trade Law 32, 137 ff.

Bronckers, Marco CEJ 'Better Rules for A New Millennium: A Warning Against Undemocratic Developments in the WTO' (1999) Journal of International Economic Law 2, 547–66.

Bronckers, Marco, CEJ, DWF Verkade and NM McNelis *TRIPs Agreement: Enforcement of Intellectual Property* (Office for Official Publications of the European Communities; Lanham, Md: Bernan Associates Luxembourg 2000).

Bulajic, Milan 'International Protection of Intellectual Property and Foreign Investment' (1987) in Detlev Dicke (ed) *Foreign Investment in the Present and a New International Economic Order* (Westview Press Boulder 1987).

Burrell, Timothy D *South African Patent Law and Practice* (2nd edn Butterworths Durban 1986).

Burstall, ML, JH Dunning and A Lake *Multinational Enterprises, Governments and Technology: Pharmaceutical Industry* (OECD Paris 1981).

Burstall, ML with Ian Senior *The Community's Pharmaceutical Industry* (Office for Official Publications of the European Communities Luxembourg 1985).

Buscaglia, Edgardo and Clarisa Long 'US Foreign Policy and Intellectual Property Rights in Latin America' (1997) Hoover Institute, Essays in Public Policy No 77 <http://www-hoover.stanford.edu/publications/epp/epp77.html> (last visited 16 January, 2002).

Byers, Michael (ed) *The Role of Law in International Politics: Essays in International Relations and International Law* (OUP Oxford 2000).

Campbell, Dennis and Susan Cotter (eds) *International Intellectual Property Law: New Developments* (J Wiley Chichester; New York 1995)

Campbell, Dennis and Susan Cotter (eds) *International Intellectual Property Law: Global Jurisdictions* (J Wiley Chichester; New York 1996).

Capling, Ann 'Intellectual Property' in Brian Hocking and Steven McGuire (eds) Trade *Politics: International, Domestic and Regional Perspectives* (Routledge London; New York 1999).

Carr, EH *The Twenty Years Crisis, 1919–1939: An Introduction to the Study of International Relations* (Macmillan London 1939).

Casella, Paulo Borba 'The Results of the Uruguay Round in Brazil: Legal and Constitutional Aspects of Implementation' in John H Jackson and Alan O Sykes (eds) *Implementing the Uruguay Round* (OUP Oxford 1997).

Challu, PM 'The Consequences of Pharmaceutical Product Patenting' (1991) World Competition 15, 65–126.

Challu, PM *Adaptation of National Legislation to the TRIPS Agreement of GATT's Uruguay Round, Aimed at Assuring Inhabitants Best Accessibility to Pharmaceuticals* (Centro Industrial de Laboratorios Farmaceuticos Argentinos Buenos Aires 1995).

Champ, Paul and Amir Attaran 'Patent Rights and Local Working Under the WTO TRIPS Agreement: An Analysis of the U.S.-Brazil Patent Dispute' (2002) Yale Journal of International Law 27, 365–93.

Chang, Y Kurt 'Special 301 and Taiwan: A Case Study of Protecting United States Intellectual Property in Foreign Countries' (1994) Northwestern Journal of International Law and Business 15, 206–30.

Chapman, Audrey R 'The Human Rights Implications of Intellectual Property Protection' (2002) Journal of International Economic Law 5, 861–82.

Charnovitz, Steve 'Participation of Nongovernmental Organizations in the World Trade Organization.' (1996) University of Pennsylvania Journal of International Economic Law 17, 331–57.

Charnovitz, Steve 'Two Centuries of Participation: NGOs and International Governance' (1997) Michigan Journal of International Law 18, 183–286.

Charnovitz, Steve 'The Legal Status of the Doha Declarations' (2002) Journal of International Economic Law 5, 207–11.

Chengsi, Zheng 'TRIPS and Intellectual Property Protection in China' (1997) European Intellectual Property Review 19, 243–6.

Chengsi, Zheng 'The TRIPS Agreement and Intellectual Property Protection in China' (1998) Duke Journal of Comparative and International Law 9, 219–27.

Cohen, Shlomo 'GATT: a TRIPS in the Right Direction' (1994/1995) Trademark World 73 32–37.

Commission on Intellectual Property Rights 'Report on Visit to India 29th—31st August 2001' (2001) <http://www.iprcommission.org/documents%5CIndia%20report.doc> (last visited 17 February 2002).

Commission on Intellectual Property Rights 'The South African Drug Case' (2001) <http://www.iprcommission.org/documents%5CS%20Africa.doc> (last visited 17 February 2002).

Corbett, Ronald JT 'Protecting and Enforcing Intellectual Property Rights in Developing Countries' (2001) International Lawyer 35, 1083–103.

Cornish, WR 'The International Relations of Intellectual Property' (1993) Cambridge Law Journal 52, 46–63.

Cornish, WR *Intellectual Property: Patents, Copyright, Trademarks and Allied Rights* (4th edn Sweet & Maxwell London 1999).

Correa, Carlos 'The GATT Agreement on Trade-Related Aspects of Intellectual Property Rights: New Standards for Patent Protection' (1994) European Intellectual Property Review 16, 327–35.

Correa, Carlos 'Intellectual Property Rights and Foreign Direct Investment' (1995) International Journal of Technology Management 10, 173–199.

Correa, Carlos 'Implementation of the TRIPs Agreement in Latin America and the Caribbean' (1997a) European Intellectual Property Review 19, 435–43.

Correa, Carlos 'The Uruguay Round and Drugs: WHO Task Force on Health Economics' (World Health Organization Geneva 1997b) <http://whqlibdoc.who.int/hq/1997/ WHO_TFHE_97.1.pdf> (last visited 16 January 2002).

Correa, Carlos 'Implementing the TRIPS Agreement in the Patents Field: Options for Developing Countries' (1998) Journal of World Intellectual Property 1, 75–100.

Correa, Carlos 'Intellectual Property Rights and the Use of Compulsory Licenses: Options for Developing Countries.' (1999) Trade-Related Agenda, Development and Equity Working Papers No 5 (October 1999) South Centre, Geneva.

Correa, Carlos *Intellectual Property Rights, the WTO, and Developing Countries: the TRIPS Agreement and Policy Options* (Zed Books New York 2000).

Correa, Carlos 'Public Health and Patent Legislation in Developing Countries' (2001) Tulane Journal of Technology and Intellectual Property 3, 1–53.

Correa, Carlos and Abdulqawi A Yusuf (eds) *Intellectual Property and International Trade: the TRIPs Agreement* (Kluwer Law International London; Boston 1998).

Cottier, Thomas 'The Prospects for Intellectual Property in GATT' (1991) Common Market Law Review 28, 383–414.

Cottier, Thomas (ed) *GATT-Uruguay Round: Nine Papers* (Verlag Stampfli+Cie AG Bern 1995).

Cox, Robert W *Production, Power and World Order: Social Forces in the Making of History* (Columbia University Press New York 1987).

Croome, John *Reshaping the World Trading System: A History of the Uruguay Round* (2nd and revised edn Kluwer Law International The Hague; Cambridge, Mass 1999).

Croskery, Patrick 'The Intellectual Property Literature: a Structured Approach' (1989) in Vivian Weil and John W Snapper (eds) *Owning Scientific and Technical Information: Value and Ethical Issues* (Rutgers UP New Brunswick; London 1989).

Cutler, A Claire 'Globalization, Law and Transnational Corporations: a Deepening of Market Discipline' (2000) in Theodore H Cohn, Stephen McBride and John Wiseman (eds) *Power in the Global Era: Grounding Globalization* (Macmillan Houndmills, Basingstoke 2000).

Czub, Kimberly A 'Argentina's Emerging Standard of Intellectual Property Protection: A Case Study of the Underlying Conflicts Between Developing Countries, TRIPS Standards, and the United States' (2001) Case Western Reserve Journal of International Law 33, 191–231.

D'Alessandro, J 'A Trade-Based Response to Intellectual Property Piracy: a Comprehensive Plan to Aid the Motion-Picture Industry' (1987) Georgetown Law Journal 76, 417–65.

Dam, Kenneth W 'The Growing Importance of International Protection of Intellectual Property' (1987) International Lawyer 21, 627–38.

Damschroder, ML 'Intellectual Property Rights and the GATT: United States Goals in the Uruguay Round' (1988) Vanderbilt Journal of Transnational Law 21, 367–400.

Daniel, Al J Jr 'Intellectual Property in the Uruguay Round: the Dunkel Draft and a Comparison of United States Intellectual Property Rights, Remedies, and Border Measures' (1993) New York University Journal of International Law and Politics 25, 751–812.

Das, Bal Gopal 'Intellectual Property Dispute, GATT, WIPO: of Playing by the Game Rules and Rules of the Game' (1994) IDEA: The Journal of Law and Technology 35, 149–81.

Davidson, Scott 'A Trip Around the Agreement on Trade Related Aspects of Intellectual Property Rights, Including Trade in Counterfeit Goods' (1997) Canterbury Law Review 6, 437–469.

Davis, Peter (ed) *Contested Ground: Public Purpose and Private Interest in the Regulation of Prescription Drugs* (OUP Oxford; New York 1996).

Davis, Theodore H Jr 'Combating Piracy of Intellectual Property in International Markets: A Proposed Modification of the Special 301 Action' (1991) Vanderbilt Journal of Transnational Law 24, 505–533.

Deardorff, Alan V 'Should Patent Protection Be Extended to All Developing Countries?' (1998) in Robert Howse (ed) *The World Trading System: Critical Perspectives on the World Economy. Vol. IV The Uruguay Round and Beyond* (Routledge London; New York 1998).

Declet, Rafael A Jr 'Protecting American Intellectual Property in China: the Persistent Problem of Software Piracy' (1997) New York International Law Review 10, 57–76.

Desai, AV 'India in the Uruguay Round' Journal of World Trade 23 (December 1989) 33–58.

Dettmann, Jean M 'GATT: An Opportunity for an Intellectual Property Rights Solution' (1991) Transnational Lawyer 4, 347–76.

DeVos, Ton *Multinational Corporations in Democratic Host Countries: US Multinationals and the Vredeling Proposal* (Dartmouth Aldershot 1989).

Dexi, Qiao 'A Survey of Intellectual Property Issues in China–U.S. Trade Negotiations Under the Special 301 Provisions' (1993) Pacific Rim Law and Policy Journal 2, 259–88.

Dhanjee, Rajan and Laurence Boisson de Chazournes 'Trade Related Aspects of Intellectual Property Rights (TRIPS): Objectives, Approaches and Basic Principles of the GATT and of Intellectual Property Conventions' (1990) Journal of World Trade 2, 5–15.

Divney, Jeffrey A and Gary J Connell 'Intellectual Property Provisions of the GATT' (1994) Colorado Lawyer 23, 1069–71.

Doane, Michael L 'TRIPS and International Intellectual Property Protection in an Age of Advancing Technology' (1994) American University Journal of International Law and Policy 9, 465–97.

Dolmo, Bess-Carolina 'Examining Global Access to Essential Pharmaceuticals in the Face of Patent Protection Rights: The South African Example' (2001) Buffalo Human Rights Law Review 7, 137–63.

Dormer, S 'Dispute Settlement and New Developments Within the Framework of TRIPs—An Interim Review' (2000) International Review of Industrial Property and Copyright Law 31, 1–36.

Drahos, Peter 'Global Property Rights in Information: the Story of TRIPs at the GATT' (1995) Prometheus 13, 6–19.

Drahos, Peter A *Philosophy of Intellectual Property* (Dartmouth Aldershot 1996).

Drahos Peter 'Intellectual Property and Human Rights' (1999) Intellectual Property Quarterly 3, 349–371.

Drahos, Peter 'Developing Countries and International Intellectual Property Standard-Setting.' (2002) Commission on Intellectual Property Rights Study Paper 8 <http://www.iprcommission.org/ documents%5CDrahos %20study.doc> (last visited 18 February 2002).

Dreyfuss, Rochelle Cooper and Andreas F Lowenfeld 'Two Achievements of the Uruguay Round: Putting TRIPS and Dispute Settlement Together' (1997) Virginia Journal of International Law 37, 275–333.

Dutfield, Graham 'Intellectual Property Rights and Development: Policy Discussion Paper' (2001) Prepared for UNCTAD/ICTSD Capacity Building Project on Intellectual Property Rights and Sustainable Development <http://www.ictsd.org/issarea/iprs-sd/docs/Policy Paper IPRs.pdf> (last visited 16 January 2002).

Dyzenhaus, David 'Positivism's Stagnant Research Programme' (2000) Oxford Journal of Legal Studies 20, 703 ff.

Ehrenhaft, Peter D 'A US View of the GATT' (1986) International Business Lawyer 14, 146–150.

El Shinawy, Azza, Hassan Salah, Ibrahim A Hassan, and Tayseer El Sawy *The Impact of GATT/TRIPS Agreement on the Egyptian Pharmaceutical Sector* (1997) Unpublished Manuscript.

Elliott, Richard 'TRIPS and Rights: International Human Rights Law, Access to Medicines, and the Interpretation of the WTO Agreement on Trade-Related Aspects of Intellectual Property Rights' Canadian HIV/AIDS Legal Network and AIDS Law Project, South Africa (November 2001) <http://www.aidslaw.ca/Maincontent/issues/cts/briefs/TRIPS-human-rights-briefPDF.pdf> (last visited 11 January 2002).

Emmert, Frank 'Intellectual Property in the Uruguay Round—Negotiating Strategies of the Western Industrialized Countries' (1990) Michigan Journal of International Law 11, 1317–1399.

Endeshaw, A *Intellectual Property For Non-Industrial Countries* (Dartmouth Aldershot 1996).

Engelberg, Alfred B 'Implementing the Doha Declaration: A Potential Strategy for Dealing with Legal and Economic Barriers to Affordable Medicines' <http://www.cptech.org/ip/health/pcontrol/engelberg-doha-pricecontrols.doc> (last visited 25 March 2002).

Enyart, J 'A GATT Intellectual Property Code' (1990) Les Nouvelles 25, 53–56.

Epstein, Stephanie and James Matthew Jones *Intellectual Property At A Crossroads: Global Piracy and International Competitiveness* (Congressional Economic Leadership Institute Arlington, Va 1990).

Evans, Gail E *Lawmaking Under the Trade Constitution: A Study in Legislation by the World Trade Organization* (Kluwer Law International The Hague; Boston 2000).

Evans, Peter, Harold Jacobson and Robert Putnam (eds) *Double-Edged Diplomacy: International Bargaining and Domestic Politics* (University of California Press Berkeley 1993).

Fagre, Nathan and Louis T Wells 'Bargaining Power of Multinationals and Host Governments'(1982) Journal of International Business Studies 13, 9–23.

Falk, Richard A, Rosalyn C Higgins, W Michael Reisman, and Burns H Weston 'Myres Smith McDougal (1906–1998)' (1998) American Journal of International Law 92, 729–733.

Feinberg, RM 'Intellectual Property, Injury and International Trade' (1988) Journal of World Trade 22, 45–56.

Felgueroso, Jose 'TRIPS and the Dispute Settlement Understanding: The First Six Years' (2002) AIPLA Quarterly Journal 30, 165–231.

Ferguson, Julia 'Developing Nations and the Agreement on Trade-Related Aspects of Intellectual Property' (2000) Colorado Journal of International Environmental Law and Policy, 49–75.

Field, Thomas G Jr 'Pharmaceuticals and Intellectual Property: Meeting Needs Throughout the World' (1990) IDEA: The Journal of Law and Technology 31, 3–26.

Fieldhouse, DK. 'The Multinational: A Critique of a Concept' in Alice Teichova, Maurice Levy-Leboyer, and Helga Nussbaum (eds) *Multinational Enterprise in Historical Perspective* (CUP Cambridge 1986).

Finger, JM and Andrzej Olechowski (eds) *The Uruguay Round: A Handbook on the Multilateral Trade Negotiations* (World Bank Washington DC 1987).

Finger, J. Michael, and Philip Schuler 'Implementation of Uruguay Round Commitments: The Development Challenge' Policy Research Working Paper No 2215 (World Bank Washington DC 1999) <http://econ.worldbank.org/docs/941.pdf> (last visited 5 March 2003).

Fink, Carsten *How Stronger Patent Protection in India Might Affect the Behavior of Transnational Pharmaceutical Industries* (World Bank Washington DC 2000).

Fink, Carsten and Carlos A Primo Braga 'How Stronger Protection of Intellectual Property Rights Affects International Trade Flows' (1999) World Bank Policy Research Working Paper No 2051 (February 1999).

Fitzmaurice, Gerald 'Vae Victis or Woe to the Negotiators! Your Treaty or Our 'Interpretation of It?" (1971) American Journal of International Law 65, 358 ff.

Fitzmaurice, Malgosia 'Actors and Factors in the Evolution of Treaty Norms: An Empirical Study' (1999) Austrian Review of International and European Law 4, 1 ff.

Fox, Eleanor M 'Trade, Competition, and Intellectual Property—TRIPS and its Antitrust Counterparts' (1996) Vanderbilt Journal of Transnational Law 29, 481–505.

Frame, J Davidson 'National Commitment to Intellectual Property Protection: An Empirical Investigation' (1987) Journal of Law and Technology 2, 209–27.

Franck, Thomas M *Fairness in International Law and Institutions* (OUP Oxford 1995).

Frumkin, Maximilian 'The Early History of Patents for Invention' (1947) Transactions of the Newcomen Society 26, 47–56.

Gad, Mohamed Omar 'Non-State Actors and the Negotiation of Multilateral Economic Instruments: A Case Study of the Multilateral Agreement on Investment' (1998) Unpublished LLM dissertation, University of Warwick.

Gadbaw, R Michael 'Intellectual Property and International Trade: Merger or Marriage of Convenience?' (1989) Vanderbilt Journal of Transnational Law 22, 223–42.

Gadbaw, R Michael, and Timothy J Richards (eds) *Intellectual Property Rights: Global Consensus, Global Conflict?* (Westview Press Boulder 1988).

Gakunu, Peter 'Intellectual Property: Perspective of the Developing World' (1989) Georgia Journal of International and Comparative Law 19, 358–365.

Gana, Ruth L 'Prospects for Developing Countries Under the TRIPS Agreement' (1996) Vanderbilt Journal of Transnational Law 29, 735–75.

Garcia, Frank J 'Trade and Inequality: Economic Justice and the Developing World' (2000) Michigan Journal of International Law 21, 975–1049.

Garcia-Castrillon and Carmen Otero 'An Approach to the WTO Ministerial Declaration on the TRIPS Agreement and Public Health' (2002) Journal of International Economic Law 5, 212–19.

Garner, Daniel 'Intellectual Property in the Uruguay Round' (1990) International Legal Perspectives 3, 51–73.

Geller, Paul Edward 'Intellectual Property in the Global Marketplace: Impact of TRIPS Dispute Settlements?' (1995) International Lawyer 29, 99–115.

Geller, Paul Edward 'From Patchwork to Network: Strategies for International Intellectual Property In Flux' (1998) Duke Journal of Comparative and International Law 9, 69–90.

General Agreement on Tariffs and Trade GATT Analytical Index: Guide to GATT Law and Practice. (6th edn GATT Geneva 1994).

Gervais, Daniel J *The TRIPS Agreement: Drafting History and Analysis* (Sweet & Maxwell London 1998).

Gervais, Daniel J 'The TRIPS Agreement After Seattle: Implementation and Dispute Settlement Issues' (2000) Journal of World Intellectual Property 3, 509–523.

Getlan, M 'TRIPs and the Future of Section 301: A Comparative Study in Trade Dispute Resolution' (1995) Columbia Journal of Transnational Law 34, 173–218.

Geuze, M and H Wager 'WTO Dispute Settlement Practice Relating to the TRIPS Agreement' (1999) Journal of International Economic Law 2, 347–84.

Ghatii, James Thuo 'The Legal Status of the Doha Declaration on TRIPS and Public Health Under the Vienna Convention on the Law of Treaties' (2002) Harvard Journal of Law and Technology 15, 291–317.

Gillespie-White, Lee 'What did Doha Accomplish?' (19 Nov 2001) <http://lists.essential.org/pipermail/ip-health/2002-February/002724.html> (last visited 19 Jan 2004).

Gilpin, Robert US *Power and the Multinational Corporation* (Basic Books New York 1975).

Gilpin, Robert *The Political Economy of International Relations* (Princeton University Press New Jersey 1987).

Giust, John E 'Noncompliance with TRIPS by Developed and Developing Countries: Is TRIPS Working?' (1997) Indiana International and Comparative Law Review 8, 69–97.

Golt, Sidney *The GATT Negotiations 1986–90: Origins, Issues and Prospects* (British-North American Committee London 1988).

Gorlin, Jacques J 'GATT—A View from the United States' (1989) Canadian Intellectual Property Review 5, 275–82.

Gorlin, Jacques J *An Analysis of the Pharmaceutical-Related Provisions of the WTO TRIPS (Intellectual Property) Agreement* (Intellectual Property Institute London 1999).

Gorlin, Jacques J 'U.S. Industries, Trade Associations, and Intellectual Property Lawmaking' (2002) Cardozo Journal of International and Comparative Law 10, 5–11.

Gosain, Rana and Henry K Sherrill 'The Effects of GATT/TRIPs on Brazil's Patent Legislation' Patent World (May 1995) 24–6.

Gowlland-Debbas Vera *Multilateral Treaty-Making: The Current Status of Challenges to and Reforms Needed in the International Legislative Process* (Kluwer Law International The Hague 2000).

Grabowski, Henry 'Patents, Innovation and Access to New Pharmaceuticals' (2002) Journal of International Economic Law 5, 849–60.

Green, Lee D 'International Protection of Intellectual Property Under the 1988 Trade Bill' (1989) Brigham Young University Law Review, 475–90.

Greenaway, David and Andre Sapir 'New Issues in the Uruguay Round: Services, TRIMs and TRIPs' (1992) European Economic Review 36, 509–18.

Grosse, Robert and Jack Behrman 'Theory in International Business' (1992) Transnational Corporations 1, 93–125.

Grubb, Philip W *Patents for Chemicals, Pharmaceuticals and Biotechnology: Fundamentals of Global Law, Practice and Strategy* (OUP Oxford 1999).

Guedes, Ana Lucia Malheiros 'Environmental Practices of Transnational Corporations in Brazil: Cases in the Chemical and Pharmaceutical Sectors' (PhD Thesis University of London 1998).

Gutowski, RJ 'The Marriage of Intellectual Property and International Trade in the TRIPs Agreement: Strange Bedfellows or a Match Made in Heaven?' (1999)Buffalo Law Review 47, 713–61.

Gutterman, Alan S 'The North-South Debate Regarding the Protection of Intellectual Property Rights' (1993) Wake Forest Law Review 28, 89–139.

Hamilton, Marci A 'The TRIPS Agreement: Imperialistic, Outdated, and Overprotective' (1996) Vanderbilt Journal of Transnational Law 29, 613–34.

Hammer, Peter J 'Differential Pricing of Essential AIDS Drugs: Markets, Politics and Public Health' (2002) Journal of International Economic Law 5, 883–912.

Hancher, Leigh and Michael Moran (eds) *Capitalism, Culture, and Economic Regulation* (OUP Oxford 1989).

Hansen, Patricia I 'Defining Unreasonableness in International Trade: Section 301 of the Trade Act of 1974' (1987) Yale Law Journal 96, 1122–46.

Harrelson, John 'TRIPS, Pharmaceutical Patents, and the HIV/AIDS Crisis: Finding the Proper Balance Between Intellectual Property Rights and Compassion' A (2001) Widener Law Symposium Journal 7, 175–201.

Hart, HLA *The Concept of Law* (OUP Oxford 1994).

Hartridge, David and Arvind Subramanian 'Intellectual Property Rights: the Issues in GATT' (1989) Vanderbilt Journal of Transnational Law 22, 893–910.

Herrington, Wayne 'Issues at the Interface of International Trade and Intellectual Property' (1992) Brooklyn Journal of International Law 18, 759–764.

Herzfeld, Shannon S S 'The Pharmaceutical Industry's Intersection With Business and Government' (2000) Florida Journal of International Law 13, 66–71.

Hettinger, Edwin C 'Justifying Intellectual Property' (1989) Philosophy and Public Affairs 18, 31–52.

Hickman, MM 'Protecting Intellectual Property in Taiwan: Non-Recognized United States Corporations and their Treaty Right of Access to Courts' (1984) Washington Law Review 60, 117–40.

Higgins, Rosalyn 'Policy Considerations and the International Judicial Process' (1968) International and Comparative Law Quarterly 17, 58 ff.

Higgins, Rosalyn *Problems and Process: International Law and How We Use It* (OUP Oxford 1994).

Higgott, Richard A, Geoffrey R D Underhill and Andreas Bieler (eds) *Non-State Actors and Authority in the Global System* (Routledge London 1999).

Hoekman, Bernard M 'New Issues in the Uruguay Round and Beyond' (1993) Economic Journal 103, 1528–39.

Hoekman, Bernard M and Michael M Kostecki *The Political Economy of the World Trading System: From GATT to WTO* (Oxford UP Oxford; New York 1995).

Hoen, Ellen 't 'TRIPS, Pharmaceutical Patents, and Access to Essential Medicines: A Long Way From Seattle to Doha' (2002) Chicago Journal of International Law 3, 27–46.

Hoffman, Gary M 'Curbing International Piracy of Intellectual Property: Policy Options for a Major Exporting Country: The Report of the International Piracy Project' (1989) The Annenberg Washington Program, Communications Policy Studies, Northwestern University.

Hoffman, Gary M, George T Marcou, and Charles Murray 'Commercial Piracy of Intellectual Property' (1989) Journal of the Patent and Trademark Office Society 71, 556–567.

Holdsworth, William *A History of English Law Vol IV* (London: Sweet & Maxwell 1937).

Hood, Christopher *Explaining Economic Policy Reversals* (Open University Press Buckingham 1994).

Hood, Neil and Stephen Young *The Economics of Multinational Enterprise* (Longman London 1979).

Horlick, Gary N 'Over the Bump in Doha?' (2002) Journal of International Economic Law 5, 195–202.

Howse, Robert 'The Canadian Generic Medicines Panel: A Dangerous Precedent in Dangerous Times' (2000) Journal of World Intellectual Property 3, 493–507.

Hughes, Justin 'The Philosophy of Intellectual Property' (1988) Georgetown Law Journal 77, 287–366.

Hunt, Alan *The Sociological Movement in Law* (Macmillan London 1978).

Ietto-Gillies, Grazia *International Production: Trends, Theories, Effects* (Polity Press Cambridge 1992).

Institute of Continuing Legal Education in Georgia *Prospects for Multilateral Agreement on Services and Intellectual Property: The Trade Act of 1988 and GATT MTNs* (Institute of Continuing Legal Education in Georgia Athens, GA 1989).

Intellectual Property Committee, Keidanren and UNICE *Basic framework of GATT Provisions on Intellectual Property: Statement of Views of the European, Japanese and United States Business Communities* (The Committee New York 1988).

International Association for the Protection of Industrial Property (AIPPI) *AIPPI and the Development of Industrial Property Protection 1897–1997* (ASIPPI Basle 1997).

International Chamber of Commerce *Intellectual Property and International Trade: A Guide to the Uruguay Round TRIPS Agreement* (International Chamber of Commerce Paris 1996).

International Chamber of Commerce *Countering Counterfeiting: A Guide to Protecting and Enforcing Intellectual Property Rights* (ICC Publishing Paris 1997).

International Federation of Pharmaceutical Manufacturers Association *GATT TRIPs and the Pharmaceutical Industry: A Review* (IFPMA Geneva 1995).

International Federation of Pharmaceutical Manufacturers Association 'Intellectual Property: Patents and Pharmaceuticals.' IFPMA Issue Paper (IFPMA Geneva February 1997).

International Intellectual Property Institute 'Patent Protection and Access to HIV/AIDS Pharmaceuticals in Sub-Saharan Africa. A Report Prepared for the World Intellectual Property Organization' (2000) WIPO Studies on Intellectual Property <http://www.wipo.int/about-ip/en/studies/pdf/iipi_hiv.pdf> (last visited 16 January 2002).

Jackson, John and AO Sykes *Implementing the Uruguay Round* (Clarendon Press New York 1997).

James, Barrie G *The global pharmaceutical industry in the 1990s: the challenge of change* (Economist Intelligence Unit London 1990).

Jayasuriya 'Pharmaceuticals, Patents and the Third World' (1988) Journal of World Trade 22, 117 ff.

Jenkins, Edgar L 'Congressional Perspective on Multilateral Trade Negotiations' (1989) Georgia Journal of International and Comparative Law 19, 320–5.

Johns, Fleur 'The Invisibility of the Transnational Corporation: An Analysis of International Law and Legal Theory' (1994) Melbourne University Law Review 19, 893 ff.

Jones, James Matthew and Stephanie Epstein *Intellectual Property at a Crossroads: Global Piracy and International Competitiveness* (Congressional Economic Leadership Institute Arlington, Va 1990).

Jordan, Kim H 'International Application of a Domestic Intellectual Property Protection Strategy: Extending a Predatory Litigation Strategy to the European Community' (1995) Santa Clara Computer and High Technology Law Journal 11, 373–401.

Julian-Arnold, Gianna 'International Compulsory Licensing: The Rationales and the Reality' (1993) IDEA: The Journal of Law and Technology 33, 349–71.

Karandikar, S *Indian Drug Industry After GATT* (World Trade Center Bombay 1994).

Kastenmeier, Robert W and David Beier 'International Trade and Intellectual Property: Promise, Risks, and Reality' (1989) Vanderbilt Journal of Transnational Law 22, 285–307.

Katzenstein, Peter Between *Power and Plenty: the Foreign Economic Policies of Advanced Industrial States* (University of Wisconsin Press Madison 1978).

Keefauver, William L 'Commentary: The Need for International Thinking in Intellectual Property Law' (1996) IDEA: The Journal of Law and Technology 37, 181–4.

Kelsen, Hans *Introduction to the Problems of Legal Theory* (Clarendon Press Oxford 1992).

Kennedy, David 'The International Style in Postwar Law and Policy' (1994) Utah Law Review 1994, 7–103.
Kennedy, David and Chris Tennant 'New Approaches to International Law: A Bibliography' (1994) Harvard International Law Journal 35, 417–430.
Keohane, Robert O and Joseph S Nye *Power and Interdependence* (2nd edn Addison Wesley Longman New York 1989).
Keohane, Robert O and Joseph S Nye Jr (eds) *Transnational Relations and World Politics* (Harvard UP Cambridge, Mass 1971).
Keohane, Robert O (ed) *Neo-Realism and Its Critics* (Columbia University Press New York 1986).
Kirchanski, Stefan 'Protection of US Patent Rights in Developing Countries: US Efforts to Enforce Pharmaceutical Patents in Thailand' (1994) Loyola of Los Angeles International and Comparative Law Journal 16, 569–608.
Kobrin, Stephen J 'Testing the Bargaining Hypothesis in the Manufacturing Sector in Developing Countries' (1987) International Organization 41, 609–38.
Koh, Harold 'Transnational Legal Process' (1996) Nebraska Law Review 75, 181–207.
Kolker, Peter L *Should Importation Be Considered As Working? A Study of Article 27 of the GATT TRIPS Agreement* (Intellectual Property Institute London 1996).
Kolker, Peter L TRIPs Agreement: Patent Protection (Office for Official Publications of the European Communities Luxembourg 2000).
Koshy, Suresh. 'The Effect of TRIPS on Indian Patent Law: A Pharmaceutical Industry Perspective' (1995) Boston University Journal of Science and Technology Law 1, 1–56.
Koskenniemi, Martti *From Apology to Utopia: The Structure of International Legal Argument* (Finnish Lawyers' Publishing Company Helsinki 1989).
Kostecki, Michel M 'Sharing Intellectual Property Between the Rich and the Poor' (1991) European Intellectual Property Review 13, 271–4.
Kraus, John *The GATT Negotiations: A Business Guide to the Results of the Uruguay Round* (International Chamber of Commerce Paris 1994).
Kronstein, Heinrich and Irene Till 'A Re-evaluation of the International Patent Convention' (1947) Law and Contemporary Problems 12, 765–81.
Kulshreshtha, A, K Trivedi and R Kumar (eds) *GATT: Critical Analysis of General Agreement on Tariffs and Trade* (ABD Publishers Jaipur 1994).
Kumar, N 'Intellectual Property Protection, Market Orientation and Location of Overseas R&D Activities by Multinational Enterprises' (1996) World Development 24, 673–88.
Kumar, Umesh *An Introduction to the African Industrial Property System*

(The Author Roma, Lesotho; Wm W Gaunt and Sons Holmes Beach, Fla, USA 1993).

Kunz-Hallstein, Hans Peter 'The Revision of the International System of Patent Protection in the Interests of the Developing Countries' (1979) IIC-International Review of Industrial Property and Copyright Law 10, 649–70.

Kunz-Hallstein, Hans Peter 'The United States Proposal for a GATT Agreement on Intellectual Property and the Paris Convention for the Protection of Industrial Property' (1989) Vanderbilt Journal of Transnational Law 22, 265–84.

Ladas, Stephen *Pericles Patents, Trademarks, and Related Rights: National and International Protection* (Harvard University Press Cambridge, Mass 1975).

Lange, David 'Public-Private Initiatives After TRIPS: Designing a Global Agenda' (1998) Duke Journal of Comparative and International Law 9, 1–9.

Lanjouw, Jean O 'The Introduction of Pharmaceutical Product Patents in India: 'Heartless Exploitation of the Poor and Suffering'?' (1997) Economic Growth Center, Yale University. Center Discussion Paper No 775 (August 1997).

Lanjouw, Jean O and Iain Cockburn 'Do Patents Matter? Empirical Evidence After GATT' (2000) National Bureau of Economic Research Working Paper W7495 (January 2000) <http://papers.nber.org/papers/W7495> (last visited 24 January 2002).

Lasswell, Harold D and Myres S McDougal *Jurisprudence for a Free Society. Volume I* (New Haven Press New Haven 1992).

Leaffer, Marshall A 'Protecting United States Intellectual Property Abroad: Towards a New Multilateralism' (1991). Iowa Law Review 76, 273–308.

Leffert, Deborah 'Special 301 Checklist: Which Countries Fail to Protect Drugs?' (1994) Patent World (December 1993/January 1994) 34–9.

Leflon, Jacques 'Uruguay Round Comments: A View from UNICE' in Jacques Bourgeois *et al* (eds) *The Uruguay Round Results: A European Lawyers' Perspective* (European University Press Brussels 1994).

Lehman, Bruce A 'Intellectual Property Under the Clinton Administration' (1993/1994) George Washington Journal of International Law and Economics 27, 395–410.

Lehman, Bruce A 'Global Intellectual Property in the Twenty-First Century' (1996) Fordham Intellectual Property, Media and Entertainment Law Journal 7 (Autumn 1996) 9–24.

Lesser, W 'The Effects of TRIPS-Mandated Intellectual Property Rights on Economic Activities in Developing Countries' (2001) WIPO Studies on Intellectual <http://www.wipo.int/about-ip/en/studies/pdf/ssa_lesser_trips.pdf> (last visited 24 January 2002).

Lever, Jack Q Jr 'The Impact of the 1988 Omnibus Trade Act on Litigation Before the International Trade Commission Under Section 337' in Carol J Holgren (ed) *1988 Patent Law Annual* (Matthew Bender and Co New York 1989).

Levy, Charles S 'Implementing TRIPS—A Test of Political Will' (2000) Law and Policy in International Business 31, 789–795.

Lewis, Theresa Beeby 'Patent Protection for the Pharmaceutical Industry: A Survey of the Patent Laws of Various Countries' (1996) International Lawyer 30, 835–65.

Liu, Paul CB 'U.S. Industry's Influence on Intellectual Property Negotiations and Special 301 Actions' (1994) UCLA Pacific Basin Law Journal 13, 87–117.

Long, Clarisa *Intellectual Property Rights in Emerging Markets* (AEI Press Washington DC 2000).

Longdin, L 'Parallel Importing Post-TRIPS: Convergence and Divergence in Australia and New Zealand' (2001) International and Comparative Law Quarterly 50, 54–89.

Love, James 'Compulsory Licensing: Models for State Practice in Developing Countries, Access to Medicine and Compliance with the WTO TRIPS Accord' (2001) Prepared for the United Nations Development Programme, (January 2001) <http://www.cptech.org/ ip/health/cl/ recommendedstatepractice.html> (last visited 11 January 2002).

Love, James Affidavit Filed on 10 April 2001 in the case of *Pharmaceutical Manufacturers' Association of South Africa, et al v Nelson Mandela, President of the Republic of South Africa et al* Case No 4183/98 (Transvaal Provincial Division, filed 18 Feb 1998) (2001) <http://www.c ptech.org/ip/health/sa/ loveaffidavit/> (last visited 19 Jan 2004).

Lutz, Martin J (ed) *International Association for the Protection of Industrial Property: Chronicle and Resolutions* (AIPPI Zurich 1997).

Macdonald, Ronald St J and Douglas M Johnston (eds) *The Structure and Process of International Law: Essays in Legal Philosophy Doctrine and Theory* (Martinus Nijhoff The Hague 1983).

Macdonald-Brown, Charles and Leon Ferera 'First WTO Decision on TRIPS: India—Patent Protection for Pharmaceutical and Agricultural Chemical Products' (1998) European Intellectual Property Review 20, 69–73.

Machlup, F and E Penrose 'The Patent Controversy in the Nineteenth Century' (1950) Journal of Economic History 10, 1–9.

MacLeod, Dylan A 'U.S. Trade Pressure and the Developing Intellectual Property Law of Thailand, Malaysia and Indonesia' (1992) University of British Columbia Law Review 26, 343–74.

Majone, Giandomenico 'The Rise of the Regulatory State in Europe' (1994) West European Politics 1994, 77.

Majone, Giandomenico (ed) *De-Regulation or Re-Regulation? Regulatory Reform in Europe and the United States* (Pinter London 1989).

Major Pharmaceutical Companies of the World 2001 (3rd edn Graham and Whiteside Ltd).

Malanczuk, Peter 'Multinational Enterprises and Treaty-Making—A Contribution to the Discussion on Non-State Actors and the 'Subjects' of International Law' in Vera Gowlland-Debbas (ed) *Multilateral Treaty-Making: The Current Status of Challenges to and Reforms Needed in the International Legislative Process* (Kluwer The Hague 2000).

Mall, Deborah 'The Inclusion of a Trade Related Intellectual Property Code Under the General Agreement on Tariffs and Trade (GATT)' (1990) Santa Clara Law Review 30, 265–91.

Malpass, Gerald D Jr 'The GATT TRIPS Agreement—Has the Competitive Position of US Inventors Changed?' (1996) Houston Journal of International Law 19, 207–44.

Mansbach, Richard W, Yale H Ferguson and Donald E Lampert *The Web of World Politics: Nonstate Actors in the Global System* (Prentice-Hall Englewood Cliffs, NJ 1976).

Mansfield, Edwin 'Intellectual Property Protection, Foreign Direct Investment, and Technology Transfer' (1994) IFC, the World Bank Discussion Paper No 19 <http://www.ifc.org/economics/pubs/dp19/dp19.pdf> (last visited 11 January 2002).

Mansfield, Edwin 'Intellectual Property Protection, Direct Investment, and Technology Transfer: Germany, Japan and the United States' (1995) IFC, the World Bank Discussion Paper No 27 <http://www.ifc.org/economics/pubs/dp27/dp27.pdf> (last visited 11 January 2002).

Markusen, James 'Contracts, Intellectual Property Rights, and Multinational Investment in Developing Countries' National Bureau of Economic Research Working Paper 6448 (March 1998) <http://papers.nber.org/papers/W6448> (last visited 22 January 2002).

Martin, Will and L Alan Winters (eds) *The Uruguay Round and the Developing Countries* (CUP Cambridge; New York; Melbourne 1996).

Martyn, W 'Decisions on Negotiating Structure and Plans for the Uruguay Round' (1988) Harvard International Law Journal 29, 199–206.

Maskus, Keith E 'Normative Concerns in the International Protection of Intellectual Property Rights.' (1990) World Economy 13, 387–410.

Maskus, Keith E 'The Role of Intellectual Property Rights in Encouraging Foreign Direct Investment and Technology Transfer' (1998) Duke Journal of Comparative and International Law 9, 109–61.

Maskus, Keith E *Intellectual Property Rights In the Global Economy* (Institute for International Economics Washington DC 2000).

Maskus, Keith E 'Parallel Imports in Pharmaceuticals: Implications for Competition and Prices in Developing Countries.' (2001) Final Report to WIPO. WIPO Studies on Intellectual Property <http://www.wipo.int/about-ip/en/studies/pdf/ssa_maskus_pi.pdf> (last visited 22 January 2002).

Maskus, Keith E and D Eby Konan 'Trade-Related Intellectual Property Rights: Issues and Exploratory Results' in A V Deardorff and R M Stern (eds) *Analytical and Negotiating Issues in the Global Trading System* (University of Michigan Press Ann Arbor 1994).

Maskus, Keith E and Mohan Penubarti 'How Trade-Related are Intellectual Property Rights?' (1995) Journal of International Economics 39, 227–48.

Matsushita, Mitsuo 'A Japanese Perspective on Intellectual Property Rights and the GATT' (1992) Columbia Business Law Review 1992, 81–95.

Matthews, Duncan *Globalising Intellectual Property Rights: the TRIPs Agreement* (Routledge London 2002).

Matthews, Duncan 'WTO Decision on the Implementation of Paragraph of the Doha Declaration on the TRIPS Agreement and Public Health: A Solution to the Access to Essential Medicines Problem?' (2004) Journal of International Economic Law 7, 73–107.

May, Christopher *A Global Political Economy of Intellectual Property Rights: The New Enclosures?* (Routledge London; New York 2000).

Mayer, Christopher S 'The Brazilian Pharmaceutical Industry Goes Walking from Ipanema to Prosperity: Will the New Intellectual Property Law Spur Domestic Investment?' (1998) Temple International and Comparative Law Journal 12, 377–401.

Mazzoleni, R and R Nelson 'Economic Theories about the Benefits and Costs of Patents' (1998) Journal of Economic Issues 32, 1031– 1052.

McDougal, Myres S 'International Law, Power and Policy: A Contemporary Conception' (1953) Recueil des Cours 82, 137.

McGrath, Michelle 'The Patent Provisions in TRIPS: Protecting Reasonable Remuneration for Services Rendered—or the Latest Development in Western Colonialism?' (1996) European Intellectual Property Review 7, 398–403.

McLeland, Le-Nhung, and J Herbert O'Toole 'Patent Systems in Less Developed Countries: The Case of India and the Andean Pact Countries' (1987) Journal of Law and Technology 2, 229–48.

McNeil, Donald 'Yale Pressed to Help Cut Drug Costs in Africa.' *New York Times* (New York 12 March 2001).

Meessen, Karl M 'Intellectual Property Rights in International Trade' (1987) Journal of World Trade 21, 67–74.

Mendes da Costa, Philip C 'Patent Harmonization through GATT: TRIP or Trap' (1992) Patent World 45, 23–7.

Merges, Robert P 'Battle of Lateralisms: Intellectual Property and Trade' (1990) Boston University International Law Journal 8, 239–46.

Milner, Helen V *Resisting Protectionism: Global Industries and the Politics of International Trade* (Princeton UP Princeton, NJ 1988).

Mirza, Zafar 'WTO/TRIPs, Pharmaceuticals and Health: Impacts and Strategies' (1999) Development 42 (December 1999) 92–7.

Mitnick, Barry M *The Political Economy of Regulation: Creating, Designing, and Removing Regulatory Forms* (Columbia UP New York 1980).

Moebes, A 'Negotiating International Copyright Protection: the United States and European Community Positions' (1992) Loyola of Los Angeles International and Comparative Law Journal 14, 301–25.

Moran, TH *Multinational Corporations and the Politics of Dependence: Copper in Chile* (Princeton University Press Princeton 1974).

Morford, Richard A 'Intellectual Property Protection: A United States Priority' (1989) Georgia Journal of International and Comparative Law 19, 336–42.

Morgenthau, Hans J *Politics Among Nations: The Struggle for Power and Peace* (Knopf New York 1948).

Mossinghoff, Gerald J 'Research-Based Pharmaceutical Companies: the Need for Improved Patent Protection Worldwide' (1987) Journal of Law and Technology 2, 307–23.

Mossinghoff, Gerald J 'National Obligations Under Intellectual Property Treaties: the Beginning of a True International Regime' (2000) Federal Circuit Bar Journal 9, 591–603.

Mossinghoff, Gerald J and Thomas Bombelles 'The Importance of Intellectual Property Protection to the American Research-Intensive Pharmaceutical Industry' (1996) Columbia Journal of World Business 31, 38–48.

Mota, Sue Ann 'TRIPS—Five Years of Disputes at the WTO' (2000) Arizona Journal of International and Comparative Law 17, 533–53.

Muchlinski, Peter T ''Global Bukowina' Examined: Viewing the Multinational Enterprise as a Transnational Law-Making Community' in Gunther Teubner (ed) *Global Law Without A State* (Dartmouth Aldershot 1997).

Muchlinski, Peter T *Multinational Enterprises and the Law* (revised paperback edn Blackwell Publishers Oxford 1999).

Mullerson, Rein *Ordering Anarchy: International Law in International Society* (Martinus Nijhoff Publishers The Hague 2000).

Murthy, Divya 'The Future of Compulsory Licensing: Deciphering the Doha Declaration on the TRIPS Agreement and Public Health' (2002) American University International Law Review 17, 1299–346.

Mutti, John and Bernard Yeung 'Section 337 and the Protection of Intellectual Property in the United States: the Complainants and the Impact' (1996) Review of Economics and Statistics 78, 510–20.

Nash, Duane 'South Africa's Medicines and Related Substances Control

Amendment Act of 1997' (2000) Berkeley Technology Law Journal 15, 485–502.

Nelson, Lester (ed) *Digest of Intellectual Property Laws of the World* (Oceana Publications Dobbs Ferry, NY 1990).

Nelson, M 'The Vredeling Directive—the EEC's Failed Attempt to Regulate Multinational Enterprises and Organize Collective Bargaining.' (1988) New York University Journal of International Law and Politics 20, 967–92.

Newman, Andrew S 'The Amendments to Section 337: Increased Protection for Intellectual Property Rights' (1989) Law and Policy in International Business 20, 571–88.

Nimmer, Raymond T and PA Krauthaus 'Globalisation of Law in Intellectual Property and Related Commercial Contexts' (1992) Law in Context 10, 80–103.

Nogues, Julio 'Patents and Pharmaceutical Drugs: Understanding the Pressures on Developing Countries' (1990) Journal of World Trade 24, 81–104.

Nogues, Julio 'Social Costs and Benefits of Introducing Patent Protection for Pharmaceutical Drugs in Developing Countries' (1993) Developing Economies 31, 24–53.

Nolff, Markus *TRIPS, PCT, and Global Patent Procurement* (Kluwer Law International Boston, MA 2000).

Norton, Joseph J, Mads Andenas and Mary Footer (eds) *The Changing World of International Law in the Twenty-First Century: A Tribute to the Late Kenneth R. Simmonds* (Kluwer Law International The Hague; Boston 1998).

Ochs, Rachel F 'Pharmaceuticals: The Battle for Control in the 21st Century' (1996) Journal of Law and Health 10, 297–341.

Oddi, A Samuel 'The International Patent System and Third World Development: Reality or Myth?' (1987) Duke Law Journal 1987, 831–77.

Oddi, A Samuel. 'TRIPS—Natural Rights and a "Polite Form of Economic Imperialism"' (1996a) Vanderbilt Journal of Transnational Law 29, 415–70.

Oddi, A Samuel 'Un-Unified Economic Theories of Patents—The Not-Quite-Holy Grail' (1996b) Notre Dame Law Review 71, 267–327.

Oh, Cecilia 'An Update on the Progress of Consultations on the Proposed Ministerial Declaration on TRIPS and Public Health' (2001) TWN Info Service on WTO Issues (26 Oct 2001). <http://lists.essential.org/pipermail/ip-health/2001-October/002266.html> (last visited 19 Jan 2004).

Olson, Mancur *The Logic of Collective Action: Public Goods and Theory of Groups* (Harvard University Press Boston 1965).

Oman, Ralph 'Intellectual Property after the Uruguay Round' (1994) Journal of the Copyright Society of the USA 42, 18–38.

Organisation for Economic Co-operation and Development *The Pharmaceutical Industry: Trade Related Issues* (OECD Paris 1985).

Organisation for Economic Cooperation and Development *Research and Development in Industry: Expenditures and Researchers, Scientists and Engineers 1976–1997* (OECD Paris 1999).

Ostergard, Robert Jr 'Intellectual Property: A Universal Human Right?' (1999) Human Rights Quarterly 21, 156–78.

Ostergard, Robert, Jr 'The Making of A Regime: Intellectual Property Rights in the International System' (PhD Thesis State University of New York, Graduate School of Binghamton University 1999),

Otten, Adrian 'Implementation of the TRIPs Agreement and Prospects for Its Further Development' (1998) Journal of International Economic Law 1, 523–36.

Otten, Adrian and Hannu Wager 'Compliance with TRIPS: the Emerging World View' (1996) Vanderbilt Journal of Transnational Law 29, 391–413.

Oxfam 'Dare to Lead: Public Health and Company Wealth' (2001) Oxfam Briefing Paper on Glaxo Smith Kline <http://www.oxfam.org.uk> (last visited 18 February 2002).

Oxfam 'Preventing the Cure: Corporate Lobbying and Fair Access to Medicines' (2001) Oxfam Briefing Paper on Pfizer <http://www.oxfam.org.uk> (last visited 18 February 2002).

Oxfam GB 'WTO Patent Rules and Access to Medicines: The Pressure Mounts' (June 2001) Oxfam Policy Paper <http://www.oxfam.org.uk/policy/papers/wtorules/wtorules.htm> (last visited 7 February 2002).

Pacon, Ana Maria 'What Will TRIPs Do For Developing Countries?' (1996) International Review of Industrial Property and Copyright Law 18, 329–57.

Paemen, Hugo, and Alexandra Bensch *From GATT to the WTO: The European Community in the Uruguay Round* (Leuven University Press Leuven 1995).

Palmer, Tom G 'Intellectual Property: A Non-Posnerian Law and Economics Approach' in Adam D Moore (ed) *Intellectual Property: Moral, Legal, and International Dilemmas* (Rowman and Littlefield Publishers, Inc Lanham, MD 1997).

Park, Anna Y 'International Trade: Agreement Between the United States and the Republic of Korea Concerning Insurance Market Access and Intellectual Property Protection in the Republic of Korea, July 21, 1986' (1987) Harvard International Law Journal 28, 166–74.

Pechman, Robert J 'Seeking Multilateral Protection for Intellectual Property: the United States 'TRIPS' Over Special 301' (1998) Minnesota Journal of Global Trade 7, 179–210.

Petersmann, Ernst-Ulrich and Meinhard Hilf (eds) *The New GATT Round of Multilateral Trade Negotiations: Legal and Economic Problems* (2nd updated edn Kluwer Law and Taxation Publishers Deventer 1991).

Peterson, Kirsten 'Recent Intellectual Property Trends in Developing Countries' (1992) Harvard International Law Journal 33, 277–90.

Petherbridge, Lee 'Intelligent TRIPS Implementation: A Strategy for Countries on the Cusp of Development' (2001) University of Pennsylvania Journal of International Economic Law 22, 1029–66.

Philip W *Patents for Chemicals, Pharmaceuticals and Biotechnology: Fundamentals of Global Law, Practice and Strategy* (Oxford University Press 1999)

Picciotto, Sol and Ruth Mayne (eds) *Regulating International Business* (Macmillan London 1999).

Politzer, Kurt *Brazilian Policies on Technological Development. Monograph Four in Transfer of Technology: The Future of Regulation* (Council of the Americas New York 1977)

Posner, Richard A 'Theories of Economic Regulation' (1974) Bell Journal of Economics 5, 335 ff.

Primo Braga, Carlos A 'The Economics of Intellectual Property Rights and the GATT: A View from the South' (1989) Vanderbilt Journal of Transnational Law 22, 243–64.

Primo Braga, Carlos A and Carsten Fink 'Reforming Intellectual Property Rights Regimes: Challenges for Developing Countries' (1998a) Journal of International Economic Law 1, 537–54.

Primo Braga, Carlos A and Carsten Fink 'The Relationship Between Intellectual Property Rights and Foreign Direct Investment' (1998b) Duke Journal of Comparative and International Law 9, 163–86.

Primo Braga, Carlos A and Carsten Fink 'Trade-Related Intellectual Property Rights: From Marrakech to Seattle' in Klaus Gunter Deutsch and Bernhard Speyer (eds) *The World Trade Organization Millennium Round: Free Trade in the Twenty-First Century* (Routledge London 2001).

Primo Braga, Carlos Alberto, Carsten Fink and Claudia Paz Sepulveda *Intellectual Property Rights and Economic Development* (World Bank Washington, DC 2000).

Putnam, Robert D 'Diplomacy and Domestic Politics: The Logic of Two-Level Games' (1988) International Organization 42, 427.

Raghavan, C *Recolonisation: GATT, the Uruguay Round and the Third World* (Zed Books London 1990)

Rapp, RT and RP Rozek 'Benefits and Costs of Intellectual Property Protection in Developing Countries' (1990) Journal of World Trade 24, 75–102.

Redwood, Heinz *New Horizons in India: The Consequences of Pharmaceutical Patent Protection* (Oldwicks Press Suffolk 1994).

Reichman, JH *Implications of the Draft TRIPS Agreement for Developing Countries as Competitors in an Integrated World Market* (UNCTAD Geneva 1993).

Reichman, JH 'Intellectual Property in International Trade: Opportunities and Risks of a GATT Connection' (1989) Vanderbilt Journal of Transnational Law 22, 747–891.

Reichman, JH 'Beyond the Historical Lines of Demarcation: Competition Law, Intellectual Property Rights, and International Trade after the GATT's Uruguay Round' (1993a) Brooklyn Journal of International Law 20, 75–119.

Reichman, JH 'The TRIPS Component of the GATT's Uruguay Round: Competitive Prospects for Intellectual Property Owners in an Integrated World Market' (1993b) Fordham Intellectual Property, Media and Entertainment Law Journal 4, 171–266.

Reichman, JH 'Universal Minimum Standards of Intellectual Property Protection Under the TRIPS Component of the WTO Agreement' (1995) International Lawyer 29, 345–88.

Reichman, JH 'The Know-How Gap in the TRIPS Agreement: Why Software Fared Badly, and What Are the Solutions?' (1995a) Hastings Communications and Entertainment Law Journal 17, 763–94.

Reichman, JH 'Compliance with TRIPS Agreement: Introduction to a Scholarly Debate' (1996) Vanderbilt Journal of Transnational Law 29, 363–90.

Reichman, JH 'Enforcing the Enforcement Procedures of the TRIPS Agreement' (1997) Virginia Journal of International Law 37, 335–56.

Reichman, JH 'Securing Compliance with the TRIPS Agreement after US v. India' (1998) Journal of International Economic Law 1, 585–601.

Reichman, JH and David Lange 'Bargaining Around the TRIPS Agreement: the Case for Ongoing Public-Private Initiatives to Facilitate Worldwide Intellectual Property Transactions' (1998) Duke Journal of Comparative and International Law 9, 11–68.

Reinbothe, Jorg and Anthony Howard 'The State of Play in the Negotiations on TRIPS' (1991) European Intellectual Property Review 13, 157–64.

Reuter, Paul *Introduction to the Law of Treaties* (Pinter London 1989)

Richards, John 'Trade Related Intellectual Property Issues' (1990) Journal of the Patent and Trademark Office Society 72, 906–23.

Richardson, Peter C 'The Need for Adequate and Effective Protection of Intellectual Property: Perspectives of the Private Sector—Patents' (1989) Georgia Journal of International and Comparative Law 19, 352–57.

Richardson, R Stephen and James D Gaisford 'North-South Disputes Over the Protection of Intellectual Property' (1996) Canadian Journal of Economics 29, 376–81.

Ricketson, S 'The Future of the Traditional Intellectual Property Conventions in the Brave New World of Trade-Related Intellectual Property Rights' (1995) IIC-International Review of Industrial Property and Copyright Law 26, 872–99.

Ricketson, S 'From GATT to TRIPs—the Agreement on Trade-Related Aspects of Intellectual Property Rights' (1998) IIC-International Review of Industrial Property and Copyright Law 29, 114–20.

Ringo, Frederick 'The Trade-Related Aspects of Intellectual Property Rights Agreement in the GATT and Legal Implications for Sub-Saharan Africa: Prospective Policy Issues for the World Trade Organization' (1994) Journal of World Trade 28, 121–39.

Risse-Kappen, Thomas (ed) *Bringing Transnational Relations Back In: Non-State Actors, Domestic Structures and International Institutions* (CUP Cambridge 1995).

Robbins, L 'Patents and US Foreign Policy' (1967–1968) IDEA: The Journal of Law and Technology 2, 521–51.

Rodau, Andrew G 'Protection of Intellectual Property: Patent, Copyright, and Trade Secret Law in the United States and Abroad' (1985) North Carolina Journal of International Law and Commercial Regulation 10, 537–78.

Rosenau, James N *The Study of Global Interdependence: Essays on the Transnationalisation of World Affairs* (Nichols New York 1980).

Rozek, Richard P 'The Consequences of Pharmaceutical Product Patenting: A Critique' (1993) World Competition—Law and Economics Review 16, 91–106.

Rubin, Seymour J and Mark L Jones (eds) *Conflict and Resolution in US-EC Trade Relations at the Opening of the Uruguay Round* (Oceana Publications New York 1989).

Ruigrok, Winfried and Rob van Tulder *The Logic of International Restructuring* (Routledge London 1995).

Rushing, Francis W and Carole-Ganz Brown (eds) *Intellectual Property Rights in Science, Technology and Economic Performance: International Comparisons* (Westview Press London 1990).

Ryan, Michael P 'The Function-Specific and Linkage-Bargain Diplomacy of International Intellectual Property Lawmaking' (1998) University of Pennsylvania Journal of International Economic Law 19, 535–86.

Ryan, Michael P *Knowledge Diplomacy: Global Competition and the Politics of Intellectual Property* (Brookings Institution Press Washington, DC 1998).

Ryan, Michael P 'Knowledge-Economy Elites, the International Law of Intellectual Property and Trade, and Economic Development' (2002) Cardozo Journal of International and Comparative Law 10, 271–303.

Sacerdoti, G (ed) *Liberalization of Services and Intellectual Property in the Uruguay Round of GATT* (Fribourg University Press Fribourg 1990).

Sadler, Brent W 'Intellectual Property Protection through International Trade' (1992) Houston Journal of International Law 14, 393–423.

Sally, R 'Multinational Enterprises, Political Economy and Institutional Theory: Domestic Embeddedness in the Context of Internationalization' (1994) Review of International Political Economy 1, 161–92.

Sally, R *States and Firms: Multinational Enterprises in Institutional Competition* (Routledge London; New York 1995).

Saxena, RB 'Trade-Related Issues of Intellectual Property Rights and the Indian Patent Act' (1988/89) World Competition 12, 81–116.

Scandizzo, Stefania 'Intellectual Property Rights and International R&D Competition' (2001) IMF Working Paper (WP/01/81) (IMF Washington DC 2001).

Scandizzo, Stefania E *International Protection of Intellectual Property Rights* (PhD Thesis University of Pennsylvania 1998).

Schapiro, Louis A 'The Role of Intellectual Property Protection and International Competitiveness' (1989) Antitrust Law Journal 58, 569–82.

Schaumberg, Tom M 'The ITC as a Forum for Protecting Intellectual Property Rights' (1988) Practising Law Institute/Commercial Law and Practice Course Handbook Series 482, 243–67.

Scherer, FM 'The Pharmaceutical Industry and World Intellectual Property Standards' (2000) Vanderbilt Law Review 53, 2245–54.

Scherer, FM and J Watal 'Post-TRIPS Options for Access to Patented Medicines in Developing Nations' (2002) Journal of International Economic Law 5, 913–39.

Schlitt, Lyn M 'Protection of Intellectual Property Rights Under Section 337 of the Tariff Act: Addressing the GATT Panel Report' (1989) Practising Law Institute/Commercial Law and Practice Course Handbook Series 510, 103–11.

Schott, Jeffrey J 'Comment on the Doha Ministerial' (2002) Journal of International Economic Law 5, 191–5.

Schug, Mary K 'Promoting Access to HIV/AIDS Pharmaceuticals in Sub-Saharan Africa Within the Framework of International Intellectual Property Law' (2001) Law and Inequality: A Journal of Theory and Practice 19, 229–57.

Sell, Susan K 'Intellectual Property Protection and Antitrust in the Developing World: Crisis, Coercion, and Choice' (1995a) International Organization 49, 315–49.

Sell, Susan K 'The Origins of a Trade-Based Approach to Intellectual Property Protection—The Role of Industry Associations' (1995b) Science Communication 17, 163–85.

Sell, Susan K *Power and Ideas: North-South Politics of Intellectual Property and Antitrust* (State University of New York Press Albany 1998).

Sell, Susan K 'Multinational Corporations as Agents of Change: The Globalization of Intellectual Property Rights' in A Claire Cutler, Virginia Haufler, and Tony Porter (eds) *Private Authority and International Affairs* (SUNY Press New York 1999a).

Sell, Susan K 'Structures, Agents and Institutions: Private Corporate Power and the Globalisation of Intellectual Property Rights' in Richard A Higgott, Geoffrey RD Underhill, and Andreas Bieler (eds) *Non-State Actors and Authority in the Global System* (Routledge London; New York 1999b).

Sell, Susan K. (2002a). 'Industry Strategies for Intellectual Property and Trade: The Quest for TRIPS, and Post-TRIPS Strategies.' Cardozo Journal of International and Comparative Law 10: 79–108.

Sell, Susan K 'Post-TRIPS Developments: The Tension Between Commercial and Social Agendas in the Context of Intellectual Property' (2002b) Florida Journal of International Law 14, 193–216.

Sell, Susan K and Christopher May 'Moments in Law: Contestation and Settlement in the History of Intellectual Property' (2001) Review of International Political Economy 8, 467–500.

Servan-Schreiber, JJ *The American Challenge* (Atheneum New York 1979).

Shanker, Daya 'Legitimacy and the TRIPS Agreement' (2002) University of Wollongong, Department of Economics Working Paper 02–01 <http://www.uow.edu.ac/ commerce/econ/workingpapers/wp02-01.pdf> (last viewed 15 October 2003).

Shechter, Yoav 'Interests, Strategies and Institutions: Lobbying in the Pharmaceutical Industry of the European Union' (PhD Thesis University of London 1999).

Sherwood, Robert M *Intellectual Property and Economic Development* (Westview Boulder Co 1990).

Sherwood, Robert M 'The TRIPS Agreement: Implications for Developing Countries' (1997) IDEA: The Journal of Law and Technology 37, 491–544.

Sherwood, Robert M 'The TRIPS Agreement: Benefits and Costs for Developing Countries' (2000) International Journal of Technology Management 19, 57–76.

Siebeck, Wolfgang E, Robert E Evenson, William Lesser and Carlos A Primo Braga (eds) 'Strengthening Protection of Intellectual Property in Developing Countries: A Survey of the Literature' Discussion Paper No 112 (World Bank Washington DC 1990).

Silverman, Milton and Philip R Lee *Pills, Profits, and Politics* (University of California Press Berkeley, CA 1974).

Silverman, Milton, Mia Lydecker and Philip R Lee *Bad Medicine: the Prescription Drug Industry in the Third World* (Stanford University Press Stanford 1992).

Simmonds, KR 'The Community and the Uruguay Round' (1988) Common Market Law Review 25, 95–107.
Simon, Emery 'U.S. Trade Policy and Intellectual Property Rights' (1986) Albany Law Review 50, 501–7.
Simon, Emery 'GATT and NAFTA Provisions on Intellectual Property' (1993) Fordham Intellectual Property, Media and Entertainment Law Journal 4, 267–86.
Simon, Emery 'Trade Law and Innovation: Section 301 of the Trade Act and Its Effect on Counterfeiting of US Technology; Current and Possible Effect of NAFTA and GATT Intellectual Property Provisions' (1995) Canada-United States Law Journal 21, 75–80.
Singham, Shanker A 'Competition Policy and the Stimulation of Innovation: TRIPS and the Interface Between Competition and Patent Protection in the Pharmaceutical Industry' (2000) Brooklyn Journal of International Law 26, 363–415.
Slaughter, Anne-Marie 'International Law in a World of Liberal States' (1995) European Journal of International Law 6, 503 ff.
Slaughter, Anne-Marie, Andrew S Tulumello and Stepan Wood 'International Law and International Relations Theory: A New Generation of Interdisciplinary Scholarship' (1998) American Journal of International Law 92, 367–97.
Slaughter, John 'TRIPS: the GATT Intellectual Property Negotiations Approach their Conclusion' (1990) European Intellectual Property Review 12, 418–20.
Smith, Michael W 'Bringing Developing Countries' Intellectual Property Laws to TRIPS Standards: Hurdles and Pitfalls Facing Vietnam's Efforts to Normalize an Intellectual Property Regime' (1999) Case Western Reserve Journal of International Law 31, 211–51.
Smith, Patricia M 'A Long and Winding Road: TRIPS and the Evolution of an International Competition Framework' (1999) Journal of International Economic Law 2, 435–40.
Smythe, Elizabeth 'State Authority and Investment Security: Non-State Actors and the Negotiation of the Multilateral Agreement on Investment at the OECD' in Richard Higgott, Geoffrey RD Underhill and Andreas Bieler (eds) *Non-State Actors and Authority in the Global System* (Routledge London 1999).
Sodipo, Bankole *Piracy and Counterfeiting: GATT TRIPS and Developing Countries* (Kluwer Law International London; Boston 1997).
Song, Sang Hyun, and Seong-Ki Kim 'The Impact of Multilateral Trade Negotiations on Intellectual Property Laws in Korea' (1994) UCLA Pacific Basin Law Journal 13, 118–39.
South Centre The TRIPS Agreement: a Guide for the South: the Uruguay Round Agreement on Trade-Related Intellectual Property Rights (Dar Es Salaam, The South Centre Geneva 1997).

South Centre Integrating Public Health Concerns into Patent Legislation in Developing Countries (South Centre Geneva 2000).

Spiers, Joseph 'Productivity Looks Promising' *Fortune* (9 March, 1992).

Stanback, WA 'International Intellectual Property Protection: An Integrated Solution to the Inadequate Protection Problem' (1989) Virginia Journal of International Law 29, 517–60.

Steidlmeier, Paul 'The Moral Legitimacy of Intellectual Property Claims: American Business and Developing Countries Perspectives' (1993) Journal of Business Ethics 12, 157–64.

Stephan, Paul B III 'Barbarians Inside the Gate: Public Choice Theory and International Economic Law' (1995) American University Journal of International Law and Policy 10, 745–67.

Stewart, George R, Myra J Tawfik, and Maureen Irish (eds) *International Trade and Intellectual Property: The Search for a Balanced System* (Westview Press Boulder Co; Oxford 1994).

Stewart, Terence P (ed) *The GATT Uruguay Round: A Negotiating History (1986–1992)* (Four Volumes, Kluwer Deventer 1993).

Stigler, George J 'The Theory of Economic Regulation' (1971) Bell Journal of Economics 2, 3 ff.

Stilwell, Matthew and Catherine Monagle 'Review of TRIPs Agreement Under Article 71.1' Trade-Related Agenda, Development and Equity Occasional Papers No 3 (South Centre Geneva December 2000).

Stilwell, Matthew and Elizabeth Tuerk 'Non-Violation Complaints and the TRIPs Agreement: Some Considerations for WTO Members' Trade-Related Agenda, Development and Equity Occasional Papers No 1 (South Centre Geneva December 2000).

Stopford, John 'Multinational Corporations' (1998–1999) Foreign Policy (1998) 12–24.

Stopford, John, Susan Strange, with John S Henley *Rival States, Rival Firms: Competition for World Market Shares* (CUP New York 1991).

Strange, Susan The Retreat of the State: The Diffusion of Power in the World Economy (CUP Cambridge 1996).

Straus, Joseph 'Bargaining Around the TRIPS Agreement: the Case for Ongoing Public-Private Initiatives to Facilitate Worldwide Intellectual Property Transactions: A Comment' (1998) Duke Journal of Comparative and International Law 9, 91–107.

Subramanian, Arvind 'Putting Some Numbers on the TRIPS Pharmaceutical Debate' (1995). International Journal of Technology Management 10, 252–68.

Subramanian, Arvind, and Jayashree Watal 'Can TRIPS Serve as an Enforcement Device for Developing Countries in the WTO?' (2000) Journal of International Economic Law 3, 403–16.

Svernlov, C 'Super 301: Gone But Not Forgotten' (1992) Journal of World Trade 26, 125–32.

Sykes, Alan O 'TRIPS, Pharmaceuticals, Developing Countries, and the Doha 'Solution'' (2002) Chicago Journal of International Law 3, 47–68.

Szymanski, Stefan 'International Exhaustion: A Review of the Economic Issues' Paper Prepared for the Intellectual Property Institute (February 1999).

Tarullo, Daniel K 'Beyond Normalcy in the Regulation of International Trade' (1987) Harvard Law Review 100, 546–628.

Tarzi, Shah M 'Multinational Corporations and American Foreign Policy: Radical, Sovereignty-at-Bay, and State-Centric Approaches' (1991) International Studies 28, 359–72.

Taylor, M Scott 'TRIPS, Trade, and Technology Transfer' (1993) Canadian Journal of Economics 26, 625–37.

Taylor, M Scott 'TRIPS, Trade, and Growth' (1994) International Economic Review 35, 361–82.

Templeman, Sydney 'Intellectual Property' (1998) Journal of International Economic Law 1, 603–6.

Teubner, Gunther, (ed) *Global Law Without a State* (Dartmouth Aldershot 1997).

Thurow, Lester C 'Needed: A New System of Intellectual Property Rights' (1997) Harvard Business Review 75, 95–103.

Timmermans, Karin and Togi Hutadjulu 'Report of an ASEAN Workshop on the TRIPs Agreement and its Impact on Pharmaceuticals' (Jakarta 2–4 May 2000) <http://www.who.int/medicines/library/dap/aseantripsagreement.pdf> (last visited 11 January 2002).

Tomar, David K 'A Look Into the WTO Pharmaceutical Patent Dispute Between the United States and India' (1999) Wisconsin International Law Journal 17, 579–603.

Trachtman, Joel P 'The International Economic Law Revolution' (1996) University of Pennsylvania Journal of International Economic Law 17, 33–61.

Trebilcock, Michael and Robert Howse 'Trade-Related Intellectual Property (TRIPs)'. Excerpts from Trebilcock and Howse (1995) chapter 10, in Robert Howse (ed) *The World Trading System: Critical Perspectives on the World Economy. Volume IV: The Uruguay Round and Beyond* (Routledge London; New York 1998).

Twinomukunzi, C 'The International Patent System—A Third World Perspective (1982) Indian Journal of International Law 22, 31–68.

UNAIDS/WHO 'Patent Situation of HIV/AIDS-Related Drugs in 80 Countries' (UNAIDS/WHO Geneva 2000) <http://www.who.int/medicines/ library/par/hivrelateddocs/ patentshivdrugs.pdf> (last visited 11 January 2002).

UNCTAD *Uruguay Round: Further Papers on Selected Issues* (United Nations New York 1990).

UNICEF/UNAIDS/WHO/MSF 'Sources and Prices of Selected Drugs and Diagnostics for People Living With HIV/AIDS' (2001) <http://www.unicef.org> (last visited 22 February 2004).

United Nations *The Role of Patents in the Transfer of Technology to Developing Countries: Report of the Secretary General* (United Nations New York 1964).

United Nations *The Role of the Patent System in the Transfer of Technology to Developing Countries* (United Nations New York 1975).

United Nations *Review of the Multilateral Treaty-Making Process* United Nations Legislative Series (United Nations New York 1985).

United Nations *Uruguay Round: Papers on Selected Issues* (United Nations New York 1989).

United Nations *New Issues in the Uruguay Round of Multilateral Trade Negotiations* (United Nations New York 1990a).

United Nations *Uruguay Round: Further Papers on Selected Issues* (United Nations New York 1990b).

United Nations *Intellectual Property Rights and Foreign Direct Investment* (United Nations New York 1993).

United Nations Centre for Human Rights *HIV/AIDS and Human Rights: International guidelines* (United Nations New York 1998).

United Nations Centre on Transnational Corporations *Transnational Corporations in the Pharmaceutical Industry of Developing Countries* (United Nations New York 1984).

United Nations Conference on Trade and Development *Guidelines on Technology Issues in the Pharmaceutical Sector in the Developing Countries* (United Nations New York 1982).

United Nations Conference on Trade and Development *The TRIPS Agreement and Developing Countries* (United Nations New York 1996).

United Nations Development Program *Human Development Report 1999* (OUP New York 1999).

United Nations 'Security Council Holds Debate on Impact of AIDS on Peace and Security in Africa' Press Release SC/6781 (10 January 2000).

United States International Trade Commission 'Global Competitiveness of US Advanced-Technology Manufacturing Industries: Pharmaceuticals: A Summary of the Report to the Committee on Finance, United States Senate, on Investigation No 332–302 Under Section 332 (g) of the Tariff Act of 1930 (USITC Publication 2438, September 1991)' (1991) World Competition 15, 27–45.

Vagts, Detlev F 'The Multinational Enterprise: A New Challenge for Transnational Law' (1970) Harvard Law Review 83, 739–92.

Velasquez, G and P Boulet *Globalization and Access to Drugs: Perspectives on the WTO/TRIPS Agreement* (2nd edn World Health Organisation. Geneva 1999) <http://www.who.int/medicines/library/dap/who-dap-98–9-rev/who-dap-98–9.htm> (last visited 7 February 2002).

Verma, SK 'TRIPs—Development and Transfer of Technology' (1996) IIC-International Review of Industrial Property and Copyright Law 27, 331–64.

Vernon, Raymond *Sovereignty at Bay: The Multinational Spread of US Enterprises* (Longman London 1971).

Vernon, Raymond *Storm Over the Multinationals: The Real Issues* (Macmillan London 1977).

Vernon, Raymond *In the Hurricane's Eye: The Troubled Prospects of Multinational Enterprises* (Harvard University Press Cambridge MA 1998).

Vicente, Wendy S 'Questionable Victory for Coerced Argentine Pharmaceutical Patent Legislation' (1998) University of Pennsylvania Journal of International Economic Law 19, 1101–40.

Viotti, Paul R and Mark V Kauppi *International Relations Theory: Realism, Pluralism, Globalism* (2nd edn Allyn and Bacon Boston 1993)

Vishwasrao, S 'Intellectual Property Rights and the Mode of Technology Transfer' (1994) Journal of Development Economics 44, 381–402.

Walker, C and M Bloomfield (eds) *Intellectual Property Rights and Capital Formation in the Next Decade* (University Press of America Lanham Md 1988).

Walker, William M 'Uruguay Round TRIPs: A Bibliographic Essay' (1989) Vanderbilt Journal of Transnational Law 22, 911–22.

Wallace, Cynthia Day *Legal Control of the Multinational Enterprise: National Regulatory Techniques and the Prospects for International Controls* (Martinus Nijhoff The Hague 1983).

Wallerstein, M, M Mogee and R Schoen (eds) *Global Dimensions of Intellectual Property Rights in Science and Technology* (National Academy Press Washington DC 1993).

Walter, Andrew 'Globalisation and Policy Convergence: The Case of Direct Investment Rules' (1999) in Richard Higgott, Geoffrey RD Underhill and Andreas Bieler (eds) *Non-State Actors and Authority in the Global System.* (Routledge London 1999).

Waltz, Kenneth N *Theory of International Politics* (Addison-Wesley Reading, MA 1979).

Watal, Jayashree 'Background Note Prepared by Jayashree Watal, Consultant to the WTO Secretariat' (2001) WHO-WTO Secretariat Workshop on Differential Pricing and Financing of Essential Drugs, Hosbjor, Norway, 8–11 April, 2001. <http://www.wto.org/english/tratop_e/trips_e/wto_background_e.pdf> (last visited 24 January 2002).

Watal, Jayashree *Intellectual Property Rights in the WTO and Developing Countries* (Kluwer Law International Boston 2001).

Watal, Jayashree and Anu P Mathai *Sectoral Impact of the Uruguay Round Agreements on Developing Countries: Pharmaceutical Industry* (United Nations Industrial Development Organization Vienna 1995).

Wegner, Harold C 'TRIPS Boomerang—Obligations for Domestic Reform' (1996) Vanderbilt Journal of Transnational Law 29, 535–58.

Weil, Prosper 'Towards Relative Normativitiy in International Law?' (1983) American Journal of International Law 77, 413–42.

Weissman, Robert 'A Long, Strange TRIPS: The Pharmaceutical Industry Drive to Harmonise Global Intellectual Property Rules, and the Remaining WTO Legal Alternatives Available to Third World Countries' (1996) University of Pennsylvania Journal of International Economic Law 17, 1069–1125.

Wilder, Richard 'Global Harmonisation of Intellectual Property' in Ian Fletcher *et al* (eds) *Foundations and Perspectives of International Trade Law* (London: Sweet & Maxwell 2001).

Wilkins, Mira 'Multinational Enterprises and Economic Change' (1998) Australian Economic History Review 38, 103–34.

Will, George 'AIDS Crushes a Continent' *Newsweek* (10 January 2000).

Wilson, David I 'A Trade Policy Goal for the 1990s: Improving the Adequacy and Effectiveness of Intellectual Property Protection in Foreign Countries' (1988) Transnational Lawyer 1, 421–47.

Wineburg, A 'Litigating Intellectual Property Disputes at the International Trade Commission' (1986) Journal of Patent and Trademark Office Society 68, 473–97.

Winter, Harvey J 'The Role of the United States Government in Improving International Intellectual Property Protection' (1987) Journal of Law and Technology 2, 325–32.

Wolfhard, E 'International Trade in Intellectual Property: The Emerging GATT Regime' (1991) University of Toronto Faculty of Law Review 49, 106–51.

World Bank *Intensifying Action Against HIV/AIDS in Africa: Responding to a Development Crisis* (World Bank Washington, DC 2000).

World Health Organization 'More Equitable Pricing for Essential Drugs: What Do We Mean and What Are the Issues?' (2001) Background Paper for the WHO-WTO Secretariat Workshop on Differential Pricing and Financing of Essential Drugs, Hosbjor, Norway, 8–11 April 2001 <http://www.wto.org/english/tratop_e/trips_e/who_background_e.pdf> (last visited 11 January 2002).

World Health Organization and World Trade Organization 'Report of the Workshop on Differential Pricing and Financing of Essential Drugs' (2001) WHO-WTO Secretariat Workshop on Differential Pricing and Financing of Essential Drugs, Hosbjor, Norway, 8–11 April 2001 <http://www.wto.org/english/tratop_e/trips_e/hosbjor_report_e.pdf> (last visited 11 January 2002).

World Intellectual Property Organization *The Situation of Industrial Property in the Countries of Asia and the Pacific* (WIPO Geneva 1984).

World Intellectual Property Organization *The Situation of Industrial Property in the Countries of Africa* (WIPO Geneva 1987).

World Intellectual Property Organization *Industrial Property Laws and Treaties* (WIPO Geneva 1978–2001).

World Intellectual Property Organization *WIPO Model Law for Developing Countries on Inventions* (WIPO Geneva 1979).

World Intellectual Property Organization *Background Reading Material on Intellectual Property* (WIPO Geneva 1988).

World Intellectual Property Organization *Implications of the TRIPS Agreement on Treaties Administered by WIPO* (WIPO Geneva 1996).

World Intellectual Property Organization *Intellectual Property Laws and Treaties* (WIPO Geneva 1998).

World Intellectual Property Organization and United Nations Economic Commission for Africa *Model Law for English-Speaking African Countries on Patents. Prepared by the Secretariats of the World Intellectual Property Organization and the United Nations Economic Commission for Africa Under the Auspices of the Committee for Patent Matters of the Conference on Industrial Property Laws of English-Speaking Africa* (World Intellectual Property Organization Geneva 1978).

World Intellectual Property Organization (ed) *Introduction to Intellectual Property: Theory and Practice* (Kluwer Law International London; Boston 1997).

World Intellectual Property Report (1987– 2001) Various Issues. Bureau of National Affairs.

World Patent Law and Practice: Patent Statutes, Regulations, and Treaties Vols 2B-2J (M Bender New York 1974).

World Trade Organization 'Pharmaceutical Patents and the TRIPS Agreement' (2001) Technical Note by the Secretariat <http://www.wto.org/ english/tratop_e/trips_e/pharma _ato186_e.htm> (last visited 17 November 2001).

World Trade Organization 'TRIPS and Pharmaceutical Patents' (2001) WTO Fact Sheet <http://www.wto.org/english/tratop_e/trips_e/tripsfact-sheet_pharma.pdf> (last visited 17 November 2001).

Worthy, John 'Intellectual Property Protection After GATT' (1994) European Intellectual Property Review 16, 195–198.

Yambrusic, Edward Slavko *Trade Based Approaches to the Protection of Intellectual Property* (Oceana Publications New York 1992).

Yang, Y 'Why Do Southern Countries Have Little Incentive to Protect Northern Intellectual Property Rights?' (1998) Canadian Journal of Economics 31, 800–16.

Yarn, Douglas H *International Protection of Intellectual Property Rights Under the United States Trade Laws* (Dean Rusk Center for International and Comparative Law Athens, Georgia: 1986).

Yu, Diane 'Punta: An Oral History of the 1986 GATT Ministerial Meeting in Punta Del Este, Uruguay' (Institute of International Economic Law, Georgetown University, Washington, DC Unpublished Manuscript November 1987).

Yusuf, AA *Developing Countries and Trade-Related Aspects of Intellectual Property Rights* (UNCTAD Geneva 1989).

Zigic, Kresimir 'Intellectual Property Rights Violations and Spillovers in North- South Trade' (1998) European Economic Review 42, 1779–99.

Zigic, Kresimir 'Strategic Trade Policy, Intellectual Property Rights Protection, and North–South Trade' (2000) Journal of Development Economics 61, 27–60.

Zutshi, BK 'Bringing TRIPS into the Multilateral Trading System' in Jagdish Bhagwati, and Mathias Hirsch (eds) *The Uruguay Round and Beyond: Essays in Honor of Arthur Dunkel* (University of Michigan Press Ann Arbor, Mich 1998).[1] For a proper definition of the term 'multinational.